discover
GREECE

KORINA MILLER
KATE ARMSTRONG, MICHAEL STAMATIOS CLARK, CHRIS DELISO,
DES HANNIGAN, VICTORIA KYRIAKOPOULOS

2

NORTHERN GREECE
p163

CENTRAL GREECE
& THE IONIAN ISLANDS
p127

ATHENS & ATTICA
p51

PELOPONNESE
& THE SARONIC
GULF ISLANDS
p93

CYCLADES, EVIA
& THE SPORADES
p195

DODECANESE
p267

CRETE
p233

DISCOVER GREECE

Athens & Attica (p51) A vibrant, cosmopolitan capital, surrounded by the impressive ruins of Attica

Peloponnese & the Saronic Gulf Islands (p93) Gorgeous, rugged landscapes and stunning coastal villages

Central Greece & the Ionian Islands (p127) Atmospheric rural peninsula and idyllic island life of Corfu or Kefallonia

Northern Greece (p163) Artistic, spirited Thessaloniki, traditional villages and the soaring peaks of Mt Olympus

Cyclades, Evia & the Sporades (p195) Island paradises of Santorini and Mykonos, ancient ruins, spas and beaches

Crete (p233) Idyllic Elafonisi, Hania's evocative Old Town, vineyards and the palace of Knossos

Dodecanese (p267) Rhodes' medieval Old Town, Nisyros volcano, Kos beaches and the spiritual atmosphere of Patmos

↘CONTENTS

NORTHERN GREECE p163

CENTRAL GREECE & THE IONIAN ISLANDS p127

ATHENS & ATTICA p51

PELOPONNESE & THE SARONIC GULF ISLANDS p93

CYCLADES, EVIA & THE SPORADES p195

DODECANESE p267

CRETE p233

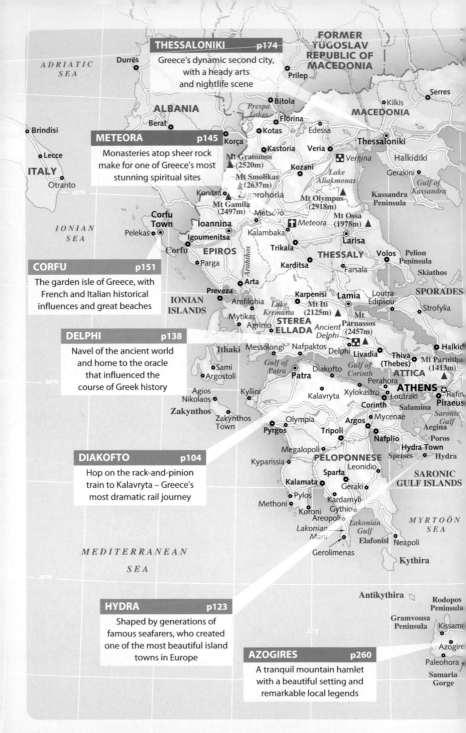

THESSALONIKI p174
Greece's dynamic second city, with a heady arts and nightlife scene

METEORA p145
Monasteries atop sheer rock make for one of Greece's most stunning spiritual sites

CORFU p151
The garden isle of Greece, with French and Italian historical influences and great beaches

DELPHI p138
Navel of the ancient world and home to the oracle that influenced the course of Greek history

DIAKOFTO p104
Hop on the rack-and-pinion train to Kalavryta – Greece's most dramatic rail journey

HYDRA p123
Shaped by generations of famous seafarers, who created one of the most beautiful island towns in Europe

AZOGIRES p260
A tranquil mountain hamlet with a beautiful setting and remarkable local legends

ADRIATIC SEA

FORMER YUGOSLAV REPUBLIC OF MACEDONIA

Durrës
Prilep
ALBANIA
Berat
Brindisi
Lecce
ITALY
Otranto

Prespa Lakes
Bitola
Florina
Kotas
Edessa
Korça
Mt Grammos (2520m)
Kastoria
Veria
Vergina
Kozani
Mt Smolikas (2637m)
Lake Aliakmonas
Konitsa
Zagorohoria
Mt Gamila (2497m)
Metsovo
Mt Olympus (2918m)
Kassandra Peninsula

Serres
Kilkis
MACEDONIA
Thessaloniki
Vergina
Halkidiki
Gerakini
Gulf of Kassandra

IONIAN SEA
Corfu Town
Pelekas
Ioannina
Igoumenitsa
Corfu
EPIROS
Parga

Kalambaka
Meteora
Trikala
THESSALY
Karditsa
Farsala
Larisa
Mt Ossa (1978m)
Volos
Pelion Peninsula
Skiathos

IONIAN ISLANDS
Preveza
Amfilohia
Mytikas
Agrinio
Arta
Karpenisi
Lake Kremasta
Mt Iti (2125m)
Lamia
STEREA ELLADA
Ancient Delphi
Mt Parnassos (2457m)
Loutra Edipsou
SPORADES
Strofylia

Ithaki
Messolongi
Nafpaktos
Delphi
Livadia
Thiva (Thebes)
Mt Parnitha (1413m)
Halkid

Sami
Argostoli
Gulf of Patra
Patra
Diakofto
Gulf of Corinth
Perahora
ATTICA
ATHENS
Rafin

Agios Nikolaos
Kyllini
Kalavryta
Xylokastro
Loutraki
Corinth
Salamina
Piraeus
Saronic Gulf
Aegina

Zakynthos
Zakynthos Town
Olympia
Pyrgos
Argos
Mycenae
Nafplio
Tripoli
Poros
Hydra Town
Speses
Hydra

Megalopoli
PELOPONNESE
Kyparissia
Sparta
Leonidio
Geraki
SARONIC GULF ISLANDS

Kalamata
Pylos
Kardamyli
Methoni
Koroni
Areopoli
Gythio
Lakonian Mani
Lakonian Gulf
Elafonisi
Neapoli
MYRTOÖN SEA

MEDITERRANEAN SEA

Gerolimenas
Kythira

Antikythira
Rodopos Peninsula
Gramvousa Peninsula
Kissamo
Azogire
Paleohora
Samaria Gorge

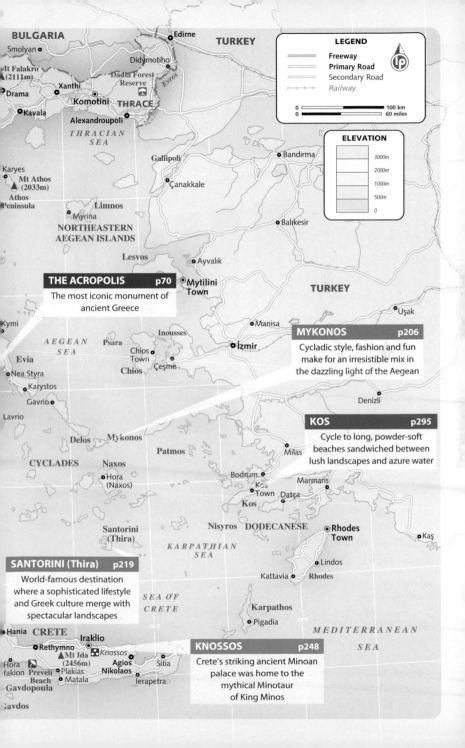

BULGARIA
Smolyan

Mt Falakro
(2111m)
Drama
Xanthi
Kavala
Komotini
THRACE

Edirne
TURKEY
Didymotiho
Dadia Forest
Reserve
Evros

Alexandroupoli

THRACIAN
SEA

Gallipoli
Çanakkale
Bandırma
Balıkesir

Karyes
Mt Athos
(2033m)
Athos
Peninsula
Myrina
Limnos

NORTHEASTERN
AEGEAN ISLANDS

Lesvos
Ayvalık
Mytilini
Town

TURKEY

THE ACROPOLIS   p70
The most iconic monument of
ancient Greece

Kymi
AEGEAN
SEA
Psara
Inousses
Chios
Town
Chios
Çeşme
İzmir
Manisa
Uşak

Evia
Nea Styra
Karystos
Gavrio

MYKONOS   p206
Cycladic style, fashion and fun
make for an irresistible mix in
the dazzling light of the Aegean

Lavrio
Delos
Mykonos
Patmos
Milas
Bodrum
Marmaris
Datça
Denizli

KOS   p295
Cycle to long, powder-soft
beaches sandwiched between
lush landscapes and azure water

CYCLADES
Naxos
Hora
(Naxos)
Kos
Town
Kos

Santorini
(Thira)
KARPATHIAN
SEA
Nisyros   DODECANESE
Rhodes
Town
Kaş
Lindos
Kattavia   Rhodes

SANTORINI (Thira)   p219
World-famous destination
where a sophisticated lifestyle
and Greek culture merge with
spectacular landscapes

SEA OF
CRETE
Karpathos
Pigadia
MEDITERRANEAN
SEA

Hania   CRETE
Rethymno
Iraklio
Mt Ida
(2456m)
Knossos
Sitia
Hora
Sfakion
Preveli
Plakias
Agios
Nikolaos
Beach
Matala
Gavdopoula
Ierapetra
Gavdos

KNOSSOS   p248
Crete's striking ancient Minoan
palace was home to the
mythical Minotaur
of King Minos

LEGEND
Freeway
Primary Road
Secondary Road
Railway

0   100 km
0   60 miles

ELEVATION
3000m
2000m
1000m
500m
0

↘ THIS IS GREECE

It's easy to understand how so many myths of gods and giants originated in this varied landscape. Greece beckons with its wide open skies and endless miles of aquamarine coastline; and then it draws you in with its infamous ancient sights, slow-paced island life and vibrant cities.

As the birthplace of drama, democracy, Western science and medicine, Greece offers a welcome balance of traditional and contemporary life. Ancient sights often take the limelight and while it's easy to find traditional villages with brilliant white buildings and roaming donkeys, Athens' firm grip on style and sophistication rivals that of any European capital. The Greek modern art scene is fresh and vibrant, fashionable clubs and cafes buzz with life and society is increasingly multicultural. There are few cultures that embrace the past so passionately while simultaneously welcoming the future with open arms.

Once you arrive, it's not difficult to find the Greece you were hoping for, whether it's the pulsing nightclubs of Mykonos, the solemnity of Meteora, or the grandeur of Delphi.

You'll quickly become acquainted with the throbbing melancholy of *rembetika* (blues songs) and the tang of homemade tzatziki, and Greece's ancient sights will unleash your imagination.

Not surprisingly, such drawcards haven't gone unnoticed. This means you need to do some preplanning and booking if you're heading for a popular city or island in the summer. Nevertheless, the sheer quantity of destinations means that most places absorb the influx of visitors with grace and ease.

Greece is essentially a laid-back place. Lounge endlessly at a cafe over a coffee, stroll along the seafront, park yourself on the beach and take your time over meals and you'll fit right in. Greeks know how to enjoy life and are renowned as some of the most hospitable people on the globe. Their generosity and warmth is as genuine as the soft sand between your toes and the warmth of the Aegean sun.

'few cultures embrace the past so passionately while simultaneously welcoming the future with open arms'

↘ GREECE'S TOP 25 EXPERIENCES

1

↘ GETTING HOOKED ON ATHENS

Greece's bustling capital, Athens (p51) has a way of surprising even the most jaded visitor. The historic centre under the magnificent Acropolis is part open-air museum, part open-air lounge, and is teeming with alfresco cafes, bars and restaurants with an almost festive atmosphere, especially at night.

Victoria Kyriakopoulos, Lonely Planet Author, Australia

↘ SOARING HIGH AT METEORA

The monasteries, precariously perched atop the sheer natural sandstone rock pillars of Meteora (p145), are spectacular to behold. Once used successfully as refuge by hermit monks seeking a retreat from expanding Turkish occupation, they now open their doors to travellers.

sunphlower, Traveller

↘ ISLAND ROAD TRIPS

A favourite island activity was to rent a car (p355) and head out across the interior. In little villages, old dames whipped up mouth-watering, traditional Greek salads and coffee so strong you could stand a spoon in it; and locals directed us to beaches and trailheads. This was 'real' island life.

Korina Miller, Lonely Planet Author, UK

1 IZZET KERIBAR; 2 PAOLO CORDELLI; 3 MARK DAFFEY

1 Streetlife in Monastiraki, Athens (p51); 2 Monasteries of Meteora (p145); 3 Island landscapes of the Cyclades (p206)

↘ MAGICAL DELPHI

Arrive early to catch the magic of the sun's rays pouring over the **Sanctuary of Athena** (p140) at Delphi, the centre of the ancient Greek world. Nearby, the Sacred Way meanders past the **Temple of Apollo** (p139), where the Delphic Oracle uttered prophecies that sent armies to battle and lovers to swoon.

Michael Stamatios Clark,
Lonely Planet Author, USA

4

5

↘ BREATHTAKING SANTORINI

Santorini (Thira; p219) is entrancing. Who would guess that something as catastrophic as an earthquake could create such breathtaking beauty? Arrive by ferry if you can – the views are incredible. And once you're there, spend at least one evening watching the sun set across the colourful cliffs of the caldera.

Krista Davis, Traveller, USA

⬐ RHODES' MEDIEVAL OLD TOWN

Getting lost in the Old Town (p281) is a must. You'll find yourself removed from the tourist throngs, meandering down twisting, cobbled alleyways with archways above and squares opening up ahead. Its beauty lies in these hidden corners, where your imagination will take off with flights of medieval fancy.

Korina Miller, Lonely Planet Author, UK

6

4 ANDREW BAIN; 5 GERHARD ZWERGER-SCHO/IMAGEBROKER; 6 WAYNE WALTON

4 Sanctuary of Athena (p140); 5 Santorini (Thira, p219); 6 Rhodes' Old Town (p281)

⬎ BESOTTED WITH PREVELI BEACH

Preveli Beach (p261) is a jewel: the palm-lined river valley offers one spar-kling pool spilling into another, then another. There is something ancient and bewitching about the place, especially at night.

Steve Slattery, Traveller

7

8

↘ UNDER THE VOLCANO

Descending into Nisyros' volcano (p293) feels like stepping onto the set of an old *Star Trek* episode. Picking your way through the scree towards the crater floor, where the lava is hubble-bubbling away, is an other-worldly experience. And when you're done here, there are still four other craters to sneak a peek at.

Paul Griffin, Traveller, UK

↘ EXPLORING THE MANI

The Mani (p115) holds a magic unlike anywhere else in Greece. With everything from rugged rocky high-lands, to hidden lush green oases, and small fishing tavernas to severe rock-solid tower houses, this pocket of the Peloponnese is well worth exploring at leisure.

Kate Armstrong,
Lonely Planet Author, Australia

9

7 CHRIS CHRISTO; 8 NEIL SETCHFIELD; 9 RICHARD GARVEY-WILLIAMS/ALAMY

7 Umbrella-lined Preveli Beach (p261); 8 Crater floor, Nisyros' volcano (p293); 9 Traditional tower houses, the Mani (p115)

10

↘ MYTHICAL KNOSSOS

Stepping into the Palace of Knossos (p248) is like finding yourself in a mythical world. Once the capital of Minoan Crete and home to King Minos' fabled Minotaur, it's imaginatively reconstructed with vibrant colours. Exploring it will take the best part of the day, while the images of amazing frescoes and towering columns will stay with you forever. Korina Miller, Lonely Planet Author, UK

↘ EXPERIENCING THE ACROPOLIS

Every August moon festival (p48) you can enter the Acropolis (p70) at night – it's stunningly beautiful, with the full moon hanging over the city and the marble magically lit up. There's a kind of quiet festival atmosphere, and there are various performances, too. You really get a sense of what it must have been like thousands of years ago.

Helen Hewitt, Traveller, UK

11

⬐ INDULGING IN GREEK CUISINE

Greek cuisine (p311) is very satisfying. You can always find fresh food, with the food stalls having the best deals. Each island seems to have its own speciality and way of preparing the food. Must-tries include baklava, Greek yoghurt with honey and *mousakas*. But beware – the *gyros* have fries in them!

Billy & Talitha Castillo, Travellers, Canada

⬐ AMBLE THE PELION PENINSULA

The Pelion Peninsula (p144) is criss-crossed by old cobblestone trails that connect mountain villages to the small bays that dot the eastern coast. Along the way, you're just as likely to encounter a small herd of goats as you are a car or motorbike. It's also likely that the trail will end near a good Greek taverna.

Michael Stamatios Clark, Lonely Planet Author, Australia

14

⭜ FEELING HISTORY AT OLYMPIA

Rub shoulders with the ghost of Milo of Kroton, the famous wrestler, or take a swipe at the boxer, Diagoras of Rhodes. At Olympia (p120), past and present merge magically. As you emerge from the tunnel into the Olympic stadium, it's hard to ignore the ghosts of thousands of cheering spectators.

Kate Armstrong, Lonely Planet Author, Australia

↘ LINGERING ON PEACEFUL PATMOS

Visiting the atmospheric Monastery of St John the Theologian (p303) is an awe-inspiring experience. Protected by giant heavy walls, the inside is filled with wafting incense, chanting priests and elaborate decor. Few sights capture the spirit of a place so well – on Patmos, artists and the spiritually inclined linger and a sense of peace flows free. Korina Miller, Lonely Planet Author, UK

15

14 GEORGE TSAFOS; 15 HOLGER LEUE

14 Foundations of the Philippeion, Ancient Olympia (p120); 15 Overlooking the Monastery of St John the Theologian (p303)

↘ LUSH SAMARIA GORGE

Visiting the Samaria Gorge (p259) is a wonderful way to see a vast variety of Greece's flora and fauna. There's beautiful scenery en route, including rushing rivers and fields of flowers. You can enjoy your packed lunch along the trail and a drink in a taverna at the end while you wait for the small ferry.

Billy & Talitha Castillo, Travellers, Canada

16

17

↘ HANIA'S PICTURE-PERFECT HARBOURSIDE

The pretty former Venetian port town of Hania (p253) features a shimmering, pastel-hued waterfront backed by an evocative old town full of winding stone lanes and atmospheric guest houses and restaurants.

Chris Deliso, Lonely Planet Author, Former Yugoslav Republic of Macedonia

↘ MOUNTAINOUS ZAGOROHORIA

An isolated mountain village in the foothills, up a multihairpin-bend road, at the end of the spectacular, but strenuous to walk along, 12km-long Vikos Gorge (p190) in the Pindos Mountains of northern Greece. The highlight of my visit to Greece!

Frances J Summers, Traveller

18

16 JOHN ELK III; 17 JOHN ELK III; 18 MARK DAFFEY

16 Hikers at Samaria Gorge (p259); 17 Waterfront architecture, Hania (p253); 18 Trail through Vikos Gorge (p190)

⬑ ATMOSPHERIC ODEON OF HERODES ATTICUS

Few theatres in the world evoke the palpable sense of history you feel when sitting on the worn marble seats of this **ancient amphitheatre** (p73), with the floodlit Acropolis as a backdrop, watching anything from the staging of ancient drama and contemporary Greek performers to the world's leading ballets.

Victoria Kyriakopoulos, Lonely Planet Author, Australia

19

20

⬇ SANDY SKIATHOS

Visit Skiathos (p228) out of season to take full advantage of its divine beaches. There are around 65 sun-drenched stretches of soft sand. Float in the waves, laze on the sand and live the dream. You'll have to pinch yourself to believe it's real.

Korina Miller, Lonely Planet Author, UK

19 Theatre-goers at the Odeon of Herodes Atticus (p73); 20 Sun-drenched beach at Skiathos (p228)

21

⬆ ECLECTIC CORFU TOWN

The story of **Corfu Town** (p152) is written across the handsome facades of its buildings. A stroll takes you from decaying Byzantine fortresses to neoclassical palaces, to Parisian-style arcades and Orthodox church towers, and the narrow, sun-dappled canyons of the Venetian Old Town.

Des Hannigan, Lonely Planet Author, UK

⬆ HEDONISM ON MYKONOS

The night on **Mykonos** (p206) always started with cocktails as we watched the sun set into the ocean. Then we'd make our way to one of the many bars in town for a bottle or two of Mythos, the local beer. The narrow, cobbled streets meant you sometimes lost your way, but all roads inevitably lead back to **Pierro's** (p211), for drag shows and dancing till the sun came back up.

James Taylor, Traveller

22

↘ GETTING LOST IN NAFPLIO

Slow seaside cafes, coastal walks to sandy coves, and the ancient theatre of Epidavros in Nafplio's (p105) backyard where classic lines were acted out beneath the stars – fantastic.

Korina Miller,
Lonely Planet Author, UK

23

24

↘ APPRECIATING THESSALONIKI

One of the best things to do in Thessaloniki (p174) is just wander along the waterfront towards the White Tower (p178) as the sun sets.

Will Gourlay, Traveller, Australia

21 JOHN ELK III; 22 INGOLF POMPE 3/ALAMY; 23 JON DAVISON; 24 GEORGE TSAFOS

21 Building facades, Corfu Town (p152); 22 Pedestrianised waterfront, Mykonos (p206); 23 Epidavros theatre (p110); 24 Illuminated White Tower (p178), Thessaloniki

↘ HYDRA HEIGHTS

Hydra (p123) is the diva of the Saronic Gulf. Its beautiful harbour town is a mix of elegant buildings and historic attractions, with a seductive veneer of fashion and celebrity. Beyond this, the island's high ground includes venerable monasteries and a glimpse of the remote, serene Hydra that locals inherit each winter.

Des Hannigan, Lonely Planet Author, UK

25

25 DIANA MAYFIELD

25 Hillside setting, Hydra (p123)

↘ GREECE'S TOP ITINERARIES

CITY LIFE

FIVE DAYS ATHENS TO THESSALONIKI

Greece's mainland cities are diverse and intriguing. In just five days you can sample the magnificent sights of Athens, take in beautiful Ioannina and experience the vibe of Thessaloniki. Buses connect these cities, but it's less than an hour's flight between each.

❶ ATHENS

Packed with big sights and quiet corners, Athens (p65) never fails to impress. Stroll along the pedestrianised **Apostolou Pavlou** (p65), sandwiched between the **Acropolis** (p70) and the stunning, brand new **Acropolis Museum** (p72), sights that will enjoyably take up the better part of your day. Get lost in the historic Turkish quarter of Plaka, on the Acropolis' northeastern slope, and spend time contemplating the local scene at one of the countless sidewalk **cafes** (p84). Spend the evening at the **National Theatre** (p85) or, if you're after something a little less formal, hang out at an atmospheric **rembetika club** (p85). The next day, take in more sights, visit the buzzing **markets** (p87) or hop on a tram to Glyfada, from where it's a short bus ride to a stretch of sandy, sun-drenched **beaches** (p78).

❷ IOANNINA

Charming Ioannina (p186) is beginning to get noticed. Beautifully positioned on the edge of Lake Pamvotis with a view to the sheer mountains, it's a vibrant mix of atmospheric sights and a hip social scene. Spend the day wandering through the **Kastro** (p186), the

GEORGE TSAFOS

Outdoor cafes, Thisio, Athens

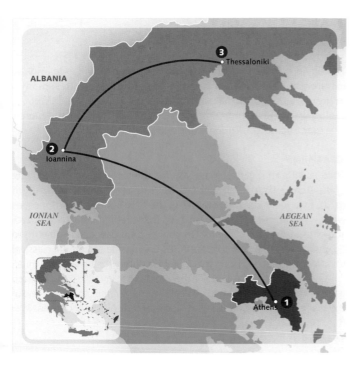

captivating old town filled with architectural wonders from Byzantine and Ottoman times. Take in the amazing **Its Kale** (p187) with its breathtaking views. Stop at some of the museums, like the fascinating **Byzantine Museum** (p187), before hopping on a relaxing **lake cruise** (p188). As the sun sinks, treat yourself to creative **cuisine** (p188) at one of the city's impressive restaurants.

❸ THESSALONIKI

Known as Greece's second city, Thessaloniki (p174) is a favourite destination with culture vultures and those after an alternative, cosmopolitan vibe. Be sure to check its packed cultural calendar before you arrive and plan your two days around any current **festivals and events** (p180). Visit the amazing interactive museum at the iconic **White Tower** (p178), the impressive mosaics at the **Church of Agios Dimitrios** (p179), and the well-respected **Archaeological Museum** (p178). Be sure to break up your sightseeing with regular visits to the city's mouth-watering **zaharoplasteia** (patisseries; p182), serving local cakes and sweets.

ANCIENT SITES

TEN DAYS ATHENS TO CRETE

The ancient ruins scattered throughout Greece will awe and inspire you. This itinerary takes in some of the top sites, many in gorgeous settings that mean you can combine your sightseeing with a little time enjoying city life, relaxing at the beach or experiencing traditional island life.

❶ ATHENS

There is little that can prepare you for the awe-inducing spectacle of the **Acropolis** (p70); be sure to visit the new **Acropolis Museum** (p72). Take in **Ancient Agora** (p73), the heart of ancient Athens, as well as the **Temple Of Olympian Zeus** (p74), remarkable for the sheer size of its Corinthian columns. On your second day, take a day trip to **Epidavros** (p110) on the Peloponnese peninsula to catch a classical theatre performance in its marvellous 3rd-century theatre. On day three, continue to explore the sites of Athens or take a day trip to the **Temple of Poseidon** (p90) in southern Attica. Return to Athens to dine in one of the many **restaurants** (p82) with views over the lit-up Acropolis.

❷ DELPHI

On day four, join a day trip from Athens to **Ancient Delphi** (p138) or reach it independently by bus and spend the night in the village of **Delphi** (p141). Fill your day exploring one of the most atmospheric archaeological sites in Greece. Spend the next morning at the fascinating **Delphi Museum** (p140) and **Sikelianos Museum** (p141), then hop on the bus back to Athens.

Tholos (p140), Sanctuary of Athena, Ancient Delphi

JOHN ELK III

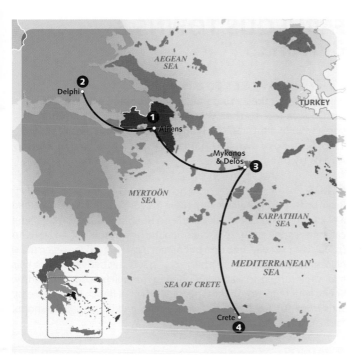

❸ MYKONOS & DELOS

Take the metro from central Athens to Piraeus and hop on the three-hour ferry to **Mykonos** (p206). Spend the rest of the day wandering through **Hora** (p207), getting lost in the narrow alleyways, boutiques, galleries and museums. Otherwise, head for the island's famous sandy **beaches** (p212). Spend the next day at the dazzling site of **Delos** (p212), one of the most important ancient sites in Greece; it's just a short boat ride from Mykonos. Return to Mykonos and join in the revelry of Hora's vibrant **nightlife** (p211).

❹ CRETE

Catch a high-speed ferry from Mykonos to **Iraklio** (p244) on Crete. You'll be there in time to visit the impressive **Archaeological Museum** (p245), a treasure trove of Minoan pottery, jewellery, sculptures and frescoes. The next day, join a day trip or hop on a bus to **Knossos** (p248), a marvellous, partially restored Minoan palace that will ignite your imagination. Spend the third and last day exploring the surrounding **Peza wine country** (p247) or visiting the Minoan site of **Phaestos** (p250).

FABULOUS TOWNS & BEACHES

TWO WEEKS KOS TO CRETE

This itinerary takes you on an island-hopping adventure from the Dodecanese to the Cyclades and on to Crete. En route you'll take in captivating villages and long stretches of divine sand. Both Kos Town and Hania on Crete are well connected to Athens by one-hour flights.

❶ KOS

Begin on Kos (p295), where Kos Town (p296) is wrapped prettily along a palm-fringed harbour. Take in the archaeological sites (p296), the cafe and restaurant (p298) scene and the nearby ruins of Asklipieion (p300). The next day, hop on a bus or rent a car to reach the seven magnificent sandy beaches of Kefalos Bay (p300), set between green hills and warm turquoise water and offering tranquil patches of paradise. Spend your third day on the long, sandy Kritika Beach (p297), an easy walk from Kos Town and backed by cafes and bars. That afternoon, take a fast ferry to Patmos (p300).

❷ PATMOS

Base yourself in Skala (p301) but spend the day exploring the hilltop old town of Hora (p303), with its winding alleyways and traditional squares. Take in the amazing Monastery of the Apocalypse (p303), where St John supposedly wrote the Book of Revelations, and the incense-filled Monastery of St John the Theologian (p303). Spend

NOBORU KOMINE

Acropolis of Lindos (p289), Rhodes

the next day at sheltered **Kambos Beach** (p305), with its shallow waters, kayaking and beach restaurant, or take an excursion boat to the idyllic, tree-shaded **Psili Ammos Beach** (p305).

❸ RHODES

Hop on a speedy hydrofoil to **Rhodes** (p280) and get yourself settled in Rhodes' magical **Old Town** (p281), enclosed within stone walls. Head out and get lost in the labyrinth of alleyways, visit the impressive **museums** (p283) and join in the buzzing **restaurant** (p286), **cafe** (p287) and **nightlife** (p287) scenes. The next day, rent a car to visit **Lindos** (p288), a pedestrianised village of whitewashed buildings, topped with an awe-inspiring **Acropolis** (p289). Just below Lindos is pretty **St Paul's Bay** (p289), a sandy cove with warm water. Spend the next day exploring the beaches along the south coast with your rented car, including beautiful **Stegna Beach** (p288) or the more remote **Glystra Beach** (p289).

❹ SANTORINI (THIRA)

Take a short flight from Rhodes to breathtaking **Santorini** (Thira; p219). Perched on the edge of the caldera, **Fira** (p220) has a few worthwhile museums and spectacular views over the multicoloured cliffs. Spend the day wandering through the town, checking out the neoclassical mansions and ancient houses dug into volcanic rock. Join a **boat cruise** (p221) across the caldera and sip cocktails at sunset in the view-filled **bars** (p222). Spend the next day on the striking east coast black-sand beaches, such as **Kamari** (p223) and **Perissa** (p224).

❺ CRETE

Take a fast, two-hour ferry from Santorini to **Rethymno** (p249) on Crete where you can settle into atmospheric **accommodation** (p251) and explore the impressive **old town** (p249). The next day, hop on a bus or rent a car to reach gorgeous **Preveli Beach** (p261), overlooked by a stunning monastery and boasting a long stretch of wide sand, palm-lined riverbanks and fresh water pools. Head for **Hania** (p253) the next morning, either by bus or car – this is Crete's most evocative city; a beautiful jumble of Venetian and Turkish architecture set on a magnificent harbour. On your last day, visit the tropical **Elafonisi Beach** (p260) on the southwest coast, with its shallow, turquoise water, tiny islets and sandy coves.

DENNIS JONES

The black sands of Perissa beach (p224), Santorini (Thira)

↘ PLANNING YOUR TRIP

PLANNING YOUR TRIP

GREECE'S BEST

GREECE'S BEST...

↘ OUTDOOR ACTIVITIES

- **Diving with dolphins** (p124) Swim alongside dolphins and delve into the Aegean's riot of colour.
- **Kayaking on Kefallonia** (p160) Explore the coastline of soaring cliffs, golden beaches and azure waters.
- **Sailing across Santorini's caldera** (p221) Join a tour on an 18th-century schooner to cruise across the breathtaking caldera.
- **Snorkelling & diving off Skiathos** (p231) Clear water, colourful reefs, sunken ships and reef beds make it ideal.
- **Skiing cross-country** (p192) Zip downhill or cross-country across the stunning Pindos Mountains.

↘ BEACHES

- **Myrtos** (p162) Greece's most idyllic beach, nestled between limestone cliffs and unbelievably blue water.
- **Preveli Beach** (p261) Palm-fringed riverbanks, freshwater pools and a hilltop monastery.
- **Koukounaries Beach** (p232) Pale sweep of golden sand that's touted as Greece's best.
- **Kefalos Bay** (p300) A paradise of wide sandy beaches and warm turquoise water.
- **Agia Anna** (p218) Long stretch of glittering sand.

↘ ARCHITECTURAL GEMS

- **Acropolis** (p70) Visually arresting monument of the ancient world.
- **Meteora** (p145) Mystical monasteries perched atop towering rock pinnacles.
- **Ancient Delphi** (p138) The atmospheric centre of the Ancient Greek world.
- **Monemvasia** (p112) A magical medieval village resting like a giant sandcastle in the sea.
- **Ancient Delos** (p212) Magnificent, sacred ruins set on a tiny island at the centre of the Cyclades.

↘ CULTURAL EXPERIENCES

- **Hellenic Festival** (p80) Greece's premier cultural festival featuring music, dance and theatre.
- **Easter on Patmos** (p300) Celebrated with atmospheric services and grand revelry.
- **Epidavros theatre** (p110) Catch a classical drama in this ancient site with near-perfect acoustics.
- **Anogia** (p253) Deep in the mountains, this rugged village offers undiluted Cretan culture.
- **Cafe Chantant** (p287) Live, traditional folk music enjoyed until the morning hours.

↘ HIKING TRAILS

- **The Mani** (p115) Wild and rugged with steep tumbling mountains, tiny coves and Maniot villages.

- **Mt Olympus** (p186) Set out across the slopes of Greece's highest peak.
- **Vikos-Aoös National Park** (p190) Watch for wildlife while hiking with semi-nomadic shepherds.
- **Samaria Gorge** (p259) Cross wooden bridges and wade through rivers in Europe's longest gorge.
- **Naxos** (p214) A lush and mountainous interior criss-crossed with ancient footpaths.

◥ GASTRONOMIC EXPERIENCES

- **Hydra's seafood** (p125) Local fish, marinated and served in front of stunning sunsets.
- **Athen's street food** (p82) Fill up on traditional cheese pies and souvlaki from streetside vendors.
- **Thessaloniki's patisseries** (p182) Sinfully scrumptious treats influenced by the Ottoman East.

- **Cretan wine** (p247) Tour the fertile Peza region for vineyards and tasting rooms.
- **Santorini's creative cuisine** (p221) Imaginative dishes like artichoke *saganaki* and smoked trout.

◥ QUIET RETREATS

- **Pelion Peninsula** (p144) Dramatic and lush, with a plunging coastline, mountain villages and quiet sandy coves.
- **Paxi** (p157) Ancient olive groves, windmills and beckoning coves.
- **Zagorohoria's villages** (p190) Preserved mountain hamlets with strong Greek traditions and gorgeous guest houses.
- **Azogires** (p260) A peaceful mountain village with rock-pool waterfalls, cave churches and overall positive vibes.
- **Lykavittos Hill** (p76) Escape the bustle of Athens on easily accessible forest paths.

HOLGER LEUE

Sailing, Santorini (Thira, p221)

THINGS YOU NEED TO KNOW

↘ AT A GLANCE

- **ATMs** In most towns and tourist areas
- **Credit cards** MasterCard and Visa are widely accepted, except on tiny islands and villages
- **Currency** Euro
- **Language** Greek, although many people speak English
- **Tipping** Restaurant bills include a service charge, but tips are appreciated; round up the fare for taxis; porters and ferry stewards expect a small gratuity (€1 to €3)
- **Visas** Most nationalities don't need a visa (see p351)

↘ ACCOMMODATION

- **Domatia** (p338) The Greek equivalent of B&B, minus the breakfast. Many are purpose-built and self-catering.
- **Hotels** (p338) Categorised according to amenities, with prices controlled by the tourist police. Maximum rates are displayed in each room.
- **Pensions** (p339) Indistinguishable from hotels.
- **Rental accommodation** (p339) Furnished apartments and villas offer good value; many require a minimum week's stay.

↘ ADVANCE PLANNING

- **Three months before** Double-check visa requirements and book flights.
- **One month before** Check ferry schedules. Book accommodation, overnight ferries and activities. Look online for festivals and events and book tickets for the larger ones.
- **Two weeks before** Book inter-island ferries and trains.

GEORGE TSAFOS

Medieval architecture, Monemvasia (p112)

- **One week before** Make reservations at any Athens restaurant with an Acropolis view.

◢ BE FOREWARNED

- **ATMs** Many banks automatically block your card after an initial withdrawal abroad; inform your bank of your travel plans. Island ATMs can lose connection for days; ensure you have a backup source of money.
- **Ferries** Weather can play havoc with schedules.

◢ COSTS

- **€50 per day** Travelling by bus, staying in hostels and occasionally eating out or taking ferries
- **€100 per day** Staying in private rooms, eating out, taking a few ferries, renting cars and seeing the sights
- **€150 per day** Comfortable rooms, good restaurants and hydrofoils all the way

◢ GETTING AROUND

- **Air** (p354) Domestic flights between major mainland cities and the larger islands.
- **Cycling** (p354) Not popular among Greeks but gaining popularity with tourists. Many regions and islands are very mountainous.

- **Boat** (p354) The true Greek island-hopping experience, ranging from slow clunkers to speedy hydrofoils.
- **Bus** (p354) Major routes serviced by safe, air-conditioned buses. Remote areas and small islands often have limited services.
- **Car** (p354) Affordable car rental available just about everywhere.

◢ GETTING THERE & AWAY

- **Air** (p352) Major hubs in Athens, Thessaloniki, Crete and Rhodes. Corfu and Mykonos take some scheduled flights. Cheap flights from Western Europe.
- **Sea** (p353) Ferries from Italian ports of Ancona, Bari, Brindisi and Venice. Busy in summer; reservations advised.
- **Train** Takes some effort; you'll need multiple tickets to cover the journey from Western Europe. Visit a travel agent or see www.raileurope.com.

◢ TECH STUFF

- **Internet** Available in major hotels, all cities and most towns
- **Wi-fi** Found in major cities and increasingly available on the islands
- **DVDs** Region code 2
- **Electricity** Two-pin adaptor, 220V AC, 50Hz

⬆ TRAVEL SEASONS

- **Summer** Mid-June to end August is high season. Beaches and sights are often crowded and accommodation can be booked solid.
- **Spring & Autumn** The best times to visit Greece; specifically May, June, September and October. The weather is warm and beaches and sites are relatively uncrowded.
- **Winter** The tourist infrastructure goes into hibernation, particularly on the islands. Many hotels and restaurants close from the end of October until mid-April; bus and ferry services are drastically reduced or cancelled.

⬆ WHAT TO BRING

- **Footwear** Sturdy shoes with ankle support is essential for managing slippery cobblestones and uneven footpaths
- **Handy distractions** Novels or a deck of cards for ferry rides
- **Sun protection** A shady hat, sunglasses and sunblock
- **Insect repellent** For mosquitoes and sand fleas

VERONICA GARBUTT

Ferry travel, Ionian islands

GET INSPIRED

BOOKS

- **Eurydice Street: A Place In Athens** (Sofka Zinovieff, 2004) An engaging tale of an expat in Athens; covers customs, etiquette, culture and modern history.
- **Falling for Icarus: A Journey Among the Cretans** (Rory Mac-Lean, 2004) The author journeys to Crete to live out his dream of constructing his own plane; the tale is entwined with history, myths and portrayals of village life.
- **It's All Greek to Me!** (John Mole, 2004) The humorous and much-acclaimed account of an English family converting a stone ruin into a home on Evia.
- **My Family and Other Animals** (Gerald Durrell, 1977) A classic, witty story of a childhood spent on Corfu, told by a now-famous naturalist and conservationist.

FILMS

- **Mediterraneo** (1991) Award-winning comedy about Italian soldiers stranded on tiny Kastellorizo during WWII.
- **For Your Eyes Only** (1981) Roger Moore travels around Greece secret-agent style.
- **Mamma Mia** (2008) Taking the world by storm, this ABBA-based musical is filmed on Skopelos, the Pelion Peninsula and Skiathos.
- **Captain Corelli's Mandolin** (2001) Based on the popular book with great scenes of Kefallonia.

- **Zorba the Greek** (1964) A steamy performance by Anthony Quinn as an uptight English writer who finds love on Crete; the famous beach dance scene was at Stavros, near Hania.

MUSIC

- **Anthologio** A musical journey with Greece's most formidable female singer, Haris Alexiou, covering hits from 1975 to 2003.
- **Itane Mia Fora** A broad range of music from Crete's favourite son, Nikos Xylouris.
- **Ta Rembetika** An excellent compilation of *rembetika* from Greece's national broadcaster, featuring all the foremost exponents of the genre.
- **To Hamogelo tis Tzokontas** Manos Hatzidakis' timeless classical recording.

WEBSITES

- **EOT** (Greek National Tourist Organisation; www.gnto.gr) For concise tourist information.
- **Greece Online** (www.greece -on-line.gr) An interactive map that lets you pinpoint things like beaches, museums, ski resorts or airports.
- **Greek Travel Pages** (www.gtp.gr) One-stop site with access to ferry schedules, accommodation listings and destination details.
- **Ministry of Culture** (www.culture .gr) Details of events, sights, galleries, monuments and museums.

PLANNING YOUR TRIP

CALENDAR

CALENDAR

JAN · FEB · MAR · APR

Easter service, Monastery of St John the Theologian (p303)

JANUARY

FEAST OF AGIOS VASILIOS
(ST BASIL)   1 JAN
Church ceremony followed by the ex-
changing of gifts, singing, dancing and
feasting. The *vasilopita* (golden glazed
cake for New Year's Eve) is cut and who-
ever gets the slice containing a coin will
supposedly have a lucky year.

EPIPHANY (BLESSING OF
THE WATERS)   6 JAN
The day of Christ's baptism by St John is
celebrated throughout Greece, with the
largest ceremony held at Piraeus. Seas,
lakes and rivers are blessed.

PATRAS CARNIVAL
This Peloponnesian festival, held between mid January and early March,
includes a wild weekend of costume
parades and colourful floats. For more
details check www.carnivalpatras.gr.

FEBRUARY

CARNIVAL SEASON
Three weeks prior to the fasting of
Lent, the carnival season begins, and
includes fancy dress, feasting, traditions
and dancing.

MARCH

INDEPENDENCE DAY   25 MAR
The anniversary of the hoisting of the
Greek flag by independence supporters at Moni Agias Lavras is celebrated
with parades and dancing. This act of
revolt marked the start of the War of
Independence.

↘ APRIL

ORTHODOX EASTER

The Lenten fast ends on Easter Sunday (40 days after the start of Lent) with the cracking of red-dyed Easter eggs, feasting and dancing. This is the most important festival in the Greek Orthodox religion. The Monastery of St John the Theologian (p303) on Patmos, in the Dodecanese, is a great place to witness it.

FEAST OF AGIOS GEORGIOS (ST GEORGE)

The feast day of St George, the country's patron saint and the patron saint of shepherds, is celebrated in many places. Expect dancing, feasting and much merriment. The day is celebrated on 23 April or the first Tuesday following Easter.

↘ MAY

MAY DAY   1 MAY

This occasion is marked by a mass exodus from towns to the country. During picnics, wildflowers are gathered and made into wreaths to decorate the house.

↘ JUNE

NAVY WEEK   EARLY JUN

Celebrating their long relationship with the sea, fishing villages and ports throughout the country host historical re-enactments and parties.

NAFPLION FESTIVAL   MID-JUN

Featuring Greek and international performers, this classical music festival in the Peloponnese uses the Palamidi fortress as one of its concert venues. Check out www.nafplionfestival.gr for details.

FEAST OF ST JOHN THE BAPTIST   24 JUN

This widely celebrated holiday sees Greeks make bonfires of the wreaths made on May Day.

ROCKWAVE FESTIVAL   END OF JUN

With major international artists (such as Moby, The Killers and Mötley Crüe) and massive crowds, this festival (p80) is held on a huge parkland at the edge of Athens.

Detail of parade float, Patras Carnival (p46)

CALENDAR

| JAN | FEB | MAR | APR |

International classical music performance, Nafplion Festival (p47)

JORN ADDE/TRONDHEIM SOLISTENE

HELLENIC FESTIVAL   JUN-AUG
The most prominent Greek summer festival (p80) features local and international music, dance and drama staged at the Odeon of Herodes Atticus in Athens and the world famous theatre of Epidavros, near Nafplio in the Peloponnese.

⬇ JULY

WINE & CULTURAL FESTIVAL
Held at Evia's coastal town of Karystos, this festival (p227) includes theatre, traditional dancing, music and visual-art exhibits. It's held in early July to the end of August and ends with a sampling of every local wine imaginable.

SPEED WORLD CUP   JUL OR AUG
Kitesurfers from around the world hit Karpathos in the Dodecanese for its excellent surfing conditions and big prize money. Event dates change annually; check www.speedworldcup.com for more details.

⬆ AUGUST

AUGUST MOON FESTIVAL   FULL MOON
The full moon is celebrated with musical performances at historical venues such as the Acropolis in Athens and other sites around the country. Check local papers for details.

FEAST OF THE ASSUMPTION   15 AUG
Assumption Day is celebrated with family reunions; the whole population seems to be on the move either side of the big day. Thousands make a pilgrimage to the miracle-working icon of Panagia Evangelistria in Tinos.

| MAY | JUN | JUL | AUG | SEP | OCT | NOV | DEC |

⬊ SEPTEMBER

GENNISIS TIS PANAGIAS   8 SEP
The birthday of the Virgin Mary is celebrated throughout Greece with religious services and feasting.

EXALTATION OF THE CROSS   14 SEP
Celebrated throughout Greece with processions and hymns.

⬊ OCTOBER & NOVEMBER

FEAST OF AGIOS DIMITRIOS   26 OCT
This feast day, commemorating St Dimitrios, is celebrated in Thessaloniki with wine drinking and revelry.

Wine tasting

GAIL MOONEY/CORBIS

OHI (NO) DAY   28 OCT
Metaxas' refusal to allow Mussolini's troops passage through Greece in WWII is commemorated with remembrance services, parades, feasting and dance.

THESSALONIKI INTERNATIONAL FILM FESTIVAL   MID-NOV
Around 150 films are crammed into 10 days of screenings around the city. For details, check out www.filmfestival.gr.

⬊ DECEMBER

CHRISTMAS DAY   25 DEC
Christmas is celebrated with religious services and feasting plus added 'Western' features, such as Christmas trees, decorations and presents.

August Moon Festival (left), Acropolis (Athens)

KATERINA MAVRONA/CORBIS

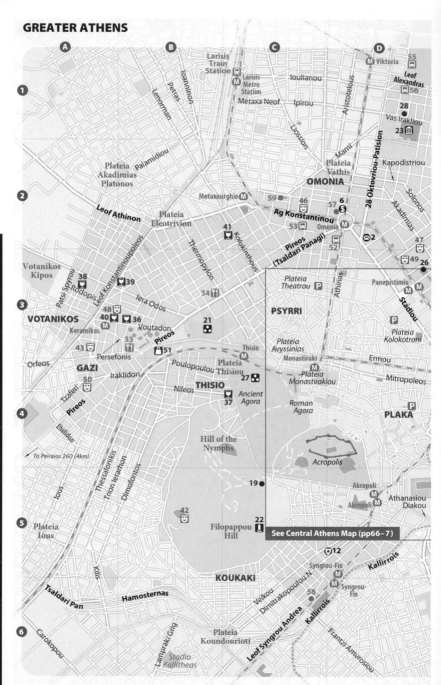

GREATER ATHENS

See Central Athens Map (pp66–7)

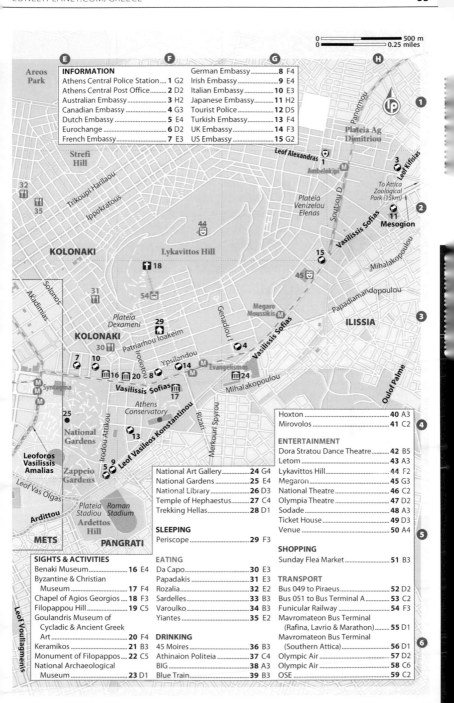

INFORMATION

Athens Central Police Station....	1 G2
Athens Central Post Office.........	2 D2
Australian Embassy	3 H2
Canadian Embassy	4 G3
Dutch Embassy	5 E4
Eurochange	6 D2
French Embassy............................	7 E3
German Embassy..........................	8 F4
Irish Embassy	9 E4
Italian Embassy	10 E3
Japanese Embassy.......................	11 H2
Tourist Police	12 D5
Turkish Embassy	13 F4
UK Embassy	14 F3
US Embassy	15 G2

SIGHTS & ACTIVITIES

Benaki Museum...........................	16 E4
Byzantine & Christian Museum	17 F4
Chapel of Agios Georgios	18 F3
Filopappou Hill	19 C5
Goulandris Museum of Cycladic & Ancient Greek Art...	20 F4
Keramikos	21 B3
Monument of Filopappos.........	22 C5
National Archaeological Museum	23 D1
National Art Gallery....................	24 G4
National Gardens	25 E4
National Library	26 D3
Temple of Hephaestus...............	27 C4
Trekking Hellas	28 D1

SLEEPING

Periscope	29 F3

EATING

Da Capo..	30 E3
Papadakis	31 E3
Rozalia..	32 E2
Sardelles.......................................	33 B3
Varoulko.......................................	34 B3
Yiantes	35 E2

DRINKING

45 Moires	36 B3
Athinaion Politeia	37 C4
BIG	38 A3
Blue Train.....................................	39 B3
Hoxton	40 A3
Mirovolos	41 C2

ENTERTAINMENT

Dora Stratou Dance Theatre..........	42 B5
Letom	43 A3
Lykavittos Hill	44 F2
Megaron	45 G3
National Theatre	46 C2
Olympia Theatre	47 D2
Sodade	48 A3
Ticket House	49 D3
Venue	50 A4

SHOPPING

Sunday Flea Market.....................	51 B3

TRANSPORT

Bus 049 to Piraeus	52 D2
Bus 051 to Bus Terminal A................	53 C2
Funicular Railway	54 F3
Mavromateon Bus Terminal (Rafina, Lavrio & Marathon).........	55 D1
Mavromateon Bus Terminal (Southern Attica).........................	56 D1
Olympic Air	57 D2
Olympic Air	58 C6
OSE	59 C2

Map labels: Areos Park, Strefi Hill, Trikoupi Harilaou, Ippokratous, KOLONAKI, Lykavittos Hill, Plateia Dexameni, KOLONAKI, Patriarhou Ioakeim, Ypsilandou, Athens Conservatory, Vasilissis Sofias, Syntagma, Akadimias, Solonos, Leof Vasileos Konstantinou, National Gardens, Leoforos Vasilissis Amalias, Zappeio Gardens, Leof Vas Olgas, Arditou, METS, Plateia Stadiou, Roman Stadium, Ardettos Hill, PANGRATI, Leof Voullagmenis, Leof Alexandras, Ambelokipi, Plateia Venizelou Elenas, Soutsou D, Vasilissis Sofias, Mesogion, Mihalakopoulou, ILISSIA, Papadiamandopoulou, Megaro Moussikis, Evangelismos, Mihalakopoulou, Genadiou I, Vasilissis Sofias, Oulof Palme, Panormou, Plateia Ag Dimitriou, Leof Kifisias, To Attica Zoological Park (15km), Plateia Venizelou Elenas

Scale: 500 m / 0.25 miles

HIGHLIGHTS

1   HELLENIC & ATHENS FESTIVAL

BY YORGOS LOUKOS, PRESIDENT & ARTISTIC DIRECTOR

The Athens Festival is quite exceptional because it takes place all over the city and there is a great variety of international artistic proposals. Our Festival partners with theatres and festivals in France, London, Berlin and New York, so audiences can discover new and co-produced works from these countries – and of course from Greece.

↘ YORGOS LOUKOS' DON'T MISS LIST

❶ ODEON OF HERODES ATTICUS

This is one of Athens' most important **venues** (p73). Get comfortable in one of the 4600 seats in this atmospheric Roman Odeon and take in a performance in much the same way ancient Greeks did in the first century. See classical music from world-famous orchestras, singers from around the world and theatre performances. The location of the venue is unique – it's in the very heart of the city on the slope beneath the Acropolis.

❷ PEIRAIOS 260

Once an abandoned factory, this **venue** (off Map pp52-3; Pireos 260, Tavros, Athens) lies in an industrial area that's being transformed into a budding arts neighbourhood. The factory is now a wonderful place of contemporary works – mostly theatre and dance from around the world, but you'll also find installations and exhibitions. This is where young people head to every night to discover the new works from all over Europe and the US.

Clockwise from top: Audiences at the Odeon of Herodes Atticus (p73); Arts venue, Peiraios 260; Megaron, Athens Concert Hall (p85); Theatre at Epidavros (p110)

❸ EPIDAVROS

Nothing beats seeing classic lines acted out in this traditional setting. Although not in Athens (it's a couple of hours from the capital), this is one of the most interesting **venues** (p110) of the Greek Festival. On Fridays and Saturdays during July and August, people travel to enjoy a performance at this 3rd-century theatre, a real jewel of ancient architecture set in the middle of the woods. The program is mainly Greek drama but not always.

❹ MEGARON

One of the most prestigious multi-purpose arts centres in Europe, the, **Megaron** (Athens Concert Hall, p85) constitutes a major focal point for music, art and education. Open since 1991, internationally acclaimed artists have praised the Megaron for its stunning environment, exceptional aesthetics and superb acoustics.

➘ THINGS YOU NEED TO KNOW

Tickets On sale from three weeks prior to a performance **Online program** www.greekfestival.gr **Average ticket price** €25 **Prices** Day trips from around €60 **Etiquette** Arrive on time or you won't be shown to your seat until intermission **See our author's review of the Hellenic & Athens Festival, p80**

HIGHLIGHTS

2 | THE ACROPOLIS

BY CATHERINE TRIANTIS, PROFESSIONAL LICENSED TOURIST GUIDE

What I love about the Acropolis is imagining what it was like 6000 years ago when it was first inhabited. I've been guiding tours here for 13 years and one thing that hasn't changed is the feeling of awe and respect I have when stepping through the monumental entranceway.

↘ CATHERINE TRIANTIS' DON'T MISS LIST

❶ PARTHENON

This is the crowning achievement of Greek architecture. Walk around the **temple** (p71) to view its geometry; stop at the northeastern corner to see its curves. Looking at the eastern steps, you can see them gradually ascend and then descend, forming a curve.

❷ ERECHTHEION

Have a look at each side of this ornate and architecturally unique **temple** (p71), characterised by elegance, grace and elaborate decoration.

The most interesting side is the porch of the Caryatids with six female Korae statues. Although copies, the artists' craftmanship is evident in the transparency of the clothing and unique hairstyles.

❸ VIEWS OF ATHENS

The Acropolis offers aerial views of the city. To the north you'll see Plaka and Ancient Agora; to the east, the Temple of Olympian Zeus and the National Gardens; to the south, the new Acropolis Museum and Filopappou Hill; and to the west, the Athenian Observatory.

Clockwise from top: Views across Athens to Lykavittos Hill (p76); Temple aspect of the Erechtheion (p71); Detail of icon painting, Acropolis (p70); Stone ruins surrounding the Parthenon (p71)

❹ COLOURFUL PAST

Built to protect the Acropolis after the Persian Wars in 479 BC, the massive northern fortification walls were made from columns taken from the sites of earlier temples. Look closely to spot hints of colour on these columns – almost everything was rendered with colour in the past.

❺ TEMPLE OF ATHENA NIKE

An absolute jewel, this **temple** (p71) was dedicated to the victory goddess, Athena Nike; it contained a wingless statue of her to keep her from flying away from Athens and therefore keeping the city victorious.

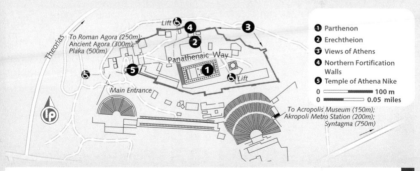

❶ Parthenon
❷ Erechtheion
❸ Views of Athens
❹ Northern Fortification Walls
❺ Temple of Athena Nike

↘ THINGS YOU NEED TO KNOW

Recommended tours See p79 **Best time** Early morning before it gets too busy and hot **How long** At least two hours **Next stop** The new Acropolis Museum (p72) **See our author's review of the Acropolis, p70**

HIGHLIGHTS

3 | ATHENS FOR KIDS

BY SIMONE GRIFFIN, SIX-YEAR-OLD TRAVELLER

I've travelled lots but Greece was one of the best places I've been. I was there for a month and it felt like a new home. The people spoiled me – they'd offer me treats and gave me lots of smiles. In Athens there were lots of interesting things to see in the busy streets.

↘ SIMONE GRIFFIN'S DON'T MISS LIST

❶ HELLENIC CHILDREN'S MUSEUM

This was a really cool **museum** (p79). The best part was the cooking class where I learned how to make Greek biscuits. The other children were all Greek and so I also learned some new words. They gave me an apron and a hat and we took turns measuring and pouring and mixing. I even got to take some of the biscuits home!

❷ NATIONAL GARDENS

Even though this **park** (p76) is in the middle of Athens, when you're in it you feel far away from the city. We went on an exciting walk past turtles and lots of birds, until we came to a playground. There were lots of great things to climb and play on. Some of them made me really dizzy!

❸ ACROPOLIS

We went to the **Acropolis** (p70) in the morning before it got too hot. It was amazing. The columns and buildings

Clockwise from top: Cooking classes at the Hellenic Children's Museum (p79); Baklava pastry (p312); Visiting the Parthenon (p71); National Gardens (p76); Beachside, Faliro (p79)

were so tall and very, very old. I really liked the old theatre where we got to sit in the marble seats and pretend it was a long time ago.

❹ EATING OUT

In Athens there were lots of yummy things to eat – little cakes, wafer-nougat treats, stuffed peppers, feta cheese and pasta. We would get lots of mezedhes (little dishes of food) to put in the middle of the table and then I'd get to try lots of different things. There were many cats in the restaurants, too. There were cats everywhere!

❺ BEACHES

Going to the **beach** (p78) was great. I'd make castles and find shells and pebbles and sometimes I'd just sit and watch the waves. But not for long. The waves were fun to jump over. Sometimes the water was cold, but lots of times it was warm and I'd get to paddle.

⬃ THINGS YOU NEED TO KNOW

Best kids' snack in the heat Ice cream and ice lollies **Essentials** Bottled water and rehydration medicine **Top tip** Teach kids a few words in Greek – it goes a long way with locals **Tickets** Kids get hefty discounts

HIGHLIGHTS

4

↘ NEW ACROPOLIS MUSEUM

Feast your eyes on the treasures unearthed from the Acropolis at the stunning, ultramodern **Acropolis Museum** (p72). The vast collection includes pieces held for years in storage as well as objects returned from abroad. In addition to the awe-inspiring sculptures, the museum contains the site and ruins of an ancient Athenian city discovered during the building's construction.

5

↘ HISTORICAL MEANDERINGS

Get lost in Athens' **historic centre** (p70). The old Turkish quarter in Plaka is virtually all that existed when Athens was declared capital of Greece. Its paved, narrow streets nestle into the northeastern slope of the Acropolis. Nearby, the former traffic-clogged thoroughfare of Apostolou Pavlou has been transformed into a lovely green pedestrian promenade and heritage trail below the Acropolis.

ATHENS & ATTICA

HIGHLIGHTS

↘ JOIN THE CAFE SCENE

Seat yourself down at a **cafe** (p84). Athenians ensconce themselves here for hours, debating, gossiping or simply people-watching. Most squares have cafes – from *kafeneia* (coffee houses) to trendy bar-like establishments – where you can work your way through a menu of frappés and small shots of traditional, strong Greek coffee.

↘ EVENING PURSUITS

Athens is a city that never sleeps. Whether you want to be wowed by phenomenal **theatre** (p85) and **opera** (p85), mesmerised by traditional **Greek folk dancing** (p85) under the stars, sung to in an atmospheric **rembetika** (Greek blues) club (p85) or danced off your feet in some of Europe's top **clubs** (p86) – the nightlife in Athens is electrifying.

↘ HEAD FOR THE BEACH

Who says you can't have the best of both worlds? When you want a break from the bustle of the city, hop on a tram to the **beach** (p78). The long stretch of sand on Athens' doorstep is a cool retreat where you can jump on a surfboard, join in the revelry of late-night summer clubbing, or simply laze by the lapping waves.

4 GEORGE TSAFOS; 5 KRZYSZTOF DYDYNSKI; 6 GEORGE TSAFOS; 7 IZZET KERIBAR; 8 GEORGE TSAFOS

4 Collections in the Acropolis Museum (p72); 5 Turkish quarter (p65); 6 Outdoor cafes, Thisio (p65); 7 Rembetika music, Stoa Athanaton (p86); 8 Glyfada (p78)

THE BEST...

⇲ PLACES TO CHILL

- **Keramikos** (p74) Stroll through the green, tranquil grounds of this ancient cemetery.
- **Lykavittos Hill** (p76) Stretch your legs on forest paths.
- **National Gardens** (p76) Relax in a shady retreat.
- **Temple of Poseidon** (p90) Be spellbound by a seaside sunset behind glimmering ruins.

⇲ GASTRO DELIGHTS

- **Diporto Agoras** (p82) Experience an eccentric eatery serving traditional cuisine and wine by the giant barrel.
- **Street Food** (p82) Fill up on scrumptious meals from streetside vendors.
- **Mani Mani** (p83) Savour regional cuisine from the Peloponnese.
- **Varoulko** (p84) Savour gourmet seafood.

⇲ ACROPOLIS VIEWS

- **Filopappou Hill** (p76) Take your camera for prime vantage points.
- **Café Avyssinia** (p83) Eat bohemian style while your eyes feast on the vista.
- **Magna Grecia** (p81) Wake up to your own view at this boutique hotel.
- **Athinaion Politeia** (p84) Nurse a strong Greek coffee with an outlook to the ruins.

⇲ WINDOWS TO THE PAST

- **Ancient Agora** (p84) Walk in Socrates' footsteps.
- **National Archaeological Museum** (p74) Get up close to the precious treasures.
- **Changing of the Guard** (p78) See the traditional presidential guards in full ceremonial dress.
- **Byzantine & Christian Museum** (p76) Be awed by icons, frescoes, textiles and manuscripts.

DIANA MAYFIELD

Temple of Poseidon (p90), Cape Sounion

THINGS YOU NEED TO KNOW

⬈ VITAL STATISTICS

- **Telephone code** ☎ 210
- **Population** Athens 3.7 million; Pireaus 175,697; Attica 4 million
- **Area** 3808 sq km

⬈ NEIGHBOURHOODS IN A NUTSHELL

- **Syntagma** The heart of modern Athens.
- **Plaka** The old Turkish quarter and home to ancient sites.
- **Monastiraki** Atmospheric market district.
- **Psyrri** Busy entertainment district.
- **Thisio** Pedestrian promenade beneath the Acropolis.
- **Kolonaki** Chic and trendy shops and galleries.
- **Makrygianni** Athens' first gay precinct.
- **Omonia** The city's dodgiest neighbourhood.
- **Exarhia** Bohemian student district.
- **Gazi** Cultural revival and gay-friendly district.

⬈ ADVANCE PLANNING

- **Two months before** Sort out your hotel and tickets for the theatre or festivals.
- **One month before** Book tours, activities and onward travel.
- **Two weeks before** Prebook top-end restaurants.

⬈ RESOURCES

- **Athens Tourism** (www.breathtaking athens.gr) Handy what's on-listings.
- **Ministry of Culture** (www.culture .gr) Guide to museums, sites and events.
- **www.elculture.gr** (in Greek) Arts and culture, including theatre, music and cinema listings.
- **Kathimerini** (www.ekathimerini.com) English-language daily with listings and ferry schedules.
- **Odyssey** (www.odyssey.gr) Includes an annual summer guide to Athens.

⬈ EMERGENCY NUMBERS

- **Police** (☎ 100)
- **Tourist police** (☎ 171; ⏲ 24hr)
- **Visitor emergency assistance** (☎ 112; ⏲ 24hr)
- **Ambulance/first-aid advice** (☎ 166)

⬈ GETTING AROUND

- **Walk** Most big sights are within easy walking distance.
- **Bus** For anywhere off the metro or train lines; 24-hour airport service.
- **Metro** The most efficient way to get around.
- **Suburban rail** Fast and comfortable service to the airport and beyond.
- **Trams** Scenic but slow.

⬈ BE FOREWARNED

- **Pickpockets** Guard your belongings on the metro and around Omonia and Monastiraki.
- **Public transport** Ensure you have a valid ticket. Fines are steep.

ATHENS & ATTICA

THINGS YOU NEED TO KNOW

DISCOVER ATHENS & ATTICA

Ancient and modern, with equal measures of grunge and grace, bustling Athens is a heady mix of history and edginess, lively cafes and alfresco dining, chaos and downright fun.

The magnificent Acropolis that rises majestically above the sprawling metropolis has stood witness to the city's many transformations. In over a decade of radical urban renewal, Athens has reinvented itself. Post-Olympics Athens is conspicuously wealthier, more sophisticated and cosmopolitan. The shift is evident in the stylish new restaurants, shops and hip hotels, and in the emerging artsy-industrial neighbourhoods and entertainment precincts. The car-free historic centre is an open-air museum, yet the city's cultural and social life that takes place around these ancient monuments, reconciling past and present. Beyond its fascinating ancient ruins and museums, Athens has a rich cultural calendar of festivals and a burgeoning contemporary arts scene.

Just beyond this seductive city lies the plain of Attica, with awe-inspiring sites, such as the glimmering Temple of Poseidon.

ATHENS IN...

Two Days

Start by climbing the glorious **Acropolis** (p70), winding down through the **Ancient Agora** (p73). Stop at a **cafe** (p84) along Adrianou before exploring **Plaka** (p65) and the **Monastiraki Flea Market** (p87). Head to the new **Acropolis Museum** (p72) for lunch and the Parthenon masterpieces. Amble around the grand promenade, then up to **Filopappou Hill** (p76) and the cafes of **Thisio** (p65), before dinner at a restaurant with an Acropolis view.

On day two, watch the **changing of the guard** (p78) at Syntagma before heading through the gardens to the **Temple of Olympian Zeus** (p74). Take a trolleybus to the **National Archaeological Museum** (p74) and spend the afternoon exploring downtown Athens or revisiting Plaka. Catch a show at the historic **Odeon of Herodes Atticus** (p73), or head to **Gazi** (p68) for dinner and nightlife.

Four Days

On the third day, head to the **Benaki Museum** (p75) and the nearby **Byzantine & Christian Museum** (p76) before lunch in **Kolonaki** (p68). Take the *teleferik* (funicular railway) up to **Lykavittos Hill** (p76) for panoramic views before having dinner in **Exarhia** (p68). Alternatively, enjoy live music at a **rembetika club** (p85).

On day four, take the tram along the coast and walk or swim at a **beach** (p78), or take a trip along the coast to the **Temple of Poseidon** (p78), then head back to the city centre to experience summer nightlife at Athens' **bars** (p84).

ATHENS ΑΘΗΝΑ

ORIENTATION

Athens' historic centre and most major sites are located within walking distance of Plateia Syntagmatos (Syntagma Sq). The city's two major landmarks, the Acropolis and Lykavittos Hill, can be seen from just about anywhere and are useful for getting one's bearings. Major streets are generally signposted in English.

Downtown Athens is a city of distinct neighbourhoods, each with its own individual character. South of Syntagma, the old Turkish quarter in Plaka is virtually all that existed when Athens was declared capital of Greece. Its paved, narrow streets pass by many of the city's ancient sites.

Centred on busy Plateia Monastirakiou (Monastiraki Sq), the area just west of Syntagma is the city's grungier but nonetheless atmospheric market district. The once clapped-out neighbourhood of Psyrri (psee-*ree*), just north of Monastiraki, has morphed into a busy entertainment precinct, with bars, restaurants, theatres and art galleries. Of late, it has lost its hip edge, and the bordering streets are rife with junkies and the city's seedier elements.

Thisio's remarkable transformation began in the late 1990s, when the former traffic-clogged, noisy thoroughfare of Apostolou Pavlou was turned into one of the most serene parts of the city. It's now a lovely green pedestrian promenade under the Acropolis, a heritage trail with its share of cafes and youth-filled bars.

CLOCKWISE FROM TOP LEFT: GEORGE TSAFOS; PAOLO CORDELLI; GEORGE TSAFOS; GEORGE TSAFOS

Clockwise from top left: Gazi nightlife (p68); Changing of the guard ceremony (p78); Views from Lykavittos Hill (p76); Stoa of Attalos (p73)

CENTRAL ATHENS

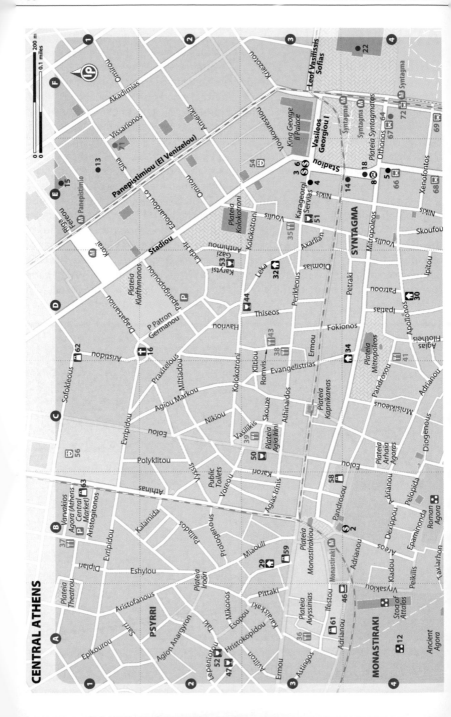

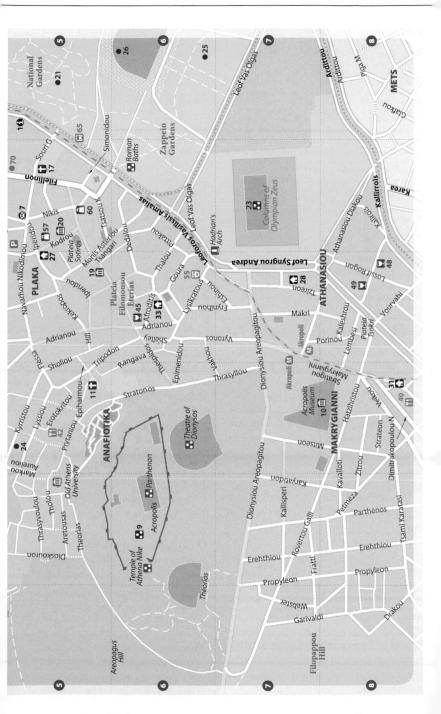

Kolonaki, east of Syntagma, is undeniably chic. Its streets are full of classy boutiques and private art galleries, as well as dozens of cafes, trendy restaurants and upscale apartment buildings. Makrygianni, between Filopappou Hill and Leoforos Syngrou, has a few upmarket hotels and restaurants, and boasts the city's first gay precincts (between Stratigou Makrygianni and Leoforos Syngrou; see boxed text, p86).

The commercial district around Omonia was once one of the city's smarter areas, but despite ongoing efforts to clean it up, it is still seedy, especially at night, when the city's less desirable elements congregate in the middle of the square (or, rather, giant roundabout). Exarhia, the bohemian graffiti-covered neighbourhood squashed between the Polytechnio and Strefi Hill, is a lively spot popular with students, artists and left-wing intellectuals. Gazi is one of the burgeoning gay-friendly neighbourhoods of Athens, with a host of gay bars and clubs.

INFORMATION
EMERGENCY
Athens central police station (Map pp52-3; ☎ 210 770 5711/17; Leoforos Alexandras 173, Ambelokipi)
ELPA road assistance (☎ 10400)
Police (☎ 100)
Tourist police (Map pp52-3; ☎ 24hr 171, 210 920 0724; Veïkou 43-45, Koukaki; ☻ 8am-10pm)
Visitor emergency assistance (☎ 112) Toll-free 24-hour service in English.

MEDICAL SERVICES
Ambulance/first-aid advice (☎ 166)
Duty doctors & hospitals (☎ 1434, in Greek) Published in *Kathimerini*.
Pharmacies (☎ 1434, in Greek) Check pharmacy windows for notice of the nearest duty pharmacy. There is a 24-hour pharmacy at the airport.
SOS Doctors (☎ 1016, 210 821 1888; ☻ 24hr) Pay service with English-speaking doctors.

MONEY

Major banks have branches around the Syntagma area and there are ATMs all over the city. Standard bank opening hours are 8am to 2.30pm Monday to Thursday and 8am to 2pm on Friday, though some banks open until 8pm weekdays and on Saturday morning.

Eurochange Syntagma (Map pp66-7; ☎ 210 331 2462; Karageorgi Servias 2; ⏰ 9am-9pm); Omonia (Map pp52-3; ☎ 210 552 2314; Kotopoulou 1); Monastiraki (Map pp66-7; ☎ 210 322 2657; Areos 1) Exchanges travellers cheques and arranges money transfers.

National Bank of Greece (Map pp66-7; ☎ 210 334 0500; cnr Karageorgi Servias & Stadiou, Syntagma) Has a 24-hour automated exchange machine.

POST

Athens central post office (Map pp52-3; www.elta.gr; Eolou 100, Omonia; ⏰ 7.30am-8pm Mon-Fri, 7.30am-2pm Sat) Unless specified otherwise, all poste restante is sent here.

Parcel post office (Map pp66-7; Nikis 33, Syntagma; ⏰ 7.30am-2pm Mon-Fri) Parcels weighing over 2kg must be brought to this post office, unwrapped, ready for inspection.

Syntagma post office (Map pp66-7; Plateia Syntagmatos, Syntagma; ⏰ 7.30am-8pm Mon-Fri, 7.30am-2pm Sat)

TOURIST INFORMATION

EOT (Greek National Tourist Organisation; www.gnto.gr) Syntagma (Map pp66-7; ☎ 210 331 0392; Leoforos Vasilissis Amalias 26a; ⏰ 9am-7pm Mon-Fri, 10am-4pm Sat & Sun); Airport (☎ 210 353 0445-7; Arrivals Hall; ⏰ 9am-7pm Mon-Fri, 10am-4pm Sat & Sun) This office has a handy free map of the city and information about public transport.

DANGERS & ANNOYANCES

Athens has its fair share of the problems found in all major cities but it is one of Europe's safest capitals. The favourite hunting grounds for pickpockets are the metro system, particularly the Piraeus-Kifisia line, and the crowded streets around Omonia, Athinas and the Monastiraki Flea Market.

SCAMS

TAXI TOUTS

Some taxi drivers work in league with overpriced, low-grade hotels around Omonia, though it's not widespread. The scam involves taxi drivers picking up late-night arrivals and persuading them that the hotel they want to go to is full – even if they have a booking. The taxi driver will pretend to phone the hotel, announce that it's full and suggest an alternative.

TRAVEL AGENTS

Some travel agents in the Plaka/Syntagma area employ touts to promote 'cheap' packages to the islands. These touts hang out at the bus and metro stops, hoping to find naive new arrivals, take them back to the agency and pressure them into buying outrageously overpriced packages.

ADULTERATED DRINKS

Some bars and clubs in Athens serve what are locally known as *bombes,* adulterated drinks that have been diluted with cheap illegal imports or methanol-based spirit substitutes. To avoid the risk, drink beer and other alcoholic drinks that are bottled, ensure that you ask for a drink with a distinctive taste; or name your brand.

TAXI DRIVERS

Most (but not all) rip-offs involve taxis picked up late at night from the ranks at the airport, train stations, bus terminals and particularly the port of Piraeus. Some drivers don't like to bother with the meter and demand whatever they think they can get away with – and refuse to take you if you insist on using the meter. Only negotiate a set fare if you have some idea of the cost; you are better off getting the driver's details to report them to the tourist police, then finding another taxi. At Piraeus, avoid the drivers at the port exit asking if you need a taxi – it's better to hail one off the street further away.

In extreme cases, drivers have accelerated meters or switch them to night rate (tariff 2 lights up) during the day. Some will also often add their tip to the price they quote. Check the extra charges for airport pick-ups and tolls, which are set and must be displayed in every taxi.

SIGHTS & ACTIVITIES
ACROPOLIS
The **Acropolis** (High City; Map pp66-7; ☎ 210 321 0219; adult/concession €12/6; ☼ 8.30am-8pm Apr-Oct, 8am-5pm Nov-Mar; ☑) is the most important ancient site in the Western world. Crowned by the Parthenon, it stands sentinel over Athens, visible from almost everywhere within the city. Its monuments of Pentelic marble gleam white in the midday sun and gradually take on a honey hue as the sun sinks, while at night they stand brilliantly illuminated above the city. A glimpse of this magnificent sight cannot fail to lift your spirits.

Inspiring as these monuments are, they are but faded remnants of Pericles' city. Pericles spared no expense – only the best materials, architects, sculptors and artists were deemed good enough for a city dedicated to the cult of Athena. The city was a showcase of lavishly coloured colossal buildings and of gargantuan statues, some of bronze, others of marble plated with gold and encrusted with precious stones.

There are several approaches to the site. The main approach from Plaka is along the path that is a continuation of Dioskouron. Anyone carrying a backpack or large bag (including camera bags) must enter from the main entrance and leave their bags at the cloakroom.

Arrive as early as possible, or go late in the afternoon, as it gets incredibly crowded. Wear shoes with rubber soles – the paths around the site are uneven and slippery. People in wheelchairs can access the site via a cage lift rising vertically up the rock face on the northern side. Those needing assistance should present at the main entrance.

HISTORY
The Acropolis was first inhabited in Neolithic times. The first temples were built during the Mycenaean era in homage to the goddess Athena. After all the buildings on the Acropolis were reduced to ashes by the Persians on the eve of the Battle of Salamis (480 BC), Pericles set about his ambitious rebuilding program. He transformed the Acropolis into a city of temples, which has come to be regarded as the zenith of classical Greek achievement.

Ravages inflicted upon them during the years of foreign occupation, pilfering by foreign archaeologists, inept renovations following Independence, visitors' footsteps, earthquakes and, more recently, acid rain and pollution have all taken their toll on the surviving monuments. The worst blow was in 1687 when the Venetians attacked the Turks, opening fire on the Acropolis and causing an explosion in the Parthenon, where the Turks were storing gunpowder, damaging all the buildings.

PROPYLAIA

The Propylaia formed the monumental entrance to the Acropolis. Built by Mnesicles between 437 BC and 432 BC, its architectural brilliance ranks with that of the Parthenon. It consists of a central hall with two wings on either side. Each section had a gate, and in ancient times these five gates were the only entrances to the 'upper city'. The ceiling of the central hall was painted with gold stars on a dark-blue background.

TEMPLE OF ATHENA NIKE

The small, exquisitely proportioned Temple of Athena Nike stands on a platform perched atop the steep southwest edge of the Acropolis, to the right of the Propylaia. Designed by Kallicrates, the temple was built of Pentelic marble between 427 BC and 424 BC. The building is almost square, with four graceful Ionic columns at either end. Only fragments remain of the frieze, which had scenes from mythology, the Battle of Plataea (479 BC) and Athenians fighting Boeotians and Persians. Parts of the frieze are in the Acropolis Museum (p72), as are some relief sculptures, including the beautiful depiction of Athena Nike fastening her sandal. The temple also housed a wooden statue of Athena.

PARTHENON

The Parthenon is the monument that more than any other epitomises the glory of ancient Greece. *Parthenon* means 'virgin's apartment' and it is dedicated to Athena Parthenos, the goddess embodying the power and prestige of the city. The largest Doric temple ever completed in Greece, and the only one built completely of Pentelic marble (apart from its wooden roof), it took 15 years to complete.

Built on the highest part of the Acropolis, the Parthenon had a dual purpose – to house the great statue of Athena commissioned by Pericles, and to serve as the new treasury. The temple consisted of eight fluted Doric columns at either end and 17 on each side. To achieve perfect form, its lines were ingeniously curved to create an optical illusion – the foundations are slightly concave and the columns are slightly convex to make both look straight.

The ceiling of the Parthenon, like that of the Propylaia, was painted blue and gilded with stars. At the eastern end was the holy cella (inner room of a temple), into which only a few privileged initiates could enter.

ERECHTHEION

Although the Parthenon was the most impressive monument of the Acropolis, it was more of a showpiece than a sanctuary. That role fell to the Erechtheion, built on the part of the Acropolis held most sacred, where Poseidon struck the ground with his trident, and where Athena produced the olive tree.

The Erechtheion is immediately recognisable by the six larger-than-life maiden columns that support its southern portico, the **Caryatids** (so called because they were

---

SIX FOR THE PRICE OF ONE

The €12 Acropolis pass includes admission to Athens' main ancient sites: Ancient Agora, Roman Agora, Keramikos, the Temple of Olympian Zeus and the Theatre of Dionysos. The ticket is valid for four days; otherwise, individual site fees apply, though this is not strictly enforced. There is free entrance to the sites on the first Sunday of the month (except for July and August) and on certain days of the year.

GEORGE TSAFOS

Excavated ruins of an ancient city neighbourhood, Acropolis Museum

↘ ACROPOLIS MUSEUM

The long-awaited **Acropolis Museum** opened with much fanfare in 2009 in the southern foothills of the Acropolis. Ten times larger than the former on-site museum, the imposing modernist building brings together the surviving treasures of the Acropolis, including items held in other museums or storage, as well as pieces returned from foreign museums. While the collection covers the Archaic and Roman periods, the emphasis is on the Acropolis of the 5th century BC, considered the apotheosis of Greece's artistic achievement.

At the entrance you can see the ruins of an ancient Athenian neighbourhood, which have been cleverly incorporated into the museum design after being uncovered during excavations.

Finds from the slopes of the Acropolis are on display in the first gallery, which has an ascending glass floor that emulates the climb up to the sacred hill, while allowing glimpses of the ruins below. Exhibits include painted vases and votive offerings from the sanctuaries where gods were worshipped, and more recent objects found in excavations of the settlement, including two clay statues of Nike at the entrance.

The museum's crowning glory is the top-floor Parthenon Gallery, a glass atrium built in alignment with the temple, and a virtual replica of the cella of the Parthenon, which can be seen from the gallery. It showcases the temple's sculptures, metopes and 160m frieze, which for the first time in more than 200 years is shown in sequence as one narrative about the Panathenaic procession.

Things you need to know: Map pp66-7; ☎ 210 900 0901; www.theacropolismuseum.gr; Dionysiou Areopagitou 15, Akropoli; ⊗ 8am-8pm Tue-Sun; admission €5; ♿

modelled on women from Karyai, modern-day Karyes, in Lakonia). Those you see are plaster casts. The originals (except for one removed by Lord Elgin that now sits in the British Museum) are in the Acropolis Museum (p72).

Architecturally, it is the most unusual monument of the Acropolis, a supreme example of Ionic architecture ingeniously built on several levels to counteract the uneven bedrock.

The northern porch consists of six Ionic columns; on the floor are the fissures supposedly left by the thunderbolt sent by Zeus to kill King Erechtheus. To the south of here was the **Cecropion** – King Cecrops' burial place.

SOUTHERN SLOPE OF THE ACROPOLIS
THEATRE OF DIONYSOS

The importance of theatre in the Athenian city-state can be gauged from the dimensions of the enormous **Theatre of Dionysos** (Map pp-66-7; ☎ 210 322 4625; Dionysiou Areopagitou; admission €2, free with Acropolis pass; ☽ 8am-8pm Apr-Oct, 8am-5pm Nov-Mar) on the southeastern slope of the Acropolis.

The first theatre on this site was a timber structure erected sometime during the 6th century BC, after the tyrant Peisistratos introduced the Festival of the Great Dionysia. The theatre was reconstructed in stone and marble by Lycurgus between 342 BC and 326 BC, with a seating capacity of 17,000 spread over 64 tiers, of which about 20 survive. Apart from the front row, the seats were built of Piraeus limestone and were occupied by ordinary citizens, although women were confined to the back rows. The front row's 67 thrones, built of Pentelic marble, were reserved for festival officials and important priests. The grandest was reserved for the Priest of Dionysos, who sat shaded from the sun under a canopy. His seat can be identified by well-preserved lion-claw feet at either side.

ODEON OF HERODES ATTICUS

The Odeon of Herodes Atticus was built in AD 161 by wealthy Roman Herodes Atticus in memory of his wife Regilla. It was excavated in 1857-58 and completely restored between 1950 and 1961. Performances of drama, music and dance are held here during the Athens Festival (p80). The theatre is only open to the public during performances.

ANCIENT AGORA

The heart of ancient Athens was the **Agora** (Market; Map pp66-7; ☎ 210 321 0185; Adrianou; adult/concession €4/2, free with Acropolis pass; ☽ 8.30am-8pm Apr-Oct, 8am-5.30pm Nov-Mar), the lively, crowded focal point of administrative, commercial, political and social activity. Socrates spent a lot of time here expounding his philosophy, and in AD 49 St Paul spent his days here winning converts to Christianity.

First developed in the 6th century BC, the site was devastated by the Persians in 480 BC, but a new Agora was built in its place almost immediately. It was flourishing by Pericles' time and continued to do so until AD 267, when it was destroyed by the Herulians, a Gothic tribe from Scandinavia. The Turks built a residential quarter on the site, but this was demolished by archaeologists after Independence and later excavated to classical and, in parts, Neolithic levels. There are a number of entrances, but the most convenient is the northern entrance from Adrianou.

STOA OF ATTALOS

The **Agora Museum**, in the reconstructed Stoa of Attalos, is a good place to start to make sense of the site. The museum has a model of the Agora as well as a collection of finds from the site. The first-ever shopping arcade, the original stoa was built by King Attalos II of Pergamum (159-138 BC), two storeys high with two aisles housing expensive shops. People also gathered here to watch the Panathenaic procession.

TEMPLE OF HEPHAESTUS

The best-preserved Doric temple in Greece, this **temple** (Map pp52-3) on the western edge of the Agora was dedicated to Hephaestus, god of the forge, and surrounded by foundries and metalwork shops. Built in 449 BC by Iktinos, one of the architects of the Parthenon, it has 34 columns and a frieze on the eastern side depicting nine of the Twelve Labours of Heracles.

CHURCH OF THE HOLY APOSTLES

This charming little church, near the southern entrance, was built in the early 10th century to commemorate St Paul's teaching in the Agora. It contains some fine Byzantine frescoes.

KERAMIKOS

The city's cemetery from the 12th century BC to Roman times was **Keramikos** (Map pp66-7; ☎ 210 346 3552; Ermou 148, Keramikos; adult/concession incl museum €2/1, free with Acropolis pass; ☯ 8.30am-8pm Apr-Oct, 8am-5.30pm Nov-Mar). Discovered in 1861 during the construction of Pireos street, it is one of the greenest and most tranquil ancient sites in Athens. Once inside, head for the small knoll ahead and to the right, where you'll find a plan of the site.

TEMPLE OF OLYMPIAN ZEUS

This is the largest **temple** (Map pp66-7; ☎ 210 922 6330; adult/concession €2/1, free with Acropolis pass; ☯ 8.30am-8pm Apr-Oct, 8am-5.30pm Nov-Mar) in Greece. The temple was begun in

the 6th century BC by Peisistratos, but was abandoned due to lack of funds. Various other leaders had stabs at completing it, but it was left to Hadrian to complete the work in AD 131. It took more than 700 years to build.

The temple is impressive for the sheer size of its 104 Corinthian columns (17m high with a base diameter of 1.7m), of which 15 remain – the fallen column was blown down in a gale in 1852. Hadrian put a colossal statue of Zeus in the cella and, in typically immodest fashion, placed an equally large one of himself next to it.

MUSEUMS & GALLERIES
NATIONAL ARCHAEOLOGICAL MUSEUM

One of the world's most important museums, the **National Archaeological Museum** (Map pp52-3; ☎ 210 821 7717; www .namuseum.gr; 28 Oktovriou-Patision 44; adult/concession €7/3; ☯ 1.30-8pm Mon, 8.30am-8pm Tue-Sun Apr-Oct, 8.30am-3pm Nov-Mar) houses the finest collection of Greek antiquities. With 10,000 sq metres of exhibition space, it could take several visits to appreciate the museum's vast holdings, but it is possible to see the highlights in half a day.

The fabulous collection of **Mycenaean antiquities** (Gallery 4) is the museum's *tour de force*. The first cabinet holds the celebrated **Mask of Agamemnon**, unearthed at Mycenae by Heinrich Schliemann, along with key finds from Grave Circle A, including bronze daggers with intricate representations of the hunt. The exquisite **Vaphio gold cups**, with scenes of men taming wild bulls, are regarded as among the finest surviving examples of Mycenaean art.

The **Cycladic collection** in Gallery 6 includes the superb figurines of the 3rd and 2nd centuries BC that inspired artists

GEORGE TSAFOS

Artefacts at the Benaki Museum

↘ IF YOU LIKE...

If you like the impressive sculptures, pottery and artefacts housed in the **National Archaeological Museum** (p74), we think you'll like what you find in these museums, too:

- **Benaki Museum** (Map pp52-3; ☎ 210 367 1000; www.benaki.gr; Koumbari 1, cnr Leoforos Vasilissis Sofias, Kolonaki; adult/concession €6/3, free Thu; ☼ 9am-5pm Mon, Wed, Fri & Sat, 9am-midnight Thu, 9am-3pm Sun) This private museum displays the vast results of 35 years of avid collecting in Europe and Asia. The collection includes Bronze Age finds from Mycenae and Thessaly; works by El Greco; ecclesiastical furniture brought from Asia Minor; pottery, copper, silver and woodwork from Egypt, Asia Minor and Mesopotamia; and a stunning collection of Greek regional costumes.
- **Goulandris Museum of Cycladic & Ancient Greek Art** (Map pp52-3; ☎ 210 722 8321; www.cycladic.gr; cnr Leoforos Vasilissis Sofias & Neofytou Douka, Kolonaki; adult/concession €7/3.50; ☼ 10am-5pm Mon, Wed, Fri & Sat, 10am-8pm Thu, 11am-5pm Sun; ♿) A private collection of Cycladic art, dating from 3000 BC to the 4th century AD. Watch for marble figurines with folded arms that inspired many 20th-century artists with their simplicity and purity of form, along with films depicting life in ancient Greece.
- **Piraeus Archaeological Museum** (☎ 210 452 1598; Harilaou Trikoupi 31, Piraeus; adult/concession €3/2; ☼ 8.30am-8pm Tue-Sun, 2-8pm Mon, closes 3pm in winter) Set your eyes on important finds from classical and Roman times, including the magnificent statue of Apollo, the *Piraeus Kouros,* the oldest larger-than-life hollow bronze statue found to date.

such as Picasso. The galleries to the left of the entrance house the oldest and most significant pieces of the **sculpture collec-** **tion**. Head up the stairs to the museum's other big crowd-puller, the spectacular **Minoan frescoes** from Santorini (Thira).

BYZANTINE & CHRISTIAN MUSEUM

This outstanding **museum** (Map pp52-3; ☎ 210 721 1027; www.culture.gr; Leoforos Vasilissis Sofias 22; adult/concession €4/2; ☼ 8.30am-7.30pm Tue-Sun May-Sep, 8.30am-3pm Tue-Sun Oct-Apr; ⑤) presents a priceless collection of Christian art, dating from the 3rd to 20th centuries. Thematic snapshots of the Byzantine and post-Byzantine world – a part of Greek history that is often ignored in favour of its ancient past – are exceptionally presented in the expansive multilevel underground galleries (the final galleries opened in 2009). The collection includes icons, frescoes, sculptures, textiles, manuscripts, vestments and mosaics.

NATIONAL ART GALLERY

Greece's premier **art gallery** (Map pp52-3; ☎ 210 723 5857; Leoforos Vasileos Konstantinou 50; adult/concession €6/5; ☼ 9am-3pm Mon & Wed-Sat, 10am-2pm Sun; ⑤) presents a rich collection of Greek art spanning four centuries from the post-Byzantine period. The 1st floor hosts works from the post-Byzantine period, the gallery's prized El Greco paintings, including *The Crucifixion* and *Symphony of the Angels,* and works from the Ionian period until 1900. On the 2nd floor are works by leading 20th-century artists, including Parthenis, Moralis, Maleas and Lytras. The gallery also has works by European masters, including paintings by Picasso, and hosts major international exhibitions.

TURKISH BATHS

The beautifully refurbished 17th-century **bathhouse** (Map pp66-7; ☎ 210 324 4340; Kyrristou 8, Plaka; admission €2; ☼ 9am-2.30pm Wed-Mon) is the only surviving public bathhouse in Athens and one of the few remnants of Ottoman times. A helpful free audio tour takes you back to the bathhouse days.

HILLS OF ATHENS

LYKAVITTOS HILL

The name Lykavittos means 'Hill of Wolves' and derives from ancient times when the hill was surrounded by countryside and its pine-covered slopes were inhabited by wolves. Today, the **hill** (Map pp52-3) rises out of a sea of concrete to offer the finest panoramas in Athens. A path leads to the summit from the top of Loukianou. Alternatively, you can take the **funicular railway** (Map pp52-3; ☎ 210 721 0701; return €6; ☼ 9am-3am, half-hourly), referred to as the '*teleferik*', from the top of Ploutarhou in Kolonaki. Perched on the summit is the little **Chapel of Agios Georgios** (Map pp52-3), floodlit like a beacon over the city at night.

WEST OF THE ACROPOLIS

Filopappou Hill (Map pp52-3), also called the Hill of the Muses, is identifiable to the southwest of the Acropolis by the **Monument of Filopappos** (Map pp52-3) at its summit. The monument was built between 114 and 116 in honour of Julius Antiochus Filopappos, who was a prominent Roman consul and administrator.

The pine-clad slopes are a pleasant place for a stroll. They offer good views of the plain and mountains of Attica and of the Saronic Gulf, and some of the best vantage points for photographing the Acropolis.

PARKS & GARDENS

NATIONAL GARDENS

A delightful, shady refuge during summer, the **National Gardens** (Map pp66-7; entrances on Leoforos Vasilissis Sofias & Leoforos Vasilissis Amalias, Syntagma; ☼ 7am-dusk) were formerly the royal gardens designed by Queen Amalia. There's also a large children's **playground**, a duck pond and a shady cafe.

KRZYSZTOF DYDYNSKI

Altar wall, Agios Nikolaos Rangavas

ATHENS & ATTICA

ATHENS

⇘ IF YOU LIKE...

If you like the frescoes and glittering collection at the **Byzantine & Christian Museum** (p76), we think you'll like these amazing Byzantine churches:

- **Church of Agii Theodori** (Map pp66-7; Syntagma) Behind Plateia Klafthmonos, this 11th-century church has a tiled dome and walls decorated with a pretty terracotta frieze of animals and plants.
- **Agios Nikolaos Rangavas** (Map pp66-7; Plaka) Built in the 11th-century, this lovely chapel was part of the palace of the Rangavas family, who counted among them Michael I, emperor of Byzantium. The church bell was the first installed in Athens after liberation from the Turks (who banned them), and was the first to ring in 1833 to announce the freedom of Athens.
- **Church of Sotira Lykodimou** (Map pp66-7; Plateia Rallou Manou) Now the Russian Orthodox Cathedral, this unique 11th-century structure, the only octagonal Byzantine church, has an imposing dome.

ZAPPEIO GARDENS

Between the National Gardens and the old Olympic stadium are the **Zappeio Gardens** (Map pp66-7; entrances on Leoforos Vasilissis Amalias & Leoforos Vasilissis Olgas), laid out in a network of wide walkways around the grand **Zappeio Palace** (Map pp66-7; www.zappeion.gr).

The Zappeio hosts conferences, events and exhibitions, and there's a pleasant cafe, restaurant and open-air cinema next door.

OTHER ATTRACTIONS
PARLIAMENT

Designed by the Bavarian architect Von Gartner and built between 1836 and 1842, Greece's **Parliament** (Map pp66-7) was originally the royal palace. The war memorial in the forecourt, known as the **Tomb of the Unknown Soldier**, is guarded by the city's famous statuesque *evzones,* the presidential guards whose uniform of short kilts and pom-pom shoes is based on the attire worn by the klephts (the mountain fighters of the War of Independence).

The changing of the guard takes place every hour, while every Sunday at 11am the *evzones* perform an extended **changing of the guard ceremony** in full ceremonial dress, accompanied by a military band.

HELLENIC COSMOS

To put the ruins and museums into perspective, take a virtual-reality trip to ancient Greece at the futuristic **Foundation for the Hellenic World** (off Map pp66-7; ☎ 212 254 0000; www.hellenic-cosmos.gr; Pireos 254, Tavros; adult €6-10, child €3.90-8, day pass €15; ☺ 9am-4pm Mon-Fri, 10am-3pm Sun Jun-Sep, closed for 2 weeks mid-Aug; ☐ ☺), about 2km from the city centre. The **Tholos virtual-reality theatre** takes you on an interactive tour of the Ancient Agora or allows you to get a feel for life in ancient Athens. The **Kivotos time machine** has 3D floor-to-ceiling screens with a live guide taking you through ancient Olympia and Miletus.

PLANETARIUM

Athens boasts the world's largest and most technologically advanced digital **planetarium** (off Map pp66-7; ☎ 210 946 9600; www.eugenfound.edu.gr; Leoforos Syngrou 387, Palio Faliro; adult €6-8, concession €4-5; ☺ 5.30-8.30pm Wed-Fri, 10.30am-8.30pm Sat & Sun, closed mid-July-late Aug). The 280-seat planetarium, with a 950-sq-metre hemispherical dome, offers 3D virtual trips into the galaxy, as well as IMAX movies and other high-tech shows. There is simultaneous narration in English (€1).

BEACHES

Athens is the only coastal European capital with beaches within easy distance of the city centre, along the coast towards **Glyfada** (Map p91). This is where Athenians cool off and where much of the summer nightlife takes place.

The better beaches are privately run and charge admission (between €4 and €15 per adult). They're usually open between 8am and dusk, May to October (later during heatwaves), and have sun

GEORGE TSAFOS

Tholos virtual-reality theatre, Hellenic Cosmos

beds and umbrellas (additional charge in some places), changing rooms, children's playgrounds and cafes.

The flashiest and most exclusive summer playground is **Astir Beach** (☎ 210 890 1621; www.astir-beach.com; admission Mon-Fri €15, Sat & Sun €25; ☉ 8am-9pm), with water sports, shops and restaurants. You can even book online.

The following can be reached by tram and then buses from Glyfada or Voula:

Akti Tou Iliou (☎ 210 985 5169; Alimo; adult/child Mon-Fri €6/3, Sat & Sun €8/4; ☉ 8am-8pm)

Asteras Beach (☎ 210 894 1620; www.balux-septem.com; Glyfada; adult/child Mon-Fri €6/3, Sat & Sun €7/3; ☉ 10am-7pm)

Yabanaki (☎ 210 897 2414; www.yabanaki.gr; Varkiza; adult/child Mon-Fri €7/4.50, Sat & Sun €8/4.50; ☉ 8am-8pm)

There are free beaches at Palio Faliro (Edem), Kavouri and Glyfada.

DIVING

Aegean Dive Centre (☎ 210 894 5409; www.adc.gr; Zamanou 53, cnr Pandoras, Glyfada; PADI certification from €390, day/night dives €35/100) organises dives between Vouliagmeni and Cape Sounion. Prices include diving equipment.

Popular with seasoned divers, the new **Planet Blue Dive Centre** (☎ 22920 26446; www.planetblue.gr; Velpex Factory, Lavrio; PADI certification from €300, dives €35-80) caters for all levels at sites around Cape Sounion. Prices include diving equipment.

ATHENS FOR CHILDREN

The shady **National Gardens** (p76) have a playground, duck pond and mini zoo. There is also a fully enclosed shady playground in the **Zappeio Gardens** (p77).

The **Hellenic Children's Museum** (Map pp66-7; ☎ 210 331 2995; Kydathineon 14, Plaka; admission free; ☉ 10am-2pm Tue-Fri, 10am-3pm

Sat & Sun) is more of a play centre, with a games room and a number of 'exhibits' – such as a mock-up of a metro tunnel – for children to explore, as well as workshops ranging from baking to bubble-making. Parents must be on hand to supervise their children at all times.

The **Museum of Greek Children's Art** (Map p66-7; ☎ 210 331 2621; Kodrou 9, Plaka; admission free; ☉ 10am-2pm Tue-Sat, 11am-2pm Sun, closed Aug) has a room set aside where children can let loose their creative energy.

The **Attica Zoological Park** (off Map pp52-3; ☎ 210 663 4724; www.atticapark.gr; Yalou, Spata; adult/3-12yr €14/10; ☉ 9am-sunset) has an expanding collection of big cats, birds, reptiles and other animals, including a monkey forest and Cheetahland, where you can walk through a tunnel. The 19-hectare site is near the airport. Take bus 319 from Doukissis Plakentias metro station.

TOURS

Athens Sightseeing Public Bus Line (Bus Route 400; tickets €5) stops at 20 key sites, such as the Acropolis, National Archaeological Museum and Panathenaic Stadium. Tickets are valid for 24 hours and can be used on all public transport, excluding airport services.

CitySightseeing Athens (Map pp66-7; ☎ 210 922 0604; www.city-sightseeing.com; adult/concession €18/8; ☉ every 30min 9am-6pm; ♿) has open-top double-decker buses cruising around town on a 90-minute circuit. You can get on and off at 15 stops on a 24-hour ticket.

Athens Happy Train (Map pp66-7; ☎ 210 725 5400; adult/concession €6/4; ☉ 9am-midnight) runs minitrain tours, with stops at Monastiraki and the Acropolis. The tours take one hour if you don't get off – or you can get on and off over five hours. Trains leave from the top of Ermou every 30 minutes and go as far as the Panathenaic Stadium.

Trekking Hellas (Map pp52-3; ☎ 210 331 0323; www.trekking.gr; Rethymnou 12, Exarhia) runs activities ranging from Athens walking tours (€22) to two-hour bike tours (€35).

FESTIVALS & EVENTS
HELLENIC FESTIVAL
Greece's premier cultural festivals, held annually under the auspices of the **Hellenic Festival** (www.greekfestival.gr) from late May to October, feature a top line-up of local and international music, dance and theatre.

Major shows in the **Athens Festival** take place at the superb Odeon of Herodes Atticus (p73), one of the world's most historic venues, with the floodlit Acropolis as a backdrop. Events are also held in various modern theatres and venues around town. The **Epidavros Festival** presents local and international productions of ancient Greek drama at the famous Epidavros ancient theatre (p110) in the Peloponnese, about two hours west of Athens. The **Musical July** festival takes place at the lovely 3rd-century-BC Ancient Epidavros Little Theatre, set among the olive groves and pine trees in the seaside village of Epidavros.

The festival program should be available from the beginning of February on the festival website and at the **festival box office** (Map pp66-7; ☎ 210 327 2000; arcade, Panepistimiou 39, Syntagma; ☽ 8.30am-4pm Mon-Fri, 9am-2pm Sat).

ROCKWAVE FESTIVAL
The annual international **Rockwave Festival** (☎ 210 882 0426; www.rockwavefestival.gr) has been growing in stature and popularity, and rock fans can expect to see some of the world's top acts – the 2009 line-up ranged from Moby, Placebo and Mötley Crüe to local artist Konstantino Bita. Tickets are available online from www.ticketpro.gr or from **Ticket House** (Map pp52-3; ☎ 210 360 8366; www.tickethouse.gr; Panepistimiou 42, Syntagma).

SLEEPING
BUDGET
Athens Style (Map pp66-7; ☎ 210 322 5010; www.athenstyle.com; Agias Theklas 10, Psyrri; dm €20-24, s/d €51/68, studios €90-124; ☒ ▯) The newest hostel in town, this bright and arty place has tasteful, well-equipped studios and hostel beds in a handy location within walking distance of the metro, major sights, restaurants and nightlife. The small rooftop bar is ideal for evening drinks under the Acropolis.

Acropolis House Pension (Map pp66-7; ☎ 210 322 2344; www.acropolishouse.gr; Kodrou 6-8, Plaka; d €59-65, s/d/tr incl breakfast €72.50/87/113.50; ☒ �) This atmospheric family-run pension is in a beautifully preserved, 19th-century house, which retains many original features and has lovely painted walls. Some rooms have bathrooms across the hall.

Hotel Phaedra (Map pp66-7; ☎ 210 323 8461; www.hotelphaedra.com; Herefontos 16, Plaka; s €65, d €65-80, tr €95; ☒ ▯) Many of the rooms at this small, family-run hotel have balconies overlooking a church or the Acropolis. The hotel had an Olympics makeover and is tastefully furnished, though room sizes vary from small to snug. Some rooms have private bathrooms across the hall. A great rooftop terrace, friendly staff and a good location make this one of the better deals in Plaka.

MIDRANGE
Hotel Achilleas (Map pp66-7; ☎ 210 323 3197; www.achilleashotel.gr; Leka 21, Syntagma; s/d/tr incl breakfast €110/135/159; ☒ ▯) From the sleek lobby with marble checkerboard floors, to the well-appointed rooms, the conveniently located Achilleas has been

Evening performance staged at Lykavittos Hill (p76)

GEORGE TSAFOS

tastefully renovated. The comfortable rooms are large and airy, and those on the top floor open onto garden balconies. There are large family rooms (€175).

Central Hotel (Map pp66-7; ☎ 210 323 4357; www.centralhotel.gr; Apollonos 21, Plaka; s/d/tr incl buffet breakfast from €111/136/185; 🅿 🖳) This stylish hotel has been tastefully decorated in light, contemporary tones. It has comfortable rooms with all the mod cons and decent bathrooms. There is a lovely roof terrace with Acropolis views, a small spa and sun lounges. Central is in a handy location between Syntagma and Plaka.

Magna Grecia (Map pp66-7; ☎ 210 324 0314; www.magnagreciahotel.com; Mitropoleos 54, Monastiraki; incl breakfast s €120, d €150-180; 🅿 🖳 🛜) This intimate boutique hotel, in a historic building opposite the cathedral, has great Acropolis views from the front rooms and rooftop terrace. Twelve individually decorated rooms with murals are named after Greek islands, and offer excellent amenities, including comfortable mattresses, DVD players and minibars.

Athens Gate (Map pp66-7; ☎ 210 923 8302; www.athensgate.gr; Leoforos Syngrou 10, Makrygianni; s/d incl breakfast €130/145; 🅿 🖳) With stunning views over the Temple of Olympian Zeus from the spacious front rooms, and a handy (if busy) location, this totally refurbished hotel is great value compared with some of the similarly priced offerings. The stylish rooms are immaculate and have all the mod cons, staff are friendly and breakfast is served on the superb rooftop terrace with a choice of 360-degree Athens views.

TOP END

Hera Hotel (Map pp66-7; ☎ 210 923 6682; www.hera hotel.gr; Falirou 9, Makrygianni; s/d incl breakfast €130/160, ste from €250; 🅿 🖳) This elegant boutique hotel, a short walk from the Acropolis and Plaka, has been totally rebuilt but the formal interior design is in keeping with the lovely neoclassical facade. There's lots of brass and timber, and stylish classic furnishings with a modern edge. The rooftop garden, restaurant and bar have spectacular views.

ourpick **Periscope** (Map pp52-3; ☎ 210 729 7200; www.periscope.gr; Haritos 22, Kolonaki; r €195-225, ste from €325 incl breakfast; ☒ ☎) Right in chic Kolonaki overlooking Lykavittos, Periscope is a smart boutique hotel with industrial decor. There are clever gadgets and design features, including the lobby slide show, the sea-level measure on the stairs, travelling TVs, aerial shots of the city on the ceilings and Korres toiletries.

EATING
BUDGET

ourpick **Filema** (Map pp66-7; ☎ 210 325 0222; Romvis 16, Syntagma; mezedhes €4.50-12; ☒ Mon-Sat) This popular *mezedhopoleio* has two shopfronts and fills tables on both sides of this narrow street, which is a busy commercial area by day but a peaceful spot when the shops close. It has a great range of mezedhes such as plump *keftedhes* (small tasty rissoles) and grilled sardines.

Rozalia (Map pp52-3; ☎ 210 330 2933; Valtetsiou 58; mains €4.50-11) An old-style Exarhia favourite on a lively pedestrian strip, this family-run taverna has a standard menu of grills and home-style fare such as *pastitsio* (layers of buttery macaroni and seasoned minced lamb). The large courtyard garden is popular in summer, when fans spraying water help keep you cool.

Pure Bliss (Map pp66-7; ☎ 210 325 0360; Romvis 24a, Syntagma; salads €7-9; ☒ 10am-1am Mon-Sat, 5-9pm Sun) One of the few places in Athens where you can get organic coffee, exotic teas and soy products. There's a range of healthy salads, juices, smoothies and mostly organic food and wine (including organic cocktails).

Diporto Agoras (Map pp66-7; ☎ 210 321 1463; cnr Theatrou & Sokratous, Omonia; ☒ 8am-6pm Mon-Sat, closed 1-20 Aug) This quirky old taverna is one of the dining gems of Athens. There's no signage, only two doors leading to a rustic cellar where there's no menu, just a few dishes that haven't changed in years. The house speciality is *revythia* (chick peas), usually followed by grilled fish and washed down with wine from one of the giant barrels lining the wall. The often erratic service is part of the appeal.

STREET FOOD

From vendors selling *koulouria* (fresh pretzel-style bread) and grilled corn or chestnuts, to the raft of fast-food offerings, there's no shortage of snacks on the run.

You can't go wrong with local *tiropites* (cheese pies) and their various permutations. **Ariston** (Map pp66-7; ☎ 210 322 7626; Voulis 10, Syntagma; pies €1.10-1.70; ☒ 10am-4pm Mon-Fri) has been around since 1910, serving the best range of tasty, freshly baked pies with all manner of fillings.

However, Greece's favourite tasty snack is the souvlaki, packing more punch for €2 than anything else. You can't miss the smells wafting from the souvlaki hub at Monastiraki, but you'll find one of the best souvlaki joints in Athens nearby at tiny **Kostas** (Map pp66-7; ☎ 210 323 2971; Plateia Agia Irini 2, Monastiraki; souvlaki €2; ☒ 5am-5pm). This old-style hole-in-the-wall joint, in a pleasant square opposite Agia Irini church, churns out tasty, freshly made pork souvlakia and kebabs, with its signature spicy tomato sauce.

MIDRANGE

ourpick Café Avyssinia (Map pp66-7; ☎ 210 321 7407; Kynetou 7, Monastiraki; mezedhes €4.50-16.50; ☷ noon-1am Tue-Sat, noon-7pm Sun) Hidden away on grungy Plateia Avyssinias, in the middle of the flea market, this bohemian *mezedhopoleio* gets top marks for atmosphere, food and friendly service. It specialises in regional Greek cuisine, from warm fava to aubergines baked with tomato and cheese, and has a great selection of ouzo, *raki* (Cretan firewater) and *tsipouro* (distilled spirit similar to ouzo but usually stronger). There are fantastic Acropolis views from the window seats upstairs.

Sardelles (Map pp52-3; ☎ 210 347 8050; Persefonis 15, Gazi; fish dishes €9-15.50) This friendly, modern fish taverna specialises in simple seafood mezedhes. It's opposite the illuminated gasworks, with tables outside, excellent service and nice touches such as the fishmonger paper tablecloths and souvenir pots of basil. Try the grilled *thrapsalo* (squid) and excellent *taramasalata* (a thick purée of fish roe, potato, oil and lemon juice).

Yiantes restaurant

NEIL SETCHFIELD

ourpick Mani Mani (Map pp66-7; ☎ 210 921 8180; Falirou 10, Makrygianni; mains €9.50-17; ☷ closed Jul & Aug) Forgo a view and head upstairs to the relaxing dining rooms of this delightful modern restaurant, which specialises in regional cuisine from Mani in the Peloponnese. The ravioli with Swiss chard, chervil and cheese, and the tangy Mani sausage with orange are standouts.

ourpick Yiantes (Map pp52-3; ☎ 210 330 1369; Valtetsiou 44, Exarhia; mains €10-17) This modern taverna set in a lovely garden courtyard is next to an open-air cinema. It is upmarket for Exarhia, but the food is superb and made with largely organic produce. There are interesting greens such as *almirikia*, the fish is perfectly grilled, and the mussels and calamari with saffron are memorable.

Palia Taverna tou Psara (Map pp66-7; ☎ 210 321 8734; Erehtheos 16, Plaka; seafood dishes €11.50-26) Hidden away from the main hustle and bustle of Plaka, this taverna is a cut above the rest, which is why they fill the tables on the street, the terrace and the place next door. There is a choice of mezedhes but it is known as the best seafood taverna in Plaka (top fresh fish €62 per kilogram).

Mono (Map pp66-7; ☎ 210 322 6711; Paleologou Venizelou 4, Plaka; mains €12-22; ☷ Mon-Sat) This classy taverna, on the outskirts of Plaka near the cathedral, is one of the new breed of restaurants serving refined contemporary Greek cuisine, not just the same old stuff in a nicer setting. Decor is subtle Greek chic, there's a lovely courtyard, and the presentation and ambience are top-rate, even if it doesn't have the picturesque setting of nearby eateries. Try the pork with rosemary mezes.

ANDERS BLOMQVIST

Brettos bar (p85)

TOP END

Papadakis (Map pp52-3; ☎ 210 360 8621; Fokylidou 15, Kolonaki; mains €18-38; ☒ Mon-Sat) In the foothills of Lykavittos, this understatedly chic restaurant specialises in seafood, with creative dishes such as stewed octopus with honey and sweet wine, delicious *salatouri* (fish salad) with small fish, and sea salad (a type of green seaweed/sea asparagus).

ourpick **Varoulko** (Map pp52-3; ☎ 210 522 8400; Pireos 80, Gazi; mains €20-35; ☒ dinner from 8pm Mon-Sat) For a magical Greek dining experience, you can't beat the winning combination of Acropolis views and delicious seafood by Lefteris Lazarou, the only Greek Michelin-rated chef. Lazarou specialises in fish and seafood creations, though there are also meat dishes on the menu. The restaurant has a superb rooftop terrace.

DRINKING
CAFES

Athens seems to have more cafes per capita than virtually any other city, inevitably packed with Athenians, prompting many a visitor to wonder if anyone ever works in this city. More recently, the burning question has been why it has Europe's most expensive coffee (between €3 and €5). One explanation is that you actually hire the chair, not just pay for coffee, as people sit on a coffee for hours.

You won't have trouble finding a cafe anywhere in town. In Kolonaki, **Da Capo** (Map pp52-3; Tsakalof 1) on the main square is known for excellent coffee and people-watching. It's self-serve if you can find a table.

Another cafe-thick area is Adrianou, along the Ancient Agora, where you'll find students and young people filling the shady tables at **Dioskouri** (Map pp66-7; Adrianou 39). Further along the pedestrian promenade along Apostolou Pavlou, you'll get great Acropolis views from **Athinaion Politeia** (Map pp52-3; Akamandos 1).

BARS

Many bars don't get busy until after 11pm and open till late.

If you can't stand the crowds at hip **Hoxton** (Map pp52-3; Voutadon 42), you can get some fresh air on the terrace of rock bar **45 Moires** (Map pp52-3; Iakhou 18, cnr Voutadon), overlooking Gazi's neon-lit chimney stacks.

Psyrri's bars come and go but a couple of staples are mainstream **Fidelio** (Map pp66-7; Ogygou 2), which has a retractable roof, and long-time favourite Lilliputian warren **Thirio** (Map pp66-7; Lepeniotou 1).

Bartessera (Map pp66-7; Kolokotroni 25) is a cool bar at the end of a narrow arcade, with great music. A safe downtown bet for 30-somethings and great cocktails is

Toy (Map pp66-7; Karytsi 10), near the cluster of bars around Plateia Karytsi, or the lively Seven Jokers (Map pp66-7; Voulis 7).

You won't find any happening bars in Plaka, but **Brettos** (Map pp66-7; Kydathineon 41) is a delightful old bar and distillery, with a stunning wall of colourful bottles and huge barrels. You can sample shots of Brettos' home brand of ouzo, brandy and other spirits, as well as the family wine.

ENTERTAINMENT

English-language entertainment information appears daily in the *Kathimerini* supplement in the *International Herald Tribune,* while *Athens News* and *Athens Plus* also have entertainment listings.

CLASSICAL MUSIC & OPERA

In summer the main cultural activity takes place at the historic Odeon of Herodes Atticus and other venues under the auspices of the Hellenic Festival (p80).

Megaron (Athens Concert Hall; Map pp52-3; ☎ 210 728 2333; www.megaron.gr; Kokkali 1, cnr Leoforos Vasilissis Sofias, Ilissia; ☽ box office 10am-6pm Mon-Fri, 10am-2pm Sat) The city's state-of-the-art concert hall presents a rich program of operas and concerts featuring world-class international and Greek performers.

The **Greek National Opera** (Ethniki Lyriki Skini; ☎ 210 360 0180; www.nationalopera.gr) season runs from November to June. Performances are usually held at the **Olympia Theatre** (Map pp52-3; ☎ 210 361 2461; Akadimias 59, Exarhia) or the Odeon of Herodes Atticus in summer.

THEATRE

Athens has more theatres than any city in Europe but, as you'd expect, most performances are in Greek. Theatre buffs may enjoy a performance of an old favourite if they know the play well enough.

National Theatre (Map pp52-3; ☎ 210 522 3243; www.n-t.gr; Agiou Konstantinou 22-24, Omonia) The recently refurbished theatre is one of the city's finest neoclassical buildings. Performances of contemporary plays and ancient theatre take place on the main stage and in venues around town. In summer, plays are performed in ancient theatres across Greece, such as at Epidavros (p110).

GREEK FOLK DANCING

Dora Stratou Dance Theatre (Map pp52-3; ☎ 210 921 4650; www.grdance.org; Filopappou Hill; adult/concession €15/10; ☽ performances 9.30pm Tue-Sat, 8.15pm Sun May-Sep) Every summer the Dora Stratou company performs its repertoire of folk dances from all over Greece at its open-air theatre on the western side of Filopappou Hill. Formed to preserve the country's folk culture, it has gained an international reputation for authenticity and professionalism. It also runs folk-dancing workshops in summer.

REMBETIKA CLUBS

Athens is where you can see some of the best *rembetika* (Greek blues) in intimate,

---

WHAT'S ON IN ATHENS

For comprehensive events listings in English, with links to online ticket sales points, try the following:

- www.elculture.gr (arts and culture listings)
- www.breathtakingathens.gr (Athens Tourism site)
- www.tickethouse.gr (Rockwave and other festivals)
- www.tickethour.com (also has sports matches)
- www.ticketservices.gr (range of events)

evocative venues. Most sets include a combination of *rembetika* and *laïka* (urban popular music). Performances start at around 11.30pm; most places do not have a cover charge, but drinks can be expensive.

ourpick **Stoa Athanaton** (Map pp66-7; ☎ 210 321 4362; Sofokleous 19, Omonia; ⏱ 3-6pm & midnight-6am Mon-Sat, closed Jun-Sep) The almost legendary Stoa Athanaton occupies a hall above the central meat market. It is a popular venue, with classic *rembetika* and *laïka* from a respected band of musicians – often starting from mid-afternoon. Access is by a lift in the arcade.

Perivoli Tou Ouranou (Map pp66-7; ☎ 210 323 5517; Lysikratous 19, Plaka; ⏱ 9pm-late Thu-Sun, closed Jul-Sep) A favourite Plaka music haunt in a rustic old-style venue where you can have dinner and listen to authentic *laïka* and *rembetika* by leading exponents.

NIGHTCLUBS

Clubs generally get busy around midnight. The majority of the top clubs close in summer or move to outdoor venues by the beach.

ourpick **Venue** (Map pp52-3; ☎ 210 341 1410; www.venue-club.com; Pireos 130, Rouf; admission €10-15; ⏱ midnight-late Fri & Sat) Arguably the city's biggest dance club, this new venue puts on the biggest dance parties with the world's biggest DJs. It has a three-stage dance floor and an energetic crowd.

Letom (Map pp52-3; ☎ 6992240000; Dekeleon 26, Gazi) Late-night clubbers flock to the dance parties at this trendy club in Gazi, with its giant mirrorball elephant, top line-

GAY & LESBIAN ATHENS

Athens' gay and lesbian scene has gained prominence in recent years, with a new breed of gay and gay-friendly clubs opening around town, predominantly in and around the Gazi, Psyrri and Metaxourghio areas. Gazi has the closest thing to a gay village, but for the most part the gay scene is relatively low-key.

The best place to start the night in Gazi is **Blue Train** (Map pp52-3; ☎ 210 346 0677; www.bluetrain.gr; Leoforos Konstantinoupoleos, Gazi), along the railway line, which has a club upstairs. **Sodade** (Map pp52-3; ☎ 210 346 8657; www.sodade.gr; Triptolemou 10, Gazi) attracts a young clubbing crowd, while **BIG** (Map pp52-3; ☎ 6946282845; Falesias 12, Gazi) is the hub of Athens' lively bear scene.

All-day hang-out **Magaze** (Map pp66-7; ☎ 210 324 3740; Eolou 33, Monastiraki) has Acropolis views from the pavement tables and becomes a lively bar after sunset.

Athens' more established gay bars and clubs are located around Makrygianni, including the veteran **Granazi** (Map pp66-7; ☎ 210 924 4185; Lembesi 20, Makrygianni) and the busy, three-level **Lamda Club** (Map pp66-7; ☎ 210 942 4202; Lembesi 15, cnr Leoforos Syngrou, Makrygianni).

The cafe-bar-restaurant **Mirovolos** (Map pp52-3; ☎ 210 522 8806; Giatrakou 12, Metaxourghio) is a popular lesbian haunt.

Check out www.athensinfoguide.com/gay or the limited English information at www.gay.gr, or look for a copy of the *Greek Gay Guide* booklet at *periptera* (street kiosks) around town.

up of international and local DJs, and gay-friendly, hip young crowd.

SUMMER CLUBS
Athens has some great open-air urban venues, but in summer much of the city's serious nightlife moves to glamorous, massive seafront clubs. Many clubs are on the tram route, which runs 24 hours on weekends. Glam up to ensure you get in the door.

Akrotiri (☎ 210 985 9147; Vasileos Georgiou B 5, Agios Kosmas; ⏱ 10pm-5am) One of the city's top beach clubs, this massive venue has a capacity for 3000, with bars, a restaurant and lounges over different levels. It hosts great party nights with top resident and visiting DJs, and pool parties during the day.

Balux (☎ 210 894 1620; Leoforos Poseidonos 58, Glyfada; ⏱ 10pm-late) This glamorous club right on the beach must be seen to be believed, with its poolside lounges and four-poster beds with flowing nets. There's a restaurant and a top line-up of local and guest DJs.

SPORT
The 2004 Olympics left a legacy of world-class sports stadiums, and Athens has begun attracting some major international and European sporting and athletic events. Sports fans should contact local clubs or sporting bodies directly for match information, or check the English-language press or www.sportingreece.com.

SOCCER
Greece's top teams are Athens-based Panathinaikos and AEK, and Piraeus-based Olympiakos, all three of which are in the European Champions League.

Generally, tickets to major games can be bought on the day at the venue. Big games take place at the Olympic Stadium in Marousi and the Karaiskaki Stadium in Piraeus, the country's best soccer stadium. Information on Greek soccer and fixtures can be found on club websites or www.greeksoccer.com. Some match tickets can be bought online at www.tickethour.gr.

SHOPPING
FLEA MARKETS
Athens' traditional Monastiraki Flea Market (Map pp66-7) has a festive atmosphere. The permanent antiques, furniture and collectables stores offer plenty to sift through and are open all week, while the streets around the station and Adrianou fill with vendors selling mostly jewellery, handicrafts and bric-a-brac.

The big Sunday Flea Market (Map pp52-3) takes place at the end of Ermou, towards Gazi, where traders peddle their stuff from the crack of dawn and you can find some bargains, interesting collectables and kitsch delights among the junk. This is the place to test your haggling skills. It winds up around 2pm.

SPECIALITY FOODS
Mesogaia (Map pp66-7; ☎ 210 322 9146; cnr Nikis & Kydathineon, Plaka) This small shop boasts a wonderful array of the finest produce from around the country, including delicious cheeses, herbs, honey, jams, olive oil and wine.

To Pantopoleion (Map pp66-7; ☎ 210 323 4612; Sofokleous 1, Omonia) This expansive store sells traditional food products from all over the country, from Santorini capers to boutique olive oils and Cretan rusks.

You can find a delectable array of food at the colourful **Athens central market** (Map pp66-7; Athinas, Omonia; ⏱ Mon-Sat).

TRADITIONAL HANDICRAFTS & SOUVENIRS
Amorgos (Map pp66-7; ☎ 210 324 3836; www.amorgosart.gr; Kodrou 3, Plaka; ⏱ 11am-3pm &

6-8pm Mon-Fri, 11am-3pm Sat) This charming store is crammed with Greek folk art, trinkets, ceramics, embroideries, and wood-carved furniture made by the owner, while his wife and daughter run the store.

Centre of Hellenic Tradition (Map pp66-7; ☎ 210 321 3023; Pandrosou 36, Plaka; ☺ 10am-7.30pm) Upstairs from the arcade you'll find great examples of traditional ceramics, sculptures and handicrafts from all parts of Greece.

Melissinos Art (Map pp66-7; ☎ 210 321 9247; www.melissinos-art.com; Agias Theklas 2, Psyrri; ☺ 10am-8pm Mon-Sat, 10am-6pm Sun) Artist Pantelis Melissinos continues the sandal-making tradition of his famous poet/sandal-maker father Stavros, whose past customers include the Beatles, Rudolph Nureyev, Sophia Loren and Jackie Onassis. It's the best place for authentic handmade leather sandals based on ancient Greek styles (€25 to €29); they can also be made to order.

GETTING THERE & AWAY
AIR
Athens is served by **Eleftherios Venizelos International Airport** (Map p91; ☎ 210 353 0000; www.aia.gr) at Spata, 27km east of Athens. The majority of domestic flights are operated by **Olympic Air** (Map pp52-3; ☎ 801 144 444, 210 926 9111; www.olympicairlines.com; Leoforos Syngrou 96, Makrygianni). Olympic takes bookings online and also has branch offices at **Syntagma** (Map pp66-7; ☎ 210 926 4444; Filellinon 15) and **Omonia** (Map pp52-3; ☎ 210 926 7218; Kotopoulou 1).

Aegean Airlines (☎ reservations 801 112 0000, 210 626 1000; www.aegeanair.com) competes with Olympic on the most popular domestic routes. There's an office in **Syntagma** (Map pp66-7; ☎ 210 331 5522; Othonos 15).

Athens Airways (☎ 8018014000; www.athensairways.com) has daily flights to several destinations on the mainland and the islands, including Crete, Mykonos, Rhodes, Santorini (Thira), Chios and Zakynthos.

BOAT
Most ferry, hydrofoil and high-speed catamaran services to the islands leave from Athens' massive port at Piraeus (p90). There are also ferry and high-speed services for Evia and the Cyclades from the smaller ports at Rafina and Lavrio.

You can check the daily schedules in the *International Herald Tribune* or search for and buy tickets online. Agents selling ferry tickets are thick on the ground around Plateia Karaïskaki in Piraeus and at the Rafina and Lavrio ports. You can also normally purchase tickets at ticket booths located on the quay, next to each ferry. Contrary to what some agents might tell you, it costs no more to buy tickets at the boat.

See also Island Hopping (p362).

BUS
Athens has two intercity (IC) KTEL bus terminals. Terminal A (from the centre, bus 051 heads there; Map pp52-3), 7km northwest of Omonia, has departures to the Peloponnese, the Ionians and western Greece. Terminal B (from the centre, bus 024 heads there; Map pp52-3), 5km north of Omonia, caters to central and northern Greece, and to Evia. The EOT office (p69) has IC bus schedules.

Buses for destinations in southern Attica leave from the **Mavromateon terminal** (Map pp52-3; ☎ 210 880 8000; cnr Leoforos Alexandras & 28 Oktovriou-Patision, Pedion Areos), about 250m north of the National Archaeological Museum.

TRAIN
Intercity trains to central and northern Greece depart from the central Larisis train station (Map pp66-7), located about 1km northwest of Plateia Omonias (metro line 2).

For the Peloponnese, take the suburban rail to Kiato and change for other OSE services there. A new rail hub (SKA) is going to be located about 20km north of the city.

OSE (☎ 1110; www.ose.gr; ✆ 24hr) offices at **Omonia** (Map pp52-3; ☎ 210 529 7005; Karolou 1; ✆ 8am-3pm Mon-Fri) and **Syntagma** (Map pp66-7; ☎ 210 362 4405; Sina 6; ✆ 8am-3pm Mon-Sat) handle advance bookings.

GETTING AROUND
TO/FROM THE AIRPORT

Express buses operate 24 hours between the airport and the city centre, Piraeus and KTEL bus terminals. Bus X95 operates 24 hours between the airport and Syntagma, departing every 30 minutes. The journey takes about an hour, depending on traffic. Tickets (€3.20) are not valid for other forms of public transport.

The metro airport service from Monastiraki is not express, so you can pick it up at any station along line 3. Just check that it is the airport train (displayed on the train and platform screen). Trains run every 30 minutes, leaving Monastiraki

between 5.50am and midnight, and the airport between 5.30am and 11.30pm. The airport ticket is valid for all forms of public transport for 90 minutes.

Unfortunately, catching a taxi from the airport can often involve an argument about the fare (see p69 for the full rundown).Check that the meter is set to the correct tariff. You will also have to pay a €3.40 airport surcharge and a €2.70 toll for using the toll road, as well as €0.35 for each piece of luggage over 10kg. Fares vary depending on traffic, but expect to pay from €25 to €30 from the airport to the city centre, and €30 to Piraeus.

PUBLIC TRANSPORT

Athens has an extensive and inexpensive integrated public transport network of buses, metro, trolleybuses and tram. **Athens Urban Transport Organisation** (OASA; ☎ 185; www.oasa.gr; Metsovou 15, Exarhia/Mouseio; ✆ 6.30am-11.30pm Mon-Fri, 7.30am-10.30pm Sat & Sun) can assist with most inquiries. Transport maps can be downloaded from its website and are also

GEORGE TSAFOS

Monastiraki Flea Market (p87)

available at the airport, at train stations and from the organisation's head office near the National Archaeological Museum.

A €1 ticket can be used on the entire Athens urban transport network, including the suburban rail (except airport services), and is valid for 90 minutes. There is also a daily €3 ticket valid for 24 hours, and a weekly €10 ticket with the same restrictions on airport travel. Children under six travel free and people under 18 and over 65 travel at half-fare.

TAXI
Hailing a taxi often involves standing on the pavement and shouting your destination. Make sure the meter is switched on when you get in. The flag fall is €1.05, with a €0.95 surcharge from ports and train and bus stations, and a €3.40 surcharge from the airport. After that, the day rate (tariff 1 on the meter) is €0.60 per kilometre. The night rate (tariff 2 on the meter) increases to €1.05 per kilometre between midnight and 5am. The minimum fare is €2.80. Most short trips around downtown Athens should cost around €4.

PIRAEUS
ΠΕΙΡΑΙΑΣ
pop 175,697
Piraeus is Greece's main port and the biggest in the Mediterranean, with more than 20 million passengers passing through annually. Central Piraeus is not a place where many visitors linger; most come only to catch a ferry from the intimidating expanse of terminals. The most attractive part is the eastern quarter around Zea Marina, and the lovely, albeit touristy, Mikrolimano harbour, lined with restaurants, bars and nightclubs.

Pireaus Dream Hotel (☎ 210 411 0555; www.pireausdreamhotel.com; Filonos 79-81; s/d/ tr incl breakfast €45/55/65; ✷ ▣) With quiet rooms starting on the 4th floor, this renovated hotel about 500m from the station has good facilities, including laptop and PlayStation rental, and serves a big American breakfast.

Buses 040 and 049 run 24 hours between Piraeus and central Athens; they run every 20 minutes from 6am until midnight and then hourly. The X96 Piraeus-Athens Airport Express bus leaves from the southwestern corner of Plateia Karaïskaki. The metro is the fastest and easiest way to get from Piraeus to central Athens.

ATTICA ΑΤΤΙΚΗ
pop 4 million
The plain of Attica is an agricultural and wine-growing region, with several large population centres. It has some fine beaches, particularly along the Apollo Coast and at Shinias, near Marathon.

TEMPLE OF POSEIDON
ΝΑΟΣ ΤΟΥ ΠΟΣΕΙΔΩΝΑ
The ancient Greeks knew how to choose a site for a temple. Nowhere is this more evident than at Cape Sounion, 70km south of Athens, where the **Temple of Poseidon** (☎ 22920 39363; adult/concession €4/2; ✷ 8am-8pm) stands on a craggy spur that plunges 65m down into the sea. Built in 444 BC, at the same time as the Parthenon, it is constructed of local marble from Agrilesa and its slender columns – of which 16 remain – are Doric.

The views from the temple are impressive. On a clear day you can see Kea, Kythnos and Serifos to the southeast, and Aegina and the Peloponnese to the west. The site also contains scanty remains of a propylaeum, a fortified tower and, to the northeast, a 6th-century temple to Athena.

ATTICA

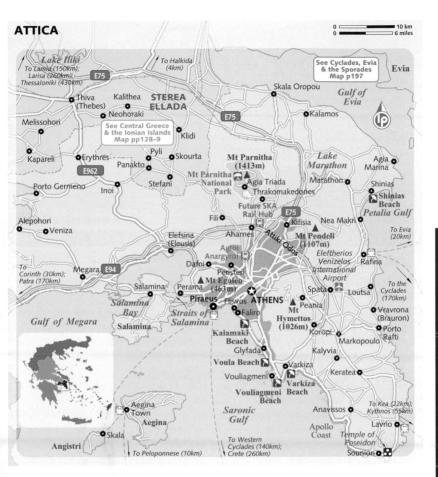

Try to visit early in the morning before the tourist buses arrive – or head there for the sunset – if you wish to indulge the sentiments of Byron's lines from *Don Juan*: 'Place me on Sunium's marbled steep, Where nothing save the waves and I, May hear our mutual murmurs sweep…'.

There are a couple of tavernas just below the site if you want to combine a visit with lunch and a swim.

You can take either the inland or the more scenic coastal bus to Cape Sounion from Athens. Coastal buses (€5.70,

1½ hours) leave Athens hourly, on the half-hour, from the Mavromateon bus terminal.

MARATHON ΜΑΡΑΘΩΝΑΣ

The plain surrounding the unremarkable, small town of Marathon, 42km northeast of Athens, is the site of one of the most celebrated battles in world history. In 490 BC an army of 9000 Greeks and 1000 Plataeans defeated the 25,000-strong Persian army, proving that the Persians were not

NEVENA TSVETANOVA/ALAMY

Burnt out slopes of Mt Parnitha

⬎ MT PARNITHA ΠΑΡΝΗΘΑ

The densely forested **Mt Parnitha National Park**, about 25km north of Athens, is the highest mountain range surrounding the city serving as the 'lungs' of Athens. Tragically, more than 4200 hectares of century-old fir and pine forest was razed in the devastating six-day fires of 2007. The state has tripled the area designated as national park and launched a major reforestation program, but it will take decades to recover.

Mt Parnitha comprises a number of smaller peaks, the highest of which is Karavola at 1413m – high enough to get snow in winter. The park is criss-crossed by numerous walking trails, is a popular hiking and mountain-biking destination and has two shelters for hikers. Trails are marked on the Road Editions trekking map of the area. There are many caves and wildlife, including red deer.

Most visitors access the park by cable car from the outer Athens suburb of Thrakomakedones, which drops you below the incongruous **Regency Casino Mont Parnes**. The casino runs a free bus service from various locations in Athens, including outside the Hilton.

Things you need to know: Mt Parnitha National Park (www.parnitha-ng.gr); Regency Casino Mont Parnes (☎ 210 242 1234; www.regencycasinos.gr; ⊗ 24hr)

invincible. The Greeks were indebted to the ingenious tactics of Miltiades, who altered the conventional battle formation so that there were fewer soldiers in the centre, but more in the wings. This lulled the Persians into thinking that the Greeks were going to be a pushover. They broke through in the centre but were then ambushed by the soldiers in the wings. At the end of the day, 6000 Persians and only 192 Greeks lay dead. The story goes that after the battle a runner was sent to Athens to announce the victory. After shouting *'Enikesame!'* ('We won!') he collapsed and died. This is the origin of today's marathon race.

PELOPONNESE & THE SARONIC GULF ISLANDS

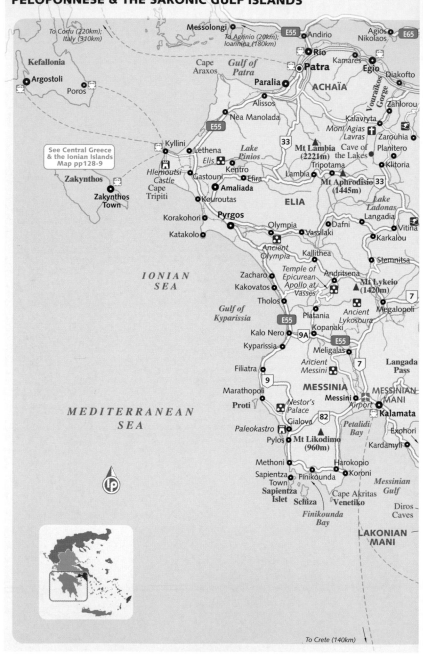

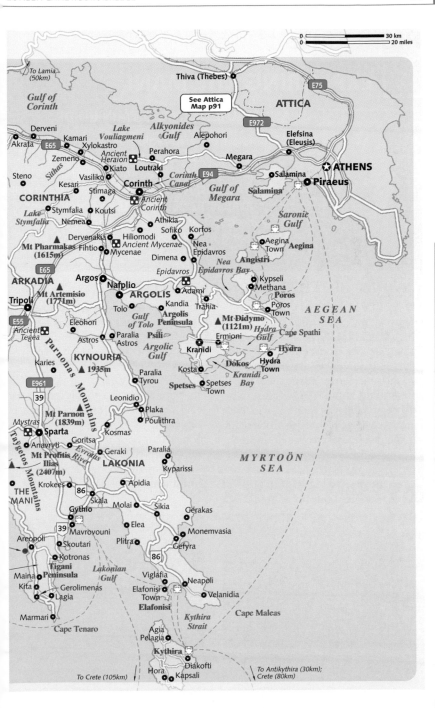

30 km
20 miles

To Lamia
(50km)

Thiva (Thebes)

ATTICA

E75

Gulf of Corinth

See Attica
Map p91

E972

Derveni
Lake Vouliagmeni
Alkyonides Gulf
Alepohori
Elefsina (Eleusis)

Kamari
Akrata E65 Xylokastro
Zemeno
Sithas
Perahora
Megara
Salamina

ATHENS

Steno
Vasiliko
Kiato
Loutraki
Salamina
Piraeus

Kesari
Stimaga
Corinth
Corinth Canal
E94
Gulf of Megara

CORINTHIA
Ancient Corinth
E65 Stymfalia Koutsi
Athikia
Saronic Gulf

Lake Stymfalia
Nemea
Sofiko
Korfos
Aegina Town
Aegina

Dervenakia
Hiliomodi
Nea Epidavros
Angistri

Mt Pharmakas (1615m)
Fihtio
Ancient Mycenae
Mycenae
Dimena
Nea Epidavros Bay
Kypseli
Methana

E65
Epidavros
Adami
Poros
Poros Town

Argos
Nafplio
ARGOLIS
*A E G E A N
S E A*

ARKADIA
Mt Artemisio (1771m)
Tolo
Kandia
Trahia
Mt Didymo (1121m)

Tripoli
Eleohori
Gulf of Tolo
Argolis Peninsula
Psili
Ermioni
Hydra Gulf
Cape Spathi

E55
Ancient Tegea
Astros
Paralia Astros
Argolic Gulf
Kranidi
Hydra
Hydra Town

Karies
KYNOURIA
1935m
Paralia Tyrou
Kosta
Dokos
Kranidi Bay

E961
Spetses
Spetses Town

39
Leonidio
Plaka

Mystras
Mt Parnon (1839m)
Poulithra
*M Y R T O O N
S E A*

Sparta
Goritsa
Kosmas

Anavryti
Geraki
Paralia

Mt Profitis Ilias (2407m)
Evrotas River
LAKONIA
Kyparissi

THE MANI
Krokees
86
Apidia

39
Skala
Molai
Sikia
Gerakas

Mavrovouni
Elea
Monemvasia

Areopoli
Skoutari
Plitra
Gefyra

Kotronas
86

Tigani Peninsula
Lakonian Gulf
Viglafia
Neapoli

Maina
Gerolimenas
Elafonisi Town
Velanidia

Kita
Lagia
Elafonisi

Marmari
Kythira Strait
Cape Maleas

Cape Tenaro
Agia Pelagia

Kythira

Diakofti

To Crete (105km)
Hora
Kapsali
To Antikythira (30km);
Crete (80km)

HIGHLIGHTS

1 EXPLORING THE MANI

BY ANNA BUTCHER, MOUNTAIN GUIDE

The Mani is a truly wild region of Greece. Huge barren mountains, soaring cliffs, labyrinthine caves, imposing stone tower houses and a sensation of exposure to the elements characterise this very unspoilt peninsula in the Peloponnese. I have worked in the Mani as a guide since 1996 – walking the old paths and accompanying genuinely interested foreigners.

⤡ ANNA BUTCHER'S DON'T MISS LIST

❶ GEROLIMENAS TO LAGIA
This is my favourite walk: from Gerolimenas (p117) via a hidden valley along an old stone mule path, over the 'Bad Mountains,' past spectacular villages and across a dramatic ridge. In spring and autumn there's an abundance of wildflowers and you can finish in Lagia with a Greek coffee in one of the traditional *kafeneia* (coffee houses).

❷ CAPE TENARO
The southernmost tip (p118) of Balkan Europe is the site of an ancient Roman city and the Oracle to Poseidon. Standing on the point that separates the Aegean and Ionian seas affords some of the most dazzling views in Greece.

❸ DIROS CAVES
The natural entrance to this spectacular cave complex (p116) is on the beach. Explore it by boat to reveal habitation dating back to the Neolithic era, along with stalactites and stalagmites with befittingly poetic names like Palm Forest and Crystal Lily.

Clockwise from top: Gerolimenas (p117); Hikers heading to Cape Tenaro (p118); Limestone interior, Diros Caves (p116); Maniot tower, the Mani (p115)

CLOCKWISE FROM TOP: PETER EASTLAND/ALAMY; PETER EASTLAND/ALAMY; TERRY HARRIS JUST GREECE PHOTO LIBRARY/ALAMY; PETER EASTLAND/ALAMY

❹ AREOPOLI

The capital of the deep Mani region retains its village feel with beautiful, traditional guest houses, wonderful tavernas and a couple of very cosy bars. From **Areopoli** (p115) there are numerous walks and great swimming opportunities in small bays and pebbly beaches.

❺ TIGANI PENINSULA

The gentle walk onto the jagged rocky promontory of **Tigani peninsula** (the Frying Pan; p117) rewards you with salt pans (which are still used today), the remains of a 5th-century basilica and the site of an old Frankish castle. Strong swimmers can take a dip off the rocks in very deep water. This is the Mani at its most extreme.

❶ Gerolimenas to Lagia   ❹ Areopoli
❷ Cape Tenaro   ❺ Tigani Peninsula
❸ Diros Caves

0 —————— 10 m
0 —————— 6 miles

LAKONIAN MANI

Lakonian Gulf

Tigani Peninsula

Gerolimenas

Agia Kyriaki

Lagia

Cape Tenaro

⤥ THINGS YOU NEED TO KNOW

Best time to visit Spring and autumn for wildflowers **Essential equipment** Walking boots with ankle support **Watch for** Around 1000 Byzantine churches on the peninsula **Only a half day?** Visit Cape Tenaro **See our author's coverage of The Mani, p115**

HIGHLIGHTS

2

⬊ MESMERISING MONEMVASIA

Resting like a giant sandcastle in the sea, Monemvasia (p112) was part of the mainland until it was cut off by an earthquake in AD 375. To reach it, you must travel through a narrow tunnel in a massive fortifying wall that conceals the enchanting town until you emerge, blinking, on the other side. Enclosed within massive walls, the island's medieval village is a wonderful place to get lost in.

3

⬊ RIDING THE RAILS

For one of the world's most dramatic rail journeys, board the train (p104) from Diakofto to Kalavryta. Still using a cog system to climb heights of over 700m, the one-hour journey will carry you past stunning, lush scenery and through the spellbinding Vouraïkos Gorge. Hop off in serene villages filled with fresh air, gushing streams and lemon and olive groves.

PELOPONNESE & THE SARONIC GULF

HIGHLIGHTS

⬂ DOLPHIN ENCOUNTERS

Head to **Hydra** (p123) to leap into the sea with dolphins. Swim alongside these local residents and scuba dive amidst the Aegean's brilliantly coloured sea life. Afterwards, return to Hydra for unexpected glamour and big nights out in one of Greece's most picturesque harbours.

⬂ ANCIENT OLYMPIA

Imbued with that special Olympic spirit, the site of the original **Olympic Games** (p120) is both impressive and fascinating. See where early sports heroes competed in chariot racing, javelin throwing, long jump and the *pankration* (a vicious form of fisticuffs). Among the surviving ruins is the stadium, complete with start and finish lines and the judges' seats. On your mark...

⬂ ENCHANTING NAFPLIO

You may arrive here simply looking for a base from which to explore the nearby ruins, but **Nafplio** (p105) will quickly charm with its picturesque harbour setting, winding streets and romantic architecture. Relax in seaside cafes beneath the hilltop Palamidi fortress, check out worthwhile local museums, and pamper yourself in boutique hotels.

2 YIORGOS DEPOLLAS/PHOTOLIBRARY; 3 NIGEL REED QEDIMAGES/ALAMY; 4 LOOK DIE BILDAGENTUR DER FOTOGRAFEN GMBH/ALAMY; 5 PANAGIOTIS KARAPANAGIOTIS/DREAMSTIME; 6 GREECE/ALAMY

2 Causeway leading to Monemvasia (p112); 3 Diakofto-Kalavryta rack-and-pinion train (p104); 4 Street scene, Hydra Town (123); 5 Stadium entrance, Ancient Olympia (p120); 6 Boats moored off Nafplio (p105)

THE BEST...

⬎ ENCOUNTERS WITH NATURE

- **Russian Bay** (p123) Dig your toes into golden sand or take a dip in the clear, sheltered bay.
- **Diros Caves** (p116) Explore deep caverns inhabited in Neolithic times.
- **Mt Eros** (p126) Haul yourself up to the top for panoramic views.
- **Cape Tenaro** (p118) Stand on Greece's most southerly point.

⬎ ARCHITECTURAL GEMS

- **Epidavros theatre** (p110) Drop a coin to check ancient acoustics.
- **Tower homes** (p115) Count traditional houses nestled in the mountains.
- **Mystras** (p110) Captivating ruins of churches, libraries and palaces.
- **Palamidi fortress** (p107) Enjoy classical music in a magical setting.

- **Moni Zoödohou Pigis** (p123) Immerse yourself in the gilded icon interior.

⬎ MANIOT VILLAGES

- **Vathia** (p118) The most dramatic traditional Mani hamlet.
- **Kardamyli** (p118) Nestled between the sea and the mountains.
- **Gerolimenas** (p117) Secluded fishing village.

⬎ MOUTH-WATERING MEALS

- **Omorfi Poli** (p108) Tasty Italian and Greek cuisine with non-Greek twists.
- **Sunset** (p125) Scrumptious fresh fish with stunning views.
- **Hotel Kirimai** (p117) Sample the creations of one of Greece's top chefs.
- **Elies** (p119) Idyllic setting and top nosh.
- **Taverna Gitoniko** (p125) Classic Greek favourites like dolmadhes.

KONRAD WOTHE/IMAGEBROKER

Tower homes (p115), Mani peninsula

THINGS YOU NEED TO KNOW

⬎ VITAL STATISTICS

- **Population** Peloponnese 1 million; Saronic Gulf Islands 45,600
- **Area** Peloponnese 21,439 sq km; Saronic Gulf Islands 318 sq km

⬎ LOCALITIES IN A NUTSHELL

- **Achaïa** (p104) Lush scenery and the dramatic Vouraïkos Gorge.
- **Corinthia** (p105) Scenic seaside towns and impressive nearby ruins.
- **Lakonia** (p110) Magical ancient Mystras and the fairytale fortress of Monemvasia.
- **The Mani** (p115) Wild, rugged and gorgeous.
- **Elia** (p119) Home of Ancient Olympia.
- **Poros** (p121) Sandy beaches and a forested interior.
- **Hydra** (p123) Picturesque and glamorous island life.

⬎ ADVANCE PLANNING

- **Two months before** Book your accommodation and tickets for plays at the Epidavros theatre.
- **One month before** Make ferry reservations for trips between the peninsula and the islands. Book tickets for the Diakofto-Kalavryta rack-and-pinion train.
- **Two weeks before** Purchase train and bus tickets.

⬎ RESOURCES

- **www.aroundpeloponnese.com** General guide, listings and accommodation.
- **www.mani.org.gr/en/** Provides information on the history, sights and customs in the Mani.
- **www.poros.gr** Includes a guide to island life.
- **www.hydradirect.com** Offers listings and news on Hydra.

⬎ EMERGENCY NUMBERS

- **Police** (☎ 100)
- **Highway Rescue** (ELPA; ☎ 104)

⬎ GETTING AROUND

- **Bus** Comprehensive routes throughout the Peloponnese.
- **Train** Useful way to reach the Peloponnese from Athens, with routes to major destinations within the peninsula.
- **Ferry** Fast boats to the Saronic Gulf Islands from Piraeus and the Peloponnese. See also Island Hopping (p361).
- **Car** The best way to explore the Peloponnese is with your own wheels.
- **Walk** Hydra is car-free.

⬎ BE FOREWARNED

- **Sights** Many have reduced hours in the winter or are totally shut.
- **Islands** The Saronic Gulf Islands are popular with Athenians and can get very busy; be sure to book ahead!

ITINERARIES

ISLAND ESCAPE Three Days

Arriving on **(1) Hydra** (p123) is like parachuting into a glamour maga-zine. Immerse yourself in the jet-setting lifestyle for a day, sipping coffee in the stylish harbourside cafes, filling up on scrumptious local cuisine and then joining the eclectic mix of visitors and locals in the energetic bars and clubs. The next day, energise yourself with a hike into the interior to serene monasteries with phenomenal views, or go diving off the coast alongside dolphins. The next day, hop on a ferry to **(2) Poros** (p121). Despite its proximity to the mainland, Poros has a remote, relaxed feel about it. Lovely Poros Town, set between the sea and the mountainous Peloponnese, makes a perfect base. From there, spend a day soaking up the sunshine and the salty sea air on the island's sandy beaches.

ARCHITECTURAL GOODIE BAG Five Days

The southern coast of the Peloponnese is home to a mixed bag of architectural treats, set in stunning surroundings. Base yourself in the engaging seaside town of **(1) Gythio** (p113), a bustling fishing village with excellent restaurants and safe swimming beaches. Offshore is the tiny Marathonisi Islet with the 18th-century Tzanetakis Grigorakis tower. From Gythio, spend a couple of days delving into **(2) The Mani** (p115). Join a hiking group or rent a car and explore the rugged set-ting – Diros Caves, Cape Tenaro and the Vyros Gorge. En route you'll see countless tower settlements built in the 17th century as defences against clan wars. Stop at one of these villages for lunch in the lively squares where you'll get great local food and soak up a bit of the Maniot culture. Next, head north of Gythio for the day to visit the fascinating Byzantine ruins of **(3) Mystras** (p110), a fortress town set against the mountains; the ruins date back to 1249. On the last day, head east of Gythio to spectacular **(4) Monemvasia** (p112), a medieval walled town suspended like an iceberg in the sea. Wander through the winding pedestrian alleys and take in the impressive churches before escaping the crowds and heading back to relaxed Gythio.

BETWEEN MOUNTAINS & SEA One Week

Begin your Peloponnese adventure in (1) Diakofto (p104), a pictur-esque village tucked between steep mountains and the lapping sea on the north coast. From here, hop on the unique (2) rack-and-pinion train (p104) for an extraordinary journey through unforgettable, lush scenery to Kalavryta and back. From Diakofto, drive or hop on a train to stunning (3) Nafplio (p105), one of the Peloponnese's most romantic seaside towns with worthwhile museums, Venetian architecture and an impressive fortress. You'll also find a hopping nightlife and snug

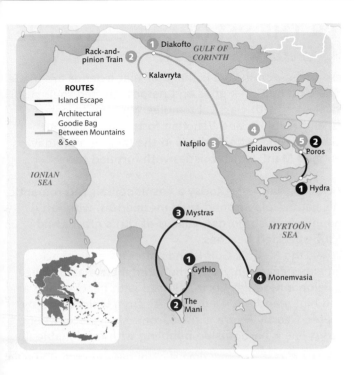

hotels. From here, take in the ruins of (4) Epidavros (p110). If you're visiting in summer, try to get tickets for a classical play at the site's amazing ancient theatre. From Nafplio, head east to catch a ferry from Methana to the coastal island of (5) Poros (p121), where you can lounge on sandy beaches as you gaze across the isthmus at the mountain views. Despite being a stone's throw from the mainland, it feels a world away. From Poros, you can easily catch a ferry to Piraeus.

DISCOVER THE PELOPONNESE & THE SARONIC GULF ISLANDS

The Peloponnese (pel-o-*pon*-ih-sos) is the stuff that legends are made of – the land where many Greek gods and heroes strutted their stuff. It boasts historical sites, with classical temples, Mycenaean palaces, Byzantine cities, and Frankish and Venetian fortresses. Flex your muscles at Ancient Olympia, cite Oedipus in the theatre of Epidavros or hike in the rugged Mani, which bristles with fortified tower houses.

Greece's first capital, Nafplio, is today a cosmopolitan and romantic city. The region's natural playground truly mesmerises, with lofty, snowcapped mountains, lush gorges, valleys of citrus groves and vineyards, and sun-speckled beaches.

Just off the coast, the Saronic Gulf Islands offer a fast track to the Greek island experience. Only a few hundred metres across the water from the Peloponnese lies Poros, blessed with beaches and a peaceful forested hinterland – it's a great base from which to enjoy the mainland's sites. Nearby Hydra is the Saronic showpiece, where pastel-hued houses line a harbourside bubbling with fashionable life.

PELOPONNESE
ΠΕΛΟΠΟΝΝΗΣΟΣ

ACHAΪA ΑΧΑΪΑ
DIAKOFTO ΔΙΑΚΟΦΤΟ
pop 2290

Diakofto (dih-ah-kof-*to*), 55km east of Patra and 80km northwest of Corinth, is a serene village, tucked between steep mountains and the sea, amid lemon and olive groves. The main reason for visiting is to board the unique rack-and-pinion train service along the Vouraïkos Gorge as far as Kalavryta (see p104).

DIAKOFTO-KALAVRYTA RAILWAY
One of the unmissable journeys to make in the Peloponnese is aboard the tiny, unique **train** (☎ in Diakofto 26910 43228) running along the railway from Diakofto to Kalavryta. It takes travellers on an unforgettable ride through the dramatic **Vouraïkos Gorge**. The train climbs over 700m in 22.5km, using a rack-and-pinion (cog) system for traction on the steep sections, effectively clamping itself to the notched girder you can see running between the rails.

The journey takes just over an hour, stopping en route at Zahlorou. At the time of research, the fare was €9.50/19 one way/return. A good website to check its status (run by a passionate trainspotter) is www.odontotos.com.

The original steam engines that first plied the route were replaced in the early 1960s by diesel cars, but the old engines can still be seen outside Diakofto and Kalavryta stations.

SLEEPING & EATING
Hotel Chris-Paul (☎ 26910 41715/855; www .chrispaul-hotel.gr; s/d/tr €35/65/78; P 🅿 🛜) This modernish, plain place has friendly management and is a block from the plat-

form – prime position for train travellers. Most rooms have balconies overlooking the garden and pool. Breakfast costs €5.

Costas (☎ 26910 43228; mains €6-10; ☽ lunch & dinner) The friendly Greek-Australian owners offer taverna-style dishes alongside the usual grilled meats. It's known for its dolmadhes (vine leaves stuffed with rice and sometimes meat; €7).

GETTING THERE & AWAY

Diakofto is on the main Corinth-Patra line; there are frequent trains in both directions (€7). The refurbished **Diakofto-Kalavryta Railway** (☎ 26910 43228) has departures daily along the rack-and-pinion line to Kalavryta to a changing schedule via Zahlorou. See p104.

CORINTHIA ΚΟΡΙΝΘΙΑ

NAFPLIO ΝΑΥΠΛΙΟ
pop 13,822

For better or worse, the secret is out about Nafplio, one of Greece's prettiest and most romantic towns. It occupies a knockout location – on a small port beneath the t owering bulk of the Palamidi fortress – and is graced with attractive narrow streets, elegant Venetian houses, neoclassical mansions with flower-bedecked balconies, and interesting museums. With good bus connections and services, the town is an ideal base from which to explore many nearby ancient sites.

ORIENTATION

Nafplio's old town occupies a narrow promontory with the Akronafplia fortress on the southern side and the promenades of Bouboulinas and Akti Miaouli on the north side. The old town's central square is Plateia Syntagmatos, at the western end of Vasileos Konstantinou.

The KTEL bus station can be found on Syngrou, which is the street separating the old town from the new.

INFORMATION

All the major banks have branches in town.

Alpha Bank (Amalias) At the western end of the street. Has ATM facilities.

Palamidi Fortress (p107), Nafplio

DIANA MAYFIELD

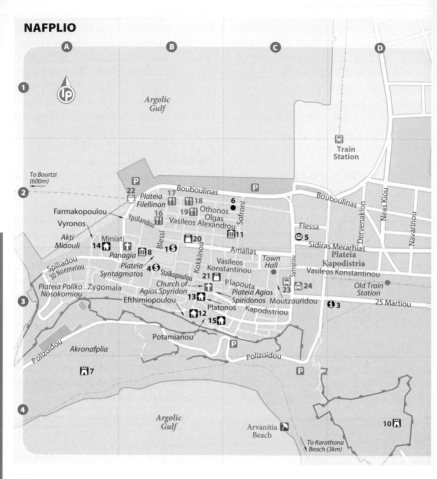

NAFPLIO

Hospital (☎ 27520 98100; cnr Asklipiou & Kolokotroni)

Municipal tourist office (☎ 27520 24444; 25 Martiou 4; �9am-1pm & 4-8pm)

Not the strongest aspect of the town's services.

National Bank of Greece (Plateia Syntagmatos) Has ATM facilities.

Scale: 0 — 200 m / 0 — 0.1 miles

To Tiryns (4km); Mycenae (25km); Corinth (65km); Athens (160km)

Argonafton

Lakos

Harmanda

Chrisostomou

Agiou Adrianou

Stadium

Thisseos

Irakleous

Leoforos Argous

Πσίου

Asklipiou

Klikis

Vas Georgiou

To Bubbles (300m); Tourist Police (350m); Tolo (10km); Epidavros (30km)

Kountouriotou

Kolokotroni

Nikitara

Moshonisiotou

Averof

Athinas

To Palamidi Fortress (3.5km)

Kyrinias

Porou

Palamidiou

summer, 8am-3pm winter) stands on a 216m-high outcrop of rock with excellent views down onto the sea and surrounding land. It was built by the Venetians between 1711 and 1714, and is regarded as a masterpiece of military architecture.

There are two main approaches to the fortress. You can go via the road (taxis cost approximately €8 one way) or the energetic can tackle the seemingly endless steps that begin southeast of the bus station.

AKRONAFPLIA FORTRESS

Rising above the old part of town, the **Akronafplia fortress** is the oldest of Nafplio's three castles, although there is much less to see here than at the other two forts. The lower sections of the walls date back to the Bronze Age, and until the arrival of the Venetians, the town was restricted to within its walls.

There's a lift up to the fortress from Plateia Poliko Nosokomiou at the western edge of town – look for the flags at the entrance of the tunnel leading to the lift.

BOURTZI

The island fortress of Bourtzi lies about 600m west of the town's port. Most of the existing structure was built by the Venetians. Boats (€4 return per person) to the island leave from the northeastern end of Akti Miaouli.

MUSEUMS

Nafplio's award-winning **Peloponnese Folklore Foundation Museum** (☎ 27520 28947; Vasileos Alexandrou 1; adult/concession €4/2; ☺ 9am-3pm & 6-9pm Mon & Wed-Sat, 9.30am-3pm Sun, closed Tue mornings) is a beautifully arranged collection of folk costumes and household items from Nafplio's former times. Not to be missed. There's also a gift shop on the ground floor.

Post office (cnr Syngrou & Sidiras Merarhias; ☺ 7.30am-2pm Mon-Fri)

Staikos Travel ☎ 27520 27950; www.staikostravel.gr; Bouboulinas 50; ☺ 8.30am-2pm & 5.30-9pm, closed Sun winter) A helpful source, as well as an efficient service for all travel services.

Tourist police (☎ 27520 98728/9; Eleftheriou 2)

SIGHTS & ACTIVITIES

PALAMIDI FORTRESS

This vast and spectacular **citadel** (☎ 27520 28036; adult/concession €4/2; ☺ 8am-7pm

An arm of the Athens National Gallery, beautiful **National Gallery – Alexandros Soutzos Museum** (☎ 27520 21915; Sidiras Merarhias 23; adult/concession €3/2, admission free Mon; ⏰ 10am-3pm Mon, Thu & Sat, 10am-3pm & 5-8pm Wed & Fri, 10am-2pm Sun) is housed in a stunningly restored neoclassical building. It displays works on the 1821 Greek War of Independence, including paintings of Greek painters Vryzakis and Tsokos, considered the most important painters of the postwar years.

Overlooking Plateia Syntagmatos and opened in 2009 following seven years of renovations, the **Archaeological Museum** (Plateia Syntagmatos; adult/concession €2/1; ⏰ 8.30am-3pm Tue-Sun) has fine exhibits on show over two light and airy floors. The oldest exhibits, fire middens, date from 32,000 BC.

FESTIVALS & EVENTS

Nafplio hosts a **classical music festival** (www.nafplionfestival.gr) over changing dates between late May and July featuring Greek and international performers. The Palamidi fortress is one of the concert venues.

SLEEPING

Dimitris Bekas (☎ 27520 24594; Efthimiopoulou 26; s/d/tr €23/29/40) A good, central budget option. The clean, homey rooms have a top-value location on the slopes of the Akronafplia.

Hotel Byron (☎ 27520 22351; www.byronhotel.gr; Platonos 2; d €60-80, tr €90; 🕸) Occupying a fine Venetian building, the Byron is a reliable favourite, with neat rooms, iron bedsteads and period furniture. Breakfast costs €5.

ourpick **Pension Marianna** (☎ 27520 24256; www.pensionmarianna.gr; Potamianou 9; s/d/tr €70/85/100, incl breakfast; P 🕸 🛜) This delightful, great-value abode – a bright yellow icon – is the pick of Nafplio. Clean

and comfortable rooms (all different, and some smaller than others) open onto terraces where you can feast on the view from your hill-top position.

Ippoliti (☎ 27520 96088; www.ippoliti.gr; Miniati; r €120-180; 🏊) The 19 rooms in this new and discretely luxurious place are decked out in tasteful muted Tuscan furnishings with neoclassical touches. There are even glass-screened fireplaces in the rooms (extra cost). It has the feel of a boutique pension with hotel services, including a gym.

EATING

Omorfi Poli (☎ 27520 29452; Bouboulinas 75; mains €6-16; ⏰ dinner) This pleasant restaurant's professional chef whips up Greek and Italian dishes. The mezedhes (€5) have a slight non-Greek twist – there's mushroom risotto as well as Greek favourites including *saganaki* (grilled cheese) and grilled sardines.

Some taverna options that are also recommended:

Arapakos (☎ 27520 27675; Bouboulinas 81; mains €7-12, fish per kilogram €30-80; ⏰ lunch & dinner) If you're feeling fishy, hook onto this upmarket morsel for quality seafood.

Alaloum (☎ 27520 29883; Papanikolaou 10; mains €7-13; ⏰ lunch & dinner) In a lovely spot on a square, and it serves up Greek Mediterranean fare.

To Koutouki (⏰ 27520 24477; Olgas 44; mains €8-18; ⏰ dinner) Good for quality grills, pastas and mezedhes. Not on the waterfront, but it is reliable and has a pleasant outdoor setting during the summer months.

DRINKING

Despite being simply jammed with cafes and bars, there still doesn't seem to be enough of them in town to hold the

KONRAD WOTHE/IMAGEBROKER

Castle ruins, near Pylos

↘ IF YOU LIKE...

If you like the colourful, picturesque town of **Nafplio** (p105), we think you'd also like to linger in these scenic coastal towns:

- **Koroni** Head for this lovely Venetian port town, situated on Messinia Bay. Medieval mansions and churches line the town's quaint narrow winding streets. These lead to a promontory, on which perches an extensive castle. Koroni's main attraction is **Zaga Beach**, a long sweep of golden sand just south of the town. Koroni also sees loggerhead turtles.
- **Methoni** South of Pylos, this is another pretty seaside town with a popular sandy beach, next to which crouches the vast and romantic 15th-century **Venetian fortress** (admission free; ☒ 8am-7pm May-Sep, to 3pm Oct-Apr).
- **Pylos** Presiding over the southern end of an immense bay which is punctuated by a castle at each end, Pylos is one of the most picturesque towns in the Peloponnese. Hang out in the delightful tree-shaded central square, walk in the surrounding pine-covered hills or hop on a boat tour to see silt-covered wrecks of sunken Turkish ships, still discernible in the clear waters.
- **Gialova** On the northeastern edge of Navarino Bay, this town boasts a fine sandy beach and safe swimming. The nearby Gialova Lagoon is a prime birdwatching site; between September and March the lagoon is home to up to 20,000 assorted waterbirds, while many others pause here on their spring migration between Africa and Eastern Europe.

throngs of trendy party animals who flock to Nafplio in summer. Most options are on Bouboulinas – just cruise along until you find an image (and the latest decor) to your taste and a musical volume you can handle.

SHOPPING

Karonis (☎ 27520 24446; www.karoniswine shop.gr; Amalias 5) Wine enthusiasts can find a fine selection of wines from all over the country, especially Nemean reds and spirits.

Museum of the Komboloi (☎ 27520 21618; www.kom boloi.gr; Staïkopoulou 25; adult/concession €3/free; ⏰ 9.30am-9pm Mon-Thu & Sun, 9.30am-9.30pm Fri & Sat) This shop – with a private museum above – sells *komboloï* (worry beads), evil-eye charms and amulets.

GETTING THERE & AROUND
The **KTEL Argolis bus station** (☎ 27520 27323; Syngrou 8) has buses to Athens (€12, 2½ hours, hourly).

For taxis call ☎ 27520 24120 or head to the rank on Syngrou.

EPIDAVROS ΕΠΙΔΑΥΡΟΣ
In its day **Epidavros** (☎ 27530 22009; adult/concession €6/3; ⏰ 8am-7.30pm summer, 7.30am-5pm winter), 30km east of Nafplio, was famed and revered as far away as Rome as a place of miraculous healing. Visitors came great distances to this sanctuary of Asclepius (god of medicine) to seek a cure for their ailments.

Today visitors are more likely to flock to the site for its amazingly well-preserved **theatre**, which remains a popular venue during the Hellenic Festival (p80) for Classical Greek theatre (along with other more modern plays, opera and music), first performed here up to 2000 years ago. It is one of the best-preserved Classical Greek structures, renowned for its amazing acoustics; a coin dropped in the centre can be heard from the highest seat.

There are two buses daily to Athens from nearby Ligourio (€12, 2½ hours).

LAKONIA ΛΑΚΩΝΙΑ
MYSTRAS ΜΥΣΤΡΑΣ
The captivating ruins of churches, libraries, strongholds and palaces in the fortress town of Mystras (miss-*trahss*), a World Heritage-listed site, spill from a spur of the Taÿgetos Mountains, 7km west of Sparta. The site is among the most important, historically speaking, in the Peloponnese. This is where the Byzantine Empire's richly artistic and intellectual culture made its last stand, almost 1000 years after its foundation, before an invading Ottoman army.

At least half a day is needed to do justice to the **ruins of Mystras** (☎ 27310 83377; adult/concession €5/3; ⏰ 8am-7.30pm summer, 8.30am-3pm winter). Wear sensible shoes and bring plenty of water. The site is divided into three sections – the *kastro* (the fortress on the summit), the *hora* (upper town) and the *kato hora* (lower town). You can approach the ruins from either direction – top to bottom or vice versa (both options are quite strenuous).

KASTRO & UPPER TOWN
The fortress was built by the Franks and extended by the Turks. The path descends from the ticket office leading to **Agia Sofia**, which served as the palace church, and where some frescoes survive. Steps descend from here to a T-junction.

A left turn leads to the **Nafplio Gate**. Near the gate, and closed for restoration at the time of research, is the huge **Palace of Despots**, a complex of several buildings constructed at different times.

From the palace, a winding, cobbled path leads down to the **Monemvasia Gate**, the entrance to the lower town.

LOWER TOWN
Through the Monemvasia Gate, turn right for the well-preserved, 14th-century **Convent of Pantanassa**. This features a beautifully ornate stone-carved facade and is still maintained by nuns, Mystras' only inhabitants. Exquisite, richly coloured, 15th-century frescoes are among the finest examples of late-

DE AGOSTINI/PHOTOLIBRARY

Tholos (beehive) tomb, Nestor's Palace

⬐ IF YOU LIKE...

If you like wandering through the absorbing ruins of **Mystras** (p110), we think you'd like stepping back in time at these other ruins:

- **Ancient Messini** These fascinating ruins lie scattered across a small valley, 25km northwest of Kalamata. Built on the site of an earlier stronghold, this Messinian capital was one of a string of defensive positions designed to keep watch over Sparta. Apart from its defensive potential, Ancient Messini was also favoured by the gods. According to local myth, Zeus was born here – not Crete.
- **Nestor's Palace** (☎ 27630 31437; site only adult/concession €3/2, site & museum adult/concession €4/2; ☒ 8.30am-3pm, museum closed Mon)) Believed to have been the court of the mythical hero Nestor, who took part in the voyage of the Argonauts and fought in the Trojan War, this is the best preserved of all Mycenaean palaces. Some of the fine frescoes discovered here are housed in the museum in the nearby village of Hora.
- **Temple of Epicurean Apollo at Vasses** (☎ 26260 22275; adult/concession €3/2; ☒ 8am-8pm) Situated on a wild, isolated spot overlooking rugged mountains and hills, this is one of Greece's most romantic and atmospheric archaeological sites. The striking and well-preserved temple stands at an altitude of 1200m. Built in 420 BC, it combines Doric and Ionic columns and a single Corinthian column – the earliest example of this order.
- **Ancient Mycenae** (☎ 27510 76585; citadel, Treasury of Atreus & museum €8; ☒ site 8am-8pm summer, 8.30am-3pm winter) In the barren foothills of Mt Agios Ilias and Mt Zara stand these sombre and mighty ruins. For 400 years (1600-1200 BC) this was the most powerful kingdom in Greece. Due to the sheer size of the citadel walls (13m high and 7m thick), the Ancient Greeks believed they must have been built by a Cyclops. Before exploring the site, it's a good idea to head to the impressive **museum** (admission incl site fee €8; ☒ noon-8pm Mon, 8am-7.30pm Tue-Sun).

Byzantine art. The nuns ask that, before entering, you cover bare legs with the cloths provided.

The path continues down to the **Monastery of Perivleptos** (☉ summer), built into a rock. Inside, the 14th-century frescoes, preserved virtually intact, equal those of Pantanassa.

The **Mitropolis** (Cathedral of Agios Dimitrios) is a complex of buildings enclosed by a high wall. The original church was built in the 1200s, but was greatly altered in the 15th century. Its impressive ecclesiastical ornaments and furniture include a marble iconostasis, an intricately carved wooden throne and a marble slab in the floor which features a two-headed eagle (symbol of Byzantium) – it's located exactly on the site where Emperor Constantine XI was crowned. The adjoining small but modern **museum** houses some quirky pieces, including female hair, buttons and embrodiery, and other everyday items of Mystras' inhabitants.

Beyond the Mitropolis is the **Vrontokhion Monastery**. Of its two churches, **Agios Theodoros** and **Aphentiko**, the latter is the most impressive, with striking frescoes.

SLEEPING

Hotel Byzantion (☎ 27310 83309; www .byzantionhotel.gr; s/d/tr incl breakfast €45/60/70; ❄ ▯ ▮) In the centre of the modern village of Nea Mystras is this small, appealing option. There's a delightful garden and the bright rooms have balconies offering arresting valley or mountain views. It's about 1km from the site.

GETTING THERE & AWAY

Frequent buses go to Mystras from Sparta (€1.40, 30 minutes, 10 daily). A radio taxi from Sparta to Mystras' lower entrance (Xenia Restaurant) costs around €9 to €10, or slightly more to the upper entrance. A cheaper option is to take a **taxi** (☎ 27310 25300) from Mystras but these can be elusive.

MONEMVASIA & GEFYRA
ΜΟΝΕΜΒΑΣΙΑ & ΓΕΦΥΡΑ

Vast, imposing, spectacular Monemvasia (mo-nem-vah-*see*-ah or mo-nem-*vah*-see-ah) is the Greek equivalent to France's Mont St-Michel. This perfect fortress is an iceberglike slab of rock moored off the coast, with sheer cliffs rising hundreds of feet from the sea, and a single highly defendable causeway.

These days Monemvasia incorporates both the rock, whose medieval village is enclosed within the walls of the rock's *kastro,* plus the modern mainland village of Gefyra just across the causeway. In summer, both places brim with visitors. Fortunately, the extraordinary visual impact of the medieval village in particular – and the delights of exploring it – override the effects of mass tourism.

ORIENTATION & INFORMATION

All the practicalities are located in Gefyra. Malvasia Travel, just before the causeway in Geyfra, acts as the bus stop. The National Bank of Greece, with an ATM, and the **post office** (☉ 7.30am-2pm Mon-Fri) are opposite. The **police** (☎ 27320 61210; Spartis 137) are in one of the few buildings in town with a street number.

SIGHTS
MONEMVASIA ARCHAEOLOGICAL MUSEUM

This small **museum** (☎ 27320 61403; admission free; ☉ 8.30am-3pm Tue-Sun winter, 8am-8pm Tue-Sun summer) displays a detailed map of Monemvasia, useful for orientating yourself. It also houses finds unearthed in the course of excavations and building around the old town.

SLEEPING

A pocket torch and sensible shoes are good options for those staying on the cobbled, dimly lit *kastro*.

Hotel Byzantino (☎ 27320 61254/351; Monemvasia; s/d/tr €60/100/120; ⚡) Great value; try to get a room with sea-facing balconies. Breakfast costs €5.

ourpick **Monopati Rooms & Apartments** (☎ 27320 61772; www.byzantine-escapade.com; Monemvasia; apt €70-85, 'little house' €110-140) These delightful stone options ooze personality, as do the hospitable owners. Stylish decor fills the apartments' quirky spaces.

Hotel Lazareto (☎ 27320 61991; www. lazareto.gr; Monemvasia; s €135, d €160-205; ⚡) Located outside the fortress walls, past the causeway, the Lazareto (occupying the handsome stone buildings of a former quarantine hospital) is the most luxurious choice. The furnishings in the well-equipped rooms are stylishly muted. But watch your head – the door frames are for little people.

EATING

Three tavernas sit cheek to cheek in Monemvasia's old town: **Matoula** (☎ 27320 61660), **Marianthi** (☎ 2732 61371) and **To Kanoni** (☎ 27320 61387). You can't really go wrong with any – choose between them for dish type (all traditional Greek) or ambience. Mains cost around €8 to €13.

GETTING THERE & AWAY

There are buses to Athens (€27, six hours, four daily) via Sparta (€9, 2½ hours), Tripoli and Corinth Isthmus.

GETTING AROUND

A **shuttle bus** (☀ 8am-midnight Jun-Sep, Christmas & Easter) ferries visitors between Geyfra and the *kastro*.

Central square, Monemvasia
GEORGE TSAFOS

⬈ KASTRO – MEDIEVAL TOWN

Monemvasia's narrow, cobbled main street is lined with souvenir shops and tavernas, flanked by winding stairways that weave between a complex network of stone houses with walled gardens and courtyards. The main street leads to the central square and the **Cathedral of Christ in Chains**, dating from the 13th century. Opposite is the **Church of Agios Pavlos**, built in 956. Further along the main street is the **Church of Myrtidiotissa**, virtually in ruins, but for a small altar and a defiantly flickering candle. Overlooking the sea is the recently restored, whitewashed 16th-century **Church of Panagia Hrysafitissa**.

GYTHIO ΓΥΘΕΙΟ

pop 4489

Once the port of ancient Sparta, Gythio (*yee*-thih-o) is the gateway to the Lakonian Mani. This attractive fishing town's bustling waterfront has pastel-coloured, 19th-century buildings, behind which crumbling old Turkish houses and scruffy streets cling to a steep, wooded hill.

ORIENTATION

Most restaurants and cafes are along the seafront on Akti Vasileos Pavlou. The bus station is at the northeastern end, past

LEE FOSTER

Harbour setting, Gythio (p113)

the small triangular park known as the Perivolaki (meaning 'tree-filled'). Behind this is the main square, Plateia Panagiotou Venetzanaki.

INFORMATION

EOT (☎ /fax 27330 24484; Vasileos Georgiou 20; ⏱ 8am-2.30pm Mon-Fri) This is the information equivalent of Monty Python's famous cheese-free cheese shop: remarkably information-free, even by EOT's lamentable standards.

Police (☎ 27330 22100; Akti Vasileos Pavlou)

Post office (cnr Ermou & Arheou Theatrou; ⏱ 7.30am-2pm Mon-Fri)

SIGHTS & ACTIVITIES

MARATHONISI ISLET

According to mythology, tranquil pine-shaded Marathonisi is ancient Cranae, where Paris (prince of Troy) and Helen (wife of Menelaus) consummated the affair that sparked the Trojan Wars. The 18th-century **Tzanetakis Grigorakis**

tower at the centre of the island houses a small **Museum of Mani History** (adult/concession €2/1; ⏱ 8am-2.30pm), which relates Maniot history through the eyes of European travellers who visited the region between the 15th and 19th centuries.

BEACHES

There's safe swimming along the 6km of sandy beaches that extend from the village of **Mavrovouni**, 2km south of Gythio.

SLEEPING & EATING

Saga Pension (☎ 27330 23220; Kranais; d €50; 🔀) This is a good-value saga-free, comfortable place with balconies. It's 150m from the port, overlooking Marathonisi Islet. The upmarket Saga Restaurant is below (mains €9 to €15, fish per kilogram €45 to €70).

Matina's (☎ 27330 22518; d/tr €60/65) A clean and comfortable abode, a house-cum-hotel, in a great location right in the heart of town. Owner Matina speaks no English but is welcoming.

Taverna Petakou (☎ 27330 22889; mains €3-7) This no-frills place beside the stadium on Xanthaki is a local favourite. The day's menu is written down in an exercise book in Greek. It may include a hearty fish soup, which comes with a large chunk of bread on the side.

GETTING THERE & AROUND

The **KTEL Lakonia bus station** (☎ 27330 22228; Evrikleos) is found northwest along the waterfront near Jande Café. Services run north to Athens (€21.40, 4½ hours, six daily) or via Sparta (€3.90, one hour); and south to Areopoli (€2.40, 30 minutes, four daily), Gerolimenas (€5.40, 1¼ hours, three daily) and the Diros Caves (€3.30, one hour, one daily).

The town **taxi rank** (☎ 27330 23400) is opposite the bus station.

THE MANI Η ΜΑΝΗ

The Mani, the region covering the central peninsula in the south of the Peloponnese, is a wild, rugged place; and Greeks from elsewhere will tell you, so are its people. For centuries the Maniots were a law unto themselves, renowned for their fierce independence, resentment of attempts to govern them and for their bitter, spectacularly murderous internal feuds. Dotted around the territory – particularly in the inner Mani – you'll find bizarre tower settlements that were built as refuges during clan wars from the 17th century onwards. Thankfully these feuds, some of which took entire armies to halt, are long forgotten and the Maniots are as friendly and hospitable as Greeks elsewhere.

It's worth including this region in your itinerary. The steep tumbling skirts of the Taÿgetos Mountains (threaded with wonderful walking trails) and the tiny coves and ports nestling beside them make for some memorably dramatic scenery. As well as the towers, there are magnificent churches, and caves.

The Mani is generally divided into the Messinian Mani (or outer Mani) and the Lakonian Mani (or inner). The Messinian Mani starts southeast of Kalamata and runs south between the coast and the Taÿgetos Mountains, while the Lakonian Mani covers the rest of the peninsula south of Itilo.

Keen explorers should ask at local shops for *Inside The Mani: A Walking Guide* by Mat Dean, and *The Mani* by Bob Barrow and Mat Dean. The books are full of walking and information gems about the region's villages, towers and churches.

LAKONIAN MANI

Grey rock, mottled with defiant clumps of green scrub, characterises the Scottish-like mountains of inner Mani. Cultivatable land is at a premium, and supports little more than a few stunted olives and figs. The wild flowers that cloak the valleys in spring exhibit nature's resilience by sprouting from the rocks. The indented coast's sheer cliffs plunge into the sea, and rocky outcrops shelter pebbled beaches.

With your own vehicle you can explore the Mani by the loop road that runs down the west coast from the main town, Areopoli, to Gerolimenas, and return via the east coast (or vice versa). Public transport exists, although is limited.

AREOPOLI ΑΡΕΟΠΟΛΗ

pop 774

Areopoli (ah-reh-o-po-lih), capital of the Mani, is aptly named after Ares, the god

Maniot village, Lakonian Mani (p115)

GEORGE TSAFOS

of war. There are some fine examples of Maniot architecture to be found in the narrow alleyways surrounding Plateia 17 Martiou. They start with the 18th-century **Church of Taxiarhes** on the southern side of the square. Look out for the extremely well-preserved relief carvings above the main door. The much older **Church of Agios Ioannis**, on the southern edge of the old town, contains a series of frescoes relating the life of Jesus.

There are numerous examples of tower houses – some in poor condition; others have been converted into smart accommodation. In the southern end of town (ask for directions), the **Religious Museum** (www.culture.gr; admission free) – off the visitor radar due to lack of signage and promotion – is a must-see. Housed in a

restored tower, the Pikoulakis Tower, it houses exquisite Byzantine pieces from Mani churches, including superb manuscripts and jewellery.

There is some fabulous walking in the area; experienced hikers should have no problem with compasses and equipment.

SLEEPING & EATING

Hotel Trapela (☎ 27330 52690; www.trapela .gr; s/d/tr €50/70/80; ⁂) The comfortable wood and stone rooms have tasteful muted colours and the design is along Maniot lines.

ourpick **Londas Pension** (☎ 27330 51360; www.londas.com; d/tr incl breakfast €80/110) This 200-year-old tower is the undisputed king of the castle: stylish whitewashed rooms are tastefully decorated in an antique and modern fusion.

To Katoi (☎ 27330 51201; mains €7-10; ⁂ dinner Mon-Fri, lunch & dinner Sat & Sun) This cosy place is recommended for its daily specials (not on the menu). It's in a lovely location near the Church of Taxiarhes.

Nicola's Corner Taverna (☎ 27330 51366; Plateia Athanaton; mains €8-10) Ignore the menu – this popular spot on the central square displays a good choice of tasty taverna staples that change daily. Don't miss the handmade maccaroni with fried local cheese.

GETTING THERE & AWAY

The **bus station** (☎ 27330 51229; Plateia Athanaton) is a few doors left of Europa Grill. There are buses to Gythio (€2.80, 30 minutes, four daily), which proceed to Athens (€23.80). There are also bus services to the Diros Caves (€1.40, 15 minutes, one daily; returns at 12.45pm) and Vathia (€3.80, one hour, two weekly).

DIROS CAVES ΣΠΗΛΑΙΟ ΔΙΡΟΥ

These extraordinary **caves** (☎ 27330 52222; adult/concession incl tour €12/7; ⁂ 8.30am-5.30pm

Jun-Sep, 8.30am-3pm Oct-May) are 11km south of Areopoli, near the village of **Pyrgos Dirou** – notable for its towers (signposted to the right off the road down to the caves).

The natural entrance to the caves is on the beach and locals like to believe the legend that they extend as far north as Sparta (speleologists have so far estimated the caves to be 14km; tourists enter to 1.5km). They were inhabited in Neolithic times, but were abandoned after an earthquake in 4 BC and weren't rediscovered until 1895. The caves are famous for their stalactites and stalagmites, which have fittingly poetic names such as the Palm Forest, Crystal Lily and the Three Wise Men.

The nearby **Neolithic Museum of Diros** (☎ 27330 52223; adult/concession €2/1; ☒ 8.30am-3pm Tue-Sun) houses items found in an adjoining Neolithic cave, the **Alepotrypa Cave**. Entrance to the museum includes entrance to this cave, which was used to store crops, and housed workshops, living areas and formal burial grounds. The inhabitants died as a result of the earthquake in 4 BC, after which the cave was sealed by boulders.

DIROU TO GEROLIMENAS ΠΥΡΓΟΣ ΔΙΡΟΥ ΠΡΟΣ ΓΕΡΟΛΙΜΕΝΑΣ

Journeying south down Mani's west coast from Pyrgos Dirou to Gerolimenas, the barren mountain landscape is broken only by deserted settlements with mighty towers. A right turn 9km south of Pyrgos Dirou leads down to the **Bay of Mezapos**, sheltered to the east by the frying pan-shaped **Tigani peninsula**. The ruins on the peninsula are those of the **Castle of Maina**, built by the Frankish leader Guillaume de Villehardouin in 1248, and subsequently adapted by the Byzantines.

GEROLIMENAS ΓΕΡΟΛΙΜΕΝΑΣ

pop 55

Gerolimenas (yeh-ro-lih-*meh*-nahss) is a tranquil fishing village built around a small, sheltered bay at the southwestern tip of the peninsula. It's the perfect place for scenic seclusion.

SLEEPING & EATING

Hotel Akrogiali (☎ 27330 54204; www.gerolimenas-hotels.com; s €25-30, d €50-80, tr €70-120, 2-/3-/4-person apt €80/100/120; ☒) The Akrogiali has a great setting overlooking the bay on the western edge of town. It offers various sleeping options, from OK doubles in the traditional hotel building and squishier rooms in a newer stone wing, to apartments nearby. Breakfast costs €6.

our pick **Hotel Kirimai** (☎ 27330 54288; www.kyrimai.gr; d €110-260, ste €300; P ☒ ☒) The luxurious Kirimai is one of Greece's most swish hospitality experiences. It sits in an idyllic setting at the far southern end of the harbour. The restaurant here is open to nonguests. It's worth splurging; the restaurant's head chef was Greek Chef of the Year 2006 and the menu changes regularly (mains €15 to €25).

GETTING THERE & AWAY

There are three buses daily from Gerolimenas to Areopoli (€3.30, 45 minutes) – and on to Athens (€27), Gythio (€5.40, 1¼ hours) and Sparta (€9.30, 2¼ hours). The bus stop is outside Hotel Akrotenaritis; tickets are bought on board.

GEROLIMENAS TO PORTO KAGIO ΓΕΡΟΛΙΜΕΝΑΣ ΠΡΟΣ ΠΟΡΤΟ ΚΑΓΙΟ

South of Gerolimenas, the road continues 4km to the small village of Alika, where it divides. The southern road follows the coast, passing pebbly beaches. It then climbs steeply inland to **Vathia**, the most dramatic of the traditional Mani villages, comprising a cluster of closely packed tower houses perched on a rocky spur.

A turn-off to the right 9km south of Alika leads to **Marmari**, with its two sandy beaches, while the main road cuts across the peninsula to the tiny east-coast fishing village of **Porto Kagio**, set on a perfect horseshoe bay.

There's a wonderful walk to one of Europe's southernmost points, **Cape Tenaro** (or Cape Matapan), whose beautiful lighthouse has been recently restored. The cape has been an important location for millenia and was first mentioned by Homer in his *Iliad*. Follow the signs from Porto Kagio; from the car park it's a 45-minute walk.

MESSINIAN MANI

This rugged coast is scattered with small coves and beaches, and backed by mountains that remain snowcapped until late May. There are glorious views and hiking opportunities.

KARDAMYLI ΚΑΡΔΑΜΥΛΗ

pop 400

This tiny village has one of the prettiest settings in the Peloponnese, nestled between the blue waters of the Messinian Gulf and the Taÿgetos Mountains. The **Vyros Gorge**, which emerges just north of town, runs to the foot of **Mt Profitis Ilias** (2407m), the highest peak of the Taÿgetos. Today the gorge and surrounding areas are very popular with hikers. Visitor numbers can swell to around 4000 in summer.

The website at www.kardamili-greece.com can provide some further, useful information.

ACTIVITIES

Hiking has become Kardamyli's biggest drawcard. The hills behind the village are criss-crossed with an extensive network of colour-coded walking trails. Many guest houses in the village can supply you with route maps (of varying detail and quality). Most of the hikes around here are strenuous, so strong footwear is essential to support your ankles on the often relentlessly rough ground, particularly if you venture into the boulder-strewn gorge itself. You will also need to carry plenty of drinking water.

Many of the walking trails pass through the mountain village of **Exohorio**, which is perched on the edge of the Vyros Gorge at an altitude of 450m. For non-walkers the village is also accessible by road, and it's a good place to do a spot of more gentle exploration. The turn-off to Exohorio is 3km south of Kardamyli.

For those who don't want to go it alone, **2407 Mountain Activities** (☎ 27210 73752; www.2407m.com) offers a range of activities including hiking (€25 to €40 per person; minimum four) and mountain-bike trips (€25 to €40; minimum two) in and around the Taÿgetos Mountains, venturing into 'secret' forested and rocky regions.

SLEEPING

Olympia Koumounakou Rooms (☎ 27210 73623/21026; s/d €30/35) Olympia loves her budget travellers (as they do her) and offers them clean, comfortable rooms and a communal kitchen. It's on the road before the pharmacy.

Hotel Vardia (☎ 27210 73777; www.vardia-hotel.gr; studio €85, apt €120-170) March into this top choice: a relaxing and stylish stone place (near a former sentry tower and situated high behind the village), whose 18 rooms have exceptional views

GEORGE TSAFOS

Coastal landscape of Kardamyli

of the Messinian Gulf. The entrance is south of town: turn at the bookshop.

Kalamitsi Hotel (☎ 27210 73131; www .kalamitsi-hotel.gr; d/ste €110/160) Situated 1km south of town, the Kalamitsi is a lovely, modern, stone-built hotel with serene, well-appointed rooms (family bungalows also available €220). Within its tree-shaded grounds, paths lead to a secluded pebbly beach. Home-cooked dinners (set menu €20, guests only) and fresh buffet breakfasts (€10) are also available.

EATING

Elies (☎ 27210 73140, 6974722819; mains €6.50-10; ⏰ lunch) Location, location. Right by the beach, 1km north of town, and nestled in olive groves. It's got a Mediterranean provincial in-a-private-garden feel with top-quality nosh to boot. Think lemon lamb casserole (€7). Worth an afternoon in your itinerary.

Taverna Dioskouri (☎ 27210 73236; mains €7.50-11.50) A safe, nothing-over-the-top option, except for the friendly owner and

the clifftop view – it overlooks the ocean from the hillside just south of town.

GETTING THERE & AROUND

Kardamyli is on the main bus route from Itilo to Kalamata (€3.10, one hour, four daily). The bus stops at the central square at the northern end of the main thoroughfare, and at the bookshop at the southern end.

ELIA ΗΛΙΑ
OLYMPIA ΟΛΥΜΠΙΑ
pop 1000

With countless overpriced souvenir shops and eateries, the modern village of Olympia (o-lim-*bee*-ah) panders unashamedly to the hundreds of thousands of tourists who continually pour through here on their way to Ancient Olympia.

SIGHTS
MUSEUM OF THE HISTORY OF THE OLYMPIC GAMES IN ANTIQUITY

This **museum** (admission free; ⏰ 1.30-8pm Mon, 8am-8pm Tue-Sun Apr-Oct, 10.30am-5pm

Mon, 8.30am-5pm Tue-Sun Nov-Mar), opened in 2004 (after the Athens Olympics), is a beautifully presented space depicting the history of all things athletic, as well as the Nemean, Panathenaic and, of course, Olympic Games. The sculptures, mosaics and other displays all pay tribute to athletes and athleticism. Women – and their involvement (or lack of) – is also acknowledged.

ARCHAEOLOGICAL MUSEUM OF OLYMPIA

This superb **museum** (☎ /fax 26240 22742; adult/concession €6/3, incl site visit €9/5; ⏱ 1.30-8pm Mon, 8am-8pm Tue-Sun Apr-Oct, 10.30am-5pm Mon, 8.30am-3pm Tue-Sun Nov-Mar) – Ancient Olympia's archaeological site

DIANA MAYFIELD

Outdoor eatery, Nafplio (p105)

museum – about 200m north of the sanctuary's ticket kiosk, is a great place to start or end your visit to the site of Ancient Olympia.

SITE OF ANCIENT OLYMPIA

The Olympics were undoubtedly the Ancient World's biggest sporting event. During the games warring states briefly halted their squabbles, corporate sponsors vied to outdo each other, and victorious competitors won great fame and considerable fortune. You could say much the same about the modern-day equivalent, the main difference being that back then only men could compete and they did most of it *sans* underpants. Held every four years until their abolition by killjoy Emperor Theodosius I in AD 394, the games lasted at least 1000 years. The World Heritage-listed site of **Ancient Olympia** (☎ 26240 22517; adult/concession €6/3, site & archaeological museum €9/5; ⏱ 8am-8pm Apr-Oct, 8.30am-3pm Nov-Mar) is still a recognisable complex of temples, priests' dwellings and public buildings. The site contains excellent explanatory boards, with depictions of what the buildings would have looked like, along with a plan and description in English.

Ancient Olympia is signposted from the modern village. The entrance is beyond the bridge over the Kladeos River. Thanks to Theodosius II and various earthquakes, little remains of the magnificent buildings of Ancient Olympia, but enough exists to sustain an absorbing visit in an idyllic, leafy setting; allow a minimum of half a day.

SLEEPING & EATING

Hotel Kronio (☎ 26240 22188; www.hotel kronio.gr; Tsoureka 1; s €46, d/tr incl breakfast €56/72; ✖ 🖳 🛜) In 2008 this place had a makeover. Its contemporary look and bright and airy rooms make it one of the best-value options around. The helpful multilingual owner adds to the overall package.

Hotel Pelops (☎ /fax 26240 22543; www .hotelpelops.gr; Varela 2; s/d/tr/ste incl breakfast €48/60/84/110; ✕ ✕ ☐ ☎) Opposite the church, this is among the town's best contenders, with comfortable rooms. The friendly Greek-Australian owners provide friendly service and a buffet breakfast fit for an athlete. On offer each night is the Pelops Platter, a massive dish of gourmet mezedhes.

No name takeaway (snacks €1.50; ☼ 7am-3pm) This nondescript blink-and-you'll-miss-it takeaway joint has been here for 20 years, and with good reason. Owner Takis makes the best *tyropita* (cheese pie) and other homemade treats in the Pelops – some would say, Greece.

Mithos (☎ 26243 00369; mains €6-8; ☼ lunch & dinner) A locally recommended place off the tourist drag. The place to get your chops around some good-quality grills. Enough said.

GETTING THERE & AWAY

BUS
There is no direct service from Olympia to Athens. Eight or so of the 16 buses (reduced schedule on Sunday) go via Pyrgos (€1.90, 30 minutes), west of Olympia, and allow time to connect for services to Athens.

TRAIN
Train services from Olympia head to Pyrgos only – there are five local departures daily (€1, 30 minutes). From Pyrgos, you can catch connections to other destinations. Note: to get to Athens, you take the train from Pyrgos (via Diakofto) and change to the *proastiako* at Kiato.

SARONIC GULF ISLANDS
ΝΗΣΙΑ ΤΟΥ ΣΑΡΩΝΙΚΟΥ
POROS ΠΟΡΟΣ
pop 4500

Poros is a popular holiday island, yet it has a refreshing sense of remoteness in its sparsely populated and forested interior. The island is separated from the mountainous Peloponnese by a narrow sea channel, and the picturesque surroundings make the main settlement of Poros Town seem more like a lakeside resort in the Swiss Alps than a Greek island port. The mainland town of Galatas lies on the opposite shore.

Poros is in fact made up of two 'almost' islands: tiny Sferia, which is occupied mainly by the town of Poros, and the much larger and mainly forested Kalavria, which has the island's beaches and its larger seasonal hotels scattered along its southern shore. An isthmus, cut by a narrow canal and spanned by a road bridge, connects the two islands.

GETTING THERE & AWAY
There are numerous daily ferries from Piraeus to Poros in summer and about four daily in winter. Fast ferries continue south to Hydra, Spetses, Ermioni and Porto Heli. Conventional ferries connect Aegina to Poros and on to Methana on the mainland.

Caïques shuttle constantly between Poros and Galatas (€0.80, five minutes) on the mainland. They leave from the quay opposite Plateia Iroön in Poros Town. Hydrofoils dock about 50m north of here and car ferries to Galatas leave from the dock several hundred metres north again, on the road to Kalavria.

GETTING AROUND

A bus operates May to October every half hour from 7am until midnight on a route that starts near the main ferry dock on Plateia Iroön in Poros Town. It crosses to Kalavria and goes east along the south coast as far as Moni Zoödohou Pigis (€1.50, 10 minutes), then turns around and heads west as far as Neorion Beach (€1.50, 15 minutes).

Some of the caïques operating between Poros and Galatas switch to ferrying tourists to beaches during summer. Operators stand on the harbour front and call out destinations.

There are several places on the road to Kalavria offering bikes for hire, both motorised and pedal-powered. Bikes start at €8 per day, and mopeds and scooters are €15 to €20.

POROS TOWN

pop 4102

Poros Town is a pleasant place where whitewashed houses with red-tiled roofs look out across the narrow channel towards the shapely mountains of the Peloponnese. Behind the harbour front a rocky bluff rises steeply to a crowning clock tower.

The town is also a useful base from which to explore the ancient sites of the adjacent Peloponnese.

INFORMATION

Poros doesn't have a tourist office, but you can find useful information at www.poros.gr.

Alpha Bank (Plateia Iroön) Has an ATM.
Bank Emporiki (Plateia Iroön) Has ATM facilities.
Family Tours (☎ 22980 25900; www.family tours.gr) On the harbour front. Sells ferry tickets and arranges accommodation, car hire, tours and cruises.

Marinos Tours (☎ 22980 23423; www.marinostours.gr) On the harbour front. Arranges hydrofoil tickets and other services.
National Bank of Greece (Papadopoulou) About 100m north of Plateia Iroön; has an ATM.
Post office (☎ 22980 22274; Tombazi; ⏱ 7.30am-2pm Mon-Fri) Next to Seven Brothers Hotel.
Tourist police (☎ 22980 22462/22256; Dimosthenous 10) Behind the Poros high school.

SLEEPING & EATING

Seven Brothers Hotel (☎ 22980 23412; www.7brothers.gr; Plateia Iroön; s/d/tr €55/65/75; 🅿 🖳) Conveniently close to the hydrofoil dock, this modern hotel has bright, comfy rooms with small balconies and tea- and coffee-making facilities.

Hotel Manessi (☎ 22980 22273/25857; www.manessi.com; Paralia; s/d €70/80; 🅿 🛜) Well-placed at the mid-point of the harbour front, the recently renovated Manessi is a central option. The business-style rooms are comfy and immaculate.

Dimitris Family Taverna (☎ 22980 23709; mains €4.50-20) The owners of this cheerful, family-run place have a butcher's business. Cuts of pork, lamb and chicken are of the finest quality, yet vegetarians can still mix and match a selection of nonmeat dishes. To get here, head north from the cathedral for 20m, turn right and then left for 100m.

Taverna Rota (☎ 22980 25627; Plateia Iroön; mains €5-15) Located on the edge of Plateia Iroön, this longstanding, family-run taverna dishes up breakfast (€4.50 to €7), traditional dishes, a range of salads, pasta and pizzas. The fish soup (€6) is excellent and they make their own flavoursome bread.

MARK DAFFEY

Poros Town, Poros

AROUND POROS

Poros has several good beaches. **Kanali Beach**, on Kalavria 1km east of the bridge, is pebbly. **Askeli Beach** is about 500m to the east and has a long sandy stretch. **Neorion Beach**, 3km west of the bridge, has waterskiing and banana-boat and air-chair rides. The best beach is at **Russian Bay**, 1.5km past Neorion.

The 18th-century **Moni Zoödohou Pigis**, on Kalavria, has a beautiful gilded iconostasis from Asia Minor. The monastery is well signposted, 4km east of Poros Town.

HYDRA ΥΔΡΑ

pop 2900

Hydra (*ee*-dhr-ah) is still the catwalk queen of the Saronic Gulf. The island has long attracted throngs of tourists, cruise passengers and yacht crews, and the occasional celebrity on their way to hidden holiday homes among the tiers of picturesque buildings that rise above the harbour. Beyond the town itself, there are corners of lovely wilderness, accessible to those willing to hike – usually uphill.

GETTING THERE & AWAY

At the time of writing only fast ferries linked Hydra with Poros and Piraeus, and Ermioni and Porto Heli on the mainland. You can buy tickets from **Idreoniki Travel** (☎ 22980 54007; www.hydreoniki.gr), opposite the ferry dock.

GETTING AROUND

In summer, there are caïques from Hydra Town to the island's beaches. There are also **water taxis** (☎ 22980 53690), which will take you anywhere you like; examples include Kamini (€11) and Vlyhos (€15).

The donkey owners clustered around the port charge around €16 to transport your bags to your hotel.

HYDRA TOWN

pop 2526

Hydra Town's red-roofed houses, with their pastel-painted walls, form a pretty amphitheatre behind the harbour, where the cobbled quayside is a colourful throng of ambling pedestrians, mules and donkeys. Behind the harbour, steep steps and alleyways paved with multi-coloured stone lead ever upwards to the rock-studded slopes of old Hydra. The harbour front and the streets leading inland are crammed with cafes and craft and souvenir shops.

INFORMATION

There is no tourist office on Hydra but a useful website is www.hydradirect.com.

There is an ATM at Saitis Tours on the harbour front. The **post office** (☻ 7.30am-2pm Mon-Fri) is found opposite the fish market on a small side street that runs between the Bank Emporiki and the National Bank of Greece, both of which have ATM facilities. The **tourist police** (☎ 22980 52205; Votsi; ☻ mid-May-Sep) can be found sharing an office with the regular police.

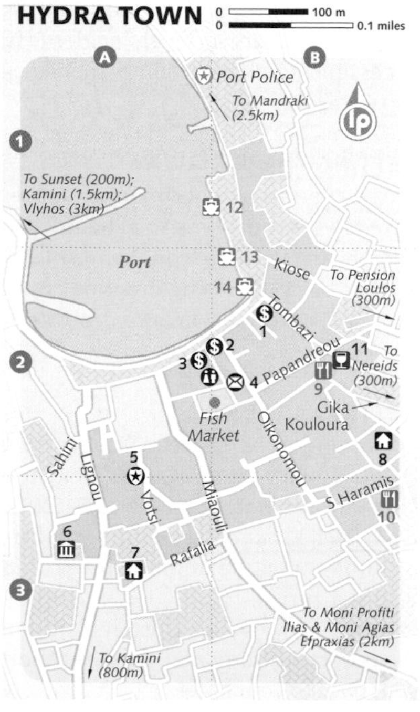

SIGHTS & ACTIVITIES

Hydra's star cultural attraction is the handsome **Lazaros Koundouriotis Historical Mansion** (☎ 22980 52421; nhmuseum@tee.gr; adult/concession €4/2; ☻ 9am-4pm Tue-Sun), an ochre-coloured building sitting high above the harbour. It was the home of one of the major players in the Greek independence struggle and is a fine example of late-18th-century traditional architecture. The main reception rooms of the 2nd floor have been restored to their full.

Kallianos Diving Center (☎ 27540 31095; www.kallianosdivingcenter.gr) is based at the private island of Kapari. Activities include a two-dive outing for €80 with full equipment supplied, or €125 with an instructor. There's a monthly diving-with-

HYDRA TOWN
0 ————— 100 m
0 ————— 0.1 miles

dolphins trip starting at €200, with a 50% refund if the dolphins decide not to turn up.

SLEEPING

Pension Erofili (☎ /fax 22980 54049; www .pensionerofili.gr; Tombazi; s/d/tr €45/55/65; ❄) Tucked away in the inner town, these pleasant, unassuming rooms are a decent budget deal for Hydra. The young family owners add a friendly sparkle. It also has a large studio room with private kitchen.

Pension Loulos (☎ 22980 52411/ 6972699381; s/d/tr €50/60/70; ❄) A grand old house brimming with seagoing history and tradition. Loulos' eponymous owner was a noted sea captain and his rooms have old-fashioned charm, but with every amenity including tea- and coffee-making facilities. Most have glorious views, and the roof terrace is sunset heaven. The pension is a few minutes inland on the slopes above Tombazi.

ourpick Nereids (☎ 22980 52875; www .nereids-hydra.com; Tombazi; s/d €60/65; ❄ 🤝) These lovely rooms represent exceptional value and quality. They are spacious, peaceful and have beautiful decor and open views to Hydra's rocky heights. Nereids is a few minutes' walk up Tombazi from the harbour, but it's worth it.

Hotel Orloff (☎ 22980 52564; www.orloff .gr; Rafalia; s/d incl breakfast €160/200; ❄ 🤝) There's a marvellous sense of historic Hydra without stuffiness at this beautiful, old mansion. The comfortable rooms have elegant furnishings and there's a lovely garden in which buffet breakfast is served. It's family-run and the welcome is warm.

EATING

ourpick Taverna Gitoniko (Manolis & Christina; ☎ 22980 53615; Spilios Haramis; mains €4-9) Classic Greek favourites, such as zucchini

DONALD C. & PRISCILLA ALEXANDER EASTMAN
Island transport, Hydra Town

balls, spinach pies and dolmadhes are tops, as is the local lamb.

Paradosiako (☎ 22980 54155; Tombazi; mains €7-15) This little streetside *mezedhopoleio* (restaurant specialising in mezedhes) is traditional Greek personified. Classic pies come in cheese, beef, shrimp and vegie varieties and favourite mezedhes are plentiful.

Sunset (☎ 22980 52067; mains €9-22) Famed by name alone for its splendid location a short distance to the west of the harbour, the Sunset throws live Greek music into the mix in summer to accompany such longstanding favourite starters as mackerel salad. Local fish are well prepared, with mains such as grilled sea bream marinated in herbs, and meat and pasta dishes are also done with flair.

Coastal path from Hydra Town to Kamini, Hydra

MARK DAFFEY

DRINKING & ENTERTAINMENT

Hydra's harbour front revs up at night, when daytime cafes become hot music bars. A few blocks inland from the harbour front, the more chilled **Amalour** (☎ 6977461357; Tombazi) does a lively line of cocktails and smoothies to a Latin rhythm.

AROUND HYDRA

Hydra's stony, arid interior, now with some regenerating pine woods, makes a robust but peaceful contrast to the clamour of the quayside.

An unbeatable Hydra experience is the long haul up to **Moni Profiti Ilias**, but you need to be fit and willing. Starting up Mialou from the harbour, it's a tough hour or more through relentless zigzags and pine trees. Just follow your nose and the occasional timely sign. You can visit the **Moni Agias Efpraxias** just before reaching Profiti Ilias itself. The latter is a wonderful complex with a central church within a rectangular walled compound.

Inside are beautiful icons and serenity; it's worth the hike.

Other paths lead to **Mt Eros** (588m), the island's highest point, and also along the island spine to east and west, but you need advanced route-finding skills or reliable walking directions from knowledgeable locals. A useful map for walkers is the *Hydra* map in the Anavasi Central Aegean series (www.mount ains.gr).

Hydra's shortcoming – or blessing – is its lack of appealing beaches to draw the crowds. There are a few strands all the same. **Kamini**, about a 1.5km walk along the coastal path from the port, has rocks and a very small pebble beach. **Vlyhos**, a 1.5km walk further on from Kamini, is an attractive village offering a slightly larger pebble beach, two tavernas and a ruined 19th-century stone bridge.

A path leads east from the port to the reasonable pebble beach at **Mandraki**, 2.5km away. **Bisti Bay**, 8km away on the southwestern side of the island, has a decent pebble beach.

CENTRAL GREECE & THE IONIAN ISLANDS

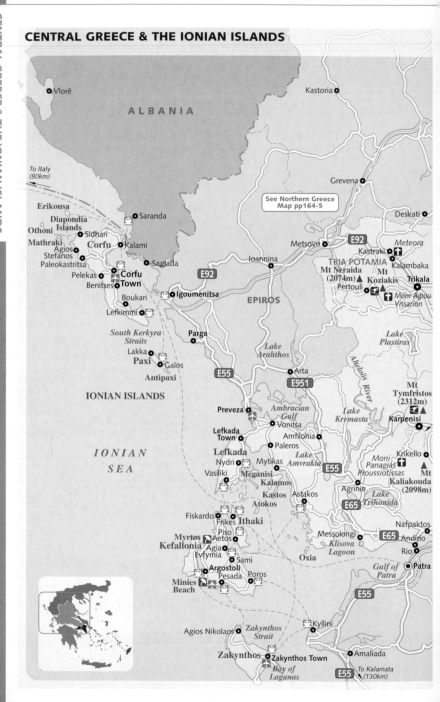

See Northern Greece
Map pp164-5

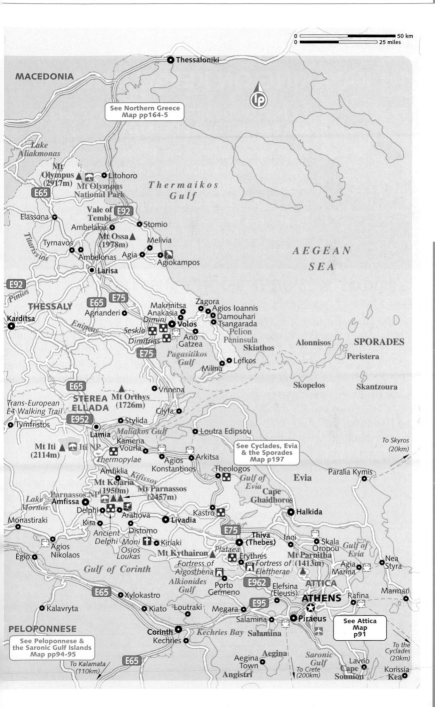

HIGHLIGHTS

1 KAYAKING ON KEFALLONIA

BY PAVLOS GEORGILAS & YVONNE WALSER, SEA KAYAK TOUR OPERATORS

We started sea kayaking 10 years ago. Sunny weather and warm, calm and amazingly clear water makes Kefallonia an ideal place for kayaking. Most of the coastline is accessible only by sea and ranges from dramatic white limestone cliffs to secluded forested coves. It's a unique experience for visitors.

➷ PAVLOS' & YVONNE'S DON'T MISS LIST

❶ MYRTOS TO ASSOS

Paddle down the dramatic west coast of Kefallonia towards gorgeous **Myrtos** (p162). From there, head for **Assos** (p162), a spectacular white-washed fishing village on the isthmus of the Assos peninsula. The cypress trees and pines that cover the surrounding hills, the impressive limestone cliffs and the fortress standing guard on the peninsula create breathtaking scenery.

❷ GULF OF MYRTOS

Head out from the fishing port of Agia Kyriaki for an easy trip along a coastline of pristine beauty. This is one of the most remote parts of Kefallonia. Stop for a swim at the white limestone cliffs, wide beaches and turquoise waters of Fteri and then paddle back to Agia Kyriaki.

❸ FISKARDO

Paddle out from the secluded cove of Emplyssi and south along the coast to **Fiskardo** (p159). This picturesque village

Clockwise from top: Village of Assos (p162); Coastal views over Myrtos (p162); Beached kayak, Fiskardo (p159)

❶ Myrtos to Assos
❷ Gulf of Myrtos
❸ Fiskardo

0 ———— 5 km
0 ———— 2.5 miles

was left untouched by the 1953 earth-quake and has traditional houses and abundant signs of an aristocratic past that make it simply unique. Continue kayaking to Phoki, a colourful little bay with crystal clear waters and a forest of cypress trees covering the surrounding slopes. From there head for Evreti Bay, paddling over three wrecked caïques.

❹ **PADDLING CALM WATER**

There are a lot of great experiences that you can enjoy while kayaking, such as complete remoteness, encounters with dolphins and breathtaking sunsets. But for us, the greatest experience of all is the unsurpassed feeling of paddling in a mirror calm sea with warm, turquoise and superbly transparent waters…as close as you can get to your soul.

↘ **THINGS YOU NEED TO KNOW**

Best months for kayaking June and September **Best times** Morning and late afternoon **Skill level** Many opportunities for complete novices **Prices** Day trips from around €60 **Only a few hours?** Paddle from Kefallonia's lighthouse at Argostoli to Minies Beach (Map pp128–9) for caves, beaches and limestone cliffs

HIGHLIGHTS

2

⬎ MESMERISING METEORA

Be awe-struck as you stand beneath the towering rock pinnacles of Meteora (p145), topped with seemingly inaccessible monasteries. Climb rock-hewn stairs into the clouds and enter a mystical place where monks continue a ten-century tradition of living atop this rock forest – the views will captivate you. Sit down and soak it all up or monastery-hop for even more wonderment.

3

⬎ ANCIENT DELPHI

Regarded by the ancient Greeks as the centre of the world, the ruins of Ancient Delphi (p138) remain one of Greece's most atmospheric sites. Pilgrims have been coming here for centuries, first to seek advice from Apollo via Delphi's famous oracle, and no w to wander through the inspiring ruins which are built into Mt Parnassos and look out toward the Gulf of Corinth.

◥ LAID-BACK PELION PENINSULA

The Pelion Peninsula (p144) is dramatic and lush, with a plunging coastline and an interior laden with fruit trees, forests and olive groves. The peninsula has always been slightly remote, creating a strong local culture and a slower pace of life from the region's villages. Get a taste by exploring mountain villages and quiet sandy coves.

◥ CORFU TOWN

With a majestic seafront, beautiful pastel architecture and a bustle that draws you in, Corfu Town (p152) is like no other Greek town. Wander the marble-paved streets, join in the lively cafe scene or take in the museums and famous Palaio Frourio. You may wonder at times if you're in Greece, Italy or France but, wherever it is, it's enchanting.

◥ SERENE PAXI

The kind of island we all daydream about, tiny Paxi (p157) seems too pretty to be true. Ancient olive groves and windmills dot the interior while tranquil coves beckon from the coastline. With colourful Venetian-style harbour towns and restaurants and hotels that beg you to stay, it's a wonder we all don't move to Paxi.

2 JOHN ELK III; 3 JOHN ELK III; 4 TERRY HARRIS JUST GREECE PHOTO LIBRARY/ALAMY; 5 PCL/ALAMY; 6 PAUL BIGLAND

2 Rock pinnacles, Meteora (p145); 3 Vistas from Ancient Delphi (p138); 4 Coastline of the Pelion Peninsula (p144); 5 The Liston, Corfu Town (p152); 6 Lakka (p158), Paxi

THE BEST...

⬆ WALKING TRAILS

- **Parnassos National Park** (p142) Take in the soaring peaks, wild animals and profusion of flowers.
- **Pelion Peninsula** (p144) Follow yesteryear's cobbled mule paths from village to village.
- **Paxi** (p157) Wander the traditional trails across this tiny island.
- **Assos** (p162) Hike to the fortress of this view-laden isthmus.
- **Meteora** (p145) Step along the once-secret *monopatia* (monk paths) that lead from pinnacle to pinnacle.

⬆ ATMOSPHERIC SLEEPS

- **Doupiani House** (p150) Awake in the shadow of Meteora's towering rock forest.
- **Paxos Beach Hotel** (p158) Enjoy your own private beach.
- **Hotel Appolonia** (p142) Luxuriate in swish rooms with views over Delphi.

- **Sisilianou Arhontiko** (p145) Stay in a renovated, traditional stone mansion.

⬆ ONE-OF-A-KIND BUILDINGS

- **Meteora's monasteries** (p146) Perched high on towering rocks.
- **Corfu Town** (p152) Venetian-era pastel-coloured mansions.
- **Pelion villages** (p144) White-washed half-timbered homes with overhanging balconies.
- **Ahillion Palace** (p155) An Empress' retreat of style (or is it kitsch?).
- **Ancient Delphi's tholos** (p140) The site's most striking ancient structure.

⬆ QUIET RETREATS

- **Kastraki** (p150) Enjoy Meteora after the tours have left.
- **Corfu's West Coast** (p156) Hop on a water taxi to small, sandy coves.
- **Antipaxi** (p159) Explore this tiny oasis of sand and sea.

GEORGE TSAFOS

Stone seating of the theatre (p140), Ancient Delphi

THINGS YOU NEED TO KNOW

VITAL STATISTICS

- Population Central Greece 1.9 million; Ionian Islands 223,150
- Area Central Greece 37,042 sq km; Ionian Islands 2432 sq km

LOCALITIES IN A NUTSHELL

- Sterea Ellada (p138) The southern section of central Greece; home to Ancient Delphi and dramatic Mt Parnassos.
- Thessaly (p144) The northeast of central Greece with the relaxed Pelion Peninsula and towering Meteora.
- Corfu (p151) Greenest and most popular Ionian island with lots of sand and a lively capital.
- Paxi (p157) Serene and tiny island that makes for a quiet escape.
- Kefallonia (p159) Mountains, vineyards and rugged island coastline.

ADVANCE PLANNING

- Two months before Sort out your accommodation, especially in Delphi and Corfu Town. Coordinate with any activities you'd like to book, such as hiking or kayaking tours.
- One month before Check online ferry schedules and prebook tickets in high season.

RESOURCES

- www.culture.gr Details on Delphi, including history, descriptions of the ruins and visiting info.
- www.routes.gr Hiking guide with detailed information on routes in central Greece.
- www.greeka.com/ionian The low-down on the Ionians, including accommodation bookings, maps and nightlife. For sites on specific islands, see p151.

EMERGENCY NUMBERS

- Police (☎ 100)
- Highway Rescue (ELPA; ☎ 104)

GETTING AROUND

- Bus Comprehensive routes throughout central Greece and on Corfu, as well as direct bus links from Athens to Corfu.
- Ferry Boats to the Ionians from Igoumenitsa, Mytikas and Astakos in central Greece. See also Island Hopping (p357).
- Car The best way to travel through central Greece (especially the Pelion Peninsula), as well as Corfu and Kefallonia.

BE FOREWARNED

- Delphi and Corfu Town These opular locations get very busy in summer.
- Port Towns Not often idyllic; look for a ferry sailings that don't require an overnight stay.

ITINERARIES

ARCHITECTURAL WONDERS Three Days

There are few ancient sites in the world that compare to **(1) Ancient Delphi** (p138). The ancient Greeks believed it to be the centre of the world and there's an almost palpable atmosphere when you're there. Built in a breathtaking setting on the slopes of Mt Parnassos and overlooking the sea, these ruins will undoubtedly inspire you. Spend a day taking in both the site and the nearby museums, particularly the Delphi Museum where many of the site's original artefacts are displayed. Delphi has some comfortable hotels with views, and it's worth spending the night so you're not rushed for time. From Delphi, drive or take a bus to the incredible site of **(2) Meteora** (p145). Here you can spend a couple of days exploring the numerous monasteries perched like birds' nests atop ancient pinnacles of smooth rock. Base yourself in **(3) Kastraki** (p150); with its impressive location beneath the towering rocks, it's a great spot to soak up the scenery and relax.

ISLAND LIFE Five Days

A green oasis, and supposedly the setting for Shakespeare's *The Tempest*, Corfu is a captivating island. Set up base in **(1) Corfu Town** (p152) amidst Venetian architecture, French promenades and marble, paved streets. Take in the museums, the lively harbour and the creative Greek cuisine. Try to catch a classical drama or music performance at the Municipal Theatre. When you've had your fill, rent a car and spend a day or two exploring the quiet **(2) West Coast** (p156) beaches and villages, stopping at Triklino Vineyard. From Corfu, hop on a ferry to the nearby island of **(3) Paxi** (p157). Despite being a stone's throw from Corfu, it's an entirely different beast – tranquil and slow-paced. Base yourself in the picturesque waterfront town of **(4) Gaïos** (p158) and if you're up for stretching your legs, set off on the old mule trails that criss-cross the island. From Gaïos, take a day trip to tiny **(5) Antipaxi** (p159) for dazzlingly clear water and sandy beaches.

ACTIVE ADVENTURES One Week

The region offers lots of opportunities to enjoy the great outdoors while taking in some of Greece's most spectacular scenery. Begin on the mountainous, green wonderland of the **(1) Pelion Peninsula** (p144). Its dramatic coastline and pretty villages make it a popular hiking destination. Spend a couple of days exploring, basing yourself in one of the peninsula's atmospheric traditional guest houses and filling up on regional cooking, which uses a good dose of mountain herbs. From the Pelion Peninsula, head to **(2) Parnassos National Park** (p142) for a day or two; if you haven't rented a car, you can reach it by bus. The park has three towering peaks which are the hiker's stomp-

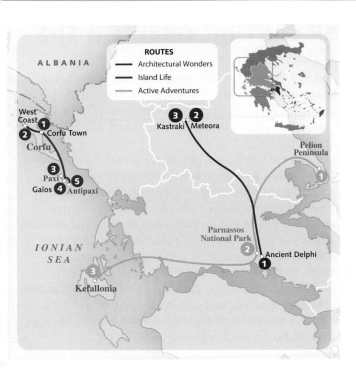

ing ground in summer and the skier's paradise in winter. You'll find unique flora, including a plethora of wildflowers in spring. From here, head for (3) Kefallonia (p159), either by bus (via Athens) or by car and ferry from Astakos in the region's southwest. The rugged mountains, fruitful vineyards, stunning coastline and golden beaches make it an excellent place to hike, kayak and unwind.

DISCOVER CENTRAL GREECE & THE IONIAN ISLANDS

A trip through central Greece and the Ionian Islands offers a blend of popular, crowd-pleasing destinations and quieter spots to linger and lounge. Outdoor enthusiasts will find countless opportunities to hike, cycle, windsurf and dive, while cultural devotees can explore some of the world's biggest sites.

The rugged and diverse landscape of central Greece ranges from rocky sea cliffs and hidden bays to inland river valleys and olive groves. The ruins at Delphi remain one of Greece's most inspiring archaeological sites, while the sheer cliffs of monastery-topped Meteora are breathtaking. The Pelion Peninsula is criss-crossed with historic cobblestone paths that link lush mountain hamlets with beaches that rival the best islands, but without the crowds.

The Ionian Islands seduce visitors with their heat, intense colour and dazzling light. Despite countless beach resorts, it's still possible to find isolated swimming coves and laid-back villages. In Corfu Town you can admire British neoclassical palaces, drink beneath Parisian-style arcades and wander through Venetian alleyways.

CENTRAL GREECE ΚΕΝΤΡΙΚΗ ΕΛΛΑΔΑ

STEREA ELLADA ΣΤΕΡΕΑ ΕΛΛΑΔΑ

DELPHI ΔΕΛΦΟΙ

pop 2500

If the ancient Greeks hadn't chosen Delphi (from *Delphis*, or womb) as the navel of their earth and built the Sanctuary of Apollo here, someone else would have thought of a good reason to make this eagle's nest village a tourist attraction. Its location on a precipitous cliff edge is spectacular, and despite its overt commercialism and the constant passage of tour buses through the modern village, it still has a special feel. Delphi is 178km northwest of Athens and is the base for exploring one of Greece's major tourist sites.

ORIENTATION & INFORMATION

Almost everything you'll need in Delphi is on Vasileon Pavlou & Friderikis. The **post office** (7.30am-2pm) and three bank ATMs are also on this street. You'll find helpful information at the **municipal tourist office** (☎ 22650 82900; 7.30am-2.30pm Mon-Fri, 8am-2pm Sat), toward the Arahova end of Vasileon Pavlou & Friderikis.

Ancient Delphi (comprising the Archaeological Museum and site itself) is 500m along the pine-shaded main road toward Arahova.

SIGHTS

ANCIENT DELPHI

Of all the archaeological sites in Greece, **Ancient Delphi** (www.culture.gr) is the one with the most potent 'spirit of place'. Built on the slopes of Mt Parnassos, overlooking the Gulf of Corinth and extending into a valley of cypress and olive trees,

ANCIENT DELPHI & SANCTUARY OF APOLLO

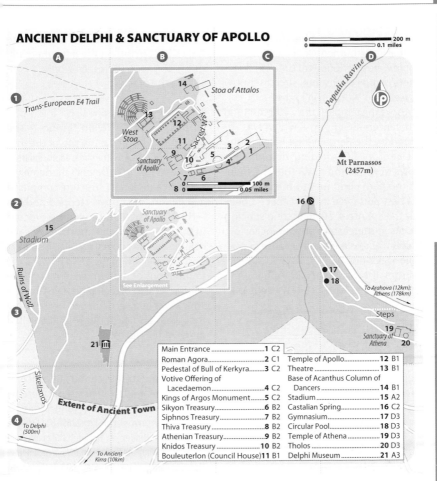

Main Entrance	1	C2
Roman Agora	2	C1
Pedestal of Bull of Kerkyra	3	C2
Votive Offering of Lacedaemon	4	C2
Kings of Argos Monument	5	C2
Sikyon Treasury	6	B2
Siphnos Treasury	7	B2
Thiva Treasury	8	B2
Athenian Treasury	9	B2
Knidos Treasury	10	B2
Bouleuterlon (Council House)	11	B1
Temple of Apollo	12	B1
Theatre	13	B1
Base of Acanthus Column of Dancers	14	B1
Stadium	15	A2
Castalian Spring	16	C2
Gymnasium	17	D3
Circular Pool	18	D3
Temple of Athena	19	D3
Tholos	20	D3
Delphi Museum	21	A3

this World Heritage Site's allure lies both in its stunning setting and its inspiring ruins. The ancient Greeks regarded Delphi as the centre of the world; according to mythology, Zeus released two eagles at opposite ends of the world and they met here. In summer, visit the site early to avoid the crowds and the heat.

Sanctuary of Apollo

The Sanctuary of Apollo is on the left of the main road as you walk toward Arahova. Just to the right of the entrance, notice the brickwork of the **Roman agora**.

From the main entrance, the steps on your right lead to the **Sacred Way**, which winds gradually up to the foundations of the Doric Temple of Apollo. In ancient times the Sacred Way was lined with treasuries and statues given by grateful city-states – Athens, Sikyon, Siphnos, Knidos and Thiva (Thebes) – all in thanks to Apollo. To the north of the reconstructed **Athenian Treasury** are the foundations of the **bouleuterion** (council house).

The 4th-century-BC **Temple of Apollo** dominated the entire sanctuary with a statue of Apollo and a hearth where an eternal flame burned. On the temple vestibule were inscriptions of Greek philosophers' words of wisdom, such as 'Know Thyself' and 'Nothing in Excess'.

Above the temple is the well-preserved 4th-century-BC **theatre**, which was restored by the Pergamenon kings in the 1st century BC, yielding magnificent views from the top row. From the theatre the path continues to the **stadium,** the best-preserved in all of Greece. Check out the sprinters' etched-stone starting blocks at the eastern end; on occasion, stadium access is limited because of possible rockslides.

From the Sanctuary of Apollo, the paved path towards Arahova runs parallel to the main road and leads to the **Castalian Spring** on the left, where pilgrims cleansed themselves before consulting the oracle.

Sanctuary of Athena

Opposite the Castalian Spring is the Sanctuary of Athena, the site of the 4th-century-BC **tholos** (rotunda; admission free), the most striking of Delphi's monuments. This graceful circular structure comprised 20 columns on a three-stepped podium – three of its columns were re-erected in the 1940s. The white portions of each column are the original marble; the darker portions are new material. To its west, the foundations of the Temple of Athena are all that remain of a rectangular structure which was heavily damaged by the same rockslides and earthquake that levelled much of the *tholos*.

DELPHI MUSEUM

From around the 8th century BC, Ancient Delphi managed to amass a considerable treasure trove, much of it reflected in its magnificent **museum** (☎ 22650 82312; www .culture.gr/war/index_en.jsp; adult site or museum €6, adult/student site & museum €9/5, free Sun Nov-Mar; ☒ 8am-7.45pm Tue-Sun, 1.30-7.45pm Mon Apr-Oct, 8.30am-2.45pm Nov-Mar).

Upon entering the museum, in room 5, you'll first notice the **Sphinx of the Naxians**, dating from 560 BC. Also residing here are well-preserved parts of the **frieze** from the Siphnian treasury, which depicts not only the battle between the gods and the giants, but also the Judgment of Paris (far left corner as you enter), who was called upon to decide which goddess was most beautiful (he chose Aphrodite).

In the rooms to the left are fragments of **metopes** (figures within the frieze) from the Athenian treasury depicting

THE DELPHIC ORACLE

The Delphic oracle, the most powerful in Greece, sat on a tripod at the entrance to a chasm that emitted intoxicating vapours. A popular story proposes that the earliest oracles were young women who regularly ran off with their advice-seeking pilgrims, leaving the post temporarily vacant. Hence it became customary for the appointed seer (Pythia) to be at least 50 years of age.

When she was consulted for divine advice, the priestess inhaled the fumes and entered a trance. Her inspired, if somewhat vague, answers were translated into verse by a priest. In fact, the oracle's reputation for infallibility may have rested with the often ambiguous or cryptic answers. Wars were fought, marriages sealed and journeys begun on the strength of the oracle's visions.

the Labours of Hercules, the Exploits of Theseus and the **Battle of the Amazons** (room 7). Further on you can't miss the tall **Acanthus Column of Dancers** (room 11), with three women dancing around its top. Next to it is the **omphalos**, a sculpted cone that once stood at what was considered the centre of the world. In the end room is the celebrated life-size **Bronze Charioteer**, which commemorates a victory in the Pythian Games of 478 or 474 BC.

SIKELIANOS MUSEUM

Fans of Greek drama should head to the intimate **Sikelianos Museum** (**Delphic Festivals Museum; ☎ 22650 82731; admission €1; 9am-3pm Thu-Mon**) in a classic mansion overlooking Delphi. The museum is dedicated to Greek poet Angelos Sikelianos and his American-born wife Eva Palmer, who together in the late 1920s established Delphi as a European centre for drama and the arts, with masks, costumes and photos on display. The town and museum sponsor a 10-day **ancient drama festival** every July.

TOURS

English-language tours of Delphi are offered by **Georgia Hasioti** (**☎ 69449 43511, 22550 82722**) who also speaks Japanese, French and Italian; **Penny Kolomvotsos** (**☎ 69446 44427**) who also speaks German; and **Electra Togia** (**☎ 69378 13215**) who also speaks Italian and Spanish.

SLEEPING

Accommodation is plentiful and high quality in Delphi, but it's advisable to book ahead in peak season (April-May and July-September) and on public holidays.

Rooms Pitho (**☎ 22650 82850; www.pithorooms.gr; Vasileon Pavlou & Friderikis 40a; s/d/tr/q incl breakfast €35/45/65/70;**) Gift shop below, small hotel above, Pitho's modern rooms, excellent service and location make it a top budget choice in Delphi.

JOHN ELK III

Sanctuary of Apollo (p139), Ancient Delphi

Hotel Hermes (**☎ 22650 82318; www.hermeshotel.gr; Vasileon Pavlou & Friderikis 27; s/d/ste incl breakfast €45/50/80;**) The welcoming and family-run Hermes is in the heart of Delphi. Most of the large wood-shuttered rooms have balconies facing the gulf. Service is excellent, and the views from the breakfast lounge are splendid.

Hotel Acropole (**☎ 22650 82675; www.delphi.com.gr; Filellinon 13; s/d/tr incl breakfast €64/79/98;**) On the quieter street below the main drag, Acropole's sharp rooms have soft beds, reading lamps, and wood and marble fittings. Top-floor rooms have great views to the gulf.

Hotel Appolonia (☎ 22650 82919; www .apollonia.gr; Syngrou; s/d/tr/ste incl breakfast €80/120/160/220; P ⚒ 🖥 ☎) The swank Appolonia has an intimate feel to it, tucked away on Delphi's upper Syngrou street. Rooms are quite modern with elegant dark-wood furnishings, carpet, large basin-sink bathrooms and balcony views over all of Delphi.

EATING

ourpick Taverna Vakhos (☎ 22650 83186; Apollonos 31; mains €4.50-11) Take the steps above the National Bank to this excellent family taverna featuring traditional local fare. You could make a meal of appetisers alone, like stuffed zucchini flowers or goat cheese with lemon, followed by *kouneli stifadho* (rabbit stew) or lamb in lemon sauce (both €8.20). Choose from an all-Greek wine list to wash it down.

Taverna To Patriko Mas (☎ 22650 82150; Vasileon Pavlou & Friderikis; mains €6-12) Set in a 19th-century stone building, this swank taverna is decidedly upscale, and the food holds up its end of the bargain. You'll find generous mezedhes and salads, great grills, including a vegie souvlaki, and a fine all-Greek wine list.

GETTING THERE & AWAY

Buses depart from the **bus station** (☎ 22650 82317; Vasileon Pavlou & Friderikis) at the Itea end of town.

MT PARNASSOS
ΠΑΡΝΑΣΣΟΣ ΟΡΟΣ

Established in 1938, **Parnassos National Park** (www.routes.gr), to the north of Delphi and Arahova, has three peaks over 2300m: Liakoura (2456m), the highest, Gerondovrachos (2396m) and Tsarkos (2416m). Kouvelos (1882m) is a popular rock-climbing face. Mt Parnassos is also part of the very elaborate Trans-European E4 international footpath *(orivatiko monopati)* from Gibraltar to Sweden, also known as the European Ramblers Path. See the **European Ramblers Association** (www.era-ewv-ferp.org) website for more information.

Between 800m and 1800m, the slopes of Parnassos support Kefallonian fir, spruce and juniper, interspersed with yellow-flowered shrubs, plum trees and the rare purple-flowered *Daphne jasminea*. Above the tree line are meadows of fescue grass. Spring flowers including crocuses, squills, tulips, orchids and irises sprout from the limestone rocks. Greece's most common mammals – foxes, hares, squirrels and jackals – may be seen, as well as vultures, passerines and hawks.

ACTIVITIES
HIKING
The most popular ascent on Parnassos is to **Liakoura Peak**. The route begins at the Parnassos refuge (1990m), 20km north of Arahova and 25km south of Amfiklia. For information, contact well-regarded local guide **Stathis Samartzis** (☎ 22670 31525, 6932566206), or the **Greek Alpine Club** (☎ 21032 12429).

SKIING
The **Parnassos Ski Centre** (☎ 22340 22694; www.parnassos-ski.gr/en; ☼ Nov-May) handles ski and snowboard operations for the most popular slope on the mountain, **Kelaria** (1950m). At last count, there were 13 lifts covering more than 20 ski runs and alpine trails. There are complete holiday facilities with accommodation, restaurants, hip cafes, babysitting services, a safety network and medical centre, along with ski and snowboarding schools. Adjacent to Kelaria are the steeper slopes of **Fterolakkas** (six lifts), popular with extreme skiers.

HEMIS/ALAMY

Timber jetty, Klisova Lagoon

⇘ IF YOU LIKE...

If you like the fresh air and adrenaline rushes offered at Mt Parnassos (p142), strap on your skis, boots or binoculars and check out central Greece's other activities:

- **Klisova Lagoon** The largest natural wetland in Greece is a favourite winter stopover for thousands of migrating birds, and an important breeding ground for the endangered Dalmatian pelican. The nearby town of Messolongi makes a decent base.

- **Delphi** (p138) Two popular **day hikes**, both part of the Trans-European E4 trail, start and end at Delphi. The first connects two ancient sites, the Temple of Apollo and Korikio Antro, a sacred mountain cave-shrine for Pan and Dionysos. En route, there are awesome views of Delphi and the Amfissa plain. A second hike meanders through the shady olives groves to Ancient Kirra on the Gulf of Corinth.

- **Iti National Park** One of Greece's most beautiful, but least-developed national parks is home to forests, meadows and snow-melt pools fringed by marsh orchids, and woodpeckers, eagles, deer and boar. Trails are not uniformly well-marked. For information, contact with the Hellenic Federation of Mountaineering (☎ 210 364 5904; info@eooa.gr; Athens).

- **Tria Potamia** In central Greece's northwest mountains, this beautiful area attracts outdoor enthusiasts who come to kayak on the Aheloös River; hike on trails criss-crossing the region; or ski at the small but popular Pertouli Skiing Centre (☎ 24340 91385; www.snowreport.gr/pertouli). Contact Hellas (☎ 24310 87964, 69774 51953; gptravel@otenet) for activity details.

- **Karpenisi** (☎ 22370 23506; www.snowreport.gr/karpenissi) This ski centre on Mt Tymfristos operates six lifts with 11 runs from November to March. Karpenisi is also a mecca for hikers, rafters, mountain bikers and rock climbers.

Rock peaks of Mt Parnassos (p142), Parnassos National Park

F.R./ALAMY

GETTING THERE & AWAY

There is public transport on winter weekends between Arahova and the ski centre on Parnassos, free with the price of a lift ticket. A taxi from Delphi runs about €40.

THESSALY ΘΕΣΣΑΛΙΑ

PELION PENINSULA
ΠΗΛΙΟΝ ΟΡΟΣ

The Pelion Peninsula lies to the east and south of Volos, a dramatic mountain range whose highest peak is Pourianos Stavros (1624m). The largely inaccessible eastern flank consists of high cliffs that plunge into the sea. The gentler western flank coils round the Pagasitikos Gulf. The interior is a green wonderland where trees heavy with fruit vie with wild olive groves and forests of horse chestnut, oak, walnut, eucalyptus and beech trees to reach the light of day. The villages tucked away in this profuse foliage are characterised by whitewashed, half-timbered houses with overhanging balconies, grey slate roofs and old winding footpaths.

Many lodgings in the Pelion are traditional *arhontika* (stone mansions), tastefully converted into pensions and reasonably priced. The peninsula has an enduring tradition of regional cooking, often flavoured with mountain herbs. Local specialities include *fasoladha* (bean soup), *kouneli stifadho*, *spetsofaï* (stewed pork sausages and peppers) and *tyropsomo* (cheese bread).

HIKING

The Pelion is a hiking mecca, and a centuries-old network of frequently restored *kalderimia* (cobbled mule pathways) connect most mountain and seaside villages. A detailed booklet in English, *Walks in the Pelion* by Lance Chilton, is available (with online updates) from Marengo Publishers (www.marengowalks.com/Pilionbk .html). The detailed Anavasi Map No 6.21, *Central Pelion* 1:25,000 is available in Volos bookshops and many *periptera* (kiosks). Both the Tsangarada tourist office (☎ 24260 48993; ⏱ 10am-2pm) and Mulberry Travel (☎ 24260 49086, 6937156780;

www.pelionet.gr) are up to date with conditions and routes. **Les Hirondelles Travel Agency** (☎ 24260 31181; www.holidays-in-pelion.com.gr) arranges accommodation, car and motorbike rentals, and also organises hiking, boat, sea-kayaking and mountain-biking excursions.

SLEEPING

Pension Katerina (☎ 24260 31159, 6945762183; Agios Ioannis; s/d/f from €35/40/65; ❄) A narrow lane off the waterfront opens to a cosy courtyard anchored by a lemon tree at this welcoming gem. Rooms are light, tidy and charming. Families will like the three apartments with kitchenettes.

Hotel Kelly (☎ 24260 31231; www.hotel-kelly.gr; Agios Ioannis; s/d/tr incl breakfast €50/60/80; ❄ P ☎) Near the end of the waterfront, this modern Tuscan-red hotel has comfortable beach-side rooms, friendly service and the village's busiest lobby bar.

Sisilianou Arhontiko (☎ 24280 99556; Makrinitsa; www.arhontiko-sisilianou.gr; d/tr incl breakfast from €80/100; P ▯ ☎) This elegant, 2007-rebuilt mansion is the pick of the village. Each room is unique and tastefully decorated with period furniture. Modern touches include satellite TV, soft beds and well-appointed bathrooms. Hint: room No 7 has mountain views from the bed.

Hotel Damouhari (☎ /fax 24260 49840; Damouhari; r from €85; P ▦) You'll need to book well in advance for one of these quaint and creaky rooms – however, still stop by to check out the nautical antiques in the lobby, or to have a drink in the Kleopatra Miramar bar.

GETTING THERE & AWAY
Buses to villages throughout the Pelion leave from the Volos bus station.

METEORA ΜΕΤΕΩΡΑ
Meteora (meh-*teh*-o-rah) is an extraordinary place, and one of the most visited in all of Greece. The massive pinnacles of smooth rock are ancient and yet could be the setting for a futuristic science fiction tale. The monasteries atop them add to this strange and beautiful landscape.

Each monastery is built around a central courtyard surrounded by monks' cells, chapels and a refectory. In the centre of each courtyard is the *katholikon* (main church).

Meteora is listed as a World Heritage Site. An excellent map (available at the newsstand in Kalambaka) is the *Panoramic Map with Geology Meteora*. A detailed booklet and map in English, *The Footpaths of Meteora* by Andonis Kalogirou (Kritiki Publishers), is available from the same shop.

SIGHTS
MONASTERIES
The monasteries are linked by asphalt roads, but it's possible to explore the area on foot on the old and once-secret *monopatia* (monk paths). The main road surrounding the entire Meteora complex of rocks and monasteries is about 10km; with your own transport, you can easily visit them all. Every day, a bus (€1.20, 20 minutes) departs from Kalambaka and Kastraki at 9am, and returns at 1pm. That's enough time to explore three monasteries – Moni Megalou Meteorou, Moni Varlaam and Moni Agias Varvaras Rousanou. Perhaps the best route is to take the bus one way to the top and then

work your way down and around on foot, finishing at either Moni Agiou Nikolaou on the Kastraki side, or at Moni Agia Triada on the Kalambaka side.

Entry to each monastery is €2, and dress codes apply: no bare shoulders are allowed, men must wear trousers and women must be covered to below the knee (baggy bottoms with elastic waistbands are generally provided).

Moni Agiou Nikolaou (Monastery of St Nikolaou Anapafsa; Map p148; ☎ 24320 22375; 🕙 9am-3.30pm Sat-Thu Apr-Oct) is the nearest *moni* to Kastraki – it's just 2km from the village square to the steep steps leading to the *moni*. The monastery was built in the 15th century, and the exceptional frescoes in its *katholikon* were painted by the monk Theophanes Strelizas from Crete. Especially beautiful is the 1527 fresco *The Naming of Animals by Adam in Paradise*.

THE METEORA: HISTORY OF A ROCK FOREST

The jutting pinnacles and cliffs of the Meteora were once sediments of an inland sea. About 10 million years ago, vertical tectonic movements pushed the entire region out of the sea at a sloping angle. The same tectonic movements caused the flanking mountains to move closer, exerting extreme pressure on the hardened sedimentary deposits – the Meteora developed netlike fissures and cracks. The weathering and erosion that followed formed the towering outcrops of rock that now vault heavenwards. Where erosion was less extreme, caves and overhangs appeared in the rock face. As early as the 11th century AD, these awesome natural caves had become the solitary abodes of hermit monks.

By the 14th century, the Byzantine power of the Roman Empire was on the wane and Turkish incursions into Greece were on the rise, so monks began to seek safe havens away from the bloodshed. The inaccessibility of the rocks of Meteora made them an ideal retreat.

The earliest monasteries were reached by climbing removable ladders. Later, windlasses were used so monks could be hauled up in nets. These days, access to the monasteries is by steps that were hewn into the rocks in the 1920s, and by a convenient back road. Some windlasses can still be seen (you can have a good look at one at Agia Triada), but they are now used for hauling up provisions – and an occasional Greek Orthodox tourist-priest from abroad.

About 700m down from Moni Megalou, **Moni Varlaam** (Map p148; ☎ 24320 22277; ⏰ 9am-4pm Wed-Mon Apr-Oct, Thu-Mon Nov-Mar) has a small museum, an original rope-basket (until the 1930s, the method for hauling up provisions and monks), and fine late-Byzantine frescoes by Frangos Kastellanos. The mural *The Blessed Sisois at the Tomb of Alexander the Great* shows the great conqueror as a humble skeleton. Look just above the door, past the candles.

For a panoramic break, visit the rambling **Psaropetra** (Map p148) lookout, 300m east of the signposted fork northeast of Moni Varlaam.

Access to **Moni Agias Varvaras Rousanou** (Map p148; ☎ 24320 22649; ⏰ 9am-6pm Thu-Tue Apr-Oct, 9am-4pm Nov-Mar) is via a small wooden bridge. The beautiful coloured-glass-illuminated *katholikon* is the highlight here, with superb frescoes of the *Resurrection* (on your left entering) and *Transfiguration* (on your right).

Of all the monasteries, **Moni Agias Triados** (Map p148; Holy Trinity Monastery; ☎ 24320 22220; ⏰ 9am-5pm Fri-Wed Apr-Oct, 10am-3pm Nov-Mar) has the most remote feel about it, plus the longest approach. It was featured in the 1981 James Bond film *For Your Eyes Only*. The views here are extraordinary, and the small 17th-century *katholikon* is beautiful, in particular the *Judgement of Pilate* and the *Hospitality of Abraham*. A well-marked 1km *monopati* leads back to Kalambaka.

After the austere Moni Agias Triados, **Moni Agiou Stefanou** (Map p148; ☎ 24320 22279; ⏰ 9am-1.30pm & 3.30-5.30pm Tue-Sun Apr-Oct, 9.30am-1pm & 3-5pm Nov-Mar) resembles a return to civilisation, with efficient nuns selling religious souvenirs and DVDs of Meteora. The monastery is at the very end of the road, 1.5km beyond Agias Triados.

JOHN ELK III
Cliffside monastery, Moni Megalou Meteorou

⇘ MONI MEGALOU METEOROU

The best known of the monasteries, **Moni Megalou Meteorou** (Grand Meteora Monastery, Metamorphosis) is an imposing form built on the highest rock in the valley, 613m above sea level. Founded by St Athanasios in the 14th century, it became the richest and most powerful monastery thanks to the Serbian emperor Symeon Uros, who turned all his wealth over to the monastery and became a monk. Its *katholikon* has a magnificent 12-sided central dome. Its striking series of frescoes entitled *Martyrdom of Saints* depicts the graphic persecution of Christians by the Romans.

Things You Need to Know Map p148; ☎ 24320 22278; ⏰ 9am-5pm Wed-Mon Apr-Oct, 9am-4pm Thu-Mon Nov-Mar

ACTIVITIES
ROCK CLIMBING
Meteora has been a mecca for European rock climbers for several years. Climbers of various skill levels can choose routes from more than 100 peaks and towers with names such as the Tower of the Holy Ghost, the Great Saint, the Devil's Tower, the Corner of Madness and the

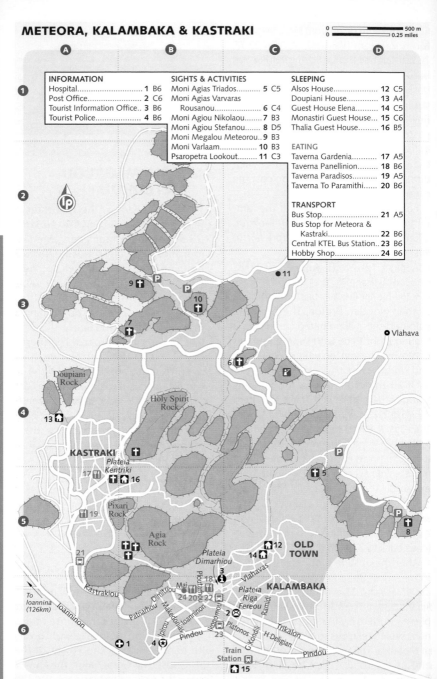

METEORA, KALAMBAKA & KASTRAKI

0 — 500 m
0 — 0.25 miles

INFORMATION
Hospital	**1**	B6
Post Office	**2**	C6
Tourist Information Office	**3**	B6
Tourist Police	**4**	B6

SIGHTS & ACTIVITIES
Moni Agias Triados	**5**	C5
Moni Agias Varvaras Rousanou	**6**	C4
Moni Agiou Nikolaou	**7**	B3
Moni Agiou Stefanou	**8**	D5
Moni Megalou Meteorou	**9**	B3
Moni Varlaam	**10**	B3
Psaropetra Lookout	**11**	C3

SLEEPING
Alsos House	**12**	C5
Doupiani House	**13**	A4
Guest House Elena	**14**	C5
Monastiri Guest House	**15**	C6
Thalia Guest House	**16**	B5

EATING
Taverna Gardenia	**17**	A5
Taverna Panellinion	**18**	B6
Taverna Paradisos	**19**	A5
Taverna To Paramithi	**20**	B6

TRANSPORT
Bus Stop	**21**	A5
Bus Stop for Meteora & Kastraki	**22**	B6
Central KTEL Bus Station	**23**	B6
Hobby Shop	**24**	B6

Vlahava

Doupiani Rock

Holy Spirit Rock

KASTRAKI

Plateia Kentriki

Pixari Rock

Agia Rock

Plateia Dimarhiou

OLD TOWN

Plateia Riga Fereou

KALAMBAKA

To Ioannina (126km)

Kastrakiou

Ioanninon

Patriarhou

Dimitriou

Makedonias

Pindou

Ioanninon

Kondili

Platonos

Trikalon

H Deligian

Pindou

Train Station

Vlahavas

Ramidi

Iron Edge. A typical climb averages three hours, and costs start from €40 per person, depending on the routes and the degree of difficulty. (All equipment is included in prices, including harness, shoes and helmet.) Contact either licensed mountain guide **Lazaros Botelis** (☎ 24320 79165, 6948043655; meteora@nolimits.com.gr; Kastraki) or mountaineering instructor **Kostas Liolos** (☎ 6972567582; kliolios@kalampaka.com; Kalambaka). For detailed information and graded routes, check out www.kalampaka.com.

KALAMBAKA ΚΑΛΑΜΠΑΚΑ
pop 8140

Kalambaka, the gateway to Meteora, is almost entirely modern, having been burned to the ground by the Nazis in WWII. It takes at least a day to see all of the monasteries of Meteora, so you'll need to spend the night either in Kalambaka or the village of Kastraki (p150).

INFORMATION
Six banks with ATMs surround the central Plateia Riga Fereou on Trikalon. There is also a currency-exchange window next to the post office.

Hospital (Map p148; ☎ 24320 22222; Pindou)
Post office (Map p148; Trikalon 24; ⌚ 7.30am-2pm Mon-Fri)
Tourist Information Office (Map p148; ☎ 24320 77734; Plateia Dimarhiou; ⌚ 8am-9pm Mon-Fri, 10am-4pm Sat & Sun) Maps and town advice, opposite the fountain.
Tourist police (Map p148; ☎ 24320 76100; cnr Ipirou & Pindou)

SLEEPING
ourpick Alsos House (Map p148; ☎ 24320 24097; www.alsoshouse.gr; Kanari 5; s/d/f incl breakfast €30/40/70; P ⊠ ⌨ ⌐) The well-managed and very comfortable Alsos House has a well-stocked communal kitchen, laundry, wide views of the rocks, and owner Yiannis Karakantas is a wealth of information about the area.

Guest House Elena (Map p148; ☎ 24320 77789; www.elenaguesthouse.gr; Kanari 3; s/d/tr incl breakfast from €35/50/75; P ⊠ ⌨ ⌐) Tastefully adorned with period furnishings, this inviting five-room bed and breakfast is immaculate. Three rooms include a Jacuzzi bath. English, Italian and French are spoken.

Monastiri Guest House (Map p148; ☎ 24320 23952; www.monastiri-guesthouse .gr; s/d/tr/ste incl breakfast €50/60/70/100; P ⊠ ⌨ ⌨ ⌐) Opposite the railway station, this converted stone mansion is a delightful addition to Kalambaka, with colourful decorations, long poster-beds and light and airy bathrooms. The handsome wood-and-stone lobby sports a fireplace and bar.

EATING
ourpick Taverna To Paramithi (Map p148; ☎ 24320 24441; Patriarhou Dimitriou 14; mains €4-9) Along with very good grills and fresh pasta, owner-cooks Makis and Eleni bring in fresh seafood daily from the coast.

Taverna Panellinion (Map p148; ☎ 24320 24735; Plateia Dimarhiou; mains €5-9) Panellinion serves first-rate mezedhes such as roasted feta, and fine versions of traditional dishes such as *pastitsio* (macaroni and meat bake) and chicken in lemon sauce. Dishes always feature fresh local ingredients, resulting in a recent culinary award for this popular eatery opposite the fountain.

GETTING THERE & AWAY
Kalambaka's **Central KTEL bus station** (Map p148; ☎ 24320 22432; Ikonomou) is 50m down from the main square and fountain, and is the arrival/departure point for Trikala bus connections.

Trains depart from the Kalambaka **train station** (☎ 24320 22451). Trains to Thessaloniki and Volos change at Paliofarsalos.

GETTING AROUND

Buses for Kastraki (€1.20) leave about every 45 minutes from the Plateia Dimarhiou fountain, and on weekends, two of these (8.20am and 1.20pm Saturday and Sunday) continue on to Moni Megalou Meteorou. But note that on weekdays the Meteora-bound buses depart from the KTEL station (9am and 1pm Monday to Friday).

Taxis (opposite the fountain) go to Kastraki (€3) and all the monasteries (for example, Moni Megalou Meteorou for €8). Some drivers speak English, German or French, and you can arrange a taxi tour from about €20 per hour.

Bikes (€8) and motorcycles (€18) can be hired for the day from the **Hobby Shop** (Map p148; ☎ /fax 24320 25262; Patriarhou Dimitriou 28) near the newsstand.

KASTRAKI ΚΑΣΤΡΑΚΙ

pop 1200

The village of Kastraki is less than 2km from Kalambaka, but its impressive location right under the rocks gives it an otherworldly feel. If you want a base for exploring the Meteora monasteries, or for climbing the rocks themselves, Kastraki is a good choice.

SLEEPING

Thalia Guest House (Map p148; ☎ 24320 23051; www.thaliarooms.gr; Kastraki; s/d €35/40; P ⊠ 🐕) With just three rooms, the new and self-catering Thalia does deliver a lot. Each room is sharp and comfortable, with balconies staring at the rocks. A modern shared kitchen is stocked by the genial French- and English-speaking hosts.

ourpick **Doupiani House** (Map p148; ☎ 24320 75326; www.doupianihouse.com; s/d/tr incl breakfast €40/50/60; P ⊠ 🖥 🛜) Incomparably set just outside the village, 500m from the town square. The spotless and balconied rooms are taste-

In the foothills of Meteora, Kastraki

fully furnished, and breakfast is served on a garden terrace overlooking the village and rocks. Hosts Thanasis and Toula are attentive and full of tips for exploring the village and monasteries.

EATING

ourpick **Taverna Paradisos** (Map p148; ☎ 24320 22723; mains €4-7.50) Look for outstanding traditional meals at the roomy Paradisos, along with spectacular views of the Meteora from the large terrace. Grilled lamb and *mousakas* are superb, along with tasty mezedhes and a choice of good Greek wines. A recent Greek cuisine award, noting the restaurant's fresh and traditional ingredients, is a source of pride to owner-cook Koula.

Taverna Gardenia (Map p148; ☎ 24320 22504; mains €4-8) Gardenia gets good marks locally for tasty taverna standards, such as lamb grills and stuffed tomatoes and peppers. Look for the patio shaded by two plane trees, just 20m south of the big church on the square.

IONIAN ISLANDS
ΤΑ ΙΟΝΙΑ ΝΗΣΙΑ
CORFU ΚΕΡΚΥΡΑ
pop 122,670

Corfu – or Kerkyra (*ker*-kih-rah) in Greek – is the greenest and second-largest Ionian island. This was Homer's 'beautiful and rich land', Shakespeare reputedly used it as a background for *The Tempest* and in the 20th century, the writers Lawrence and Gerald Durrell – among others – extolled its virtues.

Corfu is mountainous in its northern half where the east and west coastlines can be steep and dramatic and where the island's interior is a rolling expanse of peaceful countryside, where stately cypresses rise from a pelt of shimmer-

WWW.PLANNING YOUR TRIP.COM

There are countless websites devoted to the Ionians – here are some of the better ones:
- Corfu www.allcorfu.com, www.kerkyra.net
- Kefallonia www.kefalonia.gr, www.kefalonia.net.gr
- Paxi www.paxos-greece.com, www.paxos.tk

ing olive trees. South of Corfu Town, the island narrows appreciably and becomes very flat. Beaches and resorts punctuate the entire coastline, intensively so north of Corfu Town and along the north coast, but less so in the west and south.

GETTING THERE & AWAY
AIR
Corfu has several flights to/from Athens each day. There are at least three flights a week to/from Thessaloniki, Preveza and Kefallonia. **Olympic Air** (☎ 26610 22962; www.olympicairlines.com) is based at the airport. From May to September, many charter flights come from northern Europe and the UK to Corfu.

BOAT
Shipping agencies selling tickets are found in Corfu Town near the new port, along Xenofondos Stratigou and Ethnikis Antistasis.

BUS
KTEL (☎ 26610 28898) runs buses three times daily (and on Monday, Wednesday and Friday via Lefkimmi in the island's south) between Corfu Town and Athens (€39.50, 8½ hours). There's also a daily service to/from Thessaloniki (€37.70,

eight hours); for both destinations budget another €7.50 for the ferry between Corfu and the mainland. Long-distance tickets should be purchased in advance from Corfu Town's **long-distance bus station** (☎ 26610 28927/30627; I Theotoki), between Plateia San Rocco and the new port.

GETTING AROUND

A taxi between the airport and Corfu Town costs around €12.

Long-distance KTEL buses (known as green buses) travel from Corfu Town's **long-distance bus station** (☎ 26610 28927/30627; I Theotoki). Printed timetables are available at the ticket kiosk. Sunday and holiday services are reduced considerably, or don't run at all.

CORFU TOWN

pop 28,200

Corfu Town takes hold of you and never lets go. Pastel-hued Venetian-era mansions grace the old town, the Campiello. The seafront is a majestic esplanade, known as the Spianada; it's lined with handsome buildings and an arcaded promenade, the Liston, built by the French as a nostalgic nod to Paris's Rue de Rivoli. Inland from all of this historic glory, marble-paved streets lined with shops lead to the bustling modern town. Corfu Town is known also as Kerkyra.

INFORMATION

EMERGENCY

Tourist police (☎ 26610 30265; 3rd fl, Samartzi 4) Off Plateia San Rocco. There is a manned kiosk outside the entrance.

MEDICAL SERVICES

Corfu General Hospital (☎ 26610 88200; Ioulias Andreadi)

MONEY

There are banks and ATMs around Plateia San Rocco, on Georgiou Theotoki and by Paleo and Neo Limanis.

Alpha Bank (Kapodistriou) Behind the Liston.

National Bank of Greece (Voulgareos)

POST

Post office (☎ 26610 25544; 26 Leoforos Alexandras)

TOURIST INFORMATION

There is no national tourist office in Corfu Town. During high season, a municipal **tourist kiosk** (Plateia San Rocco; ☉ 9am-4pm) may operate in Plateia San Rocco, though not on Sundays from April to October. A similar kiosk may operate at the ferry arrival port in high season. English-speaking staff at **All Ways Travel** (☎ 26610 33955; www.corfuallwaystravel.com; Plateia Rocco) are very helpful. The *Corfiot* (€2), an English-language monthly newspaper with listings, is available from kiosks and from shops that sell newspapers.

SIGHTS & ACTIVITIES

The **Archaeological Museum** (☎ 26610 30680; P Vraïla 5; adult/concession €4/2, Sun free; ☉ 8.30am-3pm Tue-Sun) gives top billing to the massive Gorgon Medusa pediment, one of the best-preserved pieces of Archaic sculpture found in Greece.

Behind the eastern side of the palace is the **Municipal Art Gallery** (admission €2; ☉ 9am-5pm Tue-Sun). This fine collection features the work of leading Corfiot painters, a highlight being *The Assassination of Capodistrias* by Charalambos Pachis.

Inside the 15th-century Church of Our Lady of Antivouniotissa is the **Antivouniotissa Museum** (Byzantine Museum; ☎ 26610 38313; admission €2; ☉ 8am-7pm Tue-Sun Apr-Oct, 8.30am-2.30pm

CORFU OLD TOWN

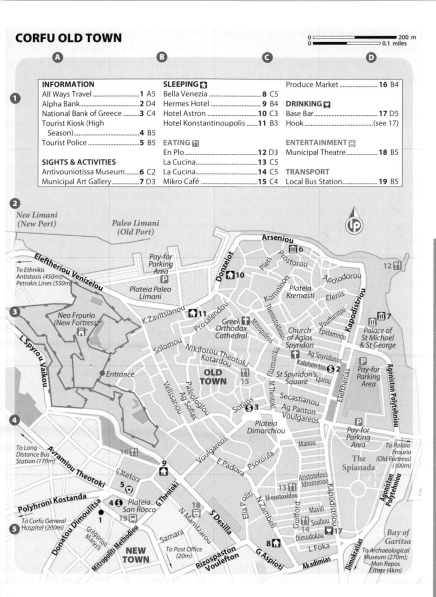

INFORMATION	
All Ways Travel	**1** A5
Alpha Bank	**2** D4
National Bank of Greece	**3** C4
Tourist Kiosk (High Season)	**4** B5
Tourist Police	**5** B5
SIGHTS & ACTIVITIES	
Antivouniotissa Museum	**6** C2
Municipal Art Gallery	**7** D3
SLEEPING	
Bella Venezia	**8** C5
Hermes Hotel	**9** B4
Hotel Astron	**10** C3
Hotel Konstantinoupolis	**11** B3
EATING	
En Plo	**12** D3
La Cucina	**13** C5
La Cucina	**14** C5
Mikro Café	**15** C4
Produce Market	**16** B4
DRINKING	
Base Bar	**17** D5
Hook	(see 17)
ENTERTAINMENT	
Municipal Theatre	**18** B5
TRANSPORT	
Local Bus Station	**19** B5

Tue-Sun Nov-Mar). This exquisite aisle-less and timber-roofed basilica, located off Arseniou, has an outstanding collection of Byzantine and post-Byzantine icons and artefacts dating from the 13th to the 17th centuries.

The **Palaio Frourio** (Old Fortress; ☎ 26610 48310; adult/concession €4/2; ⏱ 8.30am-3pm Nov-Mar, 8.30am-7pm May-Oct) was constructed by the Venetians on the remains of a 12th-century Byzantine castle. The summit of the inner outcrop is crowned by a lighthouse and can be reached by a steep climb for superb views.

On the southern outskirts of Corfu, on the Kanoni Peninsula, is the Mon Repos Estate (☺ 8am-7pm May-Oct, 8am-5pm Nov-Apr), an extensive wooded park surrounding an elegant neoclassical villa. The estate and villa were created in the 1830s by the second British commissioner of the Ionians, Sir Frederick Adam, as a tribute to his Corfiot wife. Today, the villa houses the excellent Museum of Palaeopolis (☎ 26610 41369; adult/concession €3/2; ☺ 8am-7.30pm Tue-Sun May-Oct), with entertaining displays of archaeological finds and the history of Corfu Town. Rooms on the first floor are furnished in the early-19th-century Regency style of the British era. Tracks and paths lead through the wooded grounds to the ruins of two Doric temples; the first is vestigial, but the southerly one is still quite impressive.

TOURS

Petrakis Lines (☎ 26610 31649; Ethnikis Antistasis 4) and Sarris Cruises (☎ 26610 25317; Eleftheriou Venizelou 13) both organise day trips from Corfu Town, including an excursion to ancient ruins (Butrinti) in Albania for €59; and a boat trip taking in Paxi (and the Blue Caves) and Antipaxi for €40.

SLEEPING

Hermes Hotel (☎ 26610 39268; www.hermes-hotel.gr; Markora 12; s/d/tr €50/60/75; ☒) Located in a busy part of the new town, just up from Plateia San Rocco and near the market, the Hermes has had a complete makeover in recent years and has pleasant, well-appointed rooms with double glazing. Breakfast is €7.

Hotel Astron (☎ 26610 39505; hotel_astron@hol.gr; Donzelot 15; s €75-105, d €80-110, tr €95-125; ☒ ☎) Overlooking Plateia Palaio Limani (Old Port Sq), and patiently waiting for the Old Port marina to be completed, the Astron is steadily updating its airy, good-sized rooms and installing a gym and a spa. It may rename itself the City Marina. Breakfast is €10.

Hotel Konstantinoupolis (☎ 26610 48716; www.konstantinoupolis.com.gr; K Zavitsianou 11; s/d/tr incl breakfast €88/98/118; ☒ ☎) Bright decor enhances the refurbished rooms at this atmospheric old Corfiot hotel overlooking Plateia Palaio Limani.

Bella Venezia (☎ 26610 46500; www.bellaveneziahotel.com; N Zambeli 4; d €170; ☒ ☒ ☎) Housed in what was once a girls' school, the Venezia has comfy rooms and a stylish ambience. The gazebo breakfast room in the garden is delightful.

EATING

Mikro Café (☎ 26610 31009; cnr N Theotoki 42 & Kotardhou; snacks €3.50-6) A little cafe-bar at the heart of the old town, Mikro has a leafy raised terrace and seating that clambers up a narrow lane. There's live entertainment at times and you may catch anything from acoustic riffs to very accomplished slackliners walking the wobbly walk on a shaky line slung between buildings.

En Plo (☎ 26610 81813; Faliraki; mains €5.50-12) A stylish place in a blissful waterside location looking across to Palaio Frourio, En Plo is reached down a slip road at the northern end of Kapodistriou, beyond the Palace of St Michael and St George. They do a fine seafood risotto, and mezedhes plates of meat or fish as well as pizzas and daytime snacks.

our pick La Cucina Guilford (☎ 26610 45029; Guilford 17; mains €5.50-22); Moustoxidou (☎ 26610 45799; cnr Guilford & Moustoxidou) A long-established restaurant, La Cucina shines for its well-run ethos and its creative cuisine. Hand-rolled pasta dishes are

CORFU ACTIVITIES

Corfu brims with great outdoor action. Dinghy sailing and windsurfing buffs should find **Greek Sailing Holidays** (☎ 26630 81877; www.corfu-sailing-events.com) at Avlaki, while for chartering try **Corfu Sea School** (www.corfuseaschool.com) or **Sailing Holidays Ltd** (www.sailingholidays.com), both at Gouvia marina.

For **diving** in crystal-clear waters, you'll find operators at Kassiopi, Agios Gordios, Agios Georgios, Ipsos, Gouvia and Paleokastritsa.

Corfu has some excellent walking. The **Corfu Trail** (www.corfutrail.org), developed by the devoted islander Hilary Whitton Paipeti, traverses the island north to south and takes between eight and 12 days to complete. For help with accommodation along the trail, contact **Aperghi Travel** (☎ 26610 48713; www .travelling.gr/aperghi).

For mountain-biking, especially off-road, the **Corfu Mountainbike Shop** (☎ 26610 93344; www.mountainbikecorfu.gr) is based in Dasia and rents out bikes for independent exploration, as well as organising day trips and cycling holidays. Horse riding through olive groves and on quiet trails is another excellent outdoor option with **Trailriders** (☎ 26630 23090), based in the village of Ano Korakiana.

---

at the fore – the cajun shrimp with cherry tomatoes, spring onions and mascarpone sauce is delicious. There's a range of creative mezedhes, fresh salads and pizzas, with excellent wines to go with it all.

North of Plateia San Rocco is the bustling **produce market** (☺ Mon-Sat), open morning to early afternoon and selling fresh fruit, vegetables and fish. The traditional food shop **Pogoniou** (☎ 26610 31320; G Markora 17) is crammed with cheeses, cold meats, spices, olive oil and much more.

DRINKING

The bars along the Liston are top places for preening. Clustered near the Cavalieri there are small, intimate music bars such as Hook and Base Bar.

ENTERTAINMENT

For bigger dance venues, after 11pm, head to Corfu's disco strip, 2km northwest of the new port, along Ethnikis Antistasis; take a taxi – it's a very busy unlit road without walkways.

The **Municipal Theatre** (☎ 26610 33598; Mantzarou) is Corfu's cultural power house, staging various classical music, opera, dance and drama performances, some of which are also staged at the theatre next to the Mon Repos Estate (p154).

AROUND CORFU TOWN

The coast road continues south from Corfu Town with a turn-off to the well-signposted **Ahillion Palace** (☎ 26610 56245; adult/concession €7/5; ☺ 8.30am-3pm Nov-Mar, 8am-7pm Apr-Oct) near the village of Gastouri. The Ahillion was built in the 1890s by the Empress Elizabeth of Austria, known as Sisi, as a retreat from the world and in tribute to her hero, Achilles. Kaiser Wilhelm II bought the palace in 1908, extending the themes of both imperialism and self-aggrandisement by adding a ferocious statue of Achilles Triumphant to the gardens, before leaving Corfu for something less than triumph in 1914. The palace is a major coach tour destination. Get there early for a fascinating journey through heavily accented neoclassicism, fabulous furnishings and bold statuary, walking a very thin line between style and kitsch.

WEST COAST

Some of Corfu's prettiest countryside, villages and beaches are situated on the west coast. The scenic and very popular resort of **Paleokastritsa**, 26km from Corfu Town, rambles for nearly 3km down a valley to a series of small, picturesque coves hidden between tall cliffs. Craggy mountains swathed in cypresses and olive trees tower above. You can venture to nearby grottoes or one of the dozen or so local beaches by small excursion boat (per person €8.20, 30 minutes), or water taxis can drop you off at a beach of your choice. There's a range of waterboat activities available. Cool sun-seekers can hang out at cafe-bar **La Grotta** (☎ 26630 41006; Paleokastritsa), which is set

GREG BALFOUR EVANS/ALAMY

Wooded slopes of Benitses, Corfu

↘ IF YOU LIKE...

If you like exploring the picturesque villages on Corfu's **West Coast** (p156), we think you'd like to while away a little time in Corfu's other enchanting villages:

- **Benitses** In Corfu's south, this resort has a pleasant old village, from where tracks and paths lead into the steep, wooded slopes above. Fill up at the well-known taverna **O Paxinos** (☎ 26610 72339; Benitses) on mezedhes and fish dishes (by the kilo).

- **Boukari** Also in the south, a winding coastal road leads to this tranquil village with its little harbour and waterside tavernas, including the good *psarotaverna* (fish restaurant) **Spiros Karidis** (☎ 26620 51205; Boukari).

- **Kalami** This bay-side village is famous for the picturesque **White House**, perched above the water. For a time it was home to the Durrell family who lived on the island for many years prior to WWII. Lawrence Durrell became an outstanding writer, penning *Prospero's Cell*, while his brother Gerald wrote the equally splendid, *My Family and Other Animals*. Both books are based on their life on Corfu.

in a stunning rocky cove with a cafe, sunbeds and diving board. It's reached down steps opposite the driveway up to Hotel Paleokastritsa.

The **Triklino Vineyard** (☎ 26610 58184, 69458 90285; www.triklinovineyard.gr; adult/under 6yr €7/free; ☺ noon-5pm Tue-Sun), 6km from Corfu Town on the Pelekas road near Karoubatika, blends culture with viniculture at its delightful complex where some enticing wines are produced from local vines such as Kakotrygis. There's a tour of an olive-oil mill and winery, and wine tasting and Corfiot mezedhes. They also run a series of cultural activities and performances.

SLEEPING

Rolling Stone (☎ 26610 94942; www.pelekasbeach.com; Pelekas Beach; r €30-40, apt €98) The clean and colourful apartments and double rooms surround a big sun terrace with funky trappings at this laid-back place. There's even a resident 'wellness' practitioner (relaxation treatments €10 to €30).

Hotel Zefiros (☎ 26630 41244/41088; www.hotel-zefiros.gr; Paleokastritsa; d incl breakfast €60-80, tr incl breakfast €75-105, q incl breakfast €90-130; ✗ ⚇) On the roadside near the seafront, but a delight, with immaculate, stylish rooms, some with a massive terrace. The downstairs cafe is a bright oasis.

EATING

Limani (☎ 26630 42080; Paleokastritsa Harbour; mains €4.50-11) Located down by Paleo's harbour, the well-run Limani, with its rose-bedecked terrace, does local dishes with a sure hand. Fish is by the kilo but a generous fish plate for two costs about €38.

Nereids (☎ 26630 41013; Paleokastritsa; mains €6.50-11) Halfway down the winding road to Paleokastritsa beach is this smart place, below road level and with a huge leafy courtyard. Specialities such as pork in a mustard sauce with oregano, lemon, peppers, garlic and cheese are hard to beat.

PAXI ΠΑΞΟΙ

pop 2440

Paxi packs a great deal into a bite-size island. At only 10km by 4km it's the smallest of the Ionian's main holiday islands and has hung on to a reputation for serenity and overall loveliness – a fine escape clause to Corfu's more metropolitan, quicker-paced pleasures. The dispersed inland villages sit within centuries-old olive groves, accented by winding stone walls, ancient windmills and olive presses. The old mule trails are a walker's delight. An obligatory purchase is the *Bleasdale Walking Map of Paxos* (€10 to €15), available from the island's travel agencies.

GETTING THERE & AWAY

BOAT

Ferries dock at Gaïos' new port, 1km east of the central square. Excursion boats dock along the waterfront. For information contact **Arvanitakis Travel** (☎ 26620 32007; Gaïos), or Petrakis Lines (p154) in Corfu. There's also a **ferry information office** (☎ 26650 26280) in Igoumenitsa.

Sea taxis can be a fast and effective way to travel, especially if there are other people on board. The going rate between Corfu and Paxi is around €180 per boat, shared among the passengers. Try **Nikos** (☎ 26620 32444, 69322 32072; Gaïos), or www.paxosseataxi.com.

BUS

There's a twice-weekly direct bus service between Athens and Paxi (€47, plus €7.50 for ferry ticket between Paxi and Igoumenitsa, seven hours). On Paxi, tickets are available from **Bouas Tours** (☎ 26620 32401; Gaïos).

Ahillion Palace (p155)

JOHN ELK III

GETTING AROUND

The island's bus links Gaïos and Lakka via Loggos up to four times daily in either direction (€2). Taxis between Gaïos and Lakka or Loggos cost around €12.

GAÏOS ΓΑΪΟΣ

pop 560

Gaïos hardly needs to try for the 'picturesque' label. It's the island's main town and its pink, cream and whitewashed buildings line the water's edge of a sizeable bay to either side of the main Venetian square. The town is protected from too much open water by the wooded islet of Agios Nikolaos, named after its eponymous monastery. The waterfront is lined with cafes and tavernas and can get crowded mid afternoon when excursion boats arrive.

The main street (Panagioti Kanga) runs inland from the main square towards the back of town, where you'll find the bus stop, taxi rank and car park. Banks and ATMs are near the square. There isn't a tourist office, but the helpful and efficient staff at **Paxos Magic Holidays** (☎ 26620 32269; www.paxosmagic.com) will happily direct you. They organise island excursions, including boating trips and walks. They can also arrange villa accommodation in advance.

SLEEPING

Thekli Studios (Clara Studios; ☎ 26620 32313; d €75; P ⊠ ⊠) Thekli, a local fisher-diver and energetic personality about town, runs these immaculate and well-equipped studios. She will meet you at the port if you call ahead.

Paxos Beach Hotel (☎ 26620 32211; www .paxos beachhotel.gr; s/d/tr/q incl breakfast from €88/117/146/165, ste €168-380; ⊠) In a prime location 1.5km south of Gaïos, these bungalow-style rooms step down to the sea and have a range of rooms from standard to superior. There's a private jetty, tennis court, beach, bar and restaurant.

EATING

Taka Taka (☎ 26620 32329; mains €6-22) For upmarket seafood (€40 to €75 per kilogram) in attractive surroundings, this popular place is behind the main square. Go left from the left-hand inner corner of the square, then turn right after 30m.

Taverna Vasilis (☎ 26620 32596; mains €6.50-14) The owner of this eatery is a former butcher, and knows the best meat for tasty spit-roasts and other meaty servings. It's just back from the middle of the waterfront.

Two excellent bakeries, one on the waterfront, the other near the main square, serve Paxiot delights. Gloria's, at the north end of the waterfront, tempts with some deeply sinful ice cream flavours.

ANTIPAXI ΑΝΤΙΠΑΞΟΙ

pop 25

The stunning and diminutive island of Antipaxi, 2km south of Paxi, is covered with grape vines, olives and with the occasional small hamlet here and there. Caïques and tourist boats run daily from Gaïos and pull in at two beach coves, the small, sandy **Vrika Beach** and the pretty, pebbly **Voutoumi Beach**. Floating in the water here – with its dazzling clarity – is a sensational experience.

An inland path links the two beaches (a 30-minute walk), or if you are more of an energetic person you can walk up to the village of **Vigla**, or as far as the lighthouse at the southernmost tip. Take plenty of water and allow 1½ hours minimum each way.

KEFALLONIA ΚΕΦΑΛΛΟΝΙΑ

pop 39,500

Kefallonia is the largest of the Ionian Islands and is big hearted on top of that. It boasts rugged mountain ranges, rich vineyards, soaring coastal cliffs, golden beaches, caves and grottoes, monasteries and antiquities. The 1953 earthquake devastated many of the island's settlements and much of the island's architecture is relatively modern in style. Enough untouched traditional villages and individual buildings survive, however, to make exploration worthwhile. Kefallonia also has a reputation for fine cuisine and great wines.

GETTING THERE & AWAY

AIR

There are daily flights between Kefallonia and Athens and connections to Zakynthos and Corfu. From May to September, many charter flights come from northern Europe and the UK to Kefallonia.

BOAT

Strintzis Lines (www.ferries.gr/strintzis) operates two ferries daily connecting Sami with Patra and Vathy or Piso Aetos.

BUS

Four daily buses connect Kefallonia with Athens (€37.10, seven hours), via Patra (€21, four hours). For information contact the **KTEL bus station** (☎ 26710 22276/81; kefaloniakteltours@yahoo.gr; A Tristi 5, Argostoli) on the southern waterfront in Argostoli. The office produces an excellent printed schedule.

GETTING AROUND

TO/FROM THE AIRPORT

The airport is 9km south of Argostoli. There's no airport bus service; a taxi costs around €15.

BOAT

Car ferries run hourly (more frequently in high season) from 7.30am to 10.30pm between Argostoli and Lixouri, on the island's western peninsula. The journey takes 30 minutes, and tickets cost €1.80/4.50/1.20 per person/car/motorbike.

BUS

From Argostoli's **KTEL bus station** (☎ 26710 22281, 26710 25222) on the southern waterfront, there are 11 buses daily heading to the Lassi Peninsula (€1.40), with four buses to Sami (€4), two to Poros (€4.50), two to Skala (€4.50) and two to Fiskardo (€5). There's a daily east-coast service linking Katelios with Skala, Poros, Sami, Agia Evfymia and Fiskardo. No buses operate on Sunday.

ARGOSTOLI ΑΡΓΟΣΤΟΛΙ

pop 8900

Argostoli is a hugely likeable and lively town. Today, its style is one of broad boulevards and pedestrianised shopping streets lined with the chunky, light-coloured buildings typical of Mediterranean urban architecture of the later 20th century.

ORIENTATION & INFORMATION

The main ferry quay is at the northern end of the waterfront and the bus station is at its southern end. Plateia Valianou, the large palm-treed central square, is a few blocks in from the waterfront off 21 Maïou and its nearby surrounds. Other hubs are pedestrianised Lithostrotou, lined with smart shops, and the waterfront Antoni Tristi. There are banks with ATMs along the northern waterfront and on Lithostrotou.

EOT (Greek National Tourist Organisation; ☎ 26710 22248; 8am-8pm Mon-Fri, 9am-3pm Sat Jul-Aug, 8am-2.30pm Mon-Fri Sep-Jun) The tourist office is on the northern waterfront beside the port police.

Post office (Lithostrotou)

SIGHTS & ACTIVITIES

The Korgialenio History & Folklore Museum (☎ 26710 28835; Ilia Zervou 12; admission €4; 9am-2pm Mon-Sat) and Focas-Kosmetatos Foundation (☎ 26710 26595; Vallianou; admission €3; 9.30am-1pm & 7-10pm Mon-Sat) provide interesting insights into Argostoli's cultural and political history. The Focas-Kosmetatos Foundation also manages the Cephalonia Botanica (☎ 26710 26595; 8.30am-2.30pm Tue-Sat), a lovely garden about 2km from the centre of town, full of native flora and shrubs.

Six kilometres from Argostoli in Davgata is the Museum of Natural History (☎ 26710 84400; admission €2.50; 9am-3pm), with fascinating exhibits on the geological and natural phenomena of the island, and an excellent topographical model of the island in relief.

The town's closest and largest sandy beaches are Makrys Gialos and Platys Gialos, 5km south. Regular buses serve the area.

Lourdata, 16km from Argostoli on the Argostoli-Poros road, has an attractive long beach set against a mountainous green backdrop.

To get closer to Kefalonia's coast and sea contact Monte Nero Activities (☎ 69340 10400, 69329 04360; www.monte-nero-activities.com) for well-organised sea kayaking. Day tours are €55 with lunch and snorkelling gear and there are multi-day options and instructional courses. They also organise cycling and hiking tours in the island's coastal regions. At the time of writing the company was planning a name change to Sea Kayaking Kefalonia.

TOURS

KTEL Tours (☎ 26710 23364) runs excellent-value tours of Kefallonia (€18) on Wednesdays and Sundays, visiting several towns and villages around the island. It also takes tours to Ithaki every Friday (€35). Bookings can be made at the KTEL bus station building (p159).

SLEEPING

Marina Studios (☎ 26710 26455; maristel@hol.gr; Agnis Metaxa 1; r €55, studio €65-75;) Located in a quiet street right at the northern end of the waterfront and just across from the Naval College, the rooms here are spacious and comfy and the studios have lovely beamed angle ceilings.

Vivian Villa (☎ 26710 23396; www.kefalonia-vivianvilla.gr; Deladetsima 9; s/d/tr €55/70/85,

MORELEAZE TRAVEL LONDON/ALAMY

Makrys Gialos (p160), Kefallonia

apt €120; 🔣) Highly recommended for its big, bright rooms and friendly owners. There are tea-making facilities in each room, and some have kitchens. The top-floor apartment is excellent. Prices are discounted for longer stays.

EATING

There are numerous cafes around the edges of Plateia Valianou and along Lithostrotou.

Ladokolla (☎ 26710 25522; Xarokopou 13; dishes €1.90-7; 🕑 1pm-1am) Forget table-top conventions, this is the 'Table Top' in every sense, where piping hot chicken, pork, lamb, kebabs, pittas and souvlaki are delivered without plates and onto very clean disposable covers. They'll bring a plate for anything saucy, but this is cracking down-to-earth noshing, hugely popular locally and with lively service.

ourpick **Arhontiko** (☎ 26710 27213; 5 Riso-spaston; mains €6.50-8.80; lunch & dinner) Top Kefallonian cuisine is on offer here, with starters such as a soufflé of spinach, cheese and cream, or shrimp and *saga-*

naki (fried cheese). For main try *exohiko*, pork stuffed with tomatoes, onions, peppers and feta cheese.

SAMI & SURROUNDS ΣAMH
pop 2200

Sami, 25km northeast of Argostoli and the main port of Kefallonia, was also flattened by the 1953 earthquake. Its exposed, long strip is made up of tourist-oriented cafes, but beyond this it's an attractive place, nestled in a bay and flanked by steep hills. There are several monasteries, ancient castle ruins, caves, walks and nearby beaches that reflect the region's rich history. All facilities, including a post office and banks, are in town. Buses for Argostoli usually meet ferries. Sami's **tourist office** (🕑 9am-7pm May-Sep) is at the northern end of town. An informative website is www.sami.gr.

SIGHTS & ACTIVITIES

The Municipality of Sami has published a simple brochure called *Walking Trail*, which outlines enjoyable walks through

ADINA TOVY AMSEL

Sami (p161), Kefallonia

the local area. The brochures are available from the tourist office.

Antisamos Beach, 4km northeast of Sami, is a long, stony beach in a lovely green setting backed by hills. The drive here is also a highlight, offering dramatic views from cliff edges.

About 7km from Argostoli, on the road to Sami, a side road leads south into the heart of Robola grape country where a visit to the **Cooperative of Robola Producers of Kefallonia** (☎ 26710 86301; www.robola.gr; Omala; ☻ 9am-8.30pm Mon-Fri Apr-Oct, 7am-3pm Mon-Fri Nov-Mar) is worthwhile.

ASSOS ΑΣΟΣ

Tiny Assos is an upmarket gem of white-washed and pastel houses, straddling the isthmus of a peninsula on which stands a Venetian fortress. The fortress is a pleasant place to hike to and around, with superlative views and a great historical ambience.

Cosi's Inn (☎ 26740 51420, 69367 54330; www.cosisinn.gr; 2-/3-person studio €113/129;

❂) is not typically 'Greek' but has the marks of the young and hip interior designer owner: iron beds and sofas, frosted lights and white decor feature strongly.

For eating, **Platanos** (☎ 69446 71804; mains €5.50-13) is in an attractive shady setting near the waterfront. Strong on meat dishes, there are also fish and vegetarian options such as a tasty aubergine, feta and parmesan pie.

AROUND ASSOS

One of Greece's most breathtaking and picture-perfect beaches is **Myrtos**, 8km south of Assos along an exciting stretch of the west coast road. From a roadside viewing area, you can admire and photograph the white sand and shimmering blue water set between tall limestone cliffs far below; you can reach the beach from sea level at Anomeria. Be aware that the beach drops off quickly and sharply, but once you are in the water it's a heavenly experience.

↘ NORTHERN GREECE

NORTHERN GREECE

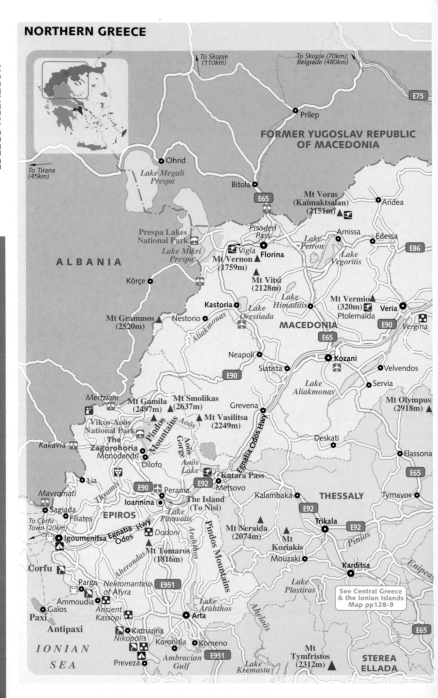

To Skopje (110km)

To Skopje (70km); Belgrade (480km)

E75

Prilep

FORMER YUGOSLAV REPUBLIC OF MACEDONIA

To Tirana (45km)

Ohrid

Lake Megali Prespa

Bitola

E65

Mt Voras (Kaïmaktsalan) (2151m)

Aridea

Arnissa

Edessa

Lake Petron

E86

Prespa Lakes National Park

Pisoderi Pass

Lake Vegoritis

Lake Mikri Prespa

Vigla

Florina

ALBANIA

Mt Vernon (1759m)

Mt Vitsi (2128m)

Mt Vermio (320m)

Veria

Körçe

Kastoria

Lake Orestiada

Lake Himaditis

Ptolemaïda

E90

Vergina

Mt Grammos (2520m)

Nestorio

MACEDONIA

E65

Aliakmonas

Neapoli

Kozani

Velvendos

E90

Siatista

Servia

Lake Aliakmonas

Mt Olympus (2918m)

Mertziani

Mt Gamila (2497m)

Mt Smolikas (2637m)

Grevena

Mt Vasilitsa (2249m)

Vikos-Aoös National Park

Pindos Mountains

Aoös

Aoös Gorge

Deskati

Elassona

Kakavia

The Zagorohoria

Monodendri

Dilofo

Aoös Lake

Katara Pass

E65

E90

Perama

E92

Metsovo

Egnatia Odos Hwy

Lia

Mavromati

The Island (To Nisi)

Kalambaka

THESSALY

Tyrnavos

Sagiada

Filiates

Ioannina

Lake Pamvotis

EPIROS

E92

Trikala

E92

To Corfu Town (20km)

Egnatia Odos

Dodoni

Pindos Mountains

Mt Neraida (2074m)

Pinios

Igoumenitsa

Mt Tomaros (1816m)

Mt Koziakis

Aherondas

Mouzaki

Karditsa

Corfu

Parga

Nekromanteio of Afyra

E951

Lake Plastiras

Epinea

Ammoudia

Gaïos

Ancient Kassopi

Lake Arahthos

See Central Greece & the Ionian Islands Map pp128-9

Paxi

Antipaxi

Kamarina

Nikopolis

Koronisia

Komeno

E65

IONIAN SEA

Preveza

Ambracian Gulf

Lake Kremasta

Mt Tymfristos (2312m)

STEREA ELLADA

E951

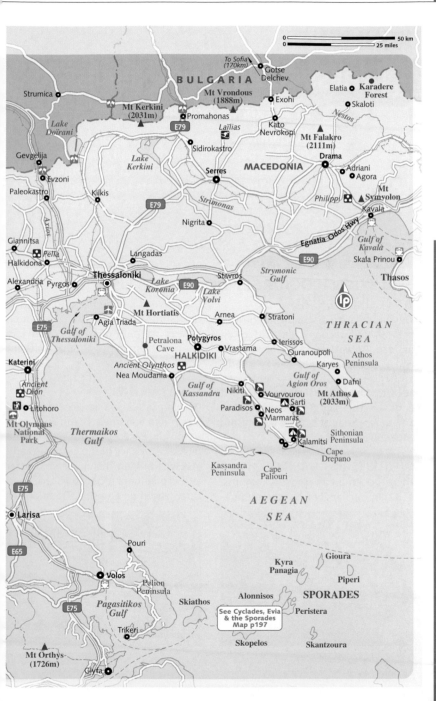

HIGHLIGHTS

1 THESSALONIKI'S BAKERIES

BY ALEXIS VALOGIORGIS, BAKER

Our family has owned a bakery for 65 years. The first pastry chef in the family was my grandfather, who taught me to bake when I was young. Thessaloniki's sweets have a unique taste because the city is at the crossroads between the East and West.

↘ ALEXIS VALOGIORGIS' DON'T MISS LIST

❶ TSOUREKI BREAD

This yummy, traditional brioche-like bread is easily recognisable as it's often braided. *Tsoureki* can be flavoured with citrus, mastic or wild cherry seeds. You'll also find it topped with nuts or, at Easter time, decorated with red dyed eggs. Eat this slightly sweet bread at any time of day; it's often a favourite with coffee at breakfast.

❷ PATISSERIE AGAPITOS

There's been a **bakery** (see Agapitos; p182) in our family for three genera-

tions. We still have the original shop on Tsimiski where you can watch bakers preparing sweets. You can choose from almost 500 different goodies to indulge in.

❸ KAZAN DIPI

Dipping into Thessaloniki's traditional *kazan dipi* (caramel cream) is akin to trying an Eastern crème brûlée. The recipe is a legacy of the Ottomans and involves boiling heavy cream, butter and vanilla until it becomes thick and caramelised on one side. Traditionally,

Clockwise from top: Pastries, Trigona Elenidis (p182); Pudding ice-cream dessert; Agapitos (p182); Tsoureki

kazan dipi was made from buffalo's milk and many bakeries continue to use this method today. You should try it at least once while in the city; it's a delicious way to round off your dinner.

❹ SYRUPY DELIGHTS

Siropiasta are sweets made from pastry soaked in syrup. They were originally brought to Greece from Turkey and every region in Greece now boasts its own variations. In Thessaloniki, *siropiasta* are generally bite-sized and soaked in honey and sugar and flavoured with, citrus, cinnamon or cloves,

for example; you'll also see many topped with chocolate or nuts. To try some, head to **Nikos** (Nikifdhroi Foka 29, Thessaloniki; ☎ 2310 276613).

❺ BAKING WITH A TWIST

In many Thessaloniki bakeries, you will find familiar sweets from other parts of Europe, but with a special Greek twist. Try *rodini* (made from almond paste and butter cream), *trigono* (puff pastry filled with fresh cream) or the ultrarich *efrosini* chocolate cake with the richest chocolate gateau. Mmmmm...

↘ THINGS YOU NEED TO KNOW

How much €1 to €4 per piece **Just one sweet?** *Efrosini* chocolate cake **Best accompaniment** Glass of water **Best time to buy** Bigger bakeries bake all day; smaller ones bring out fresh goodies mid-morning **See our author's reviews of patisseries, p182**

NORTHERN GREECE

HIGHLIGHTS

HIGHLIGHTS

⬆ THE ZAGOROHORIA'S VILLAGES

Tucked into the Pindos Mountains are the preserved hamlets of the **Zagorohoria** (p190). Tiny cottages and grand mansions nestle into the scenery, while footpaths and stone bridges link microcommunities. The isolated villages have safeguarded Greek traditions and culture through numerous invasions. These days, many of the stunning homes are guest houses where you can soak up the atmosphere in style.

⬆ NATURE ON THE DOORSTEP

Stretch your legs in the dramatic **Vikos Gorge** (p190), zip downhill or cross-country at the ski centre in **Metsovo** (p192), or explore **Perama Cave** (p192). Be spellbound by the scenery at the tranquil **Prespa Lakes** (p192), feel small beneath towering **Mt Olympus** (p186) and watch for wildlife while hiking with seminomadic shepherds in **Vikos-Aoös National Park** (p192). Northern Greece is a natural highlight.

NORTHERN GREECE

HIGHLIGHTS

4

⬋ LIVELY IOANNINA

Idyllically positioned on the edge of Lake Pamvotis and looking out to the towering mountains, Ioannina (p186) has atmospheric sights, such as the captivating old town, and a hip vibe that's nurtured by 20,000 university students. Get lost in the narrow alleyways, be dazzled by the Ottoman architecture and then live it up with top nosh, lively cafes and energetic bars.

5

⬋ THEATRE OF DODONI

A place of worship since 2000 BC, this valley site beneath majestic peaks is where an earth goddess spoke through an oracle and Zeus was heard through a sacred oak tree. It's now home to a colossal 3rd-century-BC theatre (p190) that's best enjoyed from one of the ancient stone seats during July's Festival of Ancient Drama (p190).

6

⬋ SIGHTSEEING IN THESSALONIKI

Deservedly applauded for its buzzing nightlife, shopping and packed cultural calendar, Thessaloniki (p174) is also brimming with sights. See the cool interactive museum at the White Tower, the phenomenal mosaics at the Church of Agios Dimitrios, or Greece's oldest surviving papyrus piece at the Archaeological Museum.

2 GEORGE TSAFOS; 3 MARK DAFFEY; 4 GEORGE TSAFOS; 5 NETFALLS PHOTOGRAPHY/DREAMSTIME; 6 ULRICH SPRENGEL/IMAGEBROKER

2 Stone bridge, Zagorohoria region (p190); 3 Hiking to the peak of Mt Olympus (p186); 4 Views over Lake Pamvotis (p189); 5 Stone ruins of the Theatre of Dodoni (p190), Dodoni; 6 White Tower (p178), Thessaloniki

THE BEST...

↘ CREATIVE CUISINE

- **Paparouna** (p181) Serving dishes such as chicken with peppermint and honey, washed down with organic Greek beer.
- **Gastrodromio** (p186) Traditional decor with scrumptious sauces and marinades for meat and seafood – think wine, almonds, cinnamon and nutmeg.
- **Es Aei** (p188) Ottoman flair and organic ingredients add to Ioannina specials, such as grilled pork sausage.

↘ HIKING TRAILS

- **Mt Olympus** (p186) Climb to the top of Greece's highest mountain.
- **Ioannina** (p186) Serious hikers can tackle the sheer mountains facing the city.
- **Vikos Gorge** (p190) Descend into the world's deepest gorge.

↘ ATMOSPHERIC ACCOMMODATION

- **Xenonas Papanikolaou** (p186) Romantic digs next to Mt Olympus.
- **Dafni Traditional Hotel** (p188) Unique rooms in Ioannina built into the old town's outer walls.
- **Arhontiko Dilofo** (p193) Get cosy in a 450-year-old restored mansion in the Zagorohoria.
- **Electra Palace Hotel** (p181) Comfort and class, with a mosaic-tiled pool, a *hammam* (Turkish bath) and views of Thessaloniki.

↘ SPECTACULAR VIEWS

- **Sithonia's southern tip** (p184) Rugged and dramatic with views of Mt Athos.
- **Litohoro** (p185) Admire Mt Olympus from the wooden balconies of Macedonian-style homes.
- **Lake Pamvotis** (p186) Cruise on this lake for fabulous views of Ioannina and towering peaks.

GEORGE TSAFOS

Vikos Gorge (p190), Zagorohoria

THINGS YOU NEED TO KNOW

⬎ VITAL STATISTICS

- **Population** Macedonia 2.4 million; Epiros 352,400
- **Area** Macedonia 33,785 sq km; Epiros 9203 sq km

⬎ LOCALITIES IN A NUTSHELL

- **Macedonia** (p174) As well as Thessaloniki, take in the beach-laden Sithonian Peninsula, towering Mt Olympus and mysterious Mt Athos.
- **Thessaloniki** (p174) The region's biggest city, known for its cultural clout and trendiness.
- **Epiros** (p186) In the southwest of the region and home to Ioannina, visit the impressive ruins of the Theatre of Dodoni and the magical mountain villages of the Zagorohoria.
- **Ioannina** (p186) Beautiful and energetic city with a burgeoning student population and nightlife to match.

⬎ ADVANCE PLANNING

- **Two months before** Book any activity tours and accommodation.
- **One month before** Check online for events in Thessaloniki and Ioannina and make advance bookings.

⬎ RESOURCES

- **www.greecetravel.com/macedonia** Matt Barrett's guide to the sights and cities of the region.
- **www.about-ioannina.gr** A guide to Epiros, including Ioannina, Dodoni and the Zagorohoria with background info, accommodation and sights.

⬎ EMERGENCY NUMBERS

- **Police** (☎ 100)
- **Highway Rescue** (ELPA; ☎ 104)

⬎ GETTING AROUND

- **Bus** Comprehensive routes throughout northern Greece with links to Athens.
- **Train** Fast trains between Thessaloniki and Athens.
- **Car** A great way to explore the Zagorohoria and other remote regions.

⬎ BE FOREWARNED

- **Sights** Many are closed Mondays, particularly in Thessaloniki and Ioannina.
- **Weather** Can be very unpredictable, especially on Mt Olympus. If you're setting out on a trek, always check with local hiking organisations before setting out.
- **Accommodation** Conferences and the Thessaloniki International Film Festival in November can make it next to impossible to find a bed in Thessaloniki. Be sure to book ahead.

NORTHERN GREECE

THINGS YOU NEED TO KNOW

NORTHERN GREECE

ITINERARIES

ITINERARIES

BEST OF BOTH WORLDS Three Days

Many visitors are surprised by the diversity found in northern Greece, where it's possible to enjoy cosmopolitan city life and quiet, sun-drenched beaches. **(1) Thessaloniki** (p174) is an increasingly fashionable destination with a dynamic arts and culture scene. Take in theatre, festivals and galleries before delving into the excellent shopping and nightlife. Visit the sights and Kastra, the atmospheric Turkish quarter. Be sure to stop in at a few *zaharoplasteia* (patisseries) where you can sample some of the regions unique and mouth-watering sweets. When you've gotten your fill of city life, head for the gorgeous Sithonian Peninsula (p184), accessible by bus or car, where you can laze about on golden sand backed by pine-covered hills at relatively quiet beaches like **(2) Kalogria Beach** (p184). While the peninsula is nearby, spend the night in **(3) Kalamitsi** (p185) to get a full dose of beach life. If you're up for it, you can dive here, too.

NORTHERN HIGH POINTS Five Days

Begin your tour with a couple of days in **(1) Thessaloniki** (p174), where you can take in the theatre, some impressive sights, contemporary galleries and a spirited nightlife. Enjoy the cosmopolitan cuisine and Macedonian specialities like the region's yummy Turkish-influenced sweets. Next, head by bus or car to **(2) Litohoro** (p185), a stunning village with traditional Macedonian architecture and cobbled streets. Litohoro is the base for visiting **(3) Mt Olympus** (p186), Greece's highest peak. Cloaked in thick forest and home to countless rare and endemic plants, it's the land of legends and ancient gods. The energetic can venture up the many paths on foot or you can simply admire the views from town. From Litohoro, you can also visit **(4) Ancient Dion** (p191), where the ancient Macedonians worshiped the Olympian gods, as well as the Dion museum that houses the site's original votive statues that were found virtually intact.

ALTERNATIVE NORTH One Week

Spend a couple of days in (1) Ioannina (p186), a hip, lively city with a buzzing cultural scene and great nightlife. Its seductive setting on the edge of a lake with a giant view of sheer mountains makes it an excellent base. Explore the old Turkish quarter, including the impressive Its Kale (Inner Citadel), and hop on a lake cruise for phenomenal views of the city and mountains. Take a day trip to (2) Dodoni (p190), a 3rd-century-BC theatre in a beautiful valley location. If you're visiting in July, time your visit to watch a classical drama at the theatre, performed as part of Ioannina's Festival of Ancient Drama. From Ioannina, hop on a bus to the (3) Zagorohoria (p190) region, where two days

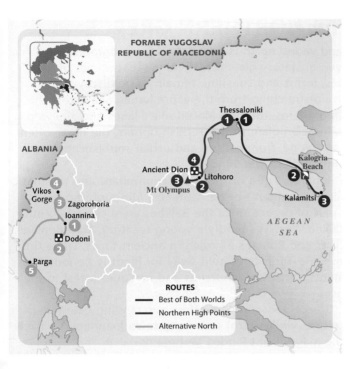

can easily melt away as you explore the villages tucked into the Pindos
Mountains. Stay in a traditional stone house and hike the awe-inspiring
(4) Vikos Gorge (p190), the world's deepest gorge at the heart of
the Vikos-Aoös National Park. After soaking up the fresh air, head for
(5) Parga (p193), a charming west-coast town tucked into the fold of
a long, sandy bay and crowned with a Venetian castle. Dig your toes
in the sand and simply relax for a couple of days.

DISCOVER NORTHERN GREECE

Greece's vast and varied north is unmatched for geographical, cultural and even gustatory diversity. Here, great stretches of mountains, lakes, forest and coastline remain to be discovered. Comprising terrain stretching from the azure Ionian Sea across the rugged Epirot mountains, through Macedonia's lakes and vineyards and across the Thracian plain to the Turkish border, the north offers something for everyone, from culture and urban sophistication to swimming, hiking and birdwatching.

The tangible reminders of a history both triumphant and traumatic remain scattered throughout northern Greece. Although the region has only been part of Greece since the Balkans were carved up in the 1912–13 Balkan Wars, it's hardly a young territory: Macedonians, Illyrians, Thracians and Romans all ruled in ancient times, while the Byzantines, Slavs and Turks later held sway for lengthy periods. Myriad monuments, fortresses, churches and mosques attest to their diverse influences.

Thessaloniki, Greece's second city, offers outstanding eateries, nightlife and culture, while Epirot university town Ioannina is a lively spot close to the magnificent Pindos Mountains.

MACEDONIA
ΜΑΚΕΔΟΝΙΑ

THESSALONIKI
ΘΕΣΣΑΛΟΝΙΚΗ

pop 363,987

Thessaloniki (thess-ah-lo-*nee*-kih) is at once the hippest, most cultured and most expensive place to sleep and eat in northern Greece – though budget options are thankfully starting to emerge. As Greece's second city, Thessaloniki (also called Salonica) offers the best nightlife, shopping, fine dining and cultural events outside of Athens, but with a friendlier, less hectic vibe.

As with Athens, the enduring symbols of a glorious history are visible here. These include the White Tower, watching over the cafe-lined waterfront, erstwhile Ottoman *hammams* (Turkish baths)-turned-art-galleries, and lengthy Byzantine walls culminating at the Ano Poli (Upper Town), an enchanting neighbourhood of colourful old houses, where little Byzantine churches peek from winding alleyways.

Thessaloniki remains lively during the long months when the more touristy parts of Greece hibernate. And, though one could easily spend weeks here, Thessaloniki and its sites are compact enough for travellers with only a few days to spare.

ORIENTATION

Thessaloniki's main squares include Plateia Eleftherias, near the port, and the grand Plateia Aristotelous, a popular meeting point that runs between Egnatia and Leoforos Nikis. Another prominent meeting point for locals is Kamara, the area around the Arch of Galerius on the northern side of Egnatia opposite Plateia Navarinou. Taking Egnatia westwards past Kamara and Plateia Aristotelous brings you to the cheap shopping/hotel district around Plateia Dimokratias. After this, Egnatia becomes Monastiriou and shortly passes the train station to the right, and continues towards the main bus station (3km further west).

INFORMATION
EMERGENCY

Farmakeio Gouva-Peraki (☎ 2310 205 544; Agias Sofias 110, Ano Poli) Up in Ano Poli, this is a handy pharmacy with experienced staff.

First-Aid Centre (☎ 2310 530 530; Navarhou Koundourioti 10)

Ippokration (☎ 2310 837 921; Papanastasiou 50) Largest public hospital; 2km east of town centre.

Port police (☎ 2310 531 504)

Tourist police (☎ 2310 554 871; 5th fl, Dodekanisou 4; ☺ 7.30am-11pm)

MONEY

Banks and ATMs are widespread, except in Ano Poli. Commission-hungry exchange offices line western Egnatia. The train station, bus station and ferry passenger terminals contain ATMs. Avoid travellers cheques if possible.

POST

Post office Aristotelous (**Aristotelous 26;** ☺ **7.30am-8pm Mon-Fri, 7.30am-2.15pm Sat, 9am-1.30pm Sun**); Koundouriotou (**Koundouriotou 6;** ☺ **7.30am-2pm**) The Koundouriotou branch is next to the port. The train station also has a post window.

TOURIST INFORMATION

Office of Tourism Directorate (☎ 2310 221 100; tour-the@otenet.gr; Tsimiski 136; ☺ 8am-8pm Mon-Fri, 8am-2pm Sat) Friendly and well-informed staff provide assistance in English and German.

GEORGE TSAFOS

Ladadika area (p181), Thessaloniki

THESSALONIKI

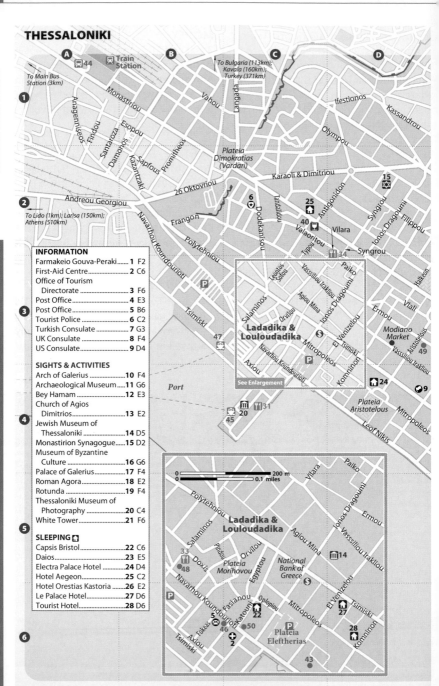

INFORMATION

Farmakeio Gouva-Peraki	1 F2
First-Aid Centre	2 C6
Office of Tourism Directorate	3 F6
Post Office	4 E3
Post Office	5 B6
Tourist Police	6 C2
Turkish Consulate	7 G3
UK Consulate	8 F4
US Consulate	9 D4

SIGHTS & ACTIVITIES

Arch of Galerius	10 F4
Archaeological Museum	11 G6
Bey Hamam	12 E3
Church of Agios Dimitrios	13 E2
Jewish Museum of Thessaloniki	14 D5
Monastirion Synagogue	15 D2
Museum of Byzantine Culture	16 G6
Palace of Galerius	17 F4
Roman Agora	18 E2
Rotunda	19 F4
Thessaloniki Museum of Photography	20 C4
White Tower	21 F6

SLEEPING

Capsis Bristol	22 C6
Daios	23 E5
Electra Palace Hotel	24 D4
Hotel Aegeon	25 C2
Hotel Orestias Kastoria	26 E2
Le Palace Hotel	27 D6
Tourist Hotel	28 D6

Ladadika & Louloudadika

See Enlargement

Port

Ladadika & Louloudadika

Plateia Morihovou

National Bank of Greece

Plateia Eleftherias

0 ——— 200 m
0 ——— 0.1 miles

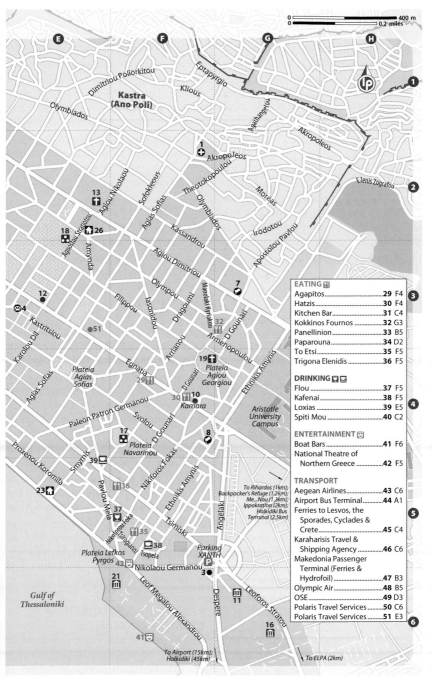

EATING

Agapitos	**29** F4
Hatzis	**30** F4
Kitchen Bar	**31** C4
Kokkinos Fournos	**32** G3
Panellinion	**33** B5
Paparouna	**34** D2
To Etsi	**35** F5
Trigona Elenidis	**36** F5

DRINKING

Flou	**37** F5
Kafenai	**38** F5
Loxias	**39** E5
Spiti Mou	**40** C2

ENTERTAINMENT

Boat Bars	**41** F6
National Theatre of Northern Greece	**42** F5

TRANSPORT

Aegean Airlines	**43** C6
Airport Bus Terminal	**44** A1
Ferries to Lesvos, the Sporades, Cyclades & Crete	**45** C4
Karaharisis Travel & Shipping Agency	**46** C6
Makedonia Passenger Terminal (Ferries & Hydrofoil)	**47** B3
Olympic Air	**48** B5
OSE	**49** D3
Polaris Travel Services	**50** C6
Polaris Travel Services	**51** E3

SIGHTS
WHITE TOWER

The history of Thessaloniki's most famous landmark, the pacific **White Tower** (☎ 2310 267 832; Lefkos Pyrgos; admission free; ☼ 8.30am-3pm Tue-Sun), is actually bathed in blood. In 1826, Ottoman Sultan Mahmud II ordered the massacre of janizaries (elite troops made up of forcibly Islamicised Christian boys) deemed disloyal. After the Greek reconquest in 1913, the 'bloody tower' was whitewashed to expunge this grisly past. Although the tower's whitewash has long been removed, the name stuck. The tower's new interactive **museum** presents the city's history through several levels of cool multimedia displays.

PALACE, ARCH & MAUSOLEUM (ROTUNDA) OF GALERIUS

Three major Roman monuments associated with the early-4th-century Emperor Galerius spill across Egnatia at Plateia Navarinou. The ruined **Palace of Galerius** (Plateia Navarinou; admission free; ☼ 8.30am-3pm Tue-Sun), sprawling east-west across the square, contains floor mosaics, columns and some walls. North of Egnatia at Kamara, the **Arch of Galerius** features sculpted soldiers in combat; it was erected in AD 303 to celebrate a victory over the Persians.

Just above the arch is the unmistakable **Rotunda** (☎ 2310 218 720; Plateia Agiou Georgiou; admission free; ☼ 8am-5pm Tue-Sun), a hulking brick structure built by Galerius as his future mausoleum (he never used it, dying in retirement in today's Serbia instead). Constantine the Great made the Rotunda Thessaloniki's first church (Agiou Georgiou), and later the Ottomans transformed it into a mosque; the minaret they added has now been restored. Some interior frescoes survive.

ROMAN AGORA

The **Roman Agora** (Plateia Dikastirion; admission free; ☼ 8am-3pm Tue-Sun) lies north of Plateia Aristotelous, across Egnatia on Plateia Dikastirion. Ancient Macedonian commercial activity, starting in the 3rd century BC, peaked under the Romans, when the area was buzzing with public affairs, services and shops. A helpful English-language placard explains the site, which contains clustered shop walls and mosaic floor remnants.

MUSEUMS

The **Archaeological Museum** (☎ 2310 830 538; Manoli Andronikou 6; admission €6, students free; ☼ 8.30am-8pm) showcases prehistoric, ancient Macedonian and Hellenistic finds. The **Derveni Treasure** contains Greece's oldest surviving papyrus piece (250-320 BC).

The snazzy **Museum of Byzantine Culture** (☎ 2310 868 570; www.mbp.gr; Leoforos Stratou 2; admission €4; ☼ 8am-8pm Tue-Sun, 1.30-8pm Mon) uses ambient lighting and features a running wall placard text explaining more than 3000 Byzantine objects, including frescoes, mosaics, embroidery, ceramics, inscriptions and icons from the early Christian period to the Fall of Constantinople (1453).

The hip **Thessaloniki Museum of Photography** (☎ 2310 566 716; www.thm photo.gr; Warehouse A, Thessaloniki Port; ☼ 11am-7pm Tue-Fri, 11am-9pm Sat & Sun), in a former portside warehouse, displays historic and contemporary Greek photography, plus dynamic temporary exhibitions, and there's a waterfront cafe.

KASTRA (ANO POLI) & THE BYZANTINE WALLS

Homes in the Kastra (Castle), also called Ano Poli (Upper Town), largely survived the 1917 fire that had originated there, as

JAPAN TRAVEL BUREAU/PHOTOLIBRARY

Interior of the Church of Agios Dimitrios

◥ CHURCH OF AGIOS DIMITRIOS

Perhaps the grandest church in Greece, the enormous 5th-century **Church of Agios Dimitrios** honours Thessaloniki's patron saint. A Roman soldier, Dimitrios was killed around AD 303 on the site (then a Roman bath), on orders from Emperor Galerius, infamous for persecuting Christians. The martyrdom site is now an eerie underground **crypt**, open during the day and for the special liturgy held here every Friday from 9pm to 11pm. In 1980, the saint's relics were returned from Italy, and they now occupy a silver reliquary inside.

The Ottomans made Agios Dimitrios a mosque, plastering over the wall frescoes. After the 1913 Greek reconquest, the plaster was removed, revealing Thessaloniki's finest church mosaics. While the 1917 fire was very damaging, five 8th-century mosaics have survived, spanning the altar.

Things you need to know: ☎ 2310 270 008; Agiou Dimitriou 97; admission free; ⏲ 8am-10pm, crypt 8am-7.30pm Tue-Thu & Sun, 1.30-7.30pm Mon, 9-11pm Fri

the wind swept the flames down towards the sea. It had been the 'Turkish quarter' during Ottoman times, and contains Thessaloniki's most atmospheric urban architecture.

Here, timber-framed, pastel-painted houses with overhanging upper storeys are clustered on small winding streets. Kastra's walls were built by Emperor Theodosius (AD 379-475), who modelled them on his own great Constantinopolitan wall system. Rebuilt in the 14th century, the walls were then strengthened with marble stones from the Jewish cemetery in 1821. It's possible to walk up the small winding streets from opposite the university (Panepistimio Aristotelion) almost to the top.

BEY HAMAM
The labyrinthine **Bey Hamam** (Paradeisos Baths; cnr Egnatia & Plateia Dikastirion; admission free; ⏲ 9am-9pm Mon-Fri, 8.30am-3pm Sat & Sun) is Thessaloniki's oldest Turkish bath (1444). The structure hosts art shows.

PETER TITMUSS/ALAMY

Winding streets of the Kastra (Ano Poli) area (p178), Thessaloniki

JEWISH SITES

Until WWII, when the occupying Nazis deported Thessaloniki's Jewish population, the city had been one of southeast Europe's most important centres of Jewish life.

The **Jewish Museum of Thessaloniki** (☎ 2310 250 406; Agiou Mina 13; admission free; ☼ 11am-2pm Tue, Fri & Sun, 11am-2pm & 5-8pm Wed & Thu) traces Thessaloniki Judaism from 140 BC to the Sephardic immigrations following 1492, ending with the Holocaust. The only synagogue to have survived the Nazis is the **Monastirioton Synagogue** (☎ 2310 524 968; Syngrou 35).

FESTIVALS & EVENTS

The **Thessaloniki International Film Festival** (☎ 2310 378 400; www.filmfestival .gr) occurs each November. Cinemas in various locations show 150 or so high-quality international films, ranging from experimental and obscure to well-known directors' works. The **Thessaloniki**

Documentary Festival (www.filmfestival.gr) is in mid-March.

The **Office of Tourism Directorate** (☎ 2310 221 100; tour-the@otenet.gr; Tsimiski 136; ☼ 8am-8pm Mon-Fri, 8am-2pm Sat), near the White Tower, can provide more info on current cultural events.

SLEEPING
BUDGET

Hotel Orestias Kastoria (☎ 2310 276 517; www.okhotel.gr; Agnostou Stratiotou 14; s/d/tr €38/49/59; ✖ ▣) An old favourite near the Church of Agios Dimitrios, the Orestias Kastoria is a friendly, small place with cosy, clean rooms. Prices rise in September, when conventions are held.

Hotel Aegeon (☎ 2310 522 921; www .aegeon-hotel.gr; Egnatia 19; s/d €45/60; ✖ 🛜) Recently renovated, this place in a historic building on Egnatia is surprisingly good value. The decent, clean rooms have low-key decor, bathrooms and most mod cons. It's a five- to 10-minute walk to the train station.

MIDRANGE

Tourist Hotel (☎ 2310 270 501; www .tourist hotel.gr; Mitropoleos 21; s/d/tr incl breakfast €55/70/90; 🗙 🖳) At this classic place (built in 1925), an old-school gated lift leads to rooms with the all mod cons and decorated with elegance. Street noise is mitigated by the soundproof windows.

Le Palace Hotel (☎ 2310 257 400; www .lepalace.gr; Tsimiski 23; s/d incl breakfast €85/100; 🗙 🛜) At night gaze down from your little balcony at twinkling Tsimiski roaring by below (there's soundproofing). Le Palace has spacious, modern rooms with all the mod cons.

Electra Palace Hotel (☎ 2310 294 000; www.electra hotels.gr; Plateia Aristotelous 9; s/d €115/130; 🗙 🛜 🖳) Even if you come only to gaze out onto the harbour from the rooftop garden cafe, the appeal of this five-star city landmark that stands splendidly over Plateia Aristotelous is instantly apparent. Rooms are spacious and with all the expected amenities, including a mosaic-tiled indoor pool, rooftop outdoor pool and *hammam*.

TOP END

Daios (☎ 2310 250 200; www.daioshotels.com; Leoforos Nikis 59; s/d with sea view €170/225; 🗙 🛜 🖳) A keen sensitivity to light and shadow pervades the whole hotel, which has a contemporary, minimalist design. Suites have enormous, sound-proofed windows and wrap-around balconies (from some you only see water, not streets).

Capsis Bristol (☎ 2310 521 321; www .capsishotel.gr; cnr Oplopiou & Katouni; s/d €192/250; 🗙 🛜) What was fated to become a stylish and friendly modern hotel was originally Thessaloniki's post office, in 1870. The Capsis Bristol's 16 rooms and four suites, decorated with ornate antiques, Persian rugs and artworks, suffuse the hotel with an old-world charm befitting its location in historic Ladadika.

EATING

The website www.tavernoxoros.gr, in Greek, listing Thessaloniki eateries and locating them on the map, is a handy online resource.

To Etsi (☎ 2310 222 469; Nikoforos Fokas 2; grills €2.50-4) This bawdily decorated, iconic eatery near the White Tower offers refreshingly light souvlaki and *soutzoukakia* (meat rissoles in tomato sauce) with vegetable dips, in Cypriot-style pitta bread. Look for the neon sign.

Panellinion (☎ 2310 567 220; Salaminos 1; mains €6-10) This friendly taverna has traditional Ladadika decor, with its wooden floors and walls lined with olive-oil bottles and tins of produce. Panellinion's varied choices include a world of ouzos and cheeses, to delicious seafood mezedhes; only organic vegetables are used.

Kitchen Bar (☎ 2310 528 108; Warehouse B, Thessaloniki Port; mains €7-13) This perennial favourite offers both drinks and artfully prepared food, in a lofty, sumptuously decorated, renovated warehouse, with outdoors waterfront tables too. The salads and risotto are as bright as the flames in the open kitchen, where the chefs, like the style-conscious clientele, are always on display.

Paparouna (☎ 2310 510852; www.papa rouna.com; Syngrou 7; mains €8-16; 🕙 1pm-1am; 🛜) Built a century ago as a bank, the lively Paparouna restaurant is marked by lofty ceilings, great bursts of red (like the name, which means 'poppy') and a checkerboard floor. The creative cuisine includes chicken with peppermint and honey, linguini with aromatic lemon-

SWEET INDULGENCES CHRIS DELISO

For a quick breakfast or sinful dessert, Thessaloniki's *zaharoplasteia* (patisseries) are hard to beat. Although classics such as baklava or chocolate profiteroles are available throughout Greece, Thessaloniki's historic ties with the mores and populations of the Ottoman East have bequeathed it with an especially rich tradition of sweets – and a discerning local population to enjoy them. While tasty places are found everywhere, the following well-polished *zaharoplasteia* are particularly famous. Most prices are by the kilo (usually around €1 to €4 per piece).

Just above the Rotunda, the classic **Kokkinos Fournos** (Apostolou Pavlou 1, Rotunda) bakery does Thessaloniki's best *koulourakia vanilias* – crunchy, slightly sweet golden cookies perfect for dipping in Greek coffee.

Since 1908, when Thessaloniki was still Ottoman, local legend **Hatzis** (☎ 2310 968 400; Egnatia 119) has been replicating the tastes of old Constantinople. After Hatzis, you'll never ask for a simple 'baklava' again. The veritable symphony of sweets served here includes *vezir parmak* (*politika* syrup cake with cream filling), *hanoum bourek* (handmade pastry with raisins, peanuts and cream) and *malempi mastiha* (cream from milk and rice porridge, flavoured with *mastiha*, a sweet liquor from Chios, and served with rose syrup).

The posh **Agapitos** (☎ 2310 268 368; Egnatia 134) offers a taste of the Continent. Its cakes, fruit concoctions and profiteroles (chocolate pudding with a crunchy base and white cream) are excellent. Try the superlative *efrosini* chocolate cake, or smudge your fingers on the delicious mini-éclairs.

A veritable institution since 1960, **Trigona Elenidis** (☎ 2310 257 510; cnr D Gounari & Tsimiski) is a very rare thing in today's world: a shop specialising in only one product. Its sweet, flaky triangular cones filled with cool and unbelievably tasty cream are legendary; locals come out with 2kg boxes, but one large triangle will certainly fill you up.

---

grass and cherry tomatoes, and even organic Greek beer. It makes phenomenal desserts, too.

DRINKING

In summer many city-centre nightclubs close and reopen in bigger spaces outdoors, on the airport road.

BARS

ourpick **Spiti Mou** (cnr Egnatia & Leontos Sofou 26; ⏰ 1pm-late; 🛜) A new bar upstairs in a lofty old building in the Syngrou district, 'My House' (as the name means in Greek) was opened after its young owners realised their own parties were becoming too big to fail. The relaxed feel is enhanced by eclectic music, well-worn decor and big couches spread out on a chequered floor.

Flou (☎ 2310 261 448; Nikoforou Foka 9; ⏰ 9pm-late Mon-Sat) What the French call 'Bobo' characterises this cosy bar on a White Tower sidestreet. Exuding neon and a *je ne sais quoi* eclectic retro decor, Flou gets packed on the weekends with an early-30s crowd and it plays a shameless selection of vintage pop.

CAFES

ourpick **Loxias** (☎ 2310 233 925; Isavron 7; ⏰ noon-2am) Educated Greeks have gravitated to this whimsical *steki* (hang-out) for years, where they might discuss philosophy, politics or literature over ouzo and snacks.

Kafenai (☎ 2310 220 310; cnr Ethnikis Amynis & Tsopela; ⏰ 9am-2am) This new *kafeneio*, beside the Cretan restaurant Myrsini, impressively revives the spirit of old Salonica. With 1950s-style Greek decor, high ceilings supported by columns and low-key jazz, it's no wonder the place attracts local artists and musicians.

ENTERTAINMENT

Lido (☎ 2310 539 055; Frixou 5, Sfageia; ⏰ 9pm-late) Thessaloniki's big, mean disco machine, Lido pumps out R&B, house and more. Like most nightclubs, in summer it operates out on the airport road.

Take a booze cruise on one of several **boat bars** (⏰ 6pm-1am) moored on the waterfront south of the White Tower, in front of Alexander the Great's statue. Each boat has slightly different decorations and themes, with music ranging from pop to reggae to R&B.

The **National Theatre of Northern Greece** (☎ 2310 288 000; Ethnikis Amynis 2) offers classical Greek drama and modern theatrical works.

GETTING THERE & AWAY

AIR

Makedonia Airport (☎ 2310 473 212; www.thessalonikiairport.gr) is 16km southeast of town, and served by local bus 78. Internationally, Makedonia Airport serves a number of European destinations.

Olympic Air (☎ 2310 368 666; www.olympicairlines.com; Navarhou Koundourioti 1-3) is near the port, and **Aegean Airlines** (☎ 2310 280 050; www.aegeanair.com; Venizelou 2) is on Plateia Eleftherias.

BOAT

Many port-area travel agencies sell tickets; try **Polaris Travel Services** (Agias Sofias ☎ 2310 278 613; Egnatia 81; ⏰ 8am-8.30pm; Port ☎ 2310 548 655; polaris@otenet.gr; Navarhou Koundourioti 19; ⏰ 8am-8.30pm) or **Karaharisis Travel & Shipping Agency** (☎ 2310 524 544; Navarhou Koundourioti 8; ⏰ 8am-8.30pm).

BUS

The **main bus station** (☎ 2310 595 408; Monastiriou 319), 3km west of the centre, features different windows selling tickets to specific destinations. There's no

ALAN BENSON

Outdoor dining, Thessaloniki

general information booth and this enhances the station's unpleasant, stressful nature.

TRAIN
Cheaper, often more comfortable and not always slower than the bus, the train goes everywhere in mainland Greece. Thessaloniki's **train station** (☎ 2310 599 421; Monastiriou) is also more central than the bus station. Get tickets at the station, or from **OSE** (☎ 2310 598 120; Aristotelous 18). The station's helpful information office provides printed timetables.

GETTING AROUND
TO/FROM THE AIRPORT
Bus 78 runs from the airport west to the main bus station via the train station every 30 minutes. From town centre to the airport by taxi costs €8 to €12.

BUS
Orange articulated buses operate within Thessaloniki, and blue-and-orange buses operate both within the city centre and

the suburbs. Tickets are sold at the ubiquitous *periptera* (street kiosks) for €0.50, or from on-board ticket machines (€0.60). However, if you'll use the bus frequently, buy a 24-hour unlimited usage ticket (€2).

TAXI
Thessaloniki's blue-and-white taxis carry multiple passengers, and won't take you if you're not going in the same direction as pre-existing passengers. The minimum fare is €2.80.

HALKIDIKI ΧΑΛΚΙΔΙΚΗ
SITHONIAN PENINSULA
ΧΕΡΣΟΝΗΣΟΣ ΣΙΘΩΝΙΑΣ
Sithonia has superb beaches, spectacular natural beauty and a relaxed feel. The coast road loops around Sithonia, skirting wide bays, climbing into pine-forested hills and dipping down to the resorts.

The west coast has long sandy beaches between **Nikiti** and **Paradisos**, notably **Kalogria Beach** and **Lagomandra Beach**. Beyond, **Neos Marmaras** is Sithonia's

View of Mt Athos, Halkidiki

MT ATHOS

More than a millennium of unbroken spiritual activity has been taking place on the isolated southeastern part of Halkidiki's third finger, at the monasteries of Agion Oros (the Holy Mountain). A semi-autonomous monastic republic that still follows the Julian calendar, along with many other Byzantine edicts and mores, the Holy Mountain consists of 20 working monasteries and smaller *skites* (dependencies), with a few *very* old-school, remote mountain hermitages still inhabited by the odd ascetic. An enormous World Heritage Site that occupies most of the Athos Peninsula, Mt Athos is formally a part of the Greek state, though ecclesiastically it remains under the Orthodox Patriarchate of Constantinople (İstanbul).

Apocryphal legends say that the Virgin Mary herself visited Athos and blessed it; the Holy Mountain is considered the Garden of the Virgin, and it is dedicated exclusively to her – meaning there's no room for other women. Although frustrated Eurocrats in Brussels have contested this prohibition, they've proven no match for more than 1000 years of tradition and the gold-sealed *chrysobulls* (decrees) of Byzantine emperors, whose names are still invoked in prayers and whose edicts continue to be respected.

For men, visiting monastic Athos requires advance planning. Visits are restricted to four days, though with special permission they can be extended – a worthwhile effort, if you have the time. Experiencing the monasteries is wonderfully peaceful – and tiring. In many hosting monasteries, you follow the monks' lifestyle, eating and attending services (even at 3.30am) with them, and generally respecting the monasteries' customs.

largest resort, with a crowded beach but many domatia. Sithonia's relatively undeveloped southern tip is rocky, rugged and dramatic, with spectacular views of Mt Athos appearing as you round the southeastern tip.

Kalamitsi, with its gorgeous beach, has been overdeveloped, though it does have services such as boat rental at the **North Aegean Diving Centre** (☎ 23750 41338), which also does dives (€50) and courses (from €80).

The best rooms are at **O Giorgakis** (☎ 23750 41338; fax 23750 41013; studios €75), above the eponymous restaurant opposite the beach. The studios sleep five and are fully equipped. The quieter **Souzana Rooms** (☎ 23750 41786; apt €50) sits in a spacious garden and has good-sized apartments.

Buses leave from Thessaloniki's eastside **Halkidiki bus terminal** (☎ 23103 16555; www.in-ktel.gr, in Greek) for Sarti (€15.80, 3½ hours, five daily) and Vourvourou (€10.50, four daily). Most of the Sarti buses loop around the Sithonian Peninsula, enjoying coastal views.

LITOHORO ΛΙΤΟΧΩΡΟ

pop 7011 / elev 305m

Relaxing Litohoro (lih-*to*-ho-ro) is the base for climbing or just admiring Mt Olympus, though its winding, cobbled upper streets and lovely Macedonian-style wood-balconied houses make it appealing in its own right.

INFORMATION

Plateia Eleftheria hosts numerous ATMs.

EOS (Greek Alpine Club; ☎ 23520 84544; ⏰ 9.30am-12.30pm & 6-8pm Mon-Sat Jun-Sep) Below the public parking lot; this office distributes pamphlets with both general and hiking information on Olympus.

Medical centre (☎ 23520 22222) Five kilometres away, at the Litohoro turn-off from the main coastal highway.

Police (☎ 23520 81100; cnr Ithakisiou & Agiou Nikolaou)

Post office (28 Oktovriou 11)

Tourist information booth (Agiou Nikolaou) In a white building with wooden eaves, just before Ithakiou.

www.litohoro.gr Municipal website.

SLEEPING & EATING

ourpick Xenonas Papanikolaou (☎ 23520 81236; xenpap@otenet.gr; Nikolaou Episkopou Kitrous 1; s/d €45/50; 🍴 💻) This romantic guest house, set in a flowery garden up in the backstreets, is a world away from the tourist crowds on Litohoro's main street. To get there from the square, take 28 Oktovriou uphill and turn left on Nikolaou Episkopou Kitrous.

Hotel Olympus Mediterranean (☎ 23520 81831; www.olympusmed.gr; Dionysou 5; d/tr incl breakfast €70/90, luxury ste €100; 🍴 💻 🏊) A four-star hotel up in the backstreets, the Olympus Mediterranean occupies an imposing neoclassical building with ornate balconies, and has 20 luxurious rooms and three suites, plus an indoor pool, a mosaic-tiled Jacuzzi pool and sauna.

ourpick Gastrodromio (☎ 23520 21300; Plateia Eleftherias; mains €7-13) Litohoro's most delightfully inventive restaurant, the spacious, traditionally decorated Gastrodromio serves flavourful dishes such as octopus with peppercorn, cumin, garlic, hot pepper and wine, or rabbit cooked in wine and glazed with almonds, cinnamon and nutmeg.

GETTING THERE & AWAY

From the **bus station** (☎ 23520 81271), buses serve Katerini (€2.10, 25 minutes, 13 daily), Thessaloniki (€8, 1¼ hours, 13 daily) and Athens (€28, 5½ hours, three daily via Katerini).

Litohoro's train station, 9km away, gets 10 daily trains on the Athens-Volos-Thessaloniki train line.

MT OLYMPUS
ΟΛΥΜΠΟΣ ΟΡΟΣ

Just as it did for the ancients, the cloud-covered lair of the Ancient Greek pantheon, awe-inspiring Mt Olympus, fires the visitor's imagination today. Greece's highest mountain, Olympus also hosts around 1700 plant species, some rare and endemic. Its slopes are covered with thick forests of numerous different deciduous trees, conifers and pines. Olympus became Greece's first national park in 1937.

Although it's possible to drive up Olympus, most people come for the hike; consult the Litohoro-based hiking associations (p180) for maps and current conditions.

EPIROS ΗΠΕΙΡΟΣ
IOANNINA ΙΩΑΝΝΙΝΑ
pop 61,629

The Epirot capital and gateway to the Vikos-Aoös National Park, hip Ioannina (ih-o-*ah*-nih-nah or *yah*-nih-nah) is a bustling commercial and cultural centre, and to 20,000 university students who energise the local nightlife. Ioannina is set on the placid (though polluted) Lake Pamvotis and faces sheer mountains. This idyllic setting is further enhanced by an evocative old quarter (the Kastro),

GEORGE TSAFOS

Kastro ruins, Ioannina

interspersed with narrow lanes and architectural wonders from Byzantine and Ottoman times. The city also has excellent restaurants, bars and cafes.

ORIENTATION

Ioannina is large, though walkable; parking, however, is tough. There's a municipal car park (€2) off the main square, Plateia Pyrrou. Ioannina's new bus station is on Georgiou Papandreou, a five-minute walk to the old town (the Kastro), where the majority of Ioannina's historic sites are located. Though essentially residential, the Kastro has Ioannina's most atmospheric accommodation choices. The airport is 5km northwest of town.

INFORMATION

Plateia Pyrrou and Averof's southern end host the major banks/ATMs.

EOS (Greek Alpine Club; ☎ 26510 22138; Despotatou Ipirou 2; ☼ 7-9pm Mon-Fri)

EOT (☎ 26510 41142; fax 26510 49139; Dodonis 39; ☼ 7.30am-2.30pm Mon-Fri) Provides general information and hiking updates for the Zagorohoria and Vikos Gorge.

Post office Georgiou Papandreou (Georgiou Papandreou); Octovriou (28 Oktovriou 3)

Tourist police (☎ 26510 65938; 28 Oktovriou 11)

University Hospital (☎ 26510 99111) Eight kilometres south, inside the university campus.

SIGHTS

The Kastro's sublime **Its Kale** (Inner Citadel; ☼ 8am-5pm & 8-10pm Tue-Sun) rises from a long bluff overlooking lake and mountain. The relaxing Its Kale contains the **Tomb of Ali Pasha** and the restored **Fetiye Cami** (Victory Mosque), originally built in 1611 to reassert Ottoman dominance following a failed Greek uprising that caused Christians to be expelled from the citadel.

The adjacent **Byzantine Museum** (☎ 26510 25989; Its Kale; admission €3; ☼ 8am-5pm Tue-Sun), housed in two nearby buildings (including Ali Pasha's former palace), presents early Christian and Byzantine art,

Shepherd, Zagorohoria region (p190)

pottery, coins and silverware, and even post-Byzantine icons and manuscripts.

The **Municipal Ethnographic Museum** (☎ 26510 26356; adult/student €3/1.50; ⌚ 8am-8pm) is at the Kastro's northern end in the Aslan Pasha Mosque (1619). Local costumes and period photographs are displayed, as are tapestries and prayer shawls from the **synagogue** (Ioustinianou 16) of Ioannina's once significant Jewish community.

ACTIVITIES

The relaxing, one-hour **lake cruise** (☎ 6944470280; tickets €5; ⌚ 10am-midnight Mon-Sun summer, Sat & Sun winter) departs from near the Island ferry quay. Since swimming is not advisable, this is the only way to experience the lake.

Serious hikers should first get the map Anavasi Mountain Editions; *Pindus-Zagori* 1:50,000, available for €8 from local *periptera* (street kiosks), and then get apprised with current conditions at the EOT or EOS (see p187).

SLEEPING

Most Ioannina hotels are near the noisy central *plateia;* for tranquillity and atmosphere, stay inside the Kastro.

Filyra (☎ 26510 83560, 6932601240; Andronikou Paleologou 18; s/d €45/55) This flower-bedecked boutique hotel inside the Kastro has five spacious self-catering suites on a quiet side street, and friendly and helpful owners.

ourpick **Dafni Traditional Hotel** (☎ 26510 83560, 6932601240; Ioustinianou 12; s/d €45/65) This remarkable new yet traditional guest house is actually built into the inside of the Kastro's enormous outer walls. Rooms combine traditional and modern amenities, and there's one grand, well-decorated family room (€90). Reception is at the Filyra.

Hotel Kastro (☎ 26510 22866; Andronikou Paleologou 57; s/d €75/90; Ⓟ) This restored Kastro mansion overlooking Its Kale has a great atmosphere: antique brass beds, stained-glass windows and a tranquil courtyard create a feeling of romantic seclusion. Service is friendly and prompt.

EATING

Most of Ioannina's best places only open for dinner.

Stoa Louli (☎ 26510 71322; Anexartisias 78; mains €7-12) This tastefully lit place, fronted by grand arches, serves an alluring range of Greek favourites with contemporary twists.

Es Aei (☎ 26510 34571; Koundouriotou 50; mains €8-12) This favourite haunt of local and foreign gastronomes combines an Ottoman flair with a unique, glass-roofed courtyard dining room. Its inventive dishes include mezedhes made from organic ingredients and Ioannina specials including grilled pork sausages.

SHOPPING

Ioannina has been known for its silverwork since the 17th century; the **Center of Traditional Handcraft of Ioannina** (☎ 26510 45221; www.kepavi.gr; Arhiepiskopou Makariou 1; ⏰ 9.30am-2.30pm & 5.30-8.30pm), near the lake, brings together scores of artisans, whom you can watch as they work.

GETTING THERE & AWAY

Olympic Air (☎ 26510 26518; www.olympic airlines.com; Kendriki Plateia) has two daily Athens flights (€99). **Aegean Airlines** (☎ 26510 64444; www.aegeanair. com; Pyrsinella 11) has one Athens flight daily (€65).

From Ioannina's **bus station** (☎ 26510 26286; Georgiou Papandreou), buses serve Athens (€35.20, 6½ hours, nine daily)

and Thessaloniki (€28.50, 4¾ hours, six daily).

GETTING AROUND

Ioannina airport is 5km northwest on the Perama road; take Bus 7 (every 20 minutes, from the clock tower).

Taxis (☎ 26510 46777) wait near Plateia Pyrrou and the lake.

AROUND IOANNINA

THE ISLAND ΤΟ ΝΗΣΙ

Ioannina's closest getaway, the Island (To Nisi), lies just opposite in Lake Pamvotis. The Island's whitewashed village, built in the 17th century by refugees from Peloponnesian Mani, has around 300 permanent residents (among them four school kids). Several important monasteries decorated with very unusual frescoes are found here, plus a couple of good fish tavernas.

To reach the Island, head to Ioannina's ferry dock, below the Kastro. In summer,

GEORGE TSAFOS

The Island, Lake Pamvotis

the boat goes every 15 minutes, in winter, only hourly.

DODONI ΔΩΔΩΝΗ

The colossal, 3rd-century-BC **Theatre of Dodoni** (☎ 26510 82287; adult €2; ☼ 8am-5pm), 21km southwest of Ioannina, is Epiros' most important ancient site. An earth goddess had been worshipped at this valley spot from around 2000 BC. The oracle she spoke through was reputedly Greece's oldest, and the one most venerated (before the Delphic oracle took precedence in the 6th century BC). By the 13th century BC, Zeus was speaking through the rustling of leaves from a sacred oak tree to worshippers at the site. Around 500 BC a temple was built in his honour, though today only its foundations and a few columns remain. Under King Pyrrhus a theatre was erected. Now restored, the Theatre of Dodoni hosts Ioannina's **Festival of Ancient Drama** in July.

Buses from Ioannina leave at 6.30am and 4.30pm daily, except for Thursday and Sunday, returning at 7.30am and 5.30pm. One other bus, on Sunday, leaves at 6pm and returns at 6.45pm.

A taxi from Ioannina costs around €35 return plus €3 per hour for waiting.

THE ZAGOROHORIA
ΤΑ ΖΑΓΟΡΟΧΩΡΙΑ

A cluster of 46 providentially preserved mountain hamlets, the Zagorohoria takes its name from an old Slavonic term, *za Gora* (behind the mountain), and the Greek word for villages (*horia*). Tucked into the Pindos range, these villages conceal inexhaustible local legends and boast marvellous houses, ranging from humble cottages of stone and slate to grand, fortified mansions made of the same hardy materials. The Zagorohoria's literal and figurative centrepiece, the Vikos-Aoös National Park, bursts with pristine rivers and forests, flowering meadows, and shimmering lakes reflecting jagged mountains and endless blue sky.

VIKOS GORGE
ΧΑΡΑΔΡΑ ΤΟΥ ΒΙΚΟΥ

Bisecting the Zagorohoria is the 12km-long, 900m-deep Vikos Gorge; according to the *Guinness Book of World Records*, it is the world's deepest, though gorge lobbyists elsewhere contest the claim. In either case, Vikos is a truly awe-inspiring work of nature.

The gorge begins near Monodendri (1090m) in the south and runs north until the Papingo villages. You can start from either end, but if you want to return to where you started, you'll have to arrange transport back via the long road route.

The Ioannina **EOT office** (☎ 26510 41142; fax 26510 49139; Dodonis 39, Ioannina; ☼ 7.30am-2.30pm Mon-Fri) advises on current weather conditions and provides maps and other information (see also p187). You'll need water, stout walking boots and some endurance; the hike takes around 6½ hours.

Starting from Monodendri, walk to the 15th-century **Agia Paraskevi Monastery** for a spectacular view over the gorge. You can descend here, on a steep, marked path. From there, it's a four-hour walk to the end, from where a right-hand trail leads to Mikro Papingo (2½ hours). The larger Megalo Papingo is a further 2km west, but the track splits into two at the base of the climb. The **Klima Spring**, about halfway along the gorge, is the only water source.

ACTIVITIES

In Kato Pedina, the new, full-service **Compass Adventures** (☎ 26530 71770; 6978845232; info@ compass adventures.gr; Kato Pedina) organises

PANOS KARAPANAGIOTIS/SHUTTERSTOCK

Mosaic flooring, Pella

↘ IF YOU LIKE...

If you like exploring the ruins of **Dodoni** (p190), we think you'd like delving into these ancient ruins, too:

- **Ancient Dion** (Dion Archaeological Park; adult/student €6/2; ☾ 8am-8pm) Just north of Mt Olympus, this was where ancient Macedonians worshiped the Olympian gods. Watch for the **Sanctuary to Isis** where votive statues were found virtually intact and are now housed in the Dion's museum.

- **Vergina** (☎ 23310 92347; adult €8; ☾ noon-7.30pm Mon, 8am-7.30pm Tue-Sun summer, 8.30am-3pm winter) The legendary burial site of the Macedonian kings (and their first capital), this World Heritage–listed site is also called the **Royal Tombs**. In 336 BC, at the wedding of his daughter Cleopatra, Philip II was assassinated here and it's believed that one of the tombs is his. There are also ruins of an extensive **palatial complex**.

- **Nekromanteio of Afyra** (☎ 26840 41206; adult €2; ☾ 8.30am-3pm) Feared by the ancients as the gate of Hades, god of the underworld, these labyrinthine ruins lay at the end of a beautiful boat ride down the coast and up the Aherondas River. The ruins were only discovered in 1958, along with the ruined monastery of **Agios Ioannis Prodromos** and a **graveyard**. The eerie underground vault is probably the place into which confused ancient visitors were lowered by windlass, thinking that they were entering the realm of Hades itself.

- **Pella** (☎ 23820 31160; admission €6; ☾ 8am-7.30pm Tue-Sun, noon-7.30pm Mon) The birthplace of Alexander the Great, these ruins feature spectacular mosaics. Created with naturally coloured, subtly contrasting stones, the mosaics depict mythological scenes. They were created for ancient houses and public buildings now destroyed. Check out the **museum** (☾ 8am-7.30pm) for more mosaics.

EMMANOUIL MICHELAKIS/ISTOCK

Macedonia's Prespa Lakes

↘ IF YOU LIKE...

If you like stretching your legs in the gorgeous **Vikos Gorge** (p190), we think
you'll like these awe-inspiring outdoor experiences, too:

- **Prespa Lakes** Macedonia's magical, mountainous northwest corner holds
  the lakes **Megali Prespa** and **Mikri Prespa**. In the absence of foreign tourists, Prespes has retained its tranquil natural beauty, and boasts lovely
  traditional stone-house villages and significant Byzantine antiquities. The
  drive from Florina passes through thick forests with sweeping mountain
  views and the occasional bear-crossing sign.

- **Metsovo** East of the Zagorohoria region, this idyllic town clings to a mountainside at 1156m. The fresh mountain air and majestic setting are undeniably appealing, and the range of all-season outdoor activities is sure to keep
  the blood flowing. Metsovo's **ski centre** (☎ 26560 41211; ☽ 9.30am-3.45pm) has
  two downhill runs and a 5km cross-country run.

- **Perama Cave** (☎ 26510 81521; www.spilaio-perama.gr; adult/student €6/3; ☽ 8am-8pm)
  Just beyond Ioannina, this is one of Greece's largest and most impressive
  caves, loaded with white stalactites. Locals hiding from the Nazis discovered
  it in 1940. The enormous 1100m-long cave has three storeys of chambers
  and passageways. There's an hour-long tour.

- **Vikos-Aoös National Park** The Zagorohoria's centrepiece bursts with pristine rivers and forests, flowering meadows, and shimmering lakes reflecting
  jagged mountains and endless blue sky. Almost one-third of Greece's flora
  (some endemic) lives here, along with endemic foxes and chamois, rare
  hawks, river otters and brown bears. You'll also see the ear-popping Pindos
  Mountains and possibly seminomadic Vlach and Sarakatsani shepherds.

hiking, skiing and mountain-biking forays into the Pindos Mountains. In winter, Compass operates a ski school and trips for off-piste skiing on virgin terrain.

SLEEPING

Arhontiko Zarkada (☎ 26530 71305; www.monodendri.com; Monodendri; s/d €40/60) These clean, snug rooms have balconies with gorge views. Some rooms have spa baths for nursing bruised hikers back to health.

Xenonas Mikro Papingo 1700 (☎ 26530 41179; Mikro Papingo; s/d €45/60) The 1700 has five handsomely appointed rooms. It's a lovely choice with real character.

our pick Arhontiko Dilofo (☎ 26530 22455, 6978417715; www.dilofo.com; Dilofo; d incl breakfast from €65) One of the most wonderful guest houses in all of Zagorohoria, this 475-year-old restored mansion in placid Dilofo is ideal for anyone seeking total peace and natural harmony. Greek, English, German and Italian are spoken here.

GETTING THERE & AWAY

From Ioannina, buses serve Dilofo (€3.50) and Mikro Papingo (€4.90, two hours, 5am and 3pm Monday, Wednesday and Friday, with the Wednesday bus hitting Vikos in summer) and Monodendri (€3.10, one hour, 6am and 3pm Monday, Wednesday and Friday). All buses return to Ioannina immediately. On weekends, take a taxi: Ioannina-Monodendri fares are approximately €30 to €45, though you can negotiate.

PARGA ΠΑΡΓΑ

pop 2432

The microresort of Parga is essentially a pretty old village of white-plastered houses stacked on winding, flowery streets, in the fold of a bay crowned by a Venetian castle.

Long sandy beaches stretch out on both sides of town, and in high season its waterfront bars get busy with Greeks, Italians and other foreigners.

A former Venetian possession, Parga resembles the similarly Italian-influenced Ionian Islands opposite, and indeed makes a good base for excursions to two of them, Paxi and Antipaxi, along with the mysterious Nekromanteio of Afyra. With its good outlying beaches and even a nice one right in town, Parga is also good for families with small kids.

INFORMATION

Several ATM-equipped banks are available, along with a small medical centre.

Dr Spiros Radiotis (☎ 26840 32450; 6944162261; Alexandrou Baga 1) On call 24 hours a day for medical emergencies; his office is beside Emporiki Trapeza.

International Travel Services (ITS; ☎ 26840 31833; www.parga.net; Spyrou Livada 4) This very experienced and helpful starting point at the village entrance can find accommodation, book local tours, arrange travel tickets and provide general information.

Police (☎ 26840 31222; Alexandrou Baga 18) The tourist police are located here too.

Post office (Alexandrou Baga 18)

ACTIVITIES

Visits to the Nekromanteio of Afyra (€42), cruises on the Aherondas River (€25), day trips to Albania or Paxi and Antipaxi (€20) are available from ITS (p193), the helpful travel agency across from the bus stop. ITS can inform you about local hill walks and even organise a one-day beginner's dive course for €35.

SLEEPING

Hotel Paradise (☎ 26840 31229; Spyrou Livada 23; s/d €50/65; ✗ ▢ ▣) The friendly, central

Panoramic view over Parga

PAUL DRABOT/SHUTTERSTOCK

Hotel Paradise has a lovely courtyard pool and downstairs bar. Rooms are airy and clean, with all the mod cons.

ourpick **Acropol** (☎ 26840 31239; www.par gatravel.com; Agion Apostolon 4; s/d €60/90; ⚡) The 10 luxurious rooms have king-sized beds, hydromassage showers and hand-made Italian furniture.

Utopia Studios (☎ 26840 31133; www .utopia.com.gr; Agiou Athanasiou; d/tr €60/100; ⚘ May-Oct; ⚡ ⚐) These five spacious, sea-view apartments give the relaxing sense of being in a real house. The wood furnishings have an understated elegance, and the balconies are large and relaxing.

EATING

Taverna to Souli (☎ 26840 31658; Anexartisias 45; mezedhes €4-6, mains €6-9) This relaxing place does great mezedhes, with a focus on local treats such as *feta Souli* (grilled feta cheese with tomatoes and herbs). Try the *kleftiko* (oven-baked lamb or goat) for a filling main course.

ourpick **O Arkoudas** (☎ 26840 32553; Grigoriou Lambraki; fish €6-9) Down on the waterfront strip, 'The Bear', as it's called in Greek, is a friendly place that serves up a tasty variety of fresh fish dishes.

GETTING THERE & AWAY

From the **bus station** (☎ 26840 31218) buses serve Igoumenitsa (€5.20, one hour, five daily), Thessaloniki (€39, seven hours, one daily) and Athens (€35.30, seven hours, three daily).

Water taxis go to Voltos Beach (€4, from 9.30am to 6pm), Lihnos Beach (€7, from 11am to 5pm) and Sarakiniko (€8, from 10am).

↘CYCLADES, EVIA
& THE SPORADES

CRAIG PERSHOUSE

Stone path leading from Fira (p220) to the old port, Santorini

CYCLADES, EVIA & THE SPORADES

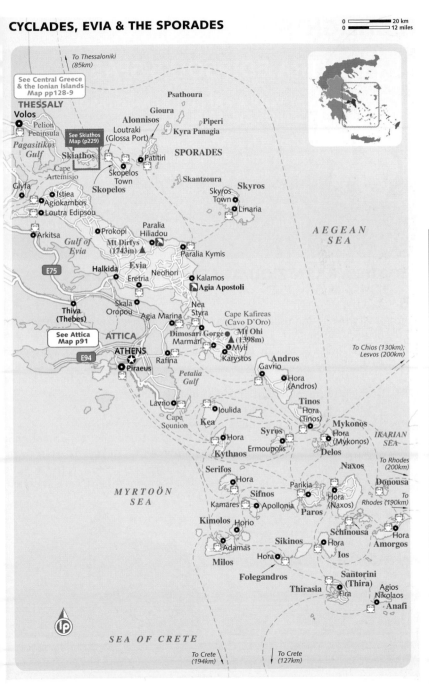

0 ⊨ 20 km
0 ⊨ 12 miles

To Thessaloniki
(85km)

See Central Greece
& the Ionian Islands
Map pp128-9

THESSALY
Volos
Pelion
Peninsula

*Pagasitikos
Gulf*

See Skiathos
Map (p229)

Skiathos

Cape
Artemisio

Glyfa

Istiea
Agiokambos
Loutra Edipsou

Arkitsa

*Gulf of
Evia*

Prokopi

Paralia
Hiliadou

Mt Dirfys
(1743m)

Halkida

Evia
Neohori

Eretria

E75

Thiva
(Thebes)

Skala
Oropou

ATTICA

See Attica
Map p91

E94

ATHENS
Piraeus

Rafina

*Petalia
Gulf*

Lavrio

Cape
Sounion

Kea

Ioulida

Hora

Kythnos

Serifos
Hora

Sifnos
Kamares
Apollonia

Kimolos
Horio

Adamas

Milos

Folegandros

Psathoura

Gioura

Alonnisos
Loutraki
(Glossa Port)

Patitiri

Piperi
Kyra Panagia

SPORADES

Skopelos
Town

Skopelos

Skantzoura

Paralia Kymis

Kalamos

Agia Apostoli

Nea
Styra

Agia Marina

Dimosari Gorge
Marmari

Mt Ohi
(1398m)

Myli

Karystos

Cape Kafireas
(Cavo D'Oro)

Skyros

Skyros
Town

Linaria

*AEGEAN
SEA*

Andros
Gavrio

Hora
(Andros)

Tinos
Hora
(Tinos)

Mykonos
Hora
(Mykonos)

Delos

Syros
Ermoupolis

Parikia

Paros

Naxos
Hora
(Naxos)

Hora

Sikinos

Hora

Ios

Schinousa
Hora

Amorgos
Hora

Donousa

Santorini
(Thira)
Fira

Thirasia

Agios
Nikolaos

Anafi

*IKARIAN
SEA*

To Chios (130km);
Lesvos (200km)

To Rhodes
(200km)

To
Rhodes (190km)

*MYRTOÖN
SEA*

SEA OF CRETE

To Crete
(194km)

To Crete
(127km)

LP

HIGHLIGHTS

1 LOUTRA EDIPSOU'S SPAS

BY VOULA KARATZIOU-ANASTASOPOULOU, SENIOR SPA EMPLOYEE

Edipsos is a famous *loutropolis* (spa town), two hours from Athens. Built above the sea, the spa town draws visitors from all over the world. Its thermal waters have been known since the Aristotle era for its therapeutic and rejuvenating qualities which treat and relax the whole body.

↘ VOULA KARATZIOU-ANASTASOPOULOU'S DON'T MISS LIST

❶ FANGO THERAPY

Brought from Italy and used in Loutra Edipsou since the Roman era, this relaxing therapy covers your body in mud made with thermal water to cleanse, detoxify, nourish and soothe your skin. It's also helpful for musculoskeletal pain and arthritis. Some spas slap it on; others let you sink into a mud bath.

❷ GRAPE FACIAL

Grapes have been grown in Greece since ancient times. A facial treatment made from local grapes and thermal water will cleanse, moisturise and tighten your skin. It's great for all skin types, especially faces that have been exposed to too much sun. It's anti-aging and will give you the feeling of instant lightness.

❸ RASUL TREATMENT

This is a traditional treatment that originated in Turkey. To start with, your body is covered in therapeutic clay. The room is then filled with steam,

Clockwise from top: Coastal view, Loutra Edipsou (p225); Therapeutic spa waters; (left & right) Thermae Sylla Hotel & Spa (p226)

which both relaxes you and helps the clay absorb toxins from your skin. And finally? A shower of therapeutic water to wash it all away. The overall result is a unique sense of cleanliness and renewal. It's exfoliating, hydrating and calming.

❹ STEAM BATH

Hippocrates first made steam baths popular when he found that they could simulate fever which could, in turn, cure many diseases. Steam baths are known for helping with respiratory problems, but they're also great for detoxifying your skin to leave you with a healthy glow. Steam baths that use aromatherapy are particularly relaxing.

❺ THERAPEUTIC BEACH TIME

What better way to experience Loutra Edipsou's therapeutic water than by taking a dip in the sea? The town lies next to magnificent beaches where the sparkling clean water is enriched by the thermal waters that pour into the sea. Combine hydrotherapy with a little beach time.

↘ THINGS YOU NEED TO KNOW

Best season to visit Spring and winter **Best time for treatment** Morning **Enhance your visit** See a local doctor to determine appropriate therapies **Only an hour?** Body peel, rasul treatment and therapeutic bath **See our author's review on p225**

HIGHLIGHTS

⬇ STUNNING SANTORINI

Prepare yourself for the beauty of **Santorini** (Thira; p219). Explore ancient houses dug into the volcanic rock, neoclassical mansions and the ruins of Ancient Thira. Hop on an 18th-century schooner across the caldera or on a water taxi to nearby active volcanic islets. And then sit back and enjoy the spectacular sunset views from the capital, perched on the caldera cliffs.

⬇ ANCIENT DELOS

Set foot on this small island at the centre of the Cyclades and you know you're somewhere special. **Ancient Delos** (p212) has had sacred status since it was determined to be the birthplace of the twins of Apollo and Artemis. Inhabited since the 3rd millennium BC, with ruins dating back to the 8th century BC, its sanctuaries, shrines, and theatres never fail to impress.

⬎ TAKING THE PLUNGE

Skiathos (p228) is blessed with a string of off-shore islets and clear water that makes the destination ideal for diving. Take your first dive or join deep dives for experts and explore colourful reefs and sunken ships. There's skin-diving, night-diving or, if you're not up for such a large plunge, you can snorkel over reef beds.

⬎ MYKONOS AFTER DARK

Glamorous **Mykonos** (p206) has a sparkling nightlife. Dubbed 'Little Venice', its bars and clubs are clustered along the water and in the old town's maze of alleyways. Sipping cocktails with a view of the sun sinking into the Aegean Sea is blissful – as is dancing the night away among a lively crowd of tourists, celebrities, cruise-ship crowds and locals.

⬎ CHARMING KARYSTOS

Little **Karystos** (p226) is nearly neighbours with Athens, but it continues to cultivate a feeling of remoteness. It's flanked by two sandy beaches, throws a wine and culture festival each summer and is the gateway for gorgeous walks through the Dimosari Gorge and climbs up Mt Ohi to 7th-century ruins. Let's keep it our little secret.

2 IZZET KERIBAR; 3 JOHN ELK III; 4 MILOS JOKIC/SHUTTERSTOCK; 5 KATJA KREDER/IMAGEBROKER; 6 TTL IMAGES/ALAMY

2 Local architecture, Santorini (p219); 3 Terrace of the Lions (p214), Ancient Delos; 4 Skiathos (p228); 5 Revellers, Mykonos (p206); 6 Castle ruins, Karystos (p226)

THE BEST...

⟴ BEACHES

- **Agios Stefanos** (p212) A popular Mykonos stretch of sand.
- **Agios Georgios** (p218) Naxos' sandy beach with shallow water; ideal for families.
- **Perivolos & Agios Georgios** (p224) Santorini's most relaxed black-sand beaches.
- **Agia Anna** (p218) A stretch of glistening white sand.
- **Koukounaries Beach** (p232) A pale sweep of golden sand that's touted as the best in Greece.

⟴ PLUSH SLEEPS

- **Atrium Hotel** (p232) Opt for a room with your own spa in these ultra-luxurious rooms over the water.
- **Aroma Suites** (p221) Charming boutique hotel on the caldera's edge.
- **Hotel Belvedere** (p210) Contemporary decor, music, movies and massage therapy.
- **Chelidonia** (p222) Traditional cliffside dwelling turned lavish.

⟴ DRINKING VENUES

- **La Scarpa** (p211) Enjoy great cocktails with sunset views.
- **Vallindras Distillery** (p218) Try local *kitron* and tour an atmospheric, traditional distillery.
- **Tropical** (p222) Sip wine amidst trendy tunes and unbeatable caldera vistas.

⟴ CHEAP EATS

- **Piccolo** (p211) Sandwiches loaded with Mykonian prosciutto and *manouri* (soft cheese).
- **Meze 2** (p216) Dine on fresh seafood with local fisherman.
- **Taverna Liofago** (p218) Beachside meals with unique Naxian flavours.
- **Mylos Café** (p221) Snacks in a converted windmill next to the caldera.
- **Cavo D'oro** (p227) Where locals dine on pasta with goat and homemade *mousakas*.

MAURITIUS IMAGES GMBH/ALAMY

Seaside lounges, Agios Stefanos (p212), Mykonos

THINGS YOU NEED TO KNOW

❯ VITAL STATISTICS

- **Population** Cyclades 109,814; Evia & the Sporades 228,750
- **Area** Cyclades 2429 sq km; Evia & the Sporades 4167 sq km

❯ LOCALITIES IN A NUTSHELL

- **Mykonos** (p206) An energetic nightlife and atmospheric old town in this fashion-conscious island.
- **Delos** (p212) Sacred, uninhabited island at the centre of the Cyclades.
- **Naxos** (p215) Green, mountainous interior, traditional villages and quiet beaches.
- **Santorini** (Thira; p219) Beautiful volcanic island with black-sand beaches.
- **Evia** (p225) A stone's throw from the mainland with hiking, natural spas and calm beaches.
- **Skiathos** (p228) Popular for its beaches and as the setting for the film *Mamma Mia*.

❯ ADVANCE PLANNING

- **Two months before** Check ferry schedules and book accommodation, especially for Mykonos, Santorini and Skiathos.
- **One month before** Check online for local events and prebook tickets.

❯ RESOURCES

- **www.mykonos-accommodation.com** Places to stay plus details on beaches.
- **www.santorini.com** History, listings, flights and ferries.
- **www.evia-greece.co.uk** Sights, accommodation and lots of links.
- **www.skiathos.gr** Listings, accommodation and general island info.

❯ EMERGENCY NUMBERS

- **Police** (☎ 100)
- **Ambulance** (☎ 166)

❯ GETTING AROUND

- **Bus** Routes across Evia and Mykonos, with less-frequent runs on Santorini and Naxos.
- **Ferry** Hop from the mainland and between the islands. For specific island services, see Island Hopping (p357).
- **Flights** From Athens to Santorini, Mykonos, Naxos and Skiathos.
- **Car** A great way to explore the larger islands.

❯ BE FOREWARNED

- **Transport** The Cyclades often experience fierce winds that can play havoc with ferry schedules.
- **Ancient Delos** The site (and therefore the island) is closed on Mondays.

ITINERARIES

SCENIC WONDERS Three Days

Revered for its surreal landscape, Santorini will mesmerise and enchant you. Stay in a guest house in **(1) Fira** (p220) with a breathtaking view over the multi-coloured cliffs and take your meals and cocktails perched on the edge of the caldera. Then sail across it on a boat trip. Spend a day on the black-sand beaches like **(2) Perivolos** (p224), located on the eastern side of the island. Stop in at **(3) Ancient Thira** (p224), the site of 9th-century-BC ruins with stunning views, then head for the pretty village of **(4) Oia** (p222) for a spectacular sunset. On your final day, take a day trip to the uninhabited **(5) volcanic islets** (p225) of Palia Kameni and Nea Kameni for hot springs and a close encounter with an active volcano.

ISLAND HOPPING Five Days

You come to Naxos for lots of reasons – the beaches, the mountains and the sights – but you also come for the fresh olives, figs and grapes. Fill your belly with the island's bounty as you explore **(1) Hora** (Naxos; p215), with its atmospheric Venetian Kastro. Dine on the freshest of seafood and then take in an evening concert at the Della Rocca-Barozzi Venetian Museum, a 13th-century tower. Spend the next day on the sandy beaches that trim much of the island's coast. Try **(2) Agia Anna** (p218) for a quiet stretch of white sand. The fit can spend the next day heading up **(3) Mt Zeus** (p218) or else visit **(4) Halki** (p218), a historic village at the heart of the island's mountainous interior where a distillery cranks out traditional *kitron*. From Naxos, catch a fast ferry to Mykonos, the glamour puss of the Cyclades. Explore **(5) Hora** (p207), the island's charming capital, letting yourself get lost in the boutiques and cafes of Little Venice and joining in the revelry of the island's infamous nightlife. On the last day, hop on a day trip to fascinating **(6) Delos** (p212), one of Greece's most important archaeological sights, before returning to Mykonos for one last sunset cocktail.

PAMPER YOURSELF One Week

Spend a couple of days on fashionable (1) Mykonos (p206), immersing yourself in the capital's atmospheric Little Venice, getting your fill of boutique shops, cafes, excellent restaurants and a nightlife that sparkles. Head for the beaches for an extra dose of relaxation and then hop on a ferry to Marmari via Rafina on the mainland. Once there, head south to nearby (2) Karystos (p226), a lovely town set on a wide bay below Mt Ohi. Relax on the two sandy beaches and replenish your soul and palate at the summer Wine & Cultural Festival. Next, make a beeline for the spa resort of (3) Loutra Edipsou (p225) to soak in the therapeutic sulphur waters. Treat yourself to a massage treatment at

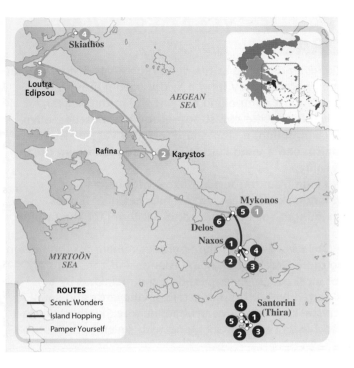

one of the local spas before hoping on a ferry from Agiokambos to
(4) Skiathos (p228) via Glyfa on the mainland. Relive the scenes from
Mamma Mia as you visit the island's film locations – this will involve
taking in some of the Aegean's most beautiful beaches. Join an excursion for a boat trip around the island or head to a diving school to
explore the deep blue.

DISCOVER THE CYCLADES, EVIA & THE SPORADES

The Cyclades (kih-*klah*-dhez) lie at the deep blue heart of the Aegean and are so named because they form a *kyklos* (circle) around the island of Delos, the most compelling ancient site in the Aegean. It's here that you'll find white cubist houses, golden beaches, olive groves, herb-strewn mountain slopes and terraced valleys. Throw in a dash of hedonism and a vivid culture, and the Greek island dream can become a reality.

The Cyclades range from big fertile Naxos, with its craggy mountains and landlocked valleys, to the beaches of Mykonos awash with sun-lounger society, and iconic Santorini for the fashion conscious.

North of the Cyclades, Evia and the Sporades remain off the beaten path, attracting more Greeks than many islands and consequently retaining lots of local colour. Evia, joined to the mainland by a drawbridge, is dotted by hilltop monasteries, vineyards and small beaches with crystal-clear bays. Meanwhile, nearby Skiathos claims the sandiest beaches in the Aegean, along with several prime scuba-diving spots.

CYCLADES
ΚΥΚΛΑΔΕΣ

MYKONOS ΜΥΚΟΝΟΣ
pop 9660

Mykonos is the great glamour island of the Cyclades and it happily flaunts its camp and fashionable reputation with style. Beneath the gloss and glitter, however, this is a charming and hugely entertaining place where the sometimes frantic mix of good-time holidaymakers, cruise-ship crowds, posturing fashionistas and preening celebrities is magically subdued by the cubist charms of Mykonos town (Hora), a traditional Cycladic maze.

GETTING THERE & AWAY

Mykonos is well served by air connections to Athens, Thessaloniki and Santorini. There are also direct easyJet flights to London from about May to mid September.

With Mykonos being such a major tourist destination, ferry connections to the mainland ports of Piraeus and Rafina are very good, as are connections to neighbouring islands.

GETTING AROUND
TO/FROM THE AIRPORT

Buses from the southern bus station serve Mykonos' airport (€1.40), which is 3km southeast of the town centre. Make sure you arrange an airport transfer with your accommodation (expect to pay around €6) or take a **taxi** (☎ 22890 22400, airport 22890 23700).

BOAT

Caïque (little boat) services leave Hora (Mykonos) for Super Paradise, Agrari and Elia Beaches (June to September only) and from Platys Gialos to Paradise (€7), Super Paradise (€8), Agrari (€7) and Elia Beaches (€7).

BUS

The Mykonos bus network (☎ 22890 26797; www.ktelmykonos.gr) has two main bus stations and a pick-up point at the New Port. The **northern bus station** (Remezzo) is behind the OTE office and has frequent departures to Agios Stefanos via Tourlos (€1.40), and services to Kalafatis Beach (€1.90). The **southern bus station** (Fabrika Sq [Plateia Yialos]) serves Agios Ioannis Beach (€1.40), Ornos, (€1.40), Platys Gialos (€1.40) and Paradise Beach (€1.40).

Bus tickets are sold at machines, street kiosks, minimarkets and tourist shops. You must buy a ticket before boarding (buy return tickets if required), validate the ticket on the bus and hang on to it.

TAXI

If you're after a **taxi** (☎ 22400 23700/22400), you'll find them at Hora's Taxi Sq (Plateia Manto Mavrogenous) and by the bus stations and ports.

HORA (MYKONOS)
ΧΩΡΑ (ΜΥΚΟΝΟΣ)
pop 6467

Hora (also known as Mykonos), the island's port and capital, is a warren of narrow alleyways that wriggle between white-walled buildings, their stone surfaces webbed with white paint. In the heart of the Little Venice area (Venetia), tiny flower-bedecked churches jostle with trendy boutiques, and there's a deluge of bougainvillea around every corner. For quick-fix navigation, familiarise yourself with main junctions and the three main streets of Matogianni, Enoplon Dynameon and Mitropoleos, which form a horseshoe behind the waterfront. The streets are crowded with chic fashion salons, cool galleries, jangling jewellers, languid and loud music bars, brightly painted houses and torrents of crimson flowers – plus a catwalk cast of thousands.

DIANA MAYFIELD

Windmills backdrop, Hora (Mykonos)

ORIENTATION

The town proper is about 400m to the south of the Old Port ferry quay, beyond the tiny town beach. A busy square, Plateia Manto Mavrogenous (usually called Taxi Sq), is 100m beyond the beach and on the edge of Hora. East of Taxi Sq, the busy waterfront leads towards the Little Venice neighbourhood and the town's iconic hill-top row of windmills. South of Taxi Sq and the waterfront, the busy streets of Matogianni, Zouganelli and Mavrogenous lead into the heart of Hora.

The northern bus station is 200m south of the Old Port ferry quay, on the way into town. The southern bus station is on Fabrika Sq, on the southern edge of town. The quay from where boats leave for Delos is at the western end of the waterfront.

INFORMATION

EMERGENCY

Police station (☎ 22890 22716) On the road to the airport.
Port police (☎ 22890 22218; Akti Kambani) Midway along the waterfront.
Tourist police (☎ 22890 22482) At the airport.

MEDICAL SERVICES

First Aid Clinic (☎ 22890 22274; Agiou Ioannou)
Hospital (☎ 22890 23994) The hospital is located about 1km along the road to Ano Mera.

MONEY

Several banks by the Old Port quay have ATMs. Eurobank has ATMs at Taxi Sq and Fabrika Sq.
Eurochange (☎ /fax 22890 27024; Plateia Manto Mavrogenous) Money exchange office in Taxi Sq.

POST

Post office (☎ 22890 22238; Laka) In the southern part of town.

TOURIST INFORMATION

Tourist Information Office (☎ 22890 25250; www.mykonos.gr; Plateia Karaoli Dimitriou; ⏰ 9am-9pm Jul & Aug, 10am-5pm Easter-Jun, Sep & Oct)

TRAVEL AGENCIES

Delia Travel (☎ 22890 22322; travel@delia .gr; Akti Kambani) Halfway along the inner waterfront. Sells ferry tickets and tickets for Delos.
Mykonos Accommodation Centre (☎ 22890 23408; www.mykonos-accommoda tion.com; 1st fl, Enoplon Dynameon 10) Well organised and very helpful for a range of information.
Sea & Sky (☎ 22890 22853; Akti Kambani) Information and ferry tickets.
Windmills Travel (☎ 22890 26555; www .windmillstravel.com; Xenias) By the southern bus station on Fabrika Sq, this is another helpful office for all types of information, including gay-related. Also sells ferry tickets.

SIGHTS

The **archaeological museum** (☎ 22890 22325; adult/concession €2/1; ⏰ 8.30am-3pm Tue-Sat, 10am-3pm Sun) houses pottery from Delos and some grave stelae and jewellery from the island of Renia (Delos' necropolis).

The **Aegean Maritime Museum** (☎ 22890 22700; Tria Pigadia; adult/concession €4/1.50; ⏰ 10.30am-1pm & 6.30-9pm Apr-Oct) has a fascinating collection of nautical paraphernalia, including ships' models.

Next door, **Lena's House** (☎ 22890 22390; Tria Pigadia; admission €2; ⏰ 6.30-9.30pm Mon-Sat, 7-9pm Sun Apr-Oct) is a charming late-19th-century, middle-class Mykonian

HORA (MYKONOS)

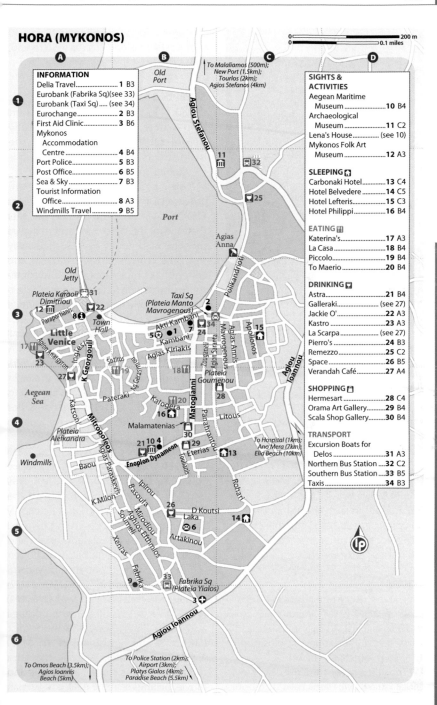

0   200 m
0   0.1 miles

INFORMATION
Delia Travel................................**1** B3
Eurobank (Fabrika Sq)........(see 33)
Eurobank (Taxi Sq) .....(see 34)
Eurochange..............................**2** B3
First Aid Clinic........................**3** B6
Mykonos
  Accommodation
  Centre....................................**4** B4
Port Police...............................**5** B3
Post Office...............................**6** B5
Sea & Sky.................................**7** B3
Tourist Information
  Office.....................................**8** A3
Windmills Travel.....................**9** B5

**SIGHTS &
ACTIVITIES**
Aegean Maritime
  Museum...............................**10** B4
Archaeological
  Museum...............................**11** C2
Lena's House................(see 10)
Mykonos Folk Art
  Museum...............................**12** A3

SLEEPING
Carbonaki Hotel.....................**13** C4
Hotel Belvedere **14** C5
Hotel Lefteris.........................**15** C3
Hotel Philippi........................**16** B4

EATING
Katerina's................................**17** A3
La Casa....................................**18** B4
Piccolo....................................**19** B4
To Maerio...............................**20** B4

DRINKING
Astra..**21** B4
Galleraki...........................(see 27)
Jackie O'..................................**22** A3
Kastro......................................**23** A3
La Scarpa.........................(see 27)
Pierro's...................................**24** B3
Remezzo..................................**25** C2
Space......................................**26** B5
Verandah Café........................**27** A4

SHOPPING
Hermesart...............................**28** C4
Orama Art Gallery..................**29** B4
Scala Shop Gallery.................**30** B4

TRANSPORT
Excursion Boats for
  Delos....................................**31** A3
Northern Bus Station.............**32** C2
Southern Bus Station **33** B5
Taxis.......................................**34** B3

Laneway eateries, Mykonos
SHANIA SHEGEDYN

house (with furnishings intact). It takes its name from its last owner, Lena Skrivanou.

The **Mykonos Folk Art Museum** (☎ 6932178330; Paraportianis; admission free; ⏲ 5.30-8.30pm Mon-Sat, 6.30-8.30pm Sun Apr-Oct), housed in an 18th-century sea captain's house, features a large collection of furnishings and other artefacts, including old musical instruments.

TOURS
Mykonos Accommodation Centre (MAC; ☎ 22890 23408; www.mykonos-accommodation.com; 1st fl, Enoplon Dynameon 10) Organises guided tours to Delos (return €15, 30 minutes; see p214).
Windmills Travel (☎ 22890 23877; www.windmillstravel.com; Plateia Yialos) The book-

ing agent for snorkelling (€25 for 30 minutes) and island cruises (€50 to €60, four weekly).

SLEEPING
If you plan to stay in Hora and want somewhere quiet, think carefully before settling for domatia on the main streets – bar noise until dawn is inevitable.

Hotel Lefteris (☎ 22890 27117; www.lefterishotel.gr; Apollonos 9; s/d €90/115, studios €190-240; 🗙) A colourful entranceway sets the tone for this welcoming international meeting place for all ages. Tucked away from the crowds, close to Taxi Sq, the Lefteris has simple but bright and comfy rooms, most with fans or air-con. There is a communal kitchen and the roof terrace is a great place to relax.

Hotel Philippi (☎ 22890 22294; chriko@otenet.gr; Kalogera 25; s/d €90/125; 🗙 🛜) A pleasant garden full of trees, flowers and shrubs makes this a good choice in the heart of Hora. There's an appealing ambience in the bright, clean rooms that open onto a railed veranda overlooking the garden.

ourpick Carbonaki Hotel (☎ 22890 24124/22461; www.carbonaki.gr; 23 Panahrantou St; s/d/tr/q €120/160/200/240; 🗙 🛜) This family-run boutique hotel, right on the edge of central Mykonos, has a delightful atmosphere and charming owners. Rooms are comfortable and bright and there are relaxing public balconies dotted round the pleasant central courtyards.

Hotel Belvedere (☎ 22890 25122; www.belvederehotel.com; Rohari; d €280-2000; 🅿 🗙 🖥 🛜 🗙) It's all billowing drapes and white linen amid the modernist landscape and furnishings of this leading Mykonos hotel. Jacuzzis, massage therapy, a fitness studio, and music and movie facilities seal the deal.

EATING

Piccolo (☎ 22890 22208; Drakopoulou 18; snacks €3.90-7.80) There are no linen-draped tables at this little food outlet, but the food is first class and ranges from crisp salads to a great selection of sandwich fillings that include Mykonian prosciutto, *manouri* (soft cheese), smoked local ham, smoked eel and crab.

La Casa (☎ 22890 24994; Matogianni 8; mains €9.90-18.90) The classic La Casa has a strong Greek basis with Italian, Arabic and Lebanese influences. Starters of smoked cheeses with mushrooms and inventive salads – including a Mykonian special with *louza* (local smoked ham), local prosciutto, cheeses and rocket – lead on to mains such as pork fillet with mustard, *pleurotus* mushrooms and tarragon.

our pick **Katerina's** (☎ 22890 23084; Agion Anargyron; mains €11-25) There's a thoughtful and creative menu of crisp salads and starters such as prawn *saganaki* (skillet-fried) or wild Porcini mushrooms. Mains include fresh sea bass or a mixed seafood plate for two (€50) or vegetarian options. The balcony view is to die for, of course, as is the 'Chocolate from Heaven' sweet.

To Maereio (☎ 22890 28825; Kalogera 16; dishes €14-21) A small, but selective menu of Mykonian favourites keeps this cosy little place popular. The mainly meat and poultry dishes can be preceded by salad mixes that include apple and pear, yoghurt and a balsamic vinegar sauce.

DRINKING

Hora's Little Venice quarter is not exactly the Grand Canal, but it does offer the Mediterranean at your feet as well as rosy sunsets, windmill views, glowing candles and a swath of colourful bars. A good spot is **Galleraki** (☎ 22890 27188), which turns out superb cocktails. Nearby, it's the sunset view at **Verandah Café** (☎ 22890 27400), while **La Scarpa** (☎ 22890 23294) lets you lean back and watch the sea from its cosy cushions.

Further down Enoplon Dynameon is **Astra** (☎ 22890 24767), where the decor is modernist Mykonos at its best, and where some of Athens' top DJs feed the ambience with rock, funk, house and drum'n'bass.

For big action into the dawn, **Space** (☎ 22890 24100; Laka) is the place. **Remezzo** (☎ 22890 24100; Polykandrioti) is run by the Space team but features lounge and dance for a more relaxing scene. Entry is around €20 to each of the clubs.

GAY BARS

Mykonos is one of the world's great gay-friendly destinations. Gay life is less overt here, but Hora has many gay-centric clubs and hang-outs from where the late-night crowds spill out onto the streets.

Kastro (☎ 22890 23072; Agion Anargyron) With a leaning towards stylish classical sounds, this is a good place to start the night with cocktails as the sun sets on Little Venice.

Jackie O' (☎ 22890 79167; www.jackieomykonos.com; Plateia Karaoli Dimitriou) Hottest gay bar in Mykonos in 2009, Jacki O' seems set to hold centre stage for some time yet.

Pierro's (☎ 22890 22177; Agias Kiriakis) Long-standing last stop for the nightwatch, where things round off with a backdrop of heavy-beat house and superbly over-the-top drag action in upstairs Ikaros. Can take over the outdoors, also.

SHOPPING

Scala Shop Gallery (☎ 22890 26992; www
.scalagallery.gr; Matogianni 48) Scala is one of
the more stylish galleries of Mykonos. It
stages changing displays of fine art and
also sells contemporary jewellery and
ceramics.

Hermesart (☎ 22890 24652; Plateia
Goumenio) There's some quirky and appealing art at this small gallery, with smaller
pieces at affordable prices.

Orama Art Gallery (☎ 22890 26339;
Fournakia) Just off Enoplon Dynameon,
Orama shows the highly original work of
Louis Orosko and Dorlies Schapitz.

AROUND MYKONOS
BEACHES

Mykonos has a good number of beaches
and most have golden sand in attractive locations. They're not big enough,
though, that you'll escape from the
crowds, and they're extremely popular and busy, especially from June
onwards.

You need to be a party person for the
likes of **Paradise** and **Super Paradise**. It
can all get very claustrophobic, but it's
heaven for the gregarious. An excellent
guide to island beaches and their specific
or mixed clientele can be found on the
beaches link of www.mykonos-accom-
modation.com.

The nearest beaches to Hora (Mykonos),
which are also the island's least glamorous beaches, are **Malaliamos**; the tiny
and crowded **Tourlos**, 2km to the north;
and **Agios Stefanos**, 4km away. About
3.5km south of Hora is the packed and
noisy **Ornos**, from where you can hop
onto boats for other beaches. Just west is
Agios Ioannis. The sizable package-holi-
day resort of **Platys Gialos** is 4km from
Hora on the southwest coast. All of the
above beaches are family orientated.

Platys Gialos is the caïque jump-
ing-off point for the glitzier beaches
to the east, such as Paradise and Super
Paradise. Mixed and gay-friendly **Elia** is
the last caïque stop, and a few minutes'
walk from here is the small and pleasant
Agrari. Nudity is fairly commonplace on
all of these beaches.

North-coast beaches can be exposed
to the *meltemi* (northeasterly wind), but
Panormos and **Agios Sostis** are fairly
sheltered and becoming more popular.

ACTIVITIES

Dive Adventures (☎ 22890 26539; www
.diveadventures.gr; Paradise Beach) offers a full
range of diving courses with multilingual
instructors.

On a great location at Kalafatis Beach,
Planet Windsailing (☎ 22890 72345; www
.pezi-huber.com) has one-hour or one-day
windsurfing for €26 or €60, respectively,
or a three-hour beginner's course for
€75.

Also at Kalafatis, the **Kalafati Dive
Center** (☎ 22890 71677; www.mykonos-diving
.com) has the full range of diving courses
including a 10-boat-dive deal with tank
and weights for €290 and with full gear
for €390.

DELOS ΔΗΛΟΣ

The Cyclades fulfil their collective name
(kyklos) by encircling the sacred island of
Delos (☎ 22890 22259; museum & sites adult/
concession €5/3; ☻ 8.30am-3pm Tue-Sun), but
Mykonos clutches the island jealously to
its heart. Delos has no permanent population and is a soothing contrast to the
relentless liveliness of modern Mykonos,
although in high summer you share it all
with fellow visitors. The island is one of
the most important archaeological sites
in Greece and the most important in the
Cyclades.

Ruins of the House of Cleopatra, Ancient Delos

ADINA TOVY AMSEL

HISTORY

Delos won early acclaim as the mythical birthplace of the twins Apollo and Artemis and was first inhabited in the 3rd millennium BC. From the 8th century BC it became a shrine to Apollo, and the oldest temples on the island date from this era. The dominant Athenians had full control of Delos – and thus the Aegean – by the 5th century BC.

Delos reached the height of its power in Hellenistic times, becoming one of the three most important religious centres in Greece and a flourishing centre of commerce.

The Romans made Delos a free port in 167 BC. This brought even greater prosperity, due largely to a lucrative slave market that sold up to 10,000 people a day. During the following century, as ancient religions lost relevance and trade routes shifted, and Delos began a long, painful decline.

EXPLORING THE SITE

The following is an outline of some significant archaeological remains on the site.

For further details, a guidebook from the ticket office is advisable, or take a guided tour.

The path to Mt Kythnos is reached by walking through the **Theatre Quarter**, where Delos' wealthiest inhabitants once built their houses. The most lavish dwellings were the **House of Dionysos**, named after the mosaic depicting the wine god riding a panther, and the **House of Cleopatra**, where headless statues of the owners were found. The **House of the Trident** was one of the grandest. The **theatre** dates from 300 BC and had a large **cistern**, the remains of which can be seen. It supplied much of the town with water.

Descending from Mt Kythnos, explore the **Sanctuaries of the Foreign Gods**. Here, at the **Shrine to the Samothracian Great Gods**, the Kabeiroi (the twins Dardanos and Aeton) were worshipped. At the **Sanctuary of the Syrian Gods** there are the remains of a theatre where an audience watched ritual orgies.

The **Sanctuary of Apollo**, to the northeast of the harbour, is the site of the much- photographed **Terrace of the Lions**. These proud beasts, carved from marble, were offerings from the people of Naxos, presented to Delos in the 7th century BC to guard the sacred area. To the northeast is the **Sacred Lake** (dry since it was drained in 1925 to prevent malarial mosquitoes breeding) where, according to legend, Leto gave birth to Apollo and Artemis.

GETTING THERE & AWAY

Boats for Delos (return €15, 30 minutes) leave Hora (Mykonos) about six times a day from about 9am in high season with the last outward boat at about 12.50pm. Departure and return times are posted on the ticket kiosk at the entrance to the Old Jetty at the south end of the harbour. There are no boats on Monday when the site is closed. Boats return from the island between 11am and 3pm. When buying tickets, establish which boat is available for your return, especially later in the day.

The Mykonos Accommodation Centre organises guided tours to Delos at 10am every day except Monday, between May and September (adult/child €40/31, three hours). Tours are in English, French, German and Italian, and in Spanish and Russian on request.

Overnight stays on Delos are forbidden and boat schedules allow a maximum of about six or seven hours there. Bring water and food, as the cafeteria's offerings are poor value for money. Wear a hat and sensible shoes.

NAXOS ΝΑΞΟΣ

pop 18,188

Naxos is more fertile than most of the other islands and produces olives, grapes, figs, citrus fruit, corn and potatoes. Mt Zeus (1004m; also known as Mt Zas or Zefs) is the Cyclades' highest peak and is the central focus of the island's mountainous interior, in which you'll find enchanting villages such as Halki and Apiranthos. There are numerous fine beaches and the island is a great place to explore on foot, as many old paths between villages, churches and other sights still survive.

DIANA MAYFIELD

Views across Naxos' interior to Hora

GETTING THERE & AWAY

Naxos is something of a ferry hub of the Cyclades, with a number of conventional and fast ferries making regular calls to and from Piraeus, and weekly links to and from the mainland ports of Thessaloniki and Lavrio and eastward to the Dodecanese. There is a daily flight to and from Athens. There are daily connections to the other main Cycladic islands in summer.

GETTING AROUND

TO/FROM THE AIRPORT

The airport is 3km south of Hora. A taxi costs €12 to €15 depending on the time of day and if booked.

BUS

Buses leave from the end of the ferry quay in Hora; timetables are posted outside the **bus information office** (☎ 22850 22291; www.naxosdestinations.com), diagonally left and across the road from the bus stop. You have to buy tickets from the office.

HORA (NAXOS) ΧΩΡΑ (ΝΑΞΟΣ)

pop 6533

Busy Hora, on the west coast of Naxos, is the island's port and capital. It's a large town, divided into two historic neighbourhoods – Bourgos, where the Greeks lived, and the hill-top Kastro, where the Venetian Catholics lived.

ORIENTATION

The ferry quay is at the northern end of the waterfront, with the bus station at its inland end. The broad waterfront, Protopapadaki, known universally as Paralia, leads off to the south from the ferry quay and is lined with cafes, tavernas and shops on its inland side.

There are a few swimming spots along the waterfront promenade below the tem-

ple. Southwest of the town is the pleasant, but busy, beach of Agios Georgios.

INFORMATION

EMERGENCY

Police station (☎ 22850 22100; Paparrigoulou) Southeast of Plateia Protodikiou.

Port police (☎ 22850 22300) Just south of the quay.

MEDICAL SERVICES

Hospital (☎ 22853 60500; Prantouna)

MONEY

All the following banks have ATMs:
Agricultural Bank of Greece (Paralia)
Alpha Bank (cnr Paralia & Papavasiliou)
National Bank of Greece (Paralia)

POST

Post office (Agios Giorgiou) Go past the OTE, across Papavasiliou, and left at the forked road.

TRAVEL AGENCIES

There is no official tourist information office on Naxos. Travel agencies can deal with most queries. Naxos Tours and Zas Travel both sell ferry tickets and organise accommodation, tours and rental cars.
Grotta Tours (☎ 22850 25782; Paralia)
Naxos Tours (☎ 22850 22095; www.naxos tours.net; Paralia)
Zas Travel (☎ 22850 23330; zas-travel@nax .forthnet.gr; Paralia)

SIGHTS

To see the Bourgos area, head into the winding backstreets behind the northern end of Paralia. The most alluring part of Hora is the residential **Kastro**. Marco Sanudo made the town the capital of his duchy in 1207, and several Venetian mansions survive.

A short distance behind the northern end of the waterfront there are several churches and chapels, and the **Mitropolis Museum** (☎ 22850 24151; Kondyli; admission free; ◷ 8.30am-3pm). The museum features fragments of a Mycenaean city of the 13th to 11th centuries BC that was abandoned because of the threat of flooding by the sea.

The **Della Rocca-Barozzi Venetian Museum** (☎ 22850 22387; **guided tours adult/student €5/3;** ◷ **10am-3pm & 7-10pm end May-mid-Sep**), a handsome old tower house of the 13th century, is within the Kastro ramparts (by the northwest gate). There are changing art exhibitions in the vaults. Tours are multilingual. The museum also runs tours (adult/student €15/10) of the Kastro at 11am Tuesday to Sunday; tours last just over two hours. Evening concerts and other events are staged in the grounds of the museum (see p217).

ACTIVITIES

Flisvos Sport Club (☎ 22850 24308; www .flisvos-sportclub.com; Agios Georgios) has a range of windsurfing options, starting with a beginner's course of six hours for €150, or a five-hour Hobie Cat sailing course for €95. The club also organises walking trips and hires out mountain bikes at a per-week rate of €60.

Naxos Horse Riding (☎ 6948809142) organises daily horse rides (10am to 1pm and 5pm to 8pm) inland and on beaches (per person €48). Beginners, young children and advanced riders are catered for.

TOURS

There are frequent excursion boats to Mykonos (adult/child €45/23), Delos (€45) and Santorini (adult/child €55/30); book through travel agents (see p215).

SLEEPING

Hotel Anixis (☎ 22850 22932; www.hotel-ani xis.gr; s/d/tr €50/60/75; ✂ 🎧) Tucked away in a quiet location in the Kastro, this pleasant hotel, in a garden setting, has bright and well-kept rooms and there are great views to the sea. Breakfast is €5.

Pension Irene II (☎ 22850 23169; www .irenepension-naxos.com; s/d €60/70; ✂ 🖥 🎧 🖼) Bright, clean rooms and a swimming pool have made this well-run place popular with a younger set.

Hotel Glaros (☎ 22850 23101; www.hotel glaros.com; Agios Georgios; s incl breakfast €65, d incl breakfast €85-95; ✂ 🖥 🎧) Service is efficient and thoughtful and the rooms are bright and clean. The hotel is only a few steps away from the beach. The owners also have attractive studios nearby (€65 to €100).

our pick **Hotel Grotta** (☎ 22850 22215; www .hotel grotta.gr; Grotta; s/d incl breakfast €70/85; P ✂ 🖥 🎧) Located on high ground to the east of the ferry quay, this fine modern hotel has comfortable and immaculate rooms, great sea views from the front, spacious public areas and a Jacuzzi. It's made even better by the cheerful, attentive atmosphere.

EATING

Meze 2 (☎ 22850 26401; Paralia; mains €3-9) The emphasis at this popular *mezedho-poleio* is on fish – and even the local fishermen eat here. Superb seafood is prepared and served by family members in an atmosphere that is never less than sociable.

O Apostolis (☎ 22850 26777; Old Market; mains €5.50-17) Right at the heart of the labyrinthine Old Market area of Bourgos, Apostolis serves up rewarding dishes such as mussels in garlic butter and parsley, and *bekri mezes,* a popular Cretan dish of casseroled beef.

Seaside setting on Andros

CHRIS RONNESETH, TREKHOLIDAYS/ISTOCK

⬐ IF YOU LIKE...

If you like the quiet corners of **Naxos** (p214) we think you'd like these other peaceful and less-visited islands in the Cyclades:

- **Andros** Satisfyingly remote in places, Andros is a mix of bare mountains, green valleys and out-of-the-way beaches. Neoclassical mansions and Venetian tower houses contrast with the rough unpainted stonework of farm buildings and patterned dovecotes. A network of footpaths is also maintained, and the island has a fascinating archaeological and cultural heritage. See also p362.

- **Amorgos** This lovely island rises from the sea in a long dragon's back of craggy mountains. There's plenty of scope for beaching, but Amorgos is much more about archaeology and the outdoor world – there's great walking, scuba diving and a burgeoning rock-climbing scene for experienced climbers. See also p362.

- **Sifnos** Sifnos seems a barren place of heavy hills as you approach by sea, until the port of Kamares appears, as if by magic. Beyond the port and between the flanking slopes of rugged mountains lies an abundant landscape of terraced olive groves, almond trees, juniper and aromatic herbs. Plenty of unspoiled paths link the island villages, and the island has a tradition of pottery making, basket weaving and cooking. See also p368.

Lucullus (☎ 22850 22569; Old Market St; mains €6.50-18) One hundred years' service and still going strong, this famous restaurant has starters such as mushroom pie, while mains include *lemonato*, tender veal in a fresh lemon juice and white wine sauce. The fisherman's pasta mixes shrimp, tomatoes, garlic and dill.

ENTERTAINMENT

Della Rocca-Barozzi Venetian Museum (☎ 22850 22387; Kastro; events admission €15-20; ⏳ 8pm Wed-Sun Apr-Oct) Special evening cultural events are held at the museum, and comprise traditional music and dance concerts, and classical and contemporary music recitals.

SHOPPING

Takis' Shop (☎ 22850 23045; Plateia Mandilara) Among the splendid wines here are such fine names as Lazaridis from northern Greece, Tslepos from the Peloponnese and Manousakis from Crete – all masterful vintages. You can also find Vallindras *kitron* (see below) and ouzo here.

Kiriakos Tziblakis (☎ 22859 22230; Papavasiliou) A fascinating cavelike place crammed with traditional produce and goods, from pots and brushes to herbs, spices, wine, *raki* and olive oil.

AROUND NAXOS
BEACHES

Conveniently located just south of the town's waterfront is **Agios Georgios**, Naxos' town beach. It's backed by hotels and tavernas at the town end and can get very crowded, but it runs for some way to the south and its shallow waters mean the beach is safe for youngsters.

The next beach south of Agios Georgios is **Agios Prokopios**, in a sheltered bay to the south of the headland of Cape Mougkri. It merges with **Agia Anna**, a stretch of shining white sand, quite narrow but long enough to feel uncrowded towards its southern end. Development is fairly solid at Prokopios and the northern end of Agia Anna. Sandy beaches continue down as far as **Pyrgaki** and include **Plaka**, **Kastraki** and **Alyko**.

Near the beach at Ágios Prokopios is **Villa Adriana** (☎ 22850 42804; www.adriana hotel.com; s/d/tr/apt €75/85/90/120; P ⚡ 🛜 🅿), a well-appointed hotel with excellent service and bright, comfortable rooms.

The beachside **Taverna Liofago** (☎ 22850 75214, 6937137737; dishes €4.50-9) has a dreamy beach location. It has been in business for decades and favours a variety of dishes with special Naxian flavour.

TRAGAEA ΤΡΑΓΑΙΑ

The Tragaea region is a vast plain of olive groves and unspoilt villages, couched beneath the central mountains.

MT ZEUS

Filoti, on the slopes of **Mt Zeus** (1004m), is the region's largest village. It has an ATM booth just down from the main bus stop.

From Filoti, you can also reach the **Cave of Zeus (Zas)**, a large, natural cavern at the foot of a cliff on the slopes of Mt Zeus. There's a junction signposted Aria Spring and Zas Cave, about 800m south of Filoti. From the road-end parking, follow a walled path past the **Aria Spring & Cave of Zeus**, a fountain and picnic area, and on to a rough track uphill to reach the cave. The path leads on from here steeply to the summit of Zas. It's quite a stiff hike of about 3km. This is not a mere stroll, so be fit and come equipped with good footwear, water and sunscreen.

HALKI ΑΛΚΕΙΟ

One of Naxos' finest experiences is a visit to the historic village of Halki, which lies at the heart of the Tragaea, about 20 minutes' drive from Naxos town. Halki is a vivid reflection of historic Naxos and is full of the handsome facades of old villas and tower houses, a legacy of a rich past as the one-time centre of Naxian commerce.

The **Vallindras Distillery** (☎ 22850 31220; 🕙 10am-11pm Jul-Aug, 10am-6pm May-Jun & Sep-Oct) in Halki's main square distils *kitron* (a liqueur made from the leaves of the citron tree) the old-fashioned way. There are free tours of the old distillery's atmospheric rooms, which still contain ancient jars and copper stills. *Kitron* tastings round off the trip and a selection of the distillery's products are on sale.

In Halki's central square, **Yianni's Taverna** (☎ 22850 31214; dishes €5.50-7.50) is noted for its good local meat dishes and fresh salads with *myzithra* (sheep's-milk cheese). Do not miss **Glikia Zoi** (Sweet Life; ☎ 22850 31602), directly opposite the L'Olivier gallery. Here Christina Falierou works her magic in a traditional cafe setting, making delicious cakes and sweets to go with coffee or drinks.

SANTORINI (THIRA)
ΣΑΝΤΟΡΙΝΗ (ΘΗΡΑ)
pop 13,670

Santorini will take your breath away. Even the most jaded traveller succumbs to the spectacle of this surreal landscape, a relic of what was probably the biggest volcanic eruption in recorded history. You do share the experience with hordes of other visitors, but the island somehow manages to cope with it all.

Santorini is not all about the caldera, however. The east side of the island has black-sand beaches at popular resorts such as Kamari and Perissa and although the famous archaeological site of Akrotiri is closed for the foreseeable future, Ancient Thira above Kamari is a major site.

GETTING THERE & AWAY
There are several flights a day to and from Athens, Thessaloniki, Crete, Mykonos and Rhodes. There are also a good number of ferries a day to and from Piraeus and to and from many of Santorini's neighbouring islands. There are daily ferries to Crete and about four ferries a week go to Rhodes and Kos in the Dodecanese.

GETTING AROUND
TO/FROM THE AIRPORT
There are frequent bus connections in summer between Fira's bus station and the airport, located southwest of Monolithos Beach. A taxi to the airport costs €12.

BUS
In summer buses leave Fira every half-hour for Oia (€1.40), Monolithos (€1.40), Kamari (€1.40) and Perissa (€2).

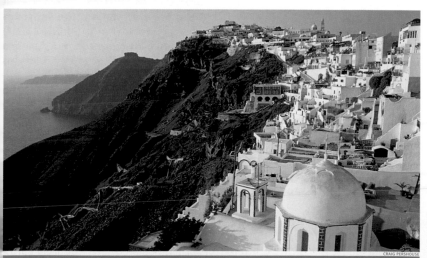

Clifftop location, Fira (p220), Santorini

CRAIG PERSHOUSE

CABLE CAR

A **cable car** (☎ 22860 22977; M Nomikou; ⏰ every 20min 7am-10pm, to 9pm winter) hums smoothly between Fira and the small port below, known as Fira Skala, from where volcanic island cruises leave. One-way cable car tickets cost €4 per adult, and €2 per child; luggage is €2.

TAXI

Fira's **taxi stand** (☎ 22860 23951/2555) is, in Dekigala, just round the corner from the bus station. A taxi from the port of Athinios to Fira costs €12, and a trip from Fira to Oia is also €12.

FIRA ΦHPA

pop 2113

A multitude of fellow admirers cannot diminish the impact of Fira's stupendous landscape. Views from the edge of the caldera over the multicoloured cliffs are breathtaking, and at night the caldera edge is a frozen cascade of lights that eclipses the displays of the gold shops in the streets behind.

ORIENTATION

The busy heart of Fira is Plateia Theotokopoulou (Central Sq). The bus station is on Mitropoleos, 150m south of Plateia Theotokopoulou. Between 25 Martiou and the caldera is the essence of Fira, a network of pedestrianised alleyways, the main ones running parallel to 25 Martiou.

Below the edge of the caldera is the paved walkway of Agiou Mina, which heads north and merges eventually with the cliff-top walkway that continues north past the pretty villages of Firostefani and Imerovigli.

INFORMATION

There are numerous ATMs scattered around town.

Aegean Pearl (☎ 22860 22170; www.aptravel.gr; Danezi) An excellent, helpful agency that sells all travel tickets and can help with accommodation, car hire and excursions.

Alpha Bank (Plateia Theotokopoulou) Represents American Express and has an ATM.

Hospital (☎ 22860 22237) On the road to Kamari. A new hospital at Karterados was under construction at the time of writing.

National Bank of Greece (Dekigala) South of Plateia Theotokopoulou, on the caldera side of the road. Has an ATM.

Pelican Tours & Travel (☎ 22860 22220; fax 22860 22570; Plateia Theotokopoulou) Sells ferry tickets and can book accommodation and excursions.

Police station (☎ 22860 22649; Karterados) About 2km from Fira.

Port police (☎ 22860 22239; 25 Martiou) North of the square.

Post office (Dekigala)

SIGHTS & ACTIVITIES

Near the bus station, the **Museum of Prehistoric Thera** (☎ 22860 23217; Mitropoleos; admission €3; ⏰ 8.30am-8pm Tue-Sun Apr-Sep, 8.30am-3pm Tue-Sun Oct-Mar) houses extraordinary finds that were excavated from Akrotiri (where, to date, only 5% of the area has been excavated). Most impressive is the glowing gold ibex figurine, measuring around 10cm in length and dating from the 17th century BC.

Megaron Gyzi Museum (☎ 22860 22244; Agiou Ioannou; adult/student €3.50/2; ⏰ 10.30am-1pm & 5-8pm Mon-Sat, 10.30am-4.30pm Sun May-Oct) has local memorabilia, including fascinating photographs of Fira before and immediately after the 1956 earthquake.

Located on the eastern tip of the island, the **Folklore Museum of Santorini** (☎ 22860 22792; adult/child €3/free; ☒ 10am-2pm & 6-8pm Apr-Oct) houses an intriguing collection that casts light on Santorini's traditions and history.

TOURS

Tour companies operate various trips to and fro across the caldera. Book at travel agencies. The *Bella Aurora,* an exact copy of an 18th-century schooner, scoots around the caldera every afternoon on a sunset buffet dinner tour (€45, from May to October), stopping for sightseeing on Nea Kameni and for ouzo on Thirasia. Most travel agencies sell tickets.

SLEEPING

Villa Roussa (☎ 22860 23220; www.villaroussa .gr; Dekigala; s/d €55/75; ℗ ☒ ☞ ☒) You don't have a caldera view but this small hotel is right at the heart of town and is hard to beat for value with its bright and immaculate rooms. It even has a swimming pool.

Maria's Rooms (☎ 22860 25143, 6973254461; Agiou Mina; d €70; ☒) A handful of charming rooms open onto a shared terrace that has unbeatable caldera and sunset views. Rooms are small but immaculate, and blissfully peaceful.

Loizos Apartments (☎ 22860 24046; www.loizos.gr; s €75, d €85-95, tr/apt €110/140; ℗ ☒ ☐ ☞ ☒) Recently refurbished and with friendly, professional service, Loizos is one of the best places in Fira. Rooms range from standard to deluxe and all are bright, clean and comfortable. Those on the front upper floor have a panoramic view towards Kamari and the sea.

Hotel Keti (☎ 22860 22324; www.hotelketi .gr; Agiou Mina; d €90-120, tr/ste €117/140; ☒ ☞) Recently refurbished, Hotel Keti is one of the smaller 'sunset view' hotels in a peace-

DIANA MAYFIELD
Aerial view of cable cars, Fira, Santorini

ful caldera niche. Its attractive traditional rooms are carved into the cliffs. Half of the rooms have Jacuzzis.

ourpick **Aroma Suites** (☎ 22860 24112; www.aromasuites.gr; Agiou Mina; s €120, d €140-160; ☒ ☞) In an excellent location at the quieter end of the caldera edge, and more accessible than similar places, this boutique hotel has charming service to match its overall ambience.

EATING

Mylos Café (☎ 22860 25640; Firostefani; ☐ ☞) On the caldera edge in Firostefani, this stylish and relaxing venue is located in a converted windmill and is the ideal place for relaxing drinks and light snacks.

Lithos (☎ 22860 24421; Agiou Mina; mains €7-19.50) Amid a swath of eateries on the caldera edge, Lithos stands out for its well-prepared dishes and attentive service. Choose from persuasive starters such as fava beans with cheese and cherry tomatoes.

Ampelos (☎ 22860 25554; Fabrika Shopping Centre; mains €10-26) There's plenty of space in this central Fira restaurant with its 2nd-floor terrace with a view. Try the grilled shrimp in a red pepper sauce with rice or the mussels *saganaki*, or settle for a selection of such starters as stuffed mushrooms with dill, garlic and parsley in white wine and the speciality pie of green onion, dill, pine nuts and Parmesan cheese.

our pick **Koukoumavlos** (☎ 22860 23807; mains €25-35) Discreet in location and outstanding for cuisine, this fine restaurant has a terrace with good views, while the interior has retained the vaulted style of its original Fira mansion. An uncrowded menu lists such certainties as lobster and monkfish terrine, or Santorini fava and smoked trout and salmon in a mandarin sauce with roasted almonds.

DRINKING & ENTERTAINMENT

Drinks prices can be cranked up in Fira, even for beer, never mind the stellar cocktail prices. You're often paying for the view, so don't glaze over too early.

Tropical (☎ 22860 23089; Marinatou) Nicely perched just before the caldera edge Tropical draws a vibrant crowd with its seductive mix of rock, soul and occasional jazz, plus unbeatable balcony views that are still there into the early hours.

Franco's Bar (☎ 22860 24428; Marinatou) Check your cuffs for this deeply stylish and ultimate sunset venue where music means classical sounds only. Expensive cocktails match the sheer elegance and impeccable musical taste.

Enigma (☎ 22860 22466; Erythrou Stavrou) A full-on dance venue when it gets going, this is the catwalk clientele's favourite spot amid coolness and floaty drapes. House and mainstream hits fit the style.

AROUND SANTORINI
OIA OIA
pop 763

The village of Oia (*ee*-ah), known locally as Pano Meria, reflects the renaissance of Santorini after the devastating earthquake of 1956. Restoration work and upmarket tourism have transformed Oia into one of the loveliest villages in the Cyclades. Built on a steep slope of the caldera, many of its dwellings nestle in niches hewn into the volcanic rock. Oia, believe it or not, gets more sunset time than Fira, and its narrow passageways get very crowded in the evenings.

INFORMATION

ATMs On Main St, outside Karvounis Tours, and also by the bus terminus.

Karvounis Tours (☎ 22860 71290; www.idogreece.com; Nikolaou Nomikou) For obtaining information, booking hotels, renting cars and bikes, and making international calls.

SIGHTS & ACTIVITIES

Ammoudi, a tiny port with good tavernas and colourful fishing boats, lies 300 steps below Oia at the base of blood-red cliffs. It can also be reached by road. In summer, boats and tours go from Ammoudi to Thirasia daily; check with travel agencies in Fira (p220) for departure times.

SLEEPING & EATING

Chelidonia (☎ 22860 71287; www.chelidonia.com; Nikolaou Nomikou; studios €155, apt €170-205, ste €220-230; ✂ ▢) Traditional cliffside dwellings that have been in the owner's family for generations offer a grand mix of old and new at Chelidonia. Modern facilities are nicely balanced by the occasional fine piece of traditional furniture and each unit has a kitchenette.

Nectar (☎ 2286071504; dishes €8-18) Quality cuisine, creative salads and main dishes such as chicken with figs, plus some seriously fine wines, ensure a rewarding meal at this bright eatery.

KAMARI KAMAPI

pop 1351

Kamari is 10km from Fira and is Santorini's best-developed resort. It has a long beach of black sand, with the rugged limestone cliffs of Cape Mesa Vouno framing its southern end with the ancient site of Ancient Thira on its summit. The beachfront road is dense with restaurants and bars. Things get very busy in high season.

Lisos Tours (☎ 22860 33765; lisostours@ san.forthnet.gr) is especially helpful and has an office on the main road into Kamari, and another just inland from the centre of the beach. It sells ferry tickets and can organise accommodation and car hire.

SLEEPING

Hotel Matina (☎ 22860 31491; www .hotel-matina.com; s/d/tr/ste incl breakfast €108/116/144/192; 🅿 🖳 🕿) A very well-run independent hotel, the Matina has spacious, brightly decorated rooms and is set back from the road in quiet grounds.

ourpick **Aegean View Hotel** (☎ 22860 32790; www.aegeanview-santorini.com; studio/apt €130/150; 🅿 🅿 🖳 🛜 🕿) Tucked below the limestone cliffs high above Kamari, this outstanding hotel has spacious studios and apartments superbly laid out and with first-class facilities, including small kitchen areas.

EATING

Amalthia (☎ 22860 32780; dishes €3.50-12) A long-established local favourite, Amalthia is a couple of blocks inland at the south-

Rock-hewn architecture of Oia, Santorini

HOLGER LEUE

SARAH PETERS/IMAGEBROKER

Ruins of Ancient Thira, Santorini

ANCIENT THIRA
ΑΡΧΑΙΑ ΘΗΡΑ

First settled by the Dorians in the 9th century BC, **Ancient Thira** consists of Hellenistic, Roman and Byzantine ruins and is an atmospheric and rewarding site to visit. The ruins include temples, houses with mosaics, an *agora* (market), a theatre and a gymnasium. There are splendid views from the site.

From March to October **Ancient Thira Tours** runs a bus every hour from 9am until 2pm, except on Monday, from Kamari to the site. If driving, take the surfaced but narrow, winding road from Kamari for just over 1km.

Things you should know: Ancient Thira (admission €4; ⏲ 8am-2.30pm Tue-Sun); Ancient Thira Tours (☎ 22860 32474; Kamari)

ern end of town, with a lovely garden area and a terrace with barbecue. There are well-prepared Greek dishes (the lamb is particularly good) and a range of pastas.

Mistral (☎ **22860 32108; mains €5.50-14**) Seafood is what this classic *psarotaverna* is all about. Fish plates for two are about €30 and the likes of bream and red mullet are by the kilo.

BEACHES

At times Santorini's black-sand beaches become so hot that a sun lounger or mat is essential. The best beaches are on the east and south coasts.

One of the main beaches is the long stretch at **Perissa**, a popular destination in summer. **Perivolos** and **Agios Georgios**, further south, are more relaxed. **Red Beach**, near Ancient Akrotiri, has high red cliffs and smooth, hand-sized pebbles submerged under clear water. **Vlyhada**, also on the south coast, is a pleasant venue. On the north coast near Oia, **Paradise** and **Pori** are both worth a stop.

Based at Perissa and **Akrotiri Beach** is the **Santorini Dive Centre** (☎ **22860 83190; www.divecenter.gr**), offering a good range of courses including 'discover scuba diving' for €55, half-day snorkelling for €40 and an open-water diving course for €380.

SLEEPING & EATING

Stelio's Place (☎ **22860 81860; www.steliosplace.com; d/tr/q €70/90/120;** ⏲ **year-round;** P ❄ 📶 🏊) In a great position set back from the main drag but barely a minute from the beach, and with immaculate, well-appointed rooms, Stelio's is great value.

Hotel Drossos (☎ **22860 81639; www.familydrossos.gr; s/d/tr incl breakfast €102/112/153;** P ❄ 💻 📶 🏊) Behind the simple facade of this fine hotel lies a lovely complex of rooms and studios with stylish decor and furnishings.

There's reliable Greek food on offer at **God's Garden** (☎ **22860 83027; dishes €4.50-11**), a decent taverna with fish dishes starting at about €6.

THIRASIA & VOLCANIC ISLETS
ΘΗΡΑΣΙΑ & ΗΦΑΙΣΤΕΙΑΚΕΣ ΝΗΣΙΔΕΣ

Unspoilt Thirasia (pop 158) was separated from Santorini by an eruption in 236 BC.

The cliff-top *hora*, **Manolas**, has tavernas and domatia. It's an attractive place, noticeably more relaxed and reflective than Fira could ever be.

The unpopulated islets of **Palia Kameni** and **Nea Kameni** are still volcanically active and can be visited on various boat excursions from Fira Skala and Athinios (see Tours, p221). A day's excursion taking in Nea Kameni, the **hot springs** on Palia Kameni, Thirasia and Oia is about €28.

EVIA & THE SPORADES
ΕΥΒΟΙΑ & ΟΙ ΣΠΟΡΑΔΕΣ

EVIA ΕΥΒΟΙΑ

Evia (*eh*-vih-ah), Greece's second-largest island after Crete and a prime holiday destination for Greeks, remains less charted by foreign tourists. Its attractions include glorious mountain roads, challenging treks, major archaeological finds and a fine selection of mostly uncrowded beaches. A mountainous spine runs north-south, dividing the island's precipitous eastern cliffs from the gentler and resort-friendly west coast.

GETTING THERE & AWAY

There are regular bus services between Halkida and Athens (€6.20, 1¼ hours, half-hourly), Ioannina (€35.50, one daily) and Thessaloniki (€36, 6 hours, twice daily).

There is also a regular train service between Halkida and Athens (normal, €5, 1½ hours, hourly), and between Halkida and Thessaloniki (normal/IC express €26/33, 5½/4½ hours, six/four daily).

CENTRAL EVIA
ERETRIA ΕΡΕΤΡΙΑ
pop 3160

Heading southeast from Halkida, Eretria is the first place of interest, with a small harbour and a lively boardwalk filled with mainland families who pack its fish tavernas on holiday weekends.

From the top of the **ancient acropolis** there are splendid views over to the mainland. West of the acropolis are the remains of a palace, temple and theatre with a subterranean passage once used by actors to reach the stage. Close by, the excellent **Archaeological Museum of Eretria** (☎ 22290 62206; admission €2; ⏰ 8.30am-3pm Tue-Sun) contains well-displayed finds from ancient Eretria. A 200m walk will bring you to the fascinating **House of Mosaics**, and ends 50m further on at the **Sanctuary of Apollo**.

GETTING THERE & AWAY

Ferries travel daily between Eretria and Skala Oropou. Tickets should be purchased from the dock kiosk at the port of Eretria.

NORTHERN EVIA
LOUTRA EDIPSOU ΛΟΥΤΡΑ ΑΙΔΗΨΟΥ
pop 3600

The classic spa resort of Loutra Edipsou has therapeutic sulphur waters, which have been celebrated since antiquity. Famous skinny dippers have included Aristotle, Plutarch and Sylla. The town's gradual expansion over the years has been tied to the improving technology required to carry the water further and further away from its thermal source. Today the town has Greece's most up-to-date hydrotherapy and physiotherapy centres. The town beach (Paralia Loutron) heats up year-round thanks to the thermal waters which spill into the sea.

ACTIVITIES

Most of the hotels offer various **spa treatments**, from simple hot baths (€6) to four-hand massages (€160).

The more relaxing (and affordable) of the resort's two big spas is the **EOT Hydrotherapy-Physiotherapy Centre** (☎ 22260 23501; 25 March St 37; ☺ 7am-1pm & 5-7pm 1 Jun-31 Oct). The spa is speckled with palm trees and has a large outdoor pool that mixes mineral and sea water, and terrace overlooking the sea. Hydro-massage bath treatments start at a modest €8.

The ultraposh **Thermae Sylla Hotel & Spa** (☎ 22260 60100; www.thermaesylla.gr; Posidonos 2), with a somewhat late-Roman ambience befitting its name, offers an assortment of health and beauty treatments, from thermal mud baths to seaweed body wraps, from around €60.

Modern spa treatments (including Thai massage) are also available from the **Knossos CitySpa Hotel** (☎ 22260 22460; www.knossos-spa.com; Vyzantinon 19).

SLEEPING & EATING

Hotel Kentrikon (☎ /fax 22260 22502; www.kentrikonhotel.com; 25th Martiou 14; s/d/tr €42/60/70; ❄ ▯ ☺ ☻) This friendly hotelspa, managed by a Greek-Irish couple, is equal parts kitsch and charm. An inviting thermal pool awaits, along with a massage therapist, Vicky Kavartziki (☎ 6945146374).

Dina's Amfilirion Restaurant (☎ 22260 60420; 28th October 26; mains €5-10) Beautifully prepared offerings change daily here. A generous plate of grilled cod with oven potatoes, a juicy tomato-cucumber salad and a worthy house wine costs about €12.

GETTING THERE & AWAY

Boat

Regular ferries run between Loutra Edipsou and mainland Arkitsa, and also between nearby Agiokambos and mainland Glyfa. Tickets should be purchased from the dock kiosk at the port of Loutra Edipsou.

Bus

From the **KTEL bus station** (☎ 22260 22250; Thermopotamou), 200m from the port, buses run to Athens (€12.30, 3½ hours, three daily via Arkitsa) and Thessaloniki (€22, five hours, daily at 10am via Glyfa).

SOUTHERN EVIA
KARYSTOS ΚΑΡΥΣΤΟΣ

pop 4960

Set on the wide Karystos Bay below Mt Ohi, and flanked by two sandy beaches, this remote but charming coastal resort is the starting point for treks to Mt Ohi and the Dimosari Gorge. The town's lively Plateia Amalias (Amalias Sq), faces the bay and boat harbour.

INFORMATION

You'll find an Alpha Bank ATM on the main square.

SIGHTS

Karystos, mentioned in Homer's *Iliad*, was a powerful city-state during the Peloponnesian Wars. The **Karystos Museum** (☎ 22240 25661; admission €2; ☺ 8.30am-3pm Tue-Sun) documents the town's archaeological heritage, including tiny Neolithic clay lamps, a stone plaque written in the Halkidian alphabet, 5th-century-BC grave stelae depicting Zeus and Athena, and an exhibit of the 6th-century *drakospita* (dragon houses) of Mt Ohi and Styra. The museum sits opposite

14th-century Venetian castle, the **Bourtzi** (admission free; ☼ year-round).

TOURS

South Evia Tours (☎ 22240 25700; fax 22240 29091; www.eviatravel.gr; Plateia Amalias) offers a range of booking services including mainland ferry tickets, excursions in the foothills of Mt Ohi, trips to the 6th-century-BC Roman-built *drakospita* near Styra, and a cruise around the Petali Islands (€35 with lunch).

FESTIVALS & EVENTS

Karystos hosts a summer **Wine & Cultural Festival** from early July until the last weekend in August. Weekend happenings include theatre performances and traditional dancing to the tune of local musicians, along with exhibits by local artists. The summer merrymaking concludes with the Wine Festival, featuring every local wine imaginable, free for the tasting. Festival schedules are available at the Karystos Museum (p226).

SLEEPING & EATING

Hotel Karystion (☎ 22240 22391; www.karystion.gr; Kriezotou 3; s/d incl breakfast €45/55; P ⊠ ��) The Karystion is the pick of town lodgings, with modern, well-appointed rooms, along with seaview balconies and helpful multilingual staff. A small stairway off the courtyard leads to a sandy beach below, great for swimming.

ourpick **Cavo d'Oro** (☎ 22240 22326; mains €4-7.50) Join the locals in this cheery alleyway restaurant, one block west of the main square, where tasty mains include goat with pasta (€7.50) and mackerel with rice (€6.50), along with homemade *mousakas* (layers of eggplant or zucchini, minced meat and potatoes, topped

with cheese sauce and baked; €6) and salads featuring only local produce and olive oil.

GETTING THERE & AWAY

Boat

There is a regular ferry service between Marmari (10km west of Karystos) and Rafina, and from Nea Styra (35km north of Karystos) to Agia Marina.

Tickets may be purchased from either the dock ticket kiosk at the port of Marmari, or in advance at **South Evia Tours** (☎ 22240 25700; fax 22240 29091; www.eviatravel.gr) in Karystos.

Bus

From the **Karystos KTEL bus station** (☎ 22240 26303), opposite Agios Nikolaos church, buses run to Athens (€8.30, three hours, four daily), and Marmari (€1.70, 20 minutes, Monday to Saturday). A taxi to Marmari is about €12.

AROUND KARYSTOS

The ruins of **Castello Rosso** (Red Castle), a 13th-century Frankish fortress, are a short walk from **Myli**, a delightful, well-watered village 4km inland from Karystos.

With your own transport, or a taxi, you can get to the base of **Mt Ohi**, where a 1½-hour hike to the summit will bring you to the ancient *drakospita* (dragon house), the finest example of a group of Stonehenge-like dwellings or temples, dating from the 7th century BC. The dwellings are hewn from rocks weighing up to several tons and are joined without mortar.

Hikers can also head north to the **Dimosari Gorge** where a beautiful and well-maintained 10km trail can be covered in four to five hours (including time for a swim).

SKIATHOS ΣΚΙΑΘΟΣ

pop 6160

Blessed with some of the Aegean's most beautiful beaches, it's little wonder that Skiathos can fill up with sun-starved Europeans in July and August, as prices soar and rooms dwindle. Despite its popularity, Skiathos remains one of the country's premier resorts. Aside from the ample sun and nightlife, the curious will find striking monasteries, hilltop tavernas and even some secluded beaches.

GETTING THERE & AWAY

AIR

Along with numerous charter flights from northern Europe, during summer there is one flight daily to/from Athens (€49). **Olympic Air** (☎ 24270 22200) has an office at the airport, not in town.

BOAT

Skiathos' main port is Skiathos Town, with links to mainland Volos and Agios Konstantinos, and to Skopelos and Alonnisos.

Tickets can be purchased from either **Hellenic Seaways** (☎ 24270 22209; fax 24270 22750) at the bottom of Papadiamantis, or from **GA Ferries** (☎ 24270 22204; fax 24270 22979), next to Alpha Bank.

GETTING AROUND

BOAT

Water taxis depart from the old port for Tzaneria and Kanapitsa beaches (€3, 20 minutes, hourly) and Achladies Bay (€2, 15 minutes, hourly).

BUS

Crowded buses leave Skiathos Town for Koukounaries Beach (€1.20 to €1.50, 30 minutes, every half-hour between 7.30am and 11pm).

TAXI

The **taxi stand** (☎ 24270 21460) is opposite the ferry dock. A taxi to/from the airport costs €5.

SKIATHOS TOWN

Skiathos Town, with its red-roofed, white-washed houses, is built on two low hills. Opposite the waterfront lies tiny and inviting **Bourtzi Islet** between the two small harbours and reached by a short causeway.

ORIENTATION

The quay is in the middle of the water-front, just north of Bourtzi Islet. Papadiamanti strikes inland from opposite the quay. Plateia Tris Ierarches (Tris Ierarches Sq) is above the old harbour, with the bus terminus is at the northern end of the new harbour.

INFORMATION

EMERGENCY

Port police (☎ 24270 22017) At the quay.
Tourist police (☎ 24270 23172; Ring Rd; ☸ 8am-9pm)

MEDICAL SERVICES

Health Centre Hospital (☎ 24270 22222) Above the old port.
Pharmacy Papantoniou (☎ 24270 24515; Papadiamanti 18)

MONEY

Numerous ATMs are on Papadiamanti and the waterfront.

POST

Post office (upper Papadiamanti; ☸ 7.30am-2pm)

TRAVEL AGENCIES

For reliable information about Skiathos, or onward travel, try the following:

SKIATHOS

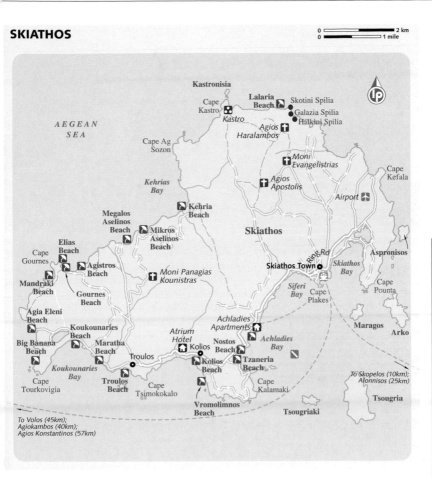

Creator Tours (☎ 24270 21384; www.crea tortours.com) On the waterfront.
Heliotropio Tourism & Travel (☎ 24270 22430; www.heliotropio.gr) On the waterfront.
Mathinos Travel (☎ 24270 23351; Papadia manti 18)

SIGHTS

Skiathos was the birthplace of famous 19th-century Greek novelist and short story writer Alexandros Papadiamanti, whose writings draw upon the hard lives of the islanders he grew up with. Papadiamanti's humble 1860-vintage

house is now a charming **museum** (☎ 24270 23843; Plateia Papadiamanti; admission €1; ☺ 9.30am-1.30pm & 5-8.30pm Tue-Sun) with books, paintings and old photos documenting his life on Skiathos.

TOURS

Excursion boats make half- and full-day trips around the island (€10 to €25, approximately four to six hours), and usually visit Cape Kastro, Lalaria Beach and the three *spilies* (caves) of Halkini, Skotini and Galazia, which are only accessible by boat. A few boats also visit the nearby

Beach-goers, Kastani Beach, Skopelos
JULIAN CASTLE/ALAMY

⬎ IF YOU LIKE...

If you're enjoying a sense of déjà vu while visiting **Skiathos Town** (p228) and find yourself uncontrollably humming *Dancing Queen*, you might like to take a day trip to neighbouring Skopelos (see p368) to track down these other *Mamma Mia* (2008) film locations:

- **Kastani Beach** The scene of *Does Your Mother Know*, this fairly remote beach is on Skopelos' sheltered west coast and is excellent for swimming. This is the island's sandiest beach, backed by a pine-cloaked hill.
- **Agios Ioannis Prodromos** Although filmed in a studio, the wedding chapel was created to look like this monastery near Glossa. Built on the top of a cliff and overlooking the sea, its location is dramatic and the views are stunning.
- **Glysteri** On the northern coast, this is where Amanda reads her diary to her friends and also the scene of *Our Last Summer*, which you can re-enact by jumping from the rocks into the aquamarine sea.

islets of Tsougria and Tsougriaki for swimming and snorkelling; you can take one boat over and return on another. At the old harbour, check out the signboards in front of each boat for a tour and schedule to your liking.

SLEEPING

For last-minute accommodation in high season, try the resourceful agents **Sotos & Maria** (☎ 24270 23219, 6974716408; sotos-2@otenet.gr).

Lena's Rooms (☎ 24270 22009; Bouboulinas St; r €55; ⌘) These six double rooms over the owner's flower shop are airy and spotless, each with fridge and balcony, plus a well-equipped common kitchen and shady, flower-filled veranda.

Villa Orsa (☎ 24270 22430; fax 24270 21952; s/d/f incl breakfast from €70/80/110; ⌘ ▢ 🛜) Perched well above the old harbour, this classic cliff-side mansion features very comfortable, traditionally styled rooms with balcony views overlooking a secluded bay. A generous breakfast is served on the garden terrace.

Hotel Bourtzi (☎ 24270 21304; www .hotelbourtzi.gr; Moraitou 8; s/d/tr incl breakfast from €90/130/150; P ✗ ☐ ☞ ☒) On upper Papadiamanti, the swank Bourtzi escapes much of the town noise, and features austere-modern rooms, an inviting garden and two small pools, one just for kids.

EATING

Taverna Alexandros (☎ 24270 22341; Mavrogiali; mains €4-9) Excellent lamb grills, traditional oven-roasted chicken and potatoes, and live acoustic Greek music await you at this friendly alleyway eatery under a canopy of mulberry trees.

Taverna Bakaliko (☎ 24270 24024; Club St; mains €4.50-9) You can't get much closer to the bay than at this popular eatery, known for well-prepared and well-priced standards like stuffed cabbage leaves, tomato and parsley salad and fish soup.

ourpick Maria's Pizza (☎ 24270 22292; mains €8-15) The pizza is just the beginning at this flower-filled gem above the old port. Highlights include stuffed garlic bread, tagliatelle pasta with prosciutto and asparagus (€12) and salads galore, each is a meal in itself.

DRINKING

ourpick Kentavros Bar (☎ 24270 22980) The long-established and handsome Kentavros, off Plateia Papadiamanti, promises rock, soul, jazz and blues, and gets the thumbs-up from locals and expats alike for its mellow ambience, artwork and good drinks.

The dancing and drinking scene heats up after midnight along the club strip past the new harbour. Best DJs are at **BBC** (☎ 24270 21190), followed by **Kahlua**

Bar (☎ 24270 23205) and **Club Pure** (☎ 6979773854), open till dawn.

SHOPPING

Loupos & His Dolphins (☎ 24270 23777; Plateia Papadiamanti; ☼ 10am-1.30pm & 6-11.30pm) Look for delicate hand-painted icons and fine Greek ceramics, along with gold and silver jewellery at this high-end gallery shop, next to Papadiamanti Museum.

Archipelagos Gallery (☎ 24270 22585; Plateia Papadiamanti; ☼ 11am-1pm & 8-10pm) Work by contemporary Greek and visiting artists stands out at this intimate shop.

AROUND SKIATHOS
SIGHTS & ACTIVITIES
DIVING

The small islets off the south shore of Skiathos make for great diving. Rates average €40 to €50 for half-day dives, equipment included.

Dive instructor team Theofanis and Eva of **Octopus Diving Centre** (☎ 24270 24549, 6944168958; www.odc-skiathos.com) at the new harbour lead dives around Tsougria and Tsougriaki islets for beginners and experts alike. **Skiathos Diving Centre** (☎ 24270 24424; www.skiathosdivingcenter.gr; Papadiamanti), and **Dolphin Diving** (☎ 24270 21599, 6944999181; www.ddiving.gr; Nostos Beach) are also popular for first-time divers, with dives off Tsougriaki Islet exploring locations 30m deep.

HIKING

A 6km-long hiking route begins at Moni Evangelistrias, eventually reaching **Cape Kastro**, before circling back through Agios Apostolis. Kastro is a spring mecca for birdwatchers, who may spot long-necked Mediterranean shags and singing blue-rock thrushes on the nearby rocky islets.

NICK HANNA/ALAMY

Thatch umbrellas, Mandraki Beach

ꙅ BEACHES

With some 65 beaches to choose from, beach-hopping on Skiathos can become a full-time occupation. The first long stretch of sand worth getting off the bus for is the pine-fringed **Vromolimnos Beach**. Further along, **Kolios Beach** and **Troulos Beach** are also good but both, alas, are very popular. The bus continues to **Koukounaries Beach**, backed by pine trees and touted as the best beach in Greece. Nowadays its crowded summer scene is best viewed at a distance, from where the 1200m long sweep of pale gold sand does indeed sparkle.

Big Banana Beach, known for its curving shape and soft white sand, lies at the other side of a narrow headland. West of Koukounaries, **Agia Eleni Beach** is a favourite with windsurfers. Sandy **Mandraki Beach**, a 1.5km walk along a pine-shaded path, is just far enough to keep it clear of the masses. The northwest coast's beaches are less crowded but are subject to the strong summer *meltemi* (northeasterly winds).

SLEEPING

Achladies Apartments (☎ 24270 22486; http://achladies.apartments.googlepages.com; Achladies Bay; d/tr/f incl breakfast €45/60/75; P) Along with self-catering rooms (two-night minimum stay) and ceiling fans, it features an ecofriendly tortoise sanctuary and a succulent garden winding down to a taverna and sandy beach.

OUR PICK **Atrium Hotel** (☎ 24270 49345; www.atriumhotel.gr; Paraskevi Beach; s/d/ste incl breakfast from €100/130/200; P ✕ ✕ ☐ ⬡ ⬡) Traditional architecture and modern touches make this hillside perch the best in its class. Rooms at the Atrium Hotel are low-key elegant, with basin sinks and large balconies.

CRETE

CRETE

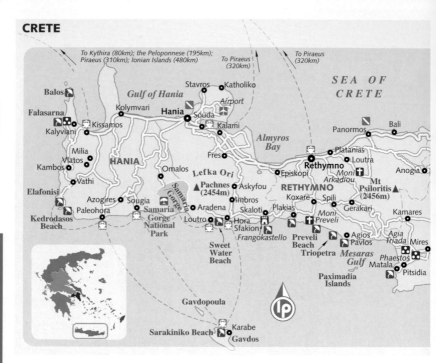

To Kythira (80km); the Peloponnese (195km); Piraeus (310km); Ionian Islands (480km)

To Piraeus (320km)

To Piraeus (320km)

SEA OF CRETE

Balos
Falasarna
Kalyviani
Kissamos
Kolymvari
Stavros
Katholiko
Hania
Airport
Souda
Kalami
Gulf of Hania
Panormos
Bali
Milia
Vlatos
Kambos
Vathi
HANIA
Omalos
Fres
Almyros Bay
Platanias
Rethymno
Loutra
Episkopi
Moni Arkadiou
Anogia
Lefka Ori
Pachnes (2454m)
Askyfou
RETHYMNO
Mt Psiloritis (2456m)
Elafonisi
Azogires
Sougia
Samaria Gorge
Aradena
Imbros
Koxare
Spili
Gerakari
Kamares
Paleohora
Samaria Gorge National Park
Loutro
Skaloti
Plakias
Moni Preveli
Kedrodasos Beach
Hora Sfakion
Frangokastello
Preveli Beach
Triopetra
Agios Pavlos
Agia Triada
Mires
Sweet Water Beach
Mesaras Gulf
Phaestos
Matala
Pitsidia
Paximadia Islands

Gavdopoula

Sarakiniko Beach
Karabe
Gavdos

CRETE

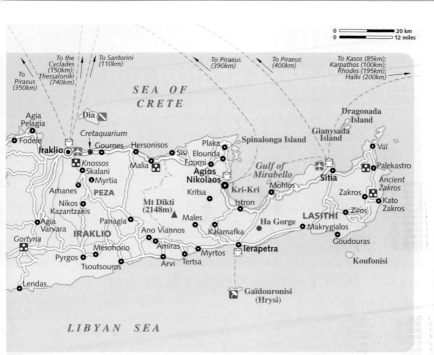

0 ⸻ 20 km
0 ⸻ 12 miles

To the Cyclades (150km); Thessaloniki (740km)

To Santorini (110km)

To Piraeus (390km)

To Piraeus (400km)

To Kasos (85km); Karpathos (100km); Rhodes (195km); Halki (200km)

To Piraeus (350km)

SEA OF CRETE

Dia

Cretaquarium

Agia Pelagia

Fodele

Iraklio

Gournes

Hersonisos

Sisi

Plaka

Elounda

Dragonada Island

Gianysada Island

Spinalonga Island

Vaï

Knossos

Skalani

Malia

Fourni

Myrtia

Agios Nikolaos

Kri-Kri

Mohlos

Sitia

Palekastro

Arhanes

PEZA

Kritsa

Gulf of Mirabello

Ancient Zakros

Nikos Kazantzakis

Mt Dikti (2148m)

Istron

Zakros

Males

Kato Zakros

Agia Varvara

Panagia

Ano Viannos

Kalamafka

LASITHI

Ziros

Gortyna

IRAKLIO

Amiras

Myrtos

Ha Gorge

Makrygialos

Mesohorio

Tertsa

Ierapetra

Goudouras

Pyrgos

Tsoutsouros

Arvi

Koufonisi

Lendas

Gaïdouronisi (Hrysi)

LIBYAN SEA

CRETE

HIGHLIGHTS

1   PEZA WINE REGION

BY EVELYNNE BAKINTA, PEZA UNION OF LOCAL PRODUCERS

My grandfather's family comes from the village of Myrtia. I left Crete to study and then came back to work for Peza Union. Peza is a fertile and blessed land, with abundant sunlight, sea breezes and special soil texture; the result offers unique-tasting wine.

HIGHLIGHTS

➘ EVELYNNE BAKINTA'S DON'T MISS LIST

❶ LOCAL RED

Kotsifali and Mantilari are two local grape varieties that balance one another in a popular Cretan red wine. A glass of this offers you the opportunity to taste red wine the way we have been producing it in our region for genera-tions. The youthful, vivid purple colour, the intense aroma and the full flavour define the unique force of this wine.

❷ LOCAL WHITE

Vilana is known for its abundance, Thrapsathiri for its delicacy and

Malvazia for its nobility. These three grape varieties complement one an-other in this much-loved Cretan white wine. The youthful shades, the subtlety and finesse in its aromas, and the full taste make it a favourite with locals.

❸ WINE TOUR

Head to Peza Union's exhibition space (see p247), located at an old wine-bottling factory 15km south of Iraklio. Watch a movie about wine-making in the area and see exhibits of early equipment. Then proceed to the

Clockwise from top: Local vineyard, Peza wine region (p247); Wine cellar interior; Antique ceramic storage jars, Knossos (p248); Regional wine selection; Grape varieties

wine-tasting area to linger over various wines, traditional mezedhes and locally produced olive oil. Then shop for your favourite bottle at the onsite market. Peza Union represents many of the region's vineyards.

❹ A GLASS WITH DINNER

My favourite Cretan meal-and-wine combination is roasted lamb with honey and sage, accompanied by a glass of Kotsifali, Mantilari and Syrah. This wine combines the local red varieties with the international Syrah grape, cultivated on Cretan slopes, adding a cosmopolitan character to this wine.

❺ WINE FESTIVAL

During the summer, the municipality of Nikos Kazantzakis organises a three-day wine festival called Oenopolitia. This takes place in various villages in the Peza region and includes wine-tasting, concerts, painting exhibitions and group visits to local museums. For dates and details, visit www.dimos-nikoskazantzakis.gr (in Greek only).

⬊ THINGS YOU NEED TO KNOW

Best time to visit Summer, when the vineyards are full of fruit, and mid-August to mid-September for harvesting **Best wine to take home for friends** Vin de pays (red, rosé or white, in easy-travel Tetra Paks) which once filled the urns of Knossos **See our author's review on p247**

HIGHLIGHTS

2

⇲ LEGENDARY KNOSSOS

The **Minoan Palace of Knossos** (p248) has been imaginatively reconstructed and gives you a window back in time. Colourful columns, vibrant frescoes and intriguing advancements, such as light wells and drainage systems, make this 3500-year-old palace all the more impressive. Watch for the Throne Room, Griffin Fresco, Grand Staircase, Dolphin Fresco and one of the earliest flushable water closets.

3

⇲ SAMARIA GORGE

Pack your hiking boots. Touted as Europe's longest gorge – and certainly one of its most gorgeous – it's worth putting up with the crowds to walk through **Samaria Gorge** (p259). You'll follow the river amidst wildflowers, cliffs of up to 500m and, if you're lucky, the shy *kri-kri*, Crete's beloved wild goat. Cross wooden bridges, wade through rivers and finish up with a refreshing dip in the sea.

CRETE

4

➘ RETHYMNO'S OLD QUARTER

Be charmed by the Venetian old town of **Rethymno** (p249). Its maze of narrow streets, which are lined with graceful houses and ornate monuments, lead down to a lively harbour. Take in the stunning Rimondi Fountain and the remnants of the town's defensive walls. Summer sees the old town relive its roots with the Renaissance Festival.

HIGHLIGHTS

5

➘ ELAFONISI & KEDRODASOS

With soft white and pink sand between your toes and warm turquoise water lapping at the shore, **Elafonisi** (p260) feels like the tropics. Tiny coves and islets and dolphins jumping offshore complete the picture. And if you don't like sharing, you can follow a coastal road to the nearby (and equally stunning) **Kedrodasos Beach**.

6

➘ RUGGED ANOGIA

Deep in the mountainous hinterland, the tiny village of **Anogia** (p253) is perched next to Mt Psiloritis and has cultivated a rebellious spirit for centuries. Here you'll find an undiluted Cretan character, evident in the old-school machismo, moustaches, traditionally dressed locals, handmade rugs and stirring local music. Sit in the main square and soak it all up.

2 Detail of Procession fresco (p245); 3 Hikers in Samaria Gorge (p259); 4 Narrow alleyway, Rethymno (p249); 5 Elafonisi (p260); 6 Traditional woven handicrafts, Anogia (p253)

CRETE

THE BEST...

THE BEST...

⬆ BEACHES

- **Golden Beach** (p263) Simply a long, long stretch of sand.
- **Preveli Beach** (p261) Sandy with palm-fringed riverbanks.
- **Gavdos island** (p261) Europe's most southerly point with a string of unspoilt beaches.
- **Falasarna** (p261) Soft coves and spectacular sunsets.
- **Frangokastello** (p261) Wide, white sand; ideal for kids.

⬆ CULTURAL EXPERIENCES

- **Summer Cultural Festival** (p263) Traditional Cretan music, theatre and art exhibits.
- **Archaeological Museum of Iraklio** (p245) Superb Minoan collection.
- **Byzantine & Post Byzantine Collection of Hania** (p256) Glittering collection in a restored fortress.
- **Phaestos** (p250) Unreconstructed ruins of a mysterious Minoan palace-city.

⬆ VIEW-FILLED HOTELS

- **Lato Hotel** (p246) Boutique lodgings, panoramic harbour views.
- **Casa Leone** (p257) Renovated 600-year-old Venetian building with water views.
- **Marin Hotel** (p246) Great waterfront vistas from a big balcony.
- **Hotel Aristea** (p253) Simple studios with magnificent mountain views.
- **Du Lac Hotel** (p263) Lakeside look-out over the pretty lagoon.

⬆ LOCAL CUISINE

- **Peri Orexeos** (p247) Creative takes like creamy chicken in angel-hair pastry.
- **Lemonokipos** (p251) Unique fare beneath lemon trees; try the pork with bitter orange leaves.
- **Bougatsa Shop** (p257) Hole-in-the-wall serving the Cretan speciality, *bougatsa*, since 1924.
- **Chrysofillis Mezedopoleio** (p264) Fresh mussels and barley pasta with prawns plus water views.

Left: Exhibits in the Archaeological Museum of Iraklio (p245); Right: Bougatsa pastries (p257)

THINGS YOU NEED TO KNOW

⤷ VITAL STATISTICS

- **Population** 540,045
- **Area** 8335 sq km

⤷ LOCALITIES IN A NUTSHELL

- **Central Crete** (p244) Bustling capital of Iraklio, celebrated Knossos, the Mediterranean's largest aquarium, picturesque Rethymno, fine beaches and mountain villages.
- **Western Crete** (p253) Magnificent Hania, the seemingly unending Samaria Gorge, unbelievable beaches and the mountainside hamlet of Azogires.
- **Eastern Crete** (p262) Photogenic Agios Nikolaos, Spinalonga Island with its massive fortress, and low-key, harbourside Sitia.

⤷ ADVANCE PLANNING

- **Two months before** Book your accommodation.
- **One month before** Check online for upcoming events and reserve tickets.
- **Two weeks before** Sort out car rental.

⤷ RESOURCES

- **www.interkriti.org** Island life, maps, city and town guides and links for accommodation bookings.
- **www.infocrete.com** Links to Crete's top 100 travel sites, including accommodation and car rentals.
- **www.explorecrete.com** Links, listings, facts, beach guides and activities.

⤷ EMERGENCY NUMBERS

- **Ambulance** (☎ 166)
- **Highway Rescue** (Elpa; ☎ 104)
- **Police** (☎ 100)

⤷ GETTING AROUND

- **Air** Direct flights from most major cities and islands in Greece.
- **Bus** Buses link the major northern towns. Less frequent services between the north-coast and southern towns, via inland mountain villages.
- **Car** If you're wanting to get out and explore (especially the countless beaches and mountain villages), it's best to have your own wheels.
- **Ferry** Direct ferry connections with the mainland and Santorini. Regular boats connect Paleohora and Hora Sfakion, including beaches between them; both towns have summer services to Gavdos island. For specific ferry services, see also Island Hopping (p357).

⤷ BE FOREWARNED

- **Flights** It's often cheaper to fly directly from Europe to Crete than via Athens.
- **Beaches** Those along the south coast can get sandblasted by strong winds.

CRETE

THINGS YOU NEED TO KNOW

ITINERARIES

CULTURAL TASTER Three Days

With only a few days, you can experience the diversity of Cretan culture. Base yourself in bustling **(1) Iraklio** (p244) to visit its very impressive archaeological museum; keep an eye out for the Griffin Fresco and the sarcophagus of Agia Triada, two of the Minoans' greatest artistic achievements. After that, hightail it out of town to the magical ruins of **(2) Knossos** (p248), a 3500-year-old palace that has been colourfully reconstructed to give you a glimpse into the legendary world of the Minoans. Next, visit the fertile **(3) Peza wine region** (p247), where you can sample local tipples. On the third day, head inland to the mountainside village of **(4) Anogia** (p253). Perched aside Mt Psiloritis, the village is known for its rebellious spirit and local musicians. Buy traditional, handmade blankets and crafts, and then get comfortable in one of the coffee shops that fringe the main square and soak up the distinctive local culture.

MIXED BAG Five Days

If you're keen to fill your vacation with a bit of everything Crete has to offer, begin your tour with a couple of days in the atmospheric seaside city of **(1) Rethymno** (p249). Get settled in characterful accommodation, dine on Cretan-style food and join in the nightlife, which is lively year-round due to the city's energetic student population. Explore the old town, including the impressive fortress, and look out for the beautiful Rimondi Fountain. Enjoy a walking tour to take in the surrounding scenery or join a dive school to explore under the sea. Take a day trip to **(2) Moni Arkadiou** (p252), a striking 16th-century Venetian baroque church. Next, head for sandy **(3) Preveli Beach** (p261), nicknamed Palm Beach for the palm-lined riverbanks that offer freshwater pools for swimming. Backed by rugged cliffs and overlooked by an impressive monastery, it's one of Crete's most photogenic beaches. Finally, head east to **(4) Phaestos** (p250), the ruins of a mysterious Minoan city set in an awe-inspiring location between mountains and a wide plain.

THE WILD WEST One Week

Base yourself in (1) Hania (p253), Crete's most evocative city. An atmospheric jumble of Venetian and Turkish architecture, set alongside a magnificent harbour, it's an excellent place to spend a couple of days exploring. Stay in one of the mansions now restored into a boutique hotel, take in the worthwhile museums and galleries and shop for local handicrafts. From Hania, take a day trip to the (2) Samaria Gorge (p259), Europe's largest gorge, boasting stunning scenery, carpets of wildflowers and a chance to see the *kri-kri*, Crete's shy wild goats.

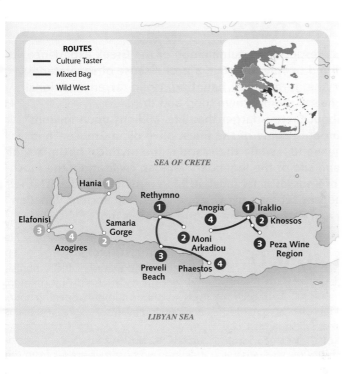

Spend a day hiking through the gorge with the crowds and then escape to (3) Elafonisi (p260). The shallow, turquoise water, tiny islets, coves and tropical setting make it Crete's top beach and a wonderful place to dig your toes into the sand for a couple of days. Finish up your tour with a visit to (4) Azogires (p260), a tranquil mountainside hamlet surrounded by woods, a stunning gorge, waterfalls and rock pools. Hole up in the fabulous hotels and taste the local honey and olive oil. Believed to be haunted by nereids and home to numerous cave churches, Azogires is a beautiful place for hill walks.

CRETE

DISCOVER CRETE

Crete is in many respects the culmination of the Greek experience. Its hospitable, spirited people maintain a proud sense of separateness, evident in everything from their haunting, violin-driven traditional music to their hearty, homegrown food and drink.

Everything about Crete is larger than life. Millions upon millions of olive trees produce some of the finest olive oil in Greece – and arguably, in the world – while the island is the mythical birthplace of Zeus himself, and site of the legendary Minoan civilisation; the much-visited Palace of Knossos is its most striking reminder. And, with their pretty pastel houses set on narrow stone lanes, the ancient Venetian ports of Hania and Rethymno are among Greece's most evocative towns.

DISCOVER CRETE

CENTRAL CRETE
IRAKLIO ΗΡΑΚΛΕΙΟ

pop 130,920

Iraklio (ee-rah-klee-oh), also called Heraklion, is Greece's fifth-largest city and the centre of Crete's economic and administrative life. It's a somewhat hectic place. It's full of the sounds of motorbikes throttling in unison at traffic lights, while airplanes constantly thrust off into the sky in summer over a long waterfront lined with the remnants of Venetian arsenals, fortresses and shrines.

ORIENTATION

The ferry port is 500m east of the old port. Iraklio's airport is 5km east of the city centre. From the bus station and port look towards the Hotel Megaron's parking lot; a concealed stone stairway here doubles back and up, accessing Epimenidou and the centre.

INFORMATION
EMERGENCY

Tourist police (☎ 2810 397111; Halikarnassos; ⊙ 7am-10pm)

INTERNET RESOURCES

www.heraklion-city.gr Official municipal website with useful information, such as phone numbers, opening hours and coming events.

MEDICAL SERVICES

Iraklio's two hospitals are far from the centre and work alternate days – call first to find out where to go.

Venizelio Hospital (☎ 2810 368000) On the road to Knossos, 4km south of Iraklio.

University Hospital (☎ 2810 392111) At Voutes, 5km south of Iraklio (bus 11, ticket price €1.50), this is the best-equipped medical facility.

MONEY

Banks and ATMs line 25 Avgoustou, and are widespread throughout the centre.

POST

Post office (☎ 2810 234468; Plateia Daskalogianni; ⊙ 7.30am-8pm Mon-Fri, 7.30am-2pm Sat)

TOURIST INFORMATION

EOT (Greek National Tourist Organisation; ☎ 2810 246299; Xanthoudidou 1; ⊙ 8.30am-

8.30pm Apr-Oct, 8.30am-3pm Nov-Mar) Opposite the archaeological museum.

TRAVEL AGENCIES

Magician's Travel (☎ 2810 301471; operation@driveongreece.gr; Mitsotaki 1B) This helpful, patient travel agency near the waterfront can arrange and inform about all ferry and plane tickets.
Skoutelis Travel (☎ 2810 280808; www .skoutelistravel.gr; 25 Avgoustou 24) Airline and ferry bookings, excursions, accommodation help and car hire can all be arranged here.

SIGHTS
ARCHAEOLOGICAL MUSEUM OF IRAKLIO

The outstanding Minoan collection makes Iraklio's **archaeological museum** (☎ 2810 279000; Xanthoudidou 2; admission €4, incl Knossos €10; ⏱ 8am-8pm Tue-Sun, 8am-1pm Mon Apr-Oct, 8am-3pm Tue-Sun, noon-3pm Mon late Oct-early Apr) second only to Athens' National Archaeological Museum. This treasure trove includes pottery, jewellery, figurines and sarcophagi, plus some famous frescoes. The most exciting Minoan finds come from the sites of Knossos, Phaestos, Malia, Zakros and Agia Triada.

The superlative Knossos frescoes include the **Procession fresco**, the **Griffin Fresco** (from the Throne Room), the **Dolphin Fresco** (from the Queen's Room) and the amazing **Bull-leaping Fresco**, which depicts a seemingly double-jointed acrobat somersaulting on the back of a charging bull.

Among the treasures of Minoan jewellery is the beautiful **gold bee pendant** from Malia, depicting two bees dropping honey into a comb.

From Phaestos, the most prized find is the fascinating **Phaestos Disk**, a 16cm circular clay tablet inscribed with (still undeciphered) pictographic symbols.

Also displayed is the elaborate **Kamares pottery**, named after the sacred cave of Kamares where it was discovered; a superbly decorated vase from

JOHN ELK III

Local marina, Iraklio

CRETE

CENTRAL CRETE

CRETE

CENTRAL CRETE

MYSTERIOUS MINOANS

Although it's been inhabited since Neolithic times (7000–3000 BC), Crete is most famous for its advanced Minoan civilisation. Traces of this still enigmatic society were only uncovered in the early 20th century, when British archaeologist Sir Arthur Evans discovered and then restored the palace at Knossos. Since no one knew what to call this lost race, Sir Arthur made an adjective of the mythical King Minos, the legendary former ruler of Knossos – and so emerged the name 'Minoans'.

Their actual name notwithstanding, we do know that the Minoans migrated to Crete in the 3rd millennium BC. These mysterious people were expert in metallurgy, making unprecedented artistic, engineering and cultural achievements during the Protopalatial period (3400–2100 BC); their most famous palaces (at Knossos, Phaestos, Malia and Zakros) were built then. The Minoans also began producing their exquisite Kamares pottery and silverware, and became a maritime power, trading with Egypt and Asia Minor.

Around 1700 BC, however, an earthquake destroyed the great palace complexes. Undeterred, the Minoans built bigger and better ones over the ruins, while settling more widely across Crete. Around 1450 BC, when the Minoan civilisation was in the ascendant, the palaces were mysteriously destroyed again, probably by a giant tsunami triggered by the massive volcanic eruption on Santorini (Thira). Knossos, the only palace saved, was finally burned down around 1400 BC.

Archaeological evidence shows that the Minoans lingered on for a few centuries in small, isolated settlements before disappearing as mysteriously as they had come.

Phaestos with white sculpted flowers is here, too.

Also from Knossos are **Linear A and B tablets** (the latter have been translated as household or business accounts), an ivory statue of a **bull leaper**, and some exquisite **gold seals**. The most famous of Minoan sarcophagi, and one of Minoan art's greatest achievements, is the **sarcophagus of Agia Triada**, painted with floral and abstract designs and ritual scenes.

SLEEPING

Kronos Hotel (☎ 2810 282240; www.kronos hotel.gr; Sofokli Venizelou 2; s/d €50/60; 🅿 💻) This well-maintained, older waterfront hotel has comfortable rooms with double-glazed windows and balconies, phone and TV. Most are fridge-equipped; some have sea views.

Marin Hotel (☎ 2810 300018; www.marin hotel.gr; Doukos Beaufort 12; s incl breakfast €75, d incl breakfast €95-125; 🅿 💻) This refurbished hotel has front-facing rooms with great views of the harbour and fortress, some with big balconies. Rooms are attractive and well-appointed.

Lato Hotel (☎ 2810 228103; www.lato .gr; Epimenidou 15; s/d €100/127, ste from €175; 🅿 🛜) The full boutique experience awaits at the well-designed Lato, marked by its superior service. The rooms' chic contemporary design is complemented by spectacular views, especially in the spacious suites; ascend to the atmospheric rooftop restaurant and bar for panoramic views.

EATING

Giakoumis Taverna (☎ 2810 280277; Theodosaki 5-8; mayirefta €4-8; ☒ closed Sun) One of the best of the tavernas clustered around the 1866 market side streets, Giakoumis is always busy, serving both vegetarian fare and meats hot off the grill. Cretan specialities dominate.

Parasies (☎ 2810 225009; Plateia Istorikou Mouseiou; grills €6.50-10) In the corner of the square next to the Historical Museum, this is a good lunch spot, with tasty grills.

Peri Orexeos (☎ 2810 222679; Koraï 10; mains €7-10) On the busy Koraï pedestrian strip, try excellent contemporary Greek food here, with creative takes like creamy chicken wrapped in *kataïfi* (angel-hair pastry), huge salads and solid Cretan cuisine.

GETTING THERE & AWAY

AIR

Iraklio's Nikos Kazantzakis Airport is Crete's biggest and gets many regular domestic, international and summertime charter flights.

BOAT

The portside **Iraklio Port Authority** (☎ 2810 244912) keeps ferry schedule information.

BUS

Iraklio's main transport hub, **Bus Station A** (☎ 2810 246534; www.ktel-heraklio-lassithi .gr; Leoforos Nearhou), serves eastern and western Crete (including Knossos) from its waterfront location near the quay.

Bus Station B (☎ 2810 255965), west of the city centre beyond Hania Gate, serves Phaestos, Agia Galini and Matala.

GETTING AROUND

Bus 1 serves the airport every 15 minutes between 6am and 1am. The bus terminal is near the Astoria Capsis Hotel on Plateia Eleftherias. An airport taxi costs €10 to €12; try **Ikarus Radio Taxi** (☎ 2810 211212).

CRETAQUARIUM

The massive **Cretaquarium** (☎ 2810 337788; www.cretaquarium.gr; adult/child over 4yr/under 4yr €8/6/free; ☒ 9am-9pm May-mid-Oct, 10am-5.30pm mid-Oct-Apr) at Gournes, 15km east of Iraklio, is the Eastern Mediterranean's largest aquarium. Interactive multimedia features and displays in several languages help explain things.

The north-coast buses (€1.70, 30 minutes) leaving from Iraklio's Bus Station A can drop you on the main road; from there it's a 10-minute walk.

> ## IRAKLIO'S WINE COUNTRY
>
> Just south of Iraklio and Knossos, the fertile Peza region produces 70% of Cretan wines. The **Peza Union of local producers** (☎ 2810 741945; www.pezaunion.gr; admission free; ☒ 9am-4pm Mon-Sat) has tastings, videos and a minimuseum. The state-of-the-art hilltop **Boutari Winery** (☎ 2810 731617; www.boutari.gr; Skalani; tour & tasting €4.50; ☒ 10am-6pm), about 8km from Iraklio, features a stunning tasting room and showroom overlooking the vineyard of the Fantaxometoho estate – and great wines on offer.

NEIL SETCHFIELD

Palace relief, Knossos

↘ **KNOSSOS** ΚΝΩΣΣΟΣ

Crete's must-see historical attraction is the **Minoan Palace of Knossos**, 5km south of Iraklio in Knossos (k-nos-*os*) village, and the capital of Minoan Crete.

Legendary home of King Minos' mythical Minotaur, Knossos was uncovered in the early 1900s by British archaeologist Sir Arthur Evans. After 35 years and some £250,000 of his own money, Sir Arthur had excavated the site and accomplished partial reconstructions. His efforts proved controversial, with some archaeologists claiming that accuracy was sacrificed to imagination. However, for the casual visitor, the reconstructions are more than sufficient for visualising a real live Minoan palace.

Evans' reconstruction brings to life the palace's most significant aspects, including the reconstructed columns; painted deep brown-red with gold-trimmed black capitals, they taper gracefully at the bottom. Vibrant frescoes add another dramatic dimension to the palace. Additionally, the Minoans' highly sophisticated society is revealed by details like the advanced drainage system, the placement of light wells, and the organisation of space within rooms – meant to be cool in summer and warm in winter.

Frequent buses from Iraklio's bus station (see p247) and from near Morosini Fountain serve Knossos. From the coastal road, occasional signs direct drivers. Since several free car parks exist close to the site, don't listen to touts advertising paid parking lots along the way.

Things you need to know: ☎ 2810 231940; admission €6; ⊙ 8am-7pm Jun-Oct, 8am-3pm Nov-May

RETHYMNO ΡΕΘΥΜΝΟ

pop 27,870

Delightful Rethymno (*reth*-im-no) is Crete's third largest town, noted for its picturesque old town running down to a lively harbour overlooked by a massive Venetian fortress. Although Rethymno is showing signs of urban sprawl, travellers seem to miss it (except when looking for parking), such is the attraction of the lovely old Venetian-Turkish quarter, with its maze of narrow streets, graceful wood-balconied houses and ornate Venetian monuments; minarets add an Ottoman flourish.

ORIENTATION

Rethymno's major sights and best sleeping and eating options are clustered near the harbour; a decent beach is on its eastern side.

The bus station, at the western end of Igoumenou Gavriil, is about 600m west of the Porto Guora (despite some discussions, it hadn't been relocated at the time of writing). If arriving by ferry, you'll see the old quarter opposite the quay.

INFORMATION

Alfa Odeon Holidays (☎ 28310 57610; www.odeon travel.gr; Paleologou 25) The helpful Manolis Chliaoutakis runs this full-service travel agency in the old town.
Alpha Bank (Pavlou Koundouriotou 29)
Ellotia Tours (☎ 28310 24533; www.rethymnoatcrete.com; Arkadiou 155; ☺ 9am-9pm Mar-Nov) Boat and plane tickets, currency exchange, car and bike hire and excursions can be arranged here.
Municipal Tourist Office (☎ 28310 29148; www.rethymno.gr; Delfini Bldg, Eleftheriou Venizelou; ☺ 8.30am-8.30pm Mon-Fri year-round, plus 9am-8.30pm Sat & Sun Mar-Nov)
National Bank of Greece (Dimokratias)

Post office (☎ 28310 22302; Moatsou 21; ☺ 7am-7pm Mon-Fri)
Rethymno Hospital (☎ 28210 27491; Triandalydou 17; ☺ 24hr)
Tourist police (☎ 28310 28156; Delfini Bldg, Venizelou; ☺ 7am-2.30pm) At the municipal tourist office.

SIGHTS

Rethymno's 16th-century **fortress** (fortezza; ☎ 28310 28101; Paleokastro Hill; admission €3.10; ☺ 8am-8pm Jun-Oct) was originally an ancient acropolis. Although its massive walls once sheltered numerous buildings, only a church and a mosque survive. Nevertheless, there are many ruins to explore, and great views from the ramparts.

In the old quarter, the unmissable **Rimondi Fountain**, with its spouting lion heads and Corinthian capitals, attests to former Venetian rule, as does the 16th-century **Loggia** (now a museum shop). The well-preserved **Porto Guora** (Great Gate) is a remnant of the Venetian defensive wall.

Venetian and Turkish architecture is vividly displayed at the **Centre for Byzantine Art** (☎ 28210 50120; Ethnikis Antistaseos). This former mansion's terrace cafe offers great old-town views.

The nearby **Nerantzes Mosque**, converted from a Franciscan church in 1657, and, further east, the **Kara Musa Pasha Mosque**, with its vaulted fountain, are Rethymno's major remaining Ottoman structures. The latter now houses the **Hellenic Conservatory**, and makes an atmospheric concert venue.

ACTIVITIES

The **Happy Walker** (☎ /fax 28310 52920; www.happywalker.com; Tombazi 56; ☺ 5pm-8.30pm) offers various countryside walks near Rethymno. More serious hikers should see

CRETE

CENTRAL CRETE

CRETE

CENTRAL CRETE

JOHN ELK III

Minoan palace-city ruins, Phaestos

↘ IF YOU LIKE...

If you like exploring the ruins of **Knossos** (p248), we think you'll enjoy encountering these other impressive Minoan sites:

- **Phaestos** (☎ 28920 42315; adult/student €4/2, incl Agia Triada €6/3; ☺ 8am-7.30pm Jun-Oct, 8am-5pm Nov-Apr) Only 63km from Iraklio, this was the second-most-important Minoan palace-city, enjoying the most awe-inspiring location, with panoramic views of the Mesara Plain and Mt Ida. There's an air of mystery about the desolate, unreconstructed ruins that's not found at Knossos.
- **Malia** (☎ 28970 31597; admission €4; ☺ 8.30am-3pm Tue-Sun) Smaller than Knossos, this ancient palace complex was built on a flat, fertile plain. Look for the Kernos Stone, a disc with 34 holes around its edge that archaeologists still can't explain, and the Loggia, used for religious ceremonies.
- **Agia Triada** (☎ 28920 91564; admission €3, incl Phaestos €6; ☺ 10am-4.30pm summer, 8.30am-3pm winter) This was possibly a royal summer villa, judging by the opulence of the objects discovered here. North of the palace, the stoa (long, colonnaded building) of an erstwhile settlement has been unearthed.
- **Gortyna** (☎ 28920 31144; admission €4; ☺ 8am-7.30pm, to 5pm winter) This vast and intriguing site was inhabited from Minoan to Christian times, and became capital of Rome's Cyrenaica province. The massive stone tablets inscribed with the wide-ranging Laws of Gortyna (5th century BC) comprise Gortyna's most significant exhibit.
- **Zakros** (☎ 28430 26897; Kato Zakros; admission €3; ☺ 8am-7.30pm Jul-Oct, 8.30am-3pm Nov-Jun) Once a major Minoan port, this palace comprised royal apartments, storerooms and workshops on a low plain near the shore. Rising water levels have since have submerged parts of the palace. While the ruins are sparse, the wildness and remoteness of the setting make it attractive.

EOS (Greek Mountaineering Club; ☎ 28310 57766; www.eos.rethymnon.com; Dimokratias 12) for detailed info on mountain climbing and other outdoor adventures in Rethymno prefecture.

The **Paradise Dive Centre** (☎ 28310 26317; www.diving-center.gr) runs diving activities and PADI courses for all levels. Its dive base is at Petres, 15 minutes west of Rethymno.

FESTIVALS & EVENTS

The annual **Renaissance Festival** (☎ 28310 51199; www.rfr.gr) is Rethymno's biggest event. Activities primarily take place in the fortress's Erofili Theatre from July to September. The mid-July **Wine Festival** is held in the flower-filled municipal park, which is always good for a relaxing stroll.

SLEEPING

Atelier (☎ 28310 24440; atelier@ret.forthnet .gr; Himaras 27; r €35-55) These clean and attractively refurbished rooms attached to Frosso Bora's pottery workshop represent great value. They're marked by Venetian architecture, like the exposed stone walls – along with flat-screen TVs, new bathrooms and kitchenettes.

Casa dei Delfini (☎ 28310 55120; kzaxa@ reth.gr; Nikiforou Foka 66-68; studio €55-75, ste €80-140; ✗) Turkish and Venetian architectural features intermingle in this elegant pension, which includes an old stone trough and hammam ceiling in one of the studio bathrooms. The traditionally decorated rooms all feature kitchenettes; most impressive is the massive maisonette, with its large private terrace.

our pick **Hotel Veneto** (☎ 28310 56634; www.veneto.gr; Epimenidou 4; studio/ste incl breakfast €125/145; ✗ 🛜) For some of Rethymno's most beautiful aesthetic flourishes, visit the Veneto, which dates partially from the 14th century. Rooms feature polished wood floors, iron beds, TV and kitchenettes.

Palazzo Rimondi (☎ 28310 51289; www .palazzorimondi.com; cnr Xanthoulidou 21 & Trikoupi 16; d studio/ste incl breakfast €160/200; ✗ 🛜) This charming old-town Venetian mansion is a real treat, with its exquisite individually decorated studios with kitchenettes. The Palazzo Rimondi also has a small splash pool in the breakfast courtyard.

EATING

Fanari (☎ 28310 54849; Kefalogiannidon 15; mezedhes €2.50-10) West of the Venetian harbour on the waterfront, this taverna serves good mezedhes, fresh fish and Cretan cuisine. Try the *bekri mezes* (pork with wine and peppers) or *apaki,* the local smoked-pork speciality, as well as the homemade wine.

Samaria (☎ 28310 24681; Eleftheriou Venizelou; mayirefta €4-7) On the waterfront but still popular with locals, Samaria does good *mayirefta,* while the soups and grills are also excellent.

Lemonokipos (☎ 28310 57087; Ethnikis Antistaseos 100; mains €7-9) Dine among the lemon trees in the lovely courtyard of this old-town taverna. The traditional Cretan fare includes some unique twists, such as pork and vegetables flavoured with bitter orange leaves.

Avli (☎ 28310 26213; www.avli.com; cnr Xanthoudidou 22 & Radamanthyos; mains €13.50-30) This delightful former Venetian villa is the place for a special night out. The Nuevo Cretan-style food is superb, the wine list excellent and you dine in a charming courtyard bursting with pots of herbs, bougainvillea canopies, fruit trees and works of art.

CRETE

Venetian Baroque church, Moni Arkadiou

JOHN ELK III

CENTRAL CRETE

◥ MONI ARKADIOU ΜΟΝΗ ΑΡΚΑΔΙΟΥ

The 16th-century **Moni Arkadiou** has deep significance for Cretans. This monastery, situated in the hills 23km southeast of Rethymno, was the site of an act of mass suicidal defiance that captured European public attention.

In November 1866, massive Ottoman forces arrived to crush island-wide revolts. Hundreds of Cretan men, women and children fled their villages to find shelter at Arkadiou. However, far from being a safe haven, the monastery was soon besieged by 2000 Turkish soldiers. Rather than surrender, the Cretans set light to stored gunpowder kegs, killing everyone, Turks included; one small girl miraculously survived, and lived to a ripe old age in a village nearby. A bust of this woman and one of the abbot who lit the gunpowder stand outside the monastery.

Arkadiou's most impressive building, its Venetian baroque church, has a striking facade marked by eight slender Corinthian columns and topped by an ornate triple-belled tower. Left of it is a small **museum**. The monastery's former windmill outside it has a macabre **ossuary**, containing skulls and bones of the 1866 fighters.

From Rethymno, three daily buses go to Moni Arkadiou (€2.50, 30 minutes).

Things you need to know: Arkadi; ☎ 28310 83136; admission €2; ◷ 9am-7pm Apr-Oct

DRINKING & ENTERTAINMENT

Rethymno's nightlife is concentrated in the bars, clubs and discos around Nearhou and Salaminos, near the Venetian harbour, along with the waterfront bars off Plastira Sq. The indefatigable student population keeps Rethymno lively year-round.

Figaro (☎ 28310 29431; Vernardou 21; ◷ noon-late) Housed in an ingeniously restored old building, Figaro is an atmospheric 'art and music' all-day bar. It attracts everyone from the local intelligentsia and students to tourists drawn in by the subdued ambience and excellent music.

GETTING THERE & AWAY

BUS

From the **bus station** (☎ 28310 22212; www .bus-service-crete-ktel.com; Igoumenou Gavriil), hourly buses run in summer to both Hania (€6.50, one hour) and Iraklio (€6.50, 1½ hours).

ANOGIA ΑΝΩΓΕΙΑ

pop 2450

Perched aside **Mt Psiloritis**, 37km southwest of Iraklio, Anogia's known for its rebellious spirit and determination to express its undiluted Cretan character. It's also known for its stirring music and has spawned many of Crete's best known musicians.

Anogia's *kafeneia* (coffee shops) on the main square are frequented by black-shirted moustachioed men, the older ones often wearing traditional dress. The women stay home or flog the traditional blankets and other crafts that hang all over the village's shops.

During WWII Anogia was a centre of resistance, and suffered heavily for it. The Nazis massacred all the local men in retaliation for their role in sheltering Allied troops and aiding in the kidnap of General Kreipe.

Anogia clings to a hillside, with the textile shops in the lower half and most accommodation and businesses above. There's an ATM-equipped bank and post office.

SLEEPING & EATING

Hotel Aristea (☎ 28340 31459; d incl breakfast €40; ℗) There are good views from this upper-village location. The simple but well-outfitted rooms have bathrooms and balconies. An excellent set of new studios is next door.

Ta Skalomata (☎ 28340 31316; grills €3-7) On the upper village's eastern edge, it

serves great grills and Cretan dishes at reasonable prices. Zucchini with cheese and aubergine is very tasty, and do try the home-baked bread.

GETTING THERE & AWAY

Four daily buses reach Anogia from Iraklio (€3.60, one hour), while two daily buses operate from Rethymno (€4.90, 1¼ hours).

WESTERN CRETE

HANIA ΧΑΝΙΑ

pop 53,370

Hania (hahn-*yah*; also spelt Chania) is Crete's most evocative city, with its pretty Venetian quarter, criss-crossed by narrow lanes, culminating at a magnificent harbour. Remnants of Venetian and Turkish architecture abound, with old town-houses now restored, transformed into atmospheric restaurants and boutique hotels.

Although all this beauty means the Old Town is deluged with tourists in summer, it's still a great place to unwind. Excellent local handicrafts mean there's good shopping, too.

Crete's second biggest city, Hania is also the major transit point for hikers doing the Samaria Gorge, and is the main transport hub for all western destinations.

ORIENTATION

Hania's bus station is on Kydonias, two blocks southwest of Plateia 1866, from where the Old Harbour is a short walk north up Halidon.

Most accommodation lies in the Old Town's western half. Hania's headland separates the Venetian port from the modern town's crowded beach, Nea Hora. Koum Kapi, in the old Turkish quarter further east, has waterfront cafes; above it,

HANIA

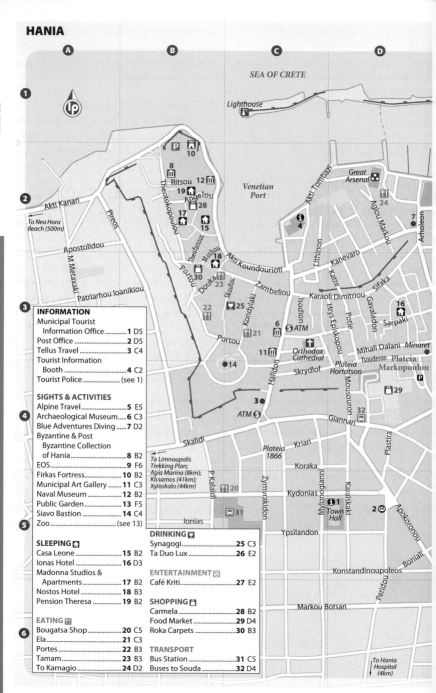

SEA OF CRETE

Lighthouse

Venetian
Port

Great
Arsenal

Akti Kanari

To Nea Hora
Beach (500m)

Apostolidou

Patriarhou Ioanikiou

To Limnoupolis
Trekking Plan;
Agia Marina (8km);
Kissamos (41km);
Xyloskalo (44km)

Plateia
1866

Plateia
Markopoulou

Orthodox
Cathedral

Town
Hall

To Hania
Hospital
(4km)

INFORMATION
Municipal Tourist
  Information Office **1** D5
Post Office **2** D5
Tellus Travel **3** C4
Tourist Information
  Booth **4** C2
Tourist Police ....(see 1)

SIGHTS & ACTIVITIES
Alpine Travel............................**5** E5
Archaeological Museum.......**6** C3
Blue Adventures Diving **7** D2
Byzantine & Post
  Byzantine Collection
  of Hania **8** B2
EOS..**9** F6
Firkas Fortress......................**10** B2
Municipal Art Gallery **11** C3
Naval Museum **12** B2
Public Garden......................**13** F5
Siavo Bastion **14** C4
Zoo..(see 13)

SLEEPING
Casa Leone **15** B2
Ionas Hotel **16** D3
Madonna Studios &
  Apartments........................**17** B2
Nostos Hotel **18** B3
Pension Theresa **19** B2

EATING
Bougatsa Shop....................**20** C5
Ela **21** C3
Portes **22** B3
Tamam **23** B3
To Karnagio **24** D2

DRINKING
Synagogi...............................**25** C3
Ta Duo Lux **26** E2

ENTERTAINMENT
Café Kriti...............................**27** E2

SHOPPING
Carmela.................................**28** B2
Food Market **29** D4
Roka Carpets **30** B3

TRANSPORT
Bus Station **31** C5
Buses to Souda **32** D4

on busy Leoforos Eleftherios Venizelos, is the Halepa district, once an upscale residential and consular district where Venizelos himself used to live (his home is now a museum).

Boats to Hania dock 7km southeast, at Souda.

INFORMATION

Most banks are in the new part of town, but ATMs exist in the Old Town on Halidon.

Hania Hospital (☎ 28210 22000; Mournies) Somewhat chaotic modern hospital 5km south; take a public bus or taxi (€8 to €10).

Municipal Tourist Information Office (☎ 28210 36155; tourism@chania.gr; Kydonias 29; ☼ 8am-2.30pm) Provides information and maps. The Old Harbour's information booth operates between noon and 2pm.

Post office (☎ 28210 28445; Peridou 10; ☼ 7.30am-8pm Mon-Fri, 7.30am-2pm Sat)

Tellus Travel (☎ 28210 91500; Halidon 108; www.tellustravel.gr; ☼ 8am-11pm) Hires out cars, changes money, arranges air and boat tickets, accommodation and excursions.

Tourist police (☎ 28210 73333; Kydonias 29; ☼ 8am-2.30pm) By the Town Hall.

www.chania.gr Municipality website; has general info. and cultural events calendar.

www.chania-guide.gr More online information.

SIGHTS
MUSEUMS

Hania's **Archaeological Museum** (☎ 28210 90334; Halidon 30; admission €2, incl Byzantine Collection €3; ☼ 8.30am-3pm Tue-Sun), in the impressive 16th-century Venetian Church of San Francisco, is marked by a Turkish fountain attesting to its former incarnation as a mosque. Its collection of

CRETE

WESTERN CRETE

finds from western Crete dating from the Neolithic to the Roman era includes statues, vases, jewellery, three splendid floor mosaics and some impressive painted sarcophagi from Armeni's Late Minoan cemetery.

The **Naval Museum** (☎ 28210 91875; Akti Koundourioti; admission €3; ☺ 9am-4pm), housed in the headland's Firkas Fortress (once a Turkish prison), exhibits model ships dating from the Bronze Age, naval instruments, paintings, photographs and Battle of Crete memorabilia.

The **Byzantine & Post Byzantine Collection of Hania** (☎ 28210 96046; Theotokopoulou; admission €2, incl Archaeological Museum €3; ☺ 8.30am-3pm Tue-Sun), in the fortress' restored Church of San Salvatore, contains a fascinating collection of artefacts, icons, jewellery and coins, including a fine mosaic floor and a prized icon of St George slaying the dragon.

OTHER ATTRACTIONS

Hania's massive **Venetian fortifications** are impressive. Best preserved is the western wall, running from the **Firkas Fortress** to the **Siavo Bastion**. The bastion offers good views of the Old Town (enter through the Naval Museum).

Hania's **Municipal Art Gallery** (☎ 28210 92294; www.pinakothiki-chania.gr; Halidon 98; admission €2, Wed free; ☺ 10am-2pm & 7-10pm Mon-Fri, 10am-2pm Sat) hosts exhibitions of modern Greek art.

Just up from the eastern waterfront, the formerly Turkish **Splantzia quarter** is a relaxing spot, where the colourful, narrow streets and leafy squares now host boutique hotels, galleries, cafes and bars.

ACTIVITIES

EOS (☎ 28210 44647; www.eoshanion.gr; Tzanakaki 90), the Greek Mountaineering Association's local branch, gives info about serious treks and climbs in the Lefka Ori, mountain refuges and the Trans-European E4 trail. It runs weekend excursions.

Friendly, English-speaking **Manolis Mesarchakis** (☎ 69769 92921; mesarchas@ yahoo.gr), an alpine ski instructor and

Former Turkish prison, Naval Museum, Hania

NEIL SETCHFIELD

hiker, provides valuable information and can help arrange guided trips for those hungry for outdoor challenges tougher than the Samaria Gorge.

Trekking Plan (☎ 28210 60861; www .cycling.gr), 8km west in Agia Marina, organises treks to the Agia Irini and Imbros gorges, climbs of Mt Gingilos, mountain-bike tours, canyoning, rappelling, rock climbing and kayaking trips. **Alpine Travel** (☎ 28210 50939; www.alpine.gr; Boniali 11-19) also organises treks.

Blue Adventures Diving (☎ 28210 40608; www.blueadventuresdiving.gr; Arholeon 11) offers a PADI certification course (€370) and daily diving trips (two dives €80), including beginner dives. Snorkelling and cruise options are offered, too.

HANIA FOR CHILDREN

The **public garden**, between Tzanakaki and Dimokratias, has a playground, a shady cafe, and a small **zoo** with two *kri-kri* (endemic Cretan wild goats). The giant water park **Limnoupolis** (☎ 28210 33246; Varypetro; day pass adult/child 6-12yr €17/12, afternoon pass €12/9; ⏱ 10am-7pm) south of town is also entertaining. Buses leave regularly from the bus station (€1.70).

TOURS

Boat excursions to the nearby **Agii Theodorou and Lazaretto islets**, and across the Gulf of Hania, leave from the harbour. The **M/S Irini** (☎ 28210 52001; cruises €15, sunset cruises €8, child under 7yr free) runs daily cruises on a lovely 1930s cruiser, including free snorkelling gear, and sunset cruises with complimentary fruit and *raki*. However, the advertised glass-bottomed boat tours aren't worth it.

SLEEPING

Pension Theresa (☎ /fax 28210 92798; Angelou 2; r €40-50; ✕ ⏻) Run by the kindly retired doctor Georgios Nikitas, this creaky old house with a steep spiral staircase and antique furniture oozes atmosphere. Some rooms have a view, though the best is from the rooftop terrace (which has a communal kitchen). Rooms have TV, air-con and lofts with an extra bed, though some are snug.

Ionas Hotel (☎ 28210 55090; www.ionas hotel.com; Sarpaki & Sorvolou; d incl breakfast €60-80, ste incl buffet breakfast €130; ✕ ⏻) This boutique hotel in the quiet but hip Splantzia quarter has a contemporary design. Rooms have all the mod cons and there's a rooftop terrace.

Nostos Hotel (☎ 28210 94743; www.nos tos-hotel.com; Zambeliou 42-46; s/d/tr incl breakfast €60/80/120; ✕) A renovated 600-year-old Venetian building, the superlative Nostos has split-level self-catering rooms; balcony rooms have harbour views.

Madonna Studios & Apartments (☎ 28210 94747; madonnastudios@yahoo.co.uk; Gamba 33; studio €70-110; ✕) This charming pension has five traditionally furnished studios with unique individual touches. The lodgings are set around a lovely flower-filled courtyard.

Casa Leone (☎ 28210 76762; www.casa -leone.com; Parodos Theotokopoulou 18; r incl breakfast €130-170; ✕) This classy former Venetian residence offers spacious, airy rooms, with balconies overlooking the harbour.

EATING

Bougatsa Shop (bougatsa €2; ⏱ 6am-2pm) Hania's most delicious *bougatsa*, made with Crete's sweet *myzithra* cheese, has been served since 1924 at this unassuming hole in the wall, opposite the bus station.

To Karnagio (☎ 28210 53366; Plateia Katehaki 8; mains €5-10.50) Near the Great Arsenal, this popular outdoor place does

ECO-ADVENTURES IN MILIA

Midway in the mountains between Paleohora and Hania, the isolated settlement of Milia (☎ 28220 51569; www.milia.gr; d from €60) is Crete's coolest eco-establishment. This abandoned village of stone farmhouses was reconstructed into eco-lodges, now using only solar energy to generate electricity. Needless to say, the food served at Milia's superb taverna comes from the settlement's own organic produce, including oil, wine, milk and cheese. (The menu changes often, depending on what's in season.) With a spectacular setting amid olive-clad mountains, and friendly staff, Milia is really one of Crete's most exceptional places. Alas, there's no bus, though if you book for at least a week the staff will usually drive you from and to Hania.

To reach Milia, drive just past **Vlatos** and take the drivable 3km dirt road up to it.

good seafood (try the grilled cuttlefish) and classic Cretan dishes.

Tamam (☎ 28210 96080; Zambeliou 49; mains €5.50-8.50) Housed in old Turkish baths, Tamam (meaning 'OK' in Turkish) does excellent vegetarian specialities and eastern-influenced dishes. Try the house salad and the Beyendi chicken with creamy aubergine purée.

ourpick Portes (☎ 28210 76261; Portou 48; mains €6-9) Set along a quiet lane in the Old Town, this excellent little place run by affable Susanna from Limerick serves Cretan treats with flair. Try the divine *gavros* (marinated anchovies) or stuffed fish

baked in paper, or the tasty meatballs with leek and tomato. The homemade bread is excellent, too.

Ela (☎ 28210 74128; Kondylaki 47; mains €8-18; ◷ noon-1am) This 14th-century building was a soap factory, then a school, distillery and cheese-processing plant. Now Ela serves Cretan specialities like goat with artichokes, while musicians create ambience.

DRINKING & ENTERTAINMENT

Synagogi (☎ 28210 96797; Skoufou 15) In a roofless Venetian building and former synagogue, this cool place with dark stone arches is a favourite of young locals.

The arty cafe-bar **Ta Duo Lux** (☎ 28210 52519; Sarpidona 8; ◷ 10am-late) is a favourite with the youths, while the rough-and-ready **Café Kriti** (☎ 28210 58661; Kalergon 22; ◷ 8pm-late) has live traditional Cretan music.

SHOPPING

Zambeliou and Theotokopoulou have excellent shopping, with traditional artisans often plying their trade. Skrydlof is 'leather lane', and the central market is worth perusing. Hania's magnificent covered **food market** (◷ 9am-5pm Mon & Wed, 9am-8pm Tue, Thu & Fri, 9am-2pm Sat) has an excellent assortment of traditional Cretan food and drink, herbs, meats and veg; the market should be seen, even if you aren't buying.

Carmela (☎ 28210 90487; Angelou 7) This exquisite store features original jewellery designs, plus Carmela's unique ceramics using ancient techniques. It also has jewellery and ceramics by leading Greek artists.

Roka Carpets (☎ 28210 74736; Zambeliou 61) Observe master weaver Mihalis Manousakis at work on his 400-year-old loom, and know you're buying genuine, handwoven rugs and other items.

GETTING THERE & AWAY

Hania's airport (CHQ) is 14km east of town on the Akrotiri Peninsula. Flights only go to/from Athens and Thessaloniki. The **port police** (☎ 28210 89240) can also provide ferry information.

Hania's main port is 7km southeast at Souda; frequent buses (€1.15) serve Hania, as do taxis (€8 to €10).

In summer, buses depart from Hania's **bus station** (KTEL; ☎ 28210 93052) during the week for numerous destinations.

GETTING AROUND

Three daily buses serve the airport (€2.60, 20 minutes); taxis cost €18 to €20.

Local blue buses (☎ 28210 27044) meet incoming ferries at Souda port, leaving from outside Hania's food market (€1.30). Buses for western beaches leave from the main bus station.

SAMARIA GORGE
ΦΑΡΑΓΓΙ ΤΗΣ ΣΑΜΑΡΙΑΣ

Although you'll have company (over 1000 people per day in summer), hiking the **Samaria Gorge** (☎ 28210 67179; admission €5; ⏲ 6am-3pm May-mid-Oct) remains an experience to remember. Remember to check climatic conditions in advance – many aspiring hikers have been disappointed when park officials close Samaria on exceptionally hot days.

At 16km, the Samaria (sah-mah-rih-*ah*) Gorge is supposedly Europe's longest. Beginning just below the Omalos Plateau, it's carved out by the river that flows between the Avlimanakou (1857m) and Volakias (2116m) peaks. Samaria's width varies from 150m to 3m, and its containing cliffs reach 500m in height. Numerous wildflowers bloom in April and May.

Samaria also shelters endangered species like Crete's beloved wild goat, the *kri-kri*. Surviving in the wild only here, the islet of Dia, north of Iraklio, and on the eastern islet of Kri-Kri, near Agios Nikolaos, the *kri-kri* is shy and seldom seen. To save it from extinction, the gorge became a national park in 1962.

HIKING THE GORGE

You can start early (before 8am) to avoid crowds, though even the first morning bus from Hania can be packed; sleeping in Omalos and getting an early lift from there allows you to get your toe on the line for the starting gun. Camping is forbidden, so time your trek (from 4½ to six hours) to finish by closing time (3pm).

Wear good hiking boots, and take sunscreen, sunglasses, hat and water bottle (springs with good water exist, though

CRETE

WESTERN CRETE

CHRIS CHRISTO
On route to Xyloskalo, Samaria Gorge

not the main stream). If it's too hard within the first hour, donkey-equipped park wardens can take you back. Look out for the elusive *kri-kri*, and for falling rocks; people have died from the latter (and from foolishly wandering off the main trail into the remote mountains).

You'll begin at **Xyloskalo**, named for the steep stone pathway flanked by wooden rails that enters the gorge, and finish at **Agia Roumeli** on the southern coast. In spring, wading through a stream is sometimes necessary; in summer, when the flow drops, the streambed rocks become stepping stones.

GETTING THERE & AWAY

Hania-Omalos buses to Xyloskalo (Omalos; €5.90, 1½ hours) leave from Hania at 6.15am, 7.30am, and 8.30am. A direct bus to Xyloskalo from Paleohora in the southwest (€5.50, 1½ hours) leaves at 6.15am.

When you finish the hike in Agia Roumeli, two daily afternoon boats to Hora Sfakion (€7.50, one hour, 3.45pm and 6pm) via Loutro (€7, 45 minutes) are timed to meet buses going back to Hania. The **ticket office** (☎ 28250 91251) is at the port.

ELAFONISI & KEDRODASOS
ΕΛΑΦΟΝΗΣΙ & ΚΕΔΡΟΔΑΣΟΣ

Arguably Crete's most beautiful beach, the white- and pink-sand **Elafonisi** is practically tropical. About an hour's drive from Paleohora, it unsurprisingly gets inundated by day-trippers who flock to the semi-detached islets, little coves, and warm, shallow turquoise waters.

For more solitude, hike about one hour eastwards from the beach on the marked E4 secondary road (or drive)

and, after some greenhouses, you'll reach the equally beautiful but less visited **Kedrodasos Beach** – as the name suggests, it's backed by a cedar forest.

Two daily buses also go from Hania (€9.60, 2½ hours) and Kissamos (€5.90, 1¼ hours), returning in the afternoon. Neither option leaves much time to relax on both beaches, so driving is ideal.

There's no accommodation on either beach, though snack bars operate at Elafonisi.

AZOGIRES ΑΖΟΓΙΡΕΣ
pop 40

It's not known whether the hippies who once frolicked in this mountainside hamlet were sworn to secrecy, but it is surprising that more travellers haven't been turned on to Azogires. In an island full of storied eccentricities, this tranquil village 7km north of Paleohora stands out for its wooded, rock-pool waterfalls haunted by nereids, cave churches where hermits once meditated, and overall positive vibes. No surprise then that Azogires, set above a stunning eponymous gorge, attracts the occasional foreign yoga and meditation group.

The village also offers plenty of hill walks, tasty local products like olive oil and honey, memorable characters and limited but excellent sleeping and eating options.

INFORMATION

Entering Azogires from the south, look left for **Alfa Restaurant** (☎ 28230 41620; Azogires Sq), the centre of local life. A free village map with all the local sights is available. There are no ATMs in Azogires.

SIGHTS & ACTIVITIES

Azogires' sights are all relatively close and connected by footpaths or roads.

ASTA PLECHAVIČIŪTĖ/DREAMSTIME

View across Falasarna

⟆ IF YOU LIKE...

if you like the sun-drenched sand of Elafonisi (p260), we think you'll like kicking back on these lovely Cretan beaches:

- **Falasarna** Some 16km west of Kissamos, this long sandy beach is one of Crete's best, comprising several coves separated by rocky spits. Falasarna's end-of-the-world feel is accentuated by spectacular sunsets, when pink hues are reflected from the sand's fine coral.
- **Frangokastello** Lying just below a magnificent 14th-century fortress, this wide, packed white-sand beach is one of Crete's best. The shallow warm water makes it ideal for kids. Be warned: when the wind's up, flying sand will chase you off quickly.
- **Vaï** Europe's only 'natural' palm-forest beach has inviting white sand. A mere 24km east of Sitia, it gets packed in summer, though you can access a more secluded beach by clambering over a rocky outcrop behind the taverna.
- **Preveli Beach** Below a monastery lies this celebrated beach, a highly photogenic stretch of sand also called Palm Beach (Paralia Finikodasous). The palm-lined riverbanks have freshwater pools good for a dip, while rugged cliffs begin where the sands end.
- **Gavdos island** Europe's most southerly point is blissful, boasting several unspoilt beaches – some accessible only by boat. It attracts campers, nudists and free spirits seeking to peace out on balmy beaches under the stars.

The side of the village west of the main road contains no less than six shrines, the two most revered being the **Holy Fathers' Cave**, accessible along a winding footpath northwest of the village, and **St John the Hermit's Cave**, somewhat closer, above Alpha Rooms. These mediaeval shrines have numerous colourful legends associated with them, and are still credited with miraculous occurrences.

CRETE

EASTERN CRETE

Just across the main road from Alpha Rooms, a short path into the woods leads to a 1m-high **waterfall**, gushing behind deep **rock pools**. Here dazzling sunlight is reflected from the water's surface through a leafy canopy where immense green dragonflies flutter; it's not hard to see why locals have, since ancient times, believed exquisitely beautiful nereids inhabit the falls and can, on certain fatal nights, steal a man's soul.

A footpath from here through the woods leads southeast to a lovely **old bridge**; cross it to reach the **Monastery of the Holy Fathers**, with its small **museum** of local ecclesiastical items and icons. Across a narrow road further east are the **Carved Caves of Ancient Azogires**, worth a peek.

You can hike the forested **Azogires Gorge** to Paleohora on shaded but rocky trails (three hours). The hike is moderately difficult and the trail not well maintained, so enquire locally about current conditions.

SLEEPING & EATING

Alfa Hotel (☎/fax 28230 41620; alfacafeneion@ aol.com; www.alfahotelazogires.blogspot.gr; Azogires; r from €25; P ✂ ⊒) Just up from the centre on the main road, the Alfa has clean, modern en suite rooms with balconies facing the far-off sea at Paleohora. There is a communal kitchen and a washing machine (€3 per load).

Alfa Restaurant (☎ 28230 41620; mains €4-6) Part coffee shop, part info centre, part restaurant, this place on the square does excellent local fare and makes a relaxing spot for a drink, too.

GETTING THERE & AWAY

Azogires is about 15 minutes from Paleohora by car; taxis cost €10.

EASTERN CRETE

AGIOS NIKOLAOS
ΑΓΙΟΣ ΝΙΚΟΛΑΟΣ

pop 10,080

Pretty Agios Nikolaos (*ah-yee-os nih-ko*-laos), is Lasithi's capital, and enjoys a unique and photogenic setting around a curving harbour connecting to a small lake said once upon a time to be bottomless. The town, which boasts five beaches of varying sizes and reasonable nightlife, has always gone in cycles. Nowadays, Agios Nikolaos gets an intriguing mix of Western and Eastern European package tourists, plus some independents and families. With a mix of services, amenities and reasonable prices, it is probably the north coast's best family holiday destination and serves as a good base for eastern explorations.

ORIENTATION

The **bus station** (KTEL; ☎ 28410 22234) is 800m from the town's centre at Plateia Venizelou, though the action for tourists is centred around Voulismeni Lake. Most banks, ATMs, travel agencies and shops are on Koundourou and the parallel 28 Oktovriou.

INFORMATION

General Hospital (☎ 28410 66000; Knosou 3)

Municipal Tourist Office (☎ 28410 22357; www.agiosnikolaos.gr; ☼ 8am-9pm Apr-Nov) Provides info, changes money and assists with accommodation.

National Bank of Greece (Nikolaou Plastira)

Post office (☎ 28410 22062; 28 Oktovriou 9; ☼ 7.30am-2pm Mon-Fri)

Tourist police (☎ 28410 91408; Erythrou Stavrou 47; ☼ 7.30am-2.30pm Mon-Fri)

SIGHTS & ACTIVITIES

The **Archaeological Museum** (☎ 28410 24943; Paleologou Konstantinou 74; admission €4; ☯ 8.30am-3pm Tue-Sun) has the island's second-most-significant Minoan collection, including clay coffins, ceramic musical instruments and gold from Mohlos.

Within town, **Ammos Beach** and **Kytroplatia Beach** are small and crowded, though convenient for a quick dip. **Almyros Beach** (1km south), is also busy but much longer, with better sand. A taxi here costs €6, or walk (20 to 30 minutes) via a coastal path starting at Kitroplateia, passing the marina and then the stadium. Further towards Sitia, **Golden Beach** (Voulisma Beach) and **Istron Bay** boast long stretches of sand.

Agios Nikolaos' **Summer Cultural Festival** has almost daily events ranging from traditional Cretan music and theatre to literary readings, art exhibits and rock concerts.

TOURS

Minotours Hellas (☎ 28410 23222; www .minotours.gr; 28 Oktovriou 6) runs numerous tours, including to the Lasithi Plateau (€40) and Knossos (€40).

Nostos Tours (☎ 28410 22819; nostos@agn .forth net.gr; Roussou Koundourou 30; ☯ 8am-noon & 5-9pm) specialises in boat excursions, one being the four-hour boat trip to Spinalonga (€20), which includes a 30-minute swim on the Kolokytha Peninsula, and an on-board bar and restaurant.

SLEEPING

Pension Mary (☎ 28410 23760; Evans 13; s/d/tr €20/25/30; ⊠) This friendly budget place has basic but clean rooms, most with private bathrooms, fridge and balconies with sea views. The upper room is cramped, though it has a terrace with barbecue. There's also a communal kitchen.

Du Lac Hotel (☎ 28410 22711; www.dulacho tel.gr; 28 Oktovriou 17; s/d/studio €40/60/80; ⊠ ᗑ) Well positioned beside the lake, this nice place has standard rooms and spacious,

CRETE

EASTERN CRETE

Boats moored harbourside, Agios Nikolaos

JOHN ELK III

CRETE

fully fitted-out studios, both with stylish furnishings and nice bathrooms.

Sgouros Hotel (☎ 28410 28931; N Pagalou 3; www.sgourosgrouphotels.com; s/d/tr incl breakfast €50/68/75; ✳ ☞) Although not Agios' cheapest hotel, the recently renovated Sgouros represents great value. Well located overlooking Kitroplateia Beach, the hotel has 22 freshly painted, clean rooms with nice bathrooms, plus one suite and four interconnected family rooms.

EATING

our pick **Chrysofillis Mezedopoleio** (☎ 28410 22705; Kitroplateia; mezedhes €4-7) A newspaperlike menu explains Cretan terminology and outlines the specials: fresh mussels, barley pasta with prawns, fried rabbit, excellent *myzithropitakia,* and lively, light salads are just some of them. The balcony water view is complemented by a stylish interior; the classic old framed photos are for sale (€22 to €40).

Aouas Taverna (☎ 28410 23231; Paleologou Konstantinou 44; mezedhes €5-9) This family-run place with a nice enclosed garden does tasty Cretan specialities such as herb pies and pickled bulbs, plus tasty grills.

Pelagos (☎ 28410 25737; Katehaki 10; fish €8-16) For fresh fish and seafood, this place, in a restored house with ambient garden, is very good – and also quite expensive. The mezedhes are excellent.

DRINKING

Nightlife is quite active in summer – just follow your ears. Places popular with Greeks and tourists alike ring the lake, and extend towards the Kitroplateia.

GETTING THERE & AWAY

Agios Nikolaos' **bus station** (☎ 28410 22234) serves Iraklio (€6.50, half-hourly), Kritsa (€1.40, 15 minutes, 10 daily) and Sitia (€7.30, one hour, seven daily). To reach

the bus station from downtown, walk (10 to 15 minutes) or take any local bus (€0.50, half-hourly), which stops precisely on the bridge, opposite the tourist info centre.

Note that to visit Elounda, you needn't start from the bus station; just go to the small **bus stop** opposite the tourist information centre. It displays timetables too.

SPINALONGA ISLAND
ΝΗΣΟΣ ΣΠΙΝΑΛΟΓΚΑΣ

Spinalonga Island lies just north of the Kolokytha Peninsula. Its massive **fortress** (☎ 28410 41773; admission €2; ☺ 9am-6.30pm) was built in 1579 to protect Elounda Bay and the Gulf of Mirabello.

When Crete joined Greece in 1913, the island became Europe's last leper colony; the final leper died here in 1953 and it's been uninhabited ever since. Locals still call it 'the island of the living dead'.

Spinalonga is fascinating to explore. After buying the entry ticket (€2), take the path going left through the tunnel and follow it clockwise around the outside of the structure until you've completed the circle. Various organised tours operate simultaneously, so you'll get free commentary in numerous European languages. More useful info is printed in various places, and you can purchase lovely copies of old Venetian maps of Crete and the area (€2 to €22). You'll pass numerous ruins of churches, fortress structures and residences, and the outer turrets offer spectacular views. The island has a small snack bar right of the ticket booth.

Ferries to Spinalonga depart half-hourly from Elounda (adults/children €10/5), giving you an hour to see the sights (though you can stay longer and return on a different boat). From Agios Nikolaos, various companies offer basic tours and longer, day-trip excursions (from €20).

EASTERN CRETE

SITIA ΣΗΤΕΙΑ

pop 8240

Sitia (si-*tee*-ah), de facto capital of easternmost Crete, is a quiet seaside town but does boast an airport and Dodecanese-bound ferries. Here, agriculture and commerce supersede tourism, and most visitors are low-key Greeks.

Sitia's architecture, strung up a terraced hillside, mixes Venetian and newer structures. The pretty harbour-side promenade features tavernas and cafes, while a sandy beach skirts the eastern bay. Sitia is always laid back, and it makes a good base for exploring nearby beaches and sights.

ORIENTATION & INFORMATION

Plateia Iroon Polytehniou is Sitia's main square. The bus station is at the eastern end of Karamanli, behind the bay. Ferries dock 500m north of Plateia Agnostou. Several ATMs are available in the centre of town.

Akasti Travel (☎ 28430 29444; www.akasti. gr; Kornarou & Metaxaki 4) Does trips and provides info.

Java Internet Cafe (☎ 28430 22263; Kornarou 113; ⏱ 9am-late)

Post office (Dimokritou; ⏱ 7.30am-3pm) Heading inland, take the first left off Venizelou.

Tourist office (☎ 28430 28300; Karamanli; ⏱ 9.30am-2.30pm & 5-8.30pm Mon-Fri, 9.30am-2.30pm Sat) This waterfront office offers maps.

SIGHTS

Sitia's excellent **Archaeological Museum** (☎ 28430 23917; Piskokefalou; admission €2; ⏱ 8.30am-3pm Tue-Sun) exhibits local finds dating from Neolithic to Roman times. Significant Minoan items include the *Palekastro Kouros* – a statue painstakingly pieced together from fragments made of hippopotamus tusks and adorned with gold. Zakros palace finds include a wine press, a bronze saw and cult objects scorched by the conflagration that destroyed the palace. Most important are the displayed Linear A tablets documenting administrative functions.

NEIL SETCHFIELD

Seaside promenade, Sitia

CRETE

EASTERN CRETE

Only the walls remain of Sitia's towering **Venetian fort** (⌚8.30am-3pm), locally called *kazarma* (from 'casa di arma') – it's used as an open-air venue.

The **folklore museum** (☎28430 22861; Kapetan Sifinos 28; admission €2; ⌚10am-1pm Mon-Fri) displays local weavings.

SLEEPING

Hotel Arhontiko (☎28430 28172; Kondylaki 16; d/studio without bathroom €30/35) Occupying an uphill neoclassical building, this hotel has old-world ambience. This spotless guest house has shared bathrooms and garden.

El Greco Hotel (☎28430 23133; info@ elgreco-sitia.gr; Arkadiou 13; s/d incl breakfast €30/40; 🅿) Offers very clean and presentable rooms with fridge.

Apostolis (☎28430 28172; Kazantzaki 27; d/tr €40/47) These domatia have ceiling fans and relatively modern bathrooms. There's a communal balcony and fridge.

Hotel Flisvos (☎28430 27135; www.flisvos-sitia.com; Karamanli 4; s/d/tr incl breakfast €50/70/80; 🅿 💻) Along the southern waterfront, this modern hotel offers well-appointed rooms with all the mod cons.

EATING

Taverna O Mihos (☎28430 22416; Kornarou 117; grills €5-8) In a traditional stone house behind the waterfront, O Mihos does great charcoal-grilled meats and Cretan fare. Eat on the beachfront terrace.

Sitia Beach (☎28430 22104; Karamanli 28; specials €5.50-9) Unexpectedly good pizza, plus home-style specials, are served at this beachfront place.

Balcony (☎28430 25084; Foundalidou 19; mains €10-19) Sitia's finest dining is upstairs in this well-decorated neoclassical building. The diverse range includes Cretan, Mexican and Asian-inspired dishes.

GETTING THERE & AWAY

AIR

Sitia's **airport** (☎28430 24666) serves national destinations, with plans for international ones too. For domestic flight info, see Island Hopping (p357).

BOAT

Sitia's ferries primarily serve the Dodecanese. For ferry info, see Island Hopping (p357).

BUS

From Sitia's **bus station** (☎28430 22272), six daily buses serve Ierapetra (€5.40, 1½ hours), and seven go to Iraklio (€13.10, three hours) via Agios Nikolaos (€6.90, 1½ hours). Four buses go to Vaï (€3, 30 minutes), and two serve Kato Zakros via Palekastro and Zakros (€4.50, one hour) in summer only.

GEORGE TSAFOS

Steps leading to a chapel entrance, Mandraki (p291), Nisyros

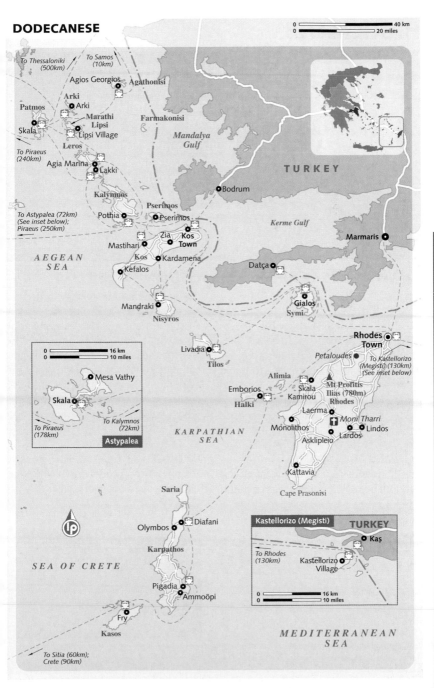

DODECANESE

0   40 km
0   20 miles

To Thessaloniki
(500km)
To Samos
(10km)

Agios Georgios   Agathonisi

Arki
Patmos   Arki
Marathi
Lipsi
Skala   Lipsi Village

Farmakonisi

Mandalya
Gulf

TURKEY

To Piraeus
(240km)
Leros
Agia Marina   Lakki

Kalymnos

Bodrum

To Astypalea (72km)
(See inset below);
Piraeus (250km)

Pothia   Pserimos
Pserimos

Kerme Gulf

AEGEAN
SEA

Mastihari   Zia   Kos
Town

Kos   Kardamena
Kefalos

Marmaris

Datça

Mandraki

Nisyros

Gialos
Symi

Rhodes
Town

Livadia

Tilos

Petaloudes

To Kastellorizo
(Megisti) (130km)
(See inset below)

Alimia

Emborios   Skala
Kamirou

Halki

Laerma

Monolithos

Asklipleio

Mt Profitis
Ilias (780m)
Rhodes

Moni Tharri
Lindos
Lardos

Kattavia

Cape Prasonisi

Astypalea inset

0   16 km
0   10 miles

Mesa Vathy

Skala

To Piraeus
(178km)
To Kalymnos
(72km)

Astypalea

KARPATHIAN
SEA

Saria

Olymbos   Diafani

Karpathos

SEA OF CRETE

Pigadia

Ammoöpi

Fry

Kasos

To Sitia (60km);
Crete (90km)

Kastellorizo (Megisti) inset

Kastellorizo (Megisti)   TURKEY

Kaş

To Rhodes
(130km)
Kastellorizo
Village

0   16 km
0   10 miles

MEDITERRANEAN
SEA

HIGHLIGHTS

1 BYZANTINE PAINTING

BY VASILEIOS PERIKLIS SIRIMIS, PROFESSIONAL PAINTER

I've been painting Byzantine icons professionally for 12 years; a family craft passed down through the generations. Our traditional method uses natural pigments mixed with egg-yolk, vinegar and holy water, and 24-karat gold leaf for some backgrounds. It makes me happy to spread the appreciation of this traditional art beyond our national borders.

⇲ VASILEIOS PERIKLIS SIRIMIS' DON'T MISS LIST

❶ BYZANTINE ART MUSEUM OF RHODES

Located in a former 11th-century Byzantine cathedral, the **Byzantine Art Museum (cnr Plateia Meg Alexandrou & Ippoton, Rhodes Old Town)** is a good place to begin your exploration, featuring high-quality icons, wall paintings and sculptures from churches throughout the Dodecanese.

❷ CHURCH OF AGIA PANAGIA, LINDOS

It's impossible not to be awed by the abundance of vibrant frescoes covering the walls of the 14th-century **Church of Agia Panagia (Plateia Eleftherias, Lindos)**. Most paintings are 19th-century. Look up at the vaulted ceiling and dome for work by the famous Gregorious of Symi, completed in 1779. And don't miss the elaborately carved wooded *iconostasis* (wall separating the nave from the sanctuary) at the front of the church.

❸ ASKLIPLEIO VILLAGE CHURCH

The tiny 11th-century **Church of Kimisis Theotokou (main square, Asklipleio)** is

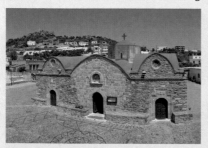

Clockwise from top: Wall frescoes of Moni Tharri; Illuminated interior of the Church of Agia Panagia, Lindos; Facade of the Church of Kimisis Theotokou, Asklipleio

Rhodes' oldest Christian church that's still in use. Inside are extraordinary 15th-century Byzantine frescoes in great condition. Next door you'll find a small folklore museum in what was once the church's olive press, and if you follow the road from the church up to the castles, you can take in some breathtaking coastal views.

❹ MONI THARRI

Set in the hilly, green countryside outside Lardos, the peaceful, atmospheric 9th-century **Moni Tharri** (entrance by donation) was Rhodes' first monastery. The monastic community has re-established itself here and welcomes you into the church to appreciate the well-preserved 13th-century frescoes that cover every square inch of the chapel's interior.

❶ Byzantine Art Museum of Rhodes
❷ Church of Agia Panagia, Lindos
❸ Asklipleio Village Church
❹ Moni Tharri

0 — 10 km
0 — 6 miles

Mt Profitis Ilias (780m)

Epta Piges

Rhodes

Vlyha Bay

Bay of Gennadi

MEDITERRANEAN SEA

↘ THINGS YOU NEED TO KNOW

Etiquette Cover bare arms and legs when entering a Greek Orthodox church and no photography **Only half a day?** Church of Kimisis Theotokou in Asklipleio **Price of icon paintings** Depends on size, theme and type of wood; from €250 to €3000 **Genuine?** Examine the thickness of the pigment and carvings

HIGHLIGHTS

2 | EASTER ON PATMOS

BY PAUL GRIFFIN, TRAVELLER

I've long been fascinated by the Book of Revelations. Patmos appealed to me for its rich cultural heritage and as the place where John experienced his visions. For many Greeks it's *the* place to spend Easter. The air is filled with excitement and veneration... plus possibly the loudest fireworks you'll ever hear!

↘ PAUL GRIFFIN'S DON'T MISS LIST

❶ FEASTING & STREET FESTIVALS

On Easter Sunday, Orthodox Greeks break the fast of Lent in a big way. Most celebrate with roasted goat and you can join in the feasting at lots of local restaurants. There's also people cracking red-dyed hard-boiled eggs and music and dancing in the streets.

❷ WITNESSING THE BIER

If you're up early on Good Friday, visit a church to see the bier being decorated with hundreds of fresh flowers. That night, people gather near churches and the air is filled with anticipation as you wait to see the bier solemnly paraded through the streets.

❸ CANDLELIT MASS

On Saturday night, head to the **Holy Monastery of Zoodohos Pigi** (p303) for the Resurrection Mass. The ceremony here is incredibly atmospheric, with flickering candle-light illuminating the stunning frescoes. At midnight, the candles are extinguished and the chapel is plunged into dark-

Clockwise from top: Monastery of the Apocalypse complex (p303); Easter tradition of cracking red-dyed eggs; Arches of the Monastery of St John the Theologian (p303); Church service, Good Friday

ness, signifying Christ's crucifixion. This is followed by fireworks throughout the town, representing his resurrection.

❹ EASTER DAY MASS

Walk up the stone Byzantine foot-path from Skala to attend mass at the **Monastery of St John the Theologian** (p303). The power and beauty of the singing is incredibly moving. Most people listen in the courtyard, taking turns to enter the ornate and intimate church for a short while. From there, visit the **Monastery of the Apocalypse** (p303) where it's believed John heard the voice of God and wrote the Book of Revelations.

❺ CHILLIN' ON THE BEACH

While it's not strictly an Easter tradition, Patmos has some great beaches where you can chill out. Some are secluded and even the more popular ones have a quiet, relaxed feel at this time of year. The beachside cafes are open and the water is just warm enough to go for a swim.

↘ THINGS YOU NEED TO KNOW

Easter greeting *Hristos anesti* (Christ is risen); reply with *Alithos anesti* (Truly He is risen) **Travel & accommodation** Book as far in advance as possible **Gifts** Decorated candles are given to friends and children **For more details about Easter in Greece p316**

HIGHLIGHTS

↘ RHODES' OLD TOWN

Enclosed within impressive stone walls, the labyrinthine passageways and alleys of Rhodes' magical **Old Town** (p283) make up a medieval city filled with life. As you are awed by intermingled Byzantine, Latin and Turkish architecture, you'll stumble upon locals drinking coffee in the squares and children playing in the courtyards. Once you find your way back out, take a stroll along the lush moat walk.

↘ STEAMING NISYROS

Early in the morning, you may find yourself standing alone in the centre of Nisyros' **volcano** (p293), surrounded only by the hissing, bubbling and steaming of the fumaroles and the red, green and orange rocks scattered on the craters' edges. Hike between the five craters in this other-worldly landscape before heading back over the top of the caldera and down the phenomenally fertile slopes to the sea.

DODECANESE

HIGHLIGHTS

5

⬎ CHARMING LINDOS

With an old-world charm that draws the crowds, **Lindos** (p288) is a dazzling white village. Its warren of narrow lanes are pedestrianised and lined with impressive 17th-century houses, tiny shops and cafes. Perched on a clifftop between the town and the sea, the spectacular Acropolis is the cherry on the cake, looking down over the town's two small, sandy bays.

6

⬎ BEACH-BUMMING ON KOS

On the calm southern side of Kos rests the vast **Kefalos Bay** (p300), home to 12km of incredible, wide sandy beaches. Nestled between green hills and warm turquoise water, these seven idyllic beaches offer everything from water sports and parties to tranquil patches of paradise.

7

⬎ MESMERISING HOHLAKIA

Remember to look down. The Dodecanese are well-known for the countless **hohlakia** (p287; p288) floors that you'll see in villages and city centres alike. Often taking decades to complete, these intricate mosaics of white and black stones are traditionally used in courtyards and are stunning works of art.

3 HERMANN DOBLER/IMAGEBROKER; 4 DIMITRIS LUCAS/DREAMSTIME ; 5 HOLGER LEUE; 6 INGOLF POMPE/ALAMY; 7 HOLGER LEUE

3 Laneways of Rhodes' Old Town (p283); 4 Craters of the volcano (p293), Nisyros; 5 Lindos village (p288); 6 Umbrella-lined Kefalos Bay (p300), Kos; 7 Detail of pebble mosaic

THE BEST...

⬎ BEACHES

- **St Paul's Bay** (p289) Warm, turquoise water in a sheltered bay below the Acropolis.
- **Glystra Beach** (p289) Perfect for swimming and often quiet.
- **Exotic Beach** (p300) An undeveloped quiet stretch of sand.
- **Kambos Beach** (p305) Swim, kayak or relax in a quiet bay.
- **Psili Ammos Beach** (p305) Sandy, shaded, idyllic and remote.

⬎ ATMOSPHERIC HOTELS

- **Melenos** (p290) Pure luxury in a 17th-century-style captain's house.
- **Hotel Anastasia** (p285) Budget beds in an Italian mansion.
- **Kalderimi Apartments** (p302) Secluded, traditional retreat with swish extras.
- **Ta Liotridia** (p292) Luxurious rooms in a traditional stone house.

⬎ INSPIRING ARCHITECTURE

- **Captains' houses** (p288) Impressive stone structures from the 17th-century.
- **Kahal Shalom Synagogue** (p284) Greece's oldest synagogue.
- **Palace of the Grand Masters** (p284) Huge and magnificent.
- **Asklipieion** (p300) Ruins of a legendary religious sanctuary.

⬎ CULTURAL EXPERIENCES

- **Cafe Chantant** (p287) Live, traditional folk music.
- **Hammam Turkish Baths** (p284) Baths in an Ottoman relic.
- **Archaeological Museum** (p292) Brand-new with intriguing exhibits.
- **Castle of the Knights** (p296) Site of Hippocrates' performances in an amazing setting.
- **Holy Monastery of Zoodohos Pigi** (p303) Candle-lit Mass on Good Friday.

JOHN SONES

Exhibits at the Museum of Archaeology (p284), Rhodes

THINGS YOU NEED TO KNOW

⬌ VITAL STATISTICS

- **Population** Dodecanese 193,480
- **Area** 2714 sq km

⬌ LOCALITIES IN A NUTSHELL

- **Rhodes** (p280) Medieval Old Town, picturesque white village of Lindos, beaches, monasteries and impressive ruins.
- **Nisyros** (p290) Volcanic island with bubbling craters, traditional villages and fertile landscape.
- **Kos** (p295) Lively Kos Town, long, sandy beaches and striking ruins of Asklipieion.
- **Patmos** (p300) Where St John wrote the Book of Revelations and a drawcard for pilgrims, artists and beach lovers.

⬌ ADVANCE PLANNING

- **Two months before** Book your accommodation.
- **One month before** Check online for upcoming events (especially in Rhodes Town) and buy tickets. Double-check ferry schedules and book activities like diving.

⬌ RESOURCES

- **www.rhodesguide.com** What's on, where to stay and where to hang out in Rhodes.
- **www.rodos.gr** Upcoming events, links and background to Rhodes.
- **www.ando.gr/eot** Official Dodecanese tourist info with ferry schedules and events.

- **www.blueislands.gr** Family-friendly accommodation in the Dodecanese.
- **www.nisyros.gr** Sights, history and environment of Nisyros.
- **www.travel-to-kos.com** A guide to Kos.
- **www.patmos-island.com** Local info and listings for Patmos.
- **www.patmosweb.gr** Listings and images of Patmos.

⬌ EMERGENCY NUMBERS

- **Police** (☎ 100)
- **Highway Rescue** (Elpa; ☎ 104)

⬌ GETTING AROUND

- **Bus** Regular routes on Rhodes and Kos, with less-frequent routes on Nisyros and Patmos.
- **Ferry** Hydrofoils zip between the Dodecanese almost daily in summer, with overnight ferries to Piraeus. For specific island services, see also Island Hopping (p357).
- **Car** The best way to explore the islands is with your own wheels.
- **Bicycle** A popular way to get around the flat terrain on Kos.

⬌ BE FOREWARNED

- **Easter** If you're hoping to visit Patmos for Easter, book well in advance.
- **Ferries** Windy weather can affect hydrofoil schedules. Don't schedule ferries and homebound flights too close together.

ITINERARIES

EXPLORING RHODES Three Days

Overflowing with opportunities to experience the diversity of island life, Rhodes has more than enough to keep you busy for a few days. Base yourself in **(1) Rhodes Town** (p281) and spend a day exploring within the walls of the Old Town. Check out the impressive museums, lose yourself in the cobbled alleyways and finish off the evening listening to live, local music in the atmospheric Cafe Chantant. On day two, rent a car and head out along the south coast, stopping at the beautifully restored **(2) Kalithea Thermi** (p287) with its amazing *hohlakia* (black-and-white pebble mosaic floors). Continue on to **(3) Moni Tsambikas** (p288) for its incredible frescoes and 360-degree views. From there, spend the day on the nearby, sandy **(4) Stegna Beach** (p288). On your final day, visit **(5) Lindos** (p288) and climb to the impressive Acropolis. Wander through the pedestrianised, whitewashed village and dine in one of the famous captains' houses. Head south to watch the sunset on remote **(6) Glystra Beach** (p289).

COASTAL CULTURE Five Days

Begin your adventure on Kos island, basing yourself in **(1) Kos Town** (p296) and spending the day taking in the ancient ruins within the town and at nearby Asklipieion. In the evening, catch a performance of Hippocrates' works in the atmospheric Castle of the Knights. The next day, hop on the bus to the soft endless sand of **(2) Kefalos Bay** (p300). Take a day trip to **(3) Nisyros** (p290) to visit the other-worldly landscape of the volcano, having lunch in Emborios and visiting the Volcanological Museum in Nikea. On day four, hop on a fast ferry to **(4) Patmos** (p300). Walk up the Byzantine footpath from the coastal town of Skala to the atmospheric Hora, visiting the Monastery of the Apocalypse where St John wrote the Book of Revelations. On your last day, hop on a bus for nearby Kambos Beach where you can swim, kayak or just soak up the sun.

ISLAND HOP One Week

Begin on Rhodes island, basing yourself in (1) Rhodes Town (p281) and spending a day in the magical Old Town. On the second day, hop on a bus to the sparkling white-washed village of (2) Lindos (p288). Climb up to the impressive Acropolis and then wander down to St Paul's Bay to swim in the warm, turquoise water. On day three, hop on a fast ferry to (3) Nisyros (p290) to visit the breathtaking volcano and the villages of Emborios and Nikea, perched on the edge of the caldera. Spend the night in friendly Mandraki and then, in the morning, hop on the ferry in nearby Kos. Fill a day wandering in (4) Kos Town (p296), with ancient ruins, cafe-lined squares and a buzzing nightlife. The next

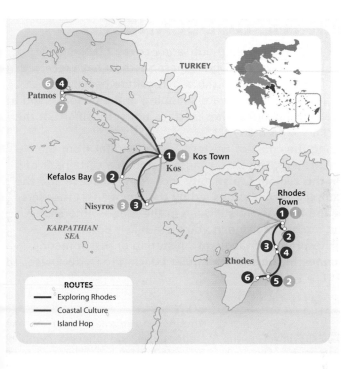

day beeline to the incredible beaches of (5) Kefalos Bay (p300). Catch a fast ferry to (6) Patmos (p300) on the next day. Base yourself in Skala, but spend the day experiencing Hora with the amazing Monastery of the Apocalypse and the Monastery of St John the Theologian. On your last day, take an excursion boat or drive and then hike to the idyllic, tree-shaded (7) Psili Ammos Beach (p305).

DISCOVER THE DODECANESE

When the Greek Gods were doling out sandy coves, blankets of wildflowers and lofty views, the Dodecanese seem to have received more than their fair share. Add to this a rich culture heavily influenced by Italian rule, azure waters lapping at their shores, and a wealth of natural and historical sites, and it's not surprising that the Dodecanese beckon to so many.

Strung out along the coast of western Turkey and far from the country's capital, Athens, the Dodecanese maintain a certain air of separateness. In this region, Christianity took root in Greece and the influences of consecutive invasions led by the Egyptians, Crusaders, Ottoman Turks and Italians are still seen in the islands' interesting architecture and regional cuisine. If you are a hiker, botanist, beachcomber, kitesurfer, archaeologist, historian or just someone longing for a lounge in the sun on a quiet beach, the Dodecanese won't disappoint.

RHODES ΡΟΔΟΣ

pop 117,000

Rhodes (*ro*-dos) is the jewel in the Dodecanese crown. It embraces you with its mild climate and charms you with the best of both worlds – the buzz of its beautiful, cultured capital and the tranquillity of its beaches and stunning scenery. It has worthwhile sights and quiet villages and offers plenty of places to get lost – from the labyrinthine back streets of the almost magical World Heritage-listed Old Town to the snaking mountain roads. Rhodes is also a great base for daytrips to surrounding islands and is very family-friendly. No wonder so many people make it their sole destination in Greece.

GETTING THERE & AWAY

AIR

Olympic Air (off Map p282; ☎ 22410 24571; Ierou Lohou 9) has flights across Greece and the Dodecanese, while **Aegean Airlines** (☎ 22410 98345; Diagoras airport) offers flights to Athens, Thessaloniki, Iraklio and Rome.

BOAT

Rhodes is the main port of the Dodecanese and offers a complex array of departures to Piraeus, Sitia, Thessaloniki and many stops in between. **Dodekanisos Seaways** (Map p282; ☎ 22410 70590; Afstralias 3) runs daily catamarans up and down the Dodecanese. Tickets are available from the kiosk at the dock. In Rhodes Town you'll also find the ANES ticket booth for long-distance ferries to Athens.

The EOT (p283) in Rhodes Town can provide you with current schedules. Tickets are available from Skevos' Travel Agency (p283).

GETTING AROUND

TO/FROM THE AIRPORT

The Diagoras airport is 16km southwest of Rhodes Town, near Paradisi. Buses depart regularly between the airport and Rhodes Town's Eastern Bus Terminal (off Map p282) from 6.30am to 11.15pm (€2.20, 25 minutes).

BICYCLE

A range of bicycles is available for hire at **Bicycle Centre** (off Map p282; ☎ 22410 28315; Griva 39; per day €5).

BOAT

There are excursion boats to Lindos and Symi (€22 return) daily in summer, leaving Mandraki Harbour at 9am and returning at 6pm.

BUS

Rhodes Town has two island bus terminals, located a block from one another, and each servicing half the island. There is regular transport across the island all week, with fewer services on Saturday and only a few on Sunday. You can pick up schedules from the kiosks at either terminal or from EOT (p283). Unlimited travel tickets are available for one/two/three days (€10/15/25).

TAXI

Rhodes Town's main taxi rank (off Map p282) is east of Plateia Rimini. Taxis prefer to use set fare rates which are posted at the rank. Sample fares: airport €18, Lindos €43, Falaraki €15 and Kalithia €8. Ring a taxi on ☎ 22410 6800, 22410 27666 or 22410 64712 within Rhodes Town and on ☎ 22410 69600 from outside the city. For disabled-accessible taxis, call ☎ 22410 77079.

RHODES TOWN

pop 56,130

The heart of Rhodes Town is the atmospheric Old Town, enclosed within massive walls and filled with winding passageways and alleys. Visit early in the day or at dusk to see the sun reflected off the stonework and to avoid the crowds.

The New Town is mainly to the north. A few blocks are dominated by package tourism, while trendy cafes, name-brand shops, fine dining and a handful of sights take you to the more enjoyable neighbourhoods. This is also where you'll find the city's best beach.

ORIENTATION

The Old Town is divided into three sectors: the Kollakio (Knights' Quarter), the

Evening activity, Plateia Ippokratous, Rhodes Town

HOLGER LEUE

DODECANESE

RHODES

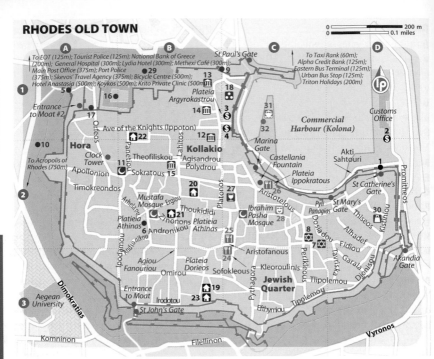

RHODES OLD TOWN

Hora and the Jewish Quarter. The Kollakio contains most of the medieval historical sights while the Hora, often referred to as the Turkish Quarter, is primarily Rhodes Town's commercial sector with shops and restaurants.

The commercial centre of the New Town lies north of the Old Town and is easily explored on foot. The Commercial Harbour (Kolona) is east of the Old Town. Excursion boats, small ferries, hydrofoils and private yachts use Mandraki Harbour, further north.

INFORMATION
INTERNET RESOURCES
www.rhodesguide.com This site includes what's on, where to stay and where to hang out in Rhodes.

www.rodos.gr A site that lists upcoming events, links and background to Rhodes.

MEDICAL SERVICES
Emergencies & ambulance (☎ 166)
General Hospital (☎ 22410 80000; Papalouka El Venizelou) Just northwest of the Old Town.

Krito Private Clinic (☎ 22410 30020; Ioannou Metaxa 3; ⏱ 24hr)

MONEY
You'll find plenty of ATMs throughout Rhodes Town and at the following banks.

You'll also find a handy ATM at the international ferry quay.

Alpha Credit Bank (Plateia Kyprou)
Commercial Bank of Greece (Plateia Symis)

National Bank of Greece New Town (Plateia Kyprou); Old Town (Plateia Mousiou)

POLICE
Port police (☎ 22410 22220; Mandrakiou)
Tourist police (☎ 22410 27423; ⏱ 24hr) Next door to the EOT office.

POST
Main post office Located on Mandraki Harbour.

TOURIST INFORMATION
EOT (☎ 22410 35226; www.ando.gr; cnr Makariou & Papagou; ⏱ 8am-2.45pm Mon-Fri) Supplies brochures, city maps and the *Rodos News,* a free English-language newspaper.

TRAVEL AGENCIES
Charalampis Travel (☎ 22410 35934; ch_trav@otenet.gr; 1 Akti Saktouri) Books flights and boat tickets.

Skevos' Travel Agency (☎ 22410 22461; skeos@rho.forthnet.gr; 111 Amerikis) Books boat and flight tickets throughout Greece.

Triton Holidays (☎ 22410 21690; www.tri tondmc.gr; Plastira 9, Mandraki) The helpful staff here book air and sea travel, hire cars, book accommodation and can plan tours throughout the Dodecanese region.

SIGHTS
OLD TOWN
KNIGHTS' QUARTER
Begin your tour of the Knights' Quarter at **Liberty Gate**, crossing the small bridge into the Old Town. The original site of the **Museum of Modern Greek Art** (☎ 22410 23766; www.mgamuseum/gr; 2 Plateia Symis; 3 sites €3; ⏱ 8am-2pm Tue-Sat) is in a medieval building. Inside you'll find maps and carvings. The main exhibition is now at the **New Art Gallery** (☎ 22410 43780; Plateia G Charitou), with an impressive collection of painting, engraving and sculpture from some of Greece's most popular 20th-century artists, including Gaitis Giannis, Vasiliou Spiros and Katraki Vaso.

Across the pebbled street from the Museum of Modern Greek Art, take in the remains of the 3rd-century-BC **Temple of Aphrodite**, one of the few ancient ruins in the Old Town.

Continuing down Plateia Argyrokastrou, the **Museum of the Decorative Arts** (☎ 22410 72674; Plateia Argyrokastrou; admission €2; ⏱ 8.30am-2.40pm Tue-Sun) houses an eclectic array of artefacts from around the Dodecanese. The museum is chock-a-block with instruments, pottery, carvings, clothing and spinning wheels and gives a colourful view into the past.

In the atmospheric 15th-century knights' hospital up the road is the **Museum of Archaeology** (☎ 22410 27657; Plateia Mousiou; admission €3; ⏰ 8am-4pm Tue-Sun). Its biggest draw is the exquisite *Aphrodite Bathing*, a 1st-century-BC marble statue that was recovered from the local seabed.

Wander up the **Avenue of the Knights** (Ippoton), once home to the knights themselves. Its lofty buildings stretch in a 600m-long unbroken wall of honey-coloured stone blocks, and its flat facade is punctuated by huge doorways and arched windows.

On the right is the truly magnificent 14th-century **Palace of the Grand Masters** (☎ 22410 23359; Ippoton; admission €6; ⏰ 8.30am-3pm Tue-Sun), which was severely damaged by the Turkish siege and then destroyed by an explosion in the mid-1800s. The Italians rebuilt the palace following old plans for the exterior but introducing a grandiose, lavish interior. Only 24 of the 158 rooms can be visited; inside you'll find antique furnishing, sculptures, frescoes and mosaic floors.

From the Palace of the Grand Masters, walk through **D'Amboise Gate**, the most atmospheric of the gates which takes you across the moat. When the palace is open, you can also gain access to the walkway along the top of the wall from here, affording great views into the Old Town and across to the sea. Another option is to follow the peaceful **Moat Walkway**, which you can access next to **St Anthony's Gate**. The walkway is a green oasis with lush lawns cushioned between trees and the old walls.

HORA

Bearing many legacies of its Ottoman past is the **Hora**. During Turkish times, churches were converted to mosques and many more Muslim houses of worship were built from scratch, although most are now dilapidated. The most important is the colourful, pink-domed **Mosque of Süleyman**, at the top of Sokratous.

Continuing through the winding pedestrian streets will bring you to the municipal **Hammam Turkish Baths** (Plateia Arionis; admission €5; ⏰ 10am-5pm Mon-Fri, 8am-5pm Sat). They are open to the public, with separate male and female baths. Warm yourself on the marble stones or opt for a massage. Lockers are available.

JEWISH QUARTER

Built in 1577, **Kahal Shalom Synagogue** (Polydorou 5) is Greece's oldest synagogue and the only one surviving on Rhodes. Have a look in at the **Jewish Synagogue Museum** (☎ 22410 22364; www.rhodesjewishmuseum.org; Dosiadou; ⏰ 10am-3pm Sun-Fri, closed winter), in the old women's prayer rooms around the corner. Exhibits include lots of early 20th-century photos, intricately decorated documents and displays about the 1673 Jews deported from Rhodes to Auschwitz in 1944. Only 151 survived.

NEW TOWN

The **Acropolis of Rhodes**, southwest of the Old Town on Monte Smith, was the site of the ancient Hellenistic city of Rhodes. The hill is named after the English admiral Sir Sydney Smith, who watched for Napoleon's fleet from here in 1802. It has superb views.

The town **beach** begins north of Mandraki and continues around the island's northernmost point and down the

Facade of the Mosque of Süleyman (p284), Rhodes Town

GREG GAWLOWSKI

west side of the New Town. The best spots will depend on the prevailing winds but tend to be on the east side, where there's usually calmer water and more sand and facilities.

ACTIVITIES

A number of diving schools operate out of Mandraki, all offering a range of courses, including a 'One Day Try Dive' for €40 to €50, and PADI certification. You can get information from their **boats** at Mandraki Harbour.

Diving Centres (☎ 22410 23780)
Diving Med College (☎ 22410 61115; www.divemedcollege.com)
Scuba Diving Trident School (☎ /fax 22410 29160)
Waterhoppers Diving Centre (☎ /fax 22410 38146, 6972500971; www .waterhoppers.com)

SLEEPING
BUDGET

Hotel Isole (☎ 22410 20682, 6937580814; www .hotelisole.com; Evdoxou 35; s/d incl breakfast €30/50; 😮 💻) With its entrance under a stone archway in the narrow passages of the Old Town's backstreets, these seven rooms offer great value for money. Decorated in white and blue, they're a cool, quiet retreat. Chat with the multilingual owners at the small bar.

our pick **Hotel Anastasia** (☎ 22410 28007; www.anastasia-hotel.com; 28 Oktovriou 46; s/d/tr €38/52/55; 😮 💻) Tucked away off the main drag in the New Town, this Italian mansion has big open rooms with lots of light. The tiled floors and high ceilings give the hotel stacks of character and the lush garden is a quiet place to sip a cocktail or enjoy a coffee at the outdoor bar.

MIDRANGE

Apollo Tourist House (☎ 22410 32003; www.apollo-touristhouse.com; Omirou 28c; s/d incl breakfast €65/70; 💻) This small pension has tastefully furnished rooms with wooden four-poster and traditional captain's beds. Splashes of colour and lengths of muslin make it all the more homey. Enjoy the

Columns of the Acropolis of Rhodes (p284)
WAYNE WALTON

TOP END

Nikos & Takis Hotel (☎ 22410 70773; www .nikostakishotel.com; Panetiou 29; d from €150; P ⊠ 🖳 🛜) This boutique hotel offers atmospheric, individually decorated rooms. Check out the Moroccan-themed Marokino, with its marble tub, ornately tiled floor and authentic slippers.

EATING

Prince Bakery Cafe (Plateia Ippokratous; snacks €1-5; ⏰ 10am-11pm) Tucked in the corner of the square, this place has a designer feel to it. Sink into the leather seats and tuck into freshly baked breads and pastries or get something to go. There's a deli for sandwiches, an orange-juicer and a well-stocked bar. If you're more peckish, go for the sausage plate or grills.

ourpick Koykos (☎ 22410 73022; Mandilana 20-26; mains €2-8) Popular with Rhodes younger crowds, Koykos is Greek kitsch. From the architecture to the copper-tray-swinging waiters, it would almost be tacky if it weren't so enjoyable. Crowds huddle around chess and card games while others focus on the savoury pies, seafood dishes, salads and mezes.

ourpick Mandala (☎ 22410 38119; Sofokleos 38; mains €8-15; ⏰ lunch Sun & dinner daily winter; lunch & dinner daily summer) Lively and popular, the hip Mandala dishes up creative cuisine, such as chèvre-and-fig starters, salmon pasta or Moroccan chicken. The eatery offers excellent service, a well-stocked bar, and frequent live music make it that much more of a treat.

Nireas (☎ 22410 31741; Sofokleous 45-47; mains €8-16) The fish will taste just as good whether you dine outside under a canopy of greenery or inside in the classy yellow rooms. Seared or sesame-encrusted tuna, steamed mussels with garlic and white wine – the list seems endless. Popular

view from your room or head out to the terrace.

Lydia Hotel (☎ 22410 22871; www.lydia hotel.com; Martiou 25; s/d €80/90; ⊠ 🖳 🛜) Close to the seaside, shopping and cafes and just a stroll away from the Old Town lies this classy hotel. What the comfortable rooms lack in character is more than made up for by the bar, lobby area and garden.

Marco Polo Mansion (☎ 22410 25562; www.marcopolomansion.gr; Agiou Fanouriou 40-42; d incl breakfast from €90) Set in a 15th-century, carefully restored mansion and bursting with atmosphere, the rooms here have a rustic yet plush feel to them with fabric and furnishings from India and Turkey. Think warm colours, high ceilings and four-poster beds.

with families for lunch, Nireas opens onto a quiet square.

DRINKING & ENTERTAINMENT
OLD TOWN

Apenadi (☎ 22410 21055; Evripidou 13-15) Step onto the set for Arabian Nights and sink into some colourful cushions, strewn beneath exquisite chandeliers. And let's not forget the funky music, mezes, cocktails and friendly service.

`ourpick` **Cafe Chantant** (☎ 22410 32277; Dimokratou 3; ☺ midnight-early) Locals sit at long wooden tables, drinking ouzo or beer and listening to live, traditional music. It's dark in here and you won't find snacks and nibbles, but the atmosphere is palpable and the band is lively.

NEW TOWN

Locals hang out along the bar-lined I Dragoum, while the tourist haunts are found along Akti Miaouli, Orfanidou and Griva.

`ourpick` **Methexi Cafe** (☎ 22410 33440; 29 Oktovriou, cnr Griva) This colonial-style mansion is filled with black-and-white photos and stacks of magazines. The comfortable, homey feeling draws a relaxed young crowd who come for live Greek music or to drink beer on the terrace.

Sound & Light Show (☎ 22410 21922; www.hellenicfestival.gr; admission €7) Squeezing many centuries of history into a show with lights, voices and music, the Sound & Light Show is something you'll either love or hate. Shows take place from Monday to Saturday next to the walls of the Old Town, off Plateia Rimini, near the D'Amboise Gate. English-language sessions are staggered, but in general begin at either 9.15pm or 11.15pm. Other languages offered are French, German and Swedish.

SHOPPING

`ourpick` **Byzantine Iconography** (☎ 22410 74127; Kisthinioy 42) Visiting the studio of Basilios Per Sirimis is an experience you shouldn't miss. A teacher and accomplished artist, he follows the traditional methods of iconography, producing paintings for churches and families throughout Greece. All of his materials are natural, including gold leaf and pigments mixed with egg and vinegar. You can see paintings in various stages of production and Basilios will fascinate you with his knowledge. Paintings go for €210 to €2000.

GETTING AROUND

Local buses leave from the **urban bus stop** (Mandraki) on Mandraki Harbour and charge a flat €1. Bus 11 does a circuit around the coast, up past the Aquarium and on to the Acropolis. Hopping on for a loop is a good way to get your bearings.

EASTERN RHODES

The majority of Rhodes' long stretches of sandy beaches are along the island's east coast. Consequently, that's much more developed, with a number of villages made over into summer resorts that tend to be filled with young package-holiday-makers and endless strips of tourist bars.

Restored to its former glory, **Kalithea Thermi** (☎ 22410 65691; Kallithea; www .kallitheasprings.gr; admission €2.50; ☺ 8am-8pm April-Oct, 8am-5pm Nov-Mar) was originally an Italian-built spa, just 9km from Rhodes Town. With grand buildings, colonnades, domed ceilings and countless archways delivering stunning sea views, it's worth a wander. Exhibitions inside show the many films made here (including scenes from *Zorba the Greek*) as well as local artwork. You'll also find a cafe and a small,

Views of the Acropolis of Lindos (p289)

JOT/IMAGEBROKER

sandy beach that's good for swimming. The as-yet-uncompleted, vast expanses of *hohlakia* (black-and-white pebble mosaic floors) have taken 14 years to complete so far.

The beaches of **Kolymbia** and **Tsambika** are sandy but can get crowded in summer. On the left, a steep sign-posted road takes you 1.5km up to the 300 steps leading to **Moni Tsambikas**. Inside the small white chapel you'll find an 11th-century icon of Mary, found on the mountaintop by an infertile couple who soon after had a child. Since then, the site has become a place of pilgrim-age for women hoping to conceive. On 18 September, the monastery's festival day, women climb up on their knees and make offerings of wax babies and silver plaques, which you'll see crowding the front of the church. The frescoes and ancient altar are worth seeing, as is the magnificent 360-degree view outside.

Further up the road is a turn-off to sandy, idyllic **Stegna Beach.**

LINDOS ΛΙΝΔΟΣ

pop 1090

Topped with an impressive acropolis and spilling down into stunning twin bays, Lindos is one of Rhodes' most pic-turesque villages. Following the narrow, winding alleyways will lead you through a maze of dazzling white **17th-century houses**, once the dwellings of wealthy admirals and many boasting courtyards with *hohlakia*.

Of course, the loveliness of Lindos has not gone unnoticed and it's become a bit of a tourist hotspot. Most of the day-trippers congregate between 10am and 4pm; you could visit early in the morning or spend the night to see Lindos *au na-turel*. Even in the bustle of the day, head off from the teeming main thoroughfares lined with tourist shops and cafes, and you'll find quiet corners of the village to explore.

ORIENTATION & INFORMATION

The village is totally pedestrianised. All vehicular traffic terminates on the central square of Plateia Eleftherias, from where the main drag, Acropolis, begins. The donkey terminus for rides up to the Acropolis itself is a little way along here. Turn right at the donkey terminus to reach the post office, after 50m.

By the donkey terminus is the Commercial Bank of Greece, with an ATM. The National Bank of Greece, located on the street opposite the Church of Agia Panagia, also has an ATM.

Lindos Sun Tours (☎ 22440 31333; www .lindosun tours.gr; Acropolis) Has room-letting services, hires cars and motorcycles and can assist with airport transfers, babysitting, etc.

Medical Clinic (☎ 22440 31224) Near the church.

Municipal Tourist Office (☎ 22440 31900; Plateia Eleftherias; ⏰ 7.30am-9pm) Helpful, although suffers from too few staff, too many tourists.

www.lindos-holiday.com A handy private website with a number of alternative villa accommodation options.

SIGHTS & ACTIVITIES
ACROPOLIS OF LINDOS
Spectacularly perched atop a 116m-high rock is the **Acropolis** (☎ 22440 31258; admission €6; ⏰ 8.30am-2.40pm Tue-Sun Sep-May, until 6pm Tue-Sun Jun-Aug). Once inside, a flight of steps leads to a large square. On the left (facing the next flight of steps) is a trireme, hewn out of the rock by the sculptor Pythocretes; a statue of Hagesandros, priest of Poseidon, originally stood on the deck of the ship. The steps ahead lead to the Acropolis itself via a vaulted corridor. A sharp left leads through an enclosed room to a row of storerooms on the right, while the stairway on the right leads to the remains of a 20-columned **Hellenistic stoa** (200 BC). The Byzantine **Church of Agios Ioannis**,

with its ancient frescoes, is to the right of this stairway. The wide stairway behind the stoa leads to a 5th-century-BC propylaeum, beyond which is the 4th-century **Temple to Athena**, the site's most important ancient ruin.

Donkey rides to the Acropolis cost €5 one way – be aware that the poor creatures should not be carrying anyone over 50kg (112lbs), though this stipulation is rarely enforced. To get here on your own steam, head straight into the village from the main square, turn left at the church and follow the signs. The last stretch is a strenuous 10-minute climb up slippery steps. There's no shade at the top; pack a hat and some water.

BEACHES
The **Main Beach** is to the east of the Acropolis and is sandy with warm water. On the western side of the Acropolis is the sheltered **St Paul's Bay** with its warm, turquoise water.

Just 2km south of Lindos, sandy **Pefki Beach** is deservedly popular. If it's too crowded, try **Glystra Beach**, just down the road and a great spot for swimming.

SLEEPING
Electra (☎ 22440 31266; s/d €45/55; 🖭) Thankfully, Lindos' true budget option is brilliant. Electra has an expansive and popular roof terrace with superb views and a beautiful shady garden of lemon trees. The 11 rooms are airy and spacious. Each has a fridge and there's a communal kitchen. Follow the donkey route to find it.

Filoxenia Guest House (☎ 22440 31266; www.lindos-filoxenia.com; d/ste incl breakfast €90/140; 🖭 🖳) Inside a traditional home, these simple rooms are embellished with wrought-iron bed frames, antique furnishing, tiled floors or raised sleeping platforms. Family rooms are also available. All rooms have fridge and kitchenette.

our pick Melenos (☎ 22440 32222; www.melenoslindos.com; ste incl breakfast €385; ✖ 🖳 🛜) The kind of place most of us dream of staying in, Melenos is pure luxury. Built in 17th-century style, almost everything has been handmade, hand-carved or hand-stitched – from the sandstone motifs to the mosaic floors, painted ceiling, woven fabrics and cedar sleeping platforms.

EATING

Captain's House (☎ 22440 31235; snacks €3-6) This atmospheric, shaded courtyard gives you a chance to peek inside one of Lindos' traditional seafarers' abodes. Sit on sofas in the shaded courtyard or head inside the traditional captain's house. Refresh with iced coffees, beer on tap, cocktails and juice or munch on baguettes or toasted sandwiches. Follow signs left from the Acropolis.

Kalypso (☎ 22440 32135; mains €6-12) Set in one of Lindos' historic buildings, this is a family-run restaurant that's stood the test of time. Ignore the touristy outdoor appearance; inside you'll find traditional decor and a warm atmosphere. Dine on the rooftop on feta flutes, fresh tuna, sausages in mustard, or rabbit stew in red wine. The menu is enormous, with vegetarian and children's options. Take the second right off the main drag to find it.

ANCIENT IALYSOS
ΑΡΧΑΙΑ ΙΑΛΥΣΟΣ

The Doric city of **Ialysos** (adult €3; ✞ 8.30am-3pm Tue-Sun) was built on Filerimos Hill, an excellent vantage point, and attracted successive invaders over the years. Over time, it became a hotchpotch of Doric, Byzantine and medieval remains. As you enter, stairs lead to the ancient remains of a 3rd-century-BC temple and the restored 14th-century **Chapel of Agios Georgios** and **Monastery of Our Lady**. All that's left of the temple are the foundations but the chapel is a peaceful retreat.

Take the path left from the entrance to a 12th-century **chapel** (looking like a bunker) filled with frescoes. They're not well preserved but worth a look.

There is a sign requesting that visitors dress 'properly'. Although there's no elaboration, out of respect, shoulders should be covered and women should wear long skirts or trousers. Ialysos is 10km from Rhodes, with buses running every half hour.

NISYROS
ΝΙΣΥΡΟΣ

pop 950

Nisyros (ni-see-ross) tumbles down to the sea from its central volcano. Nearly round and built of pumice and rock, the island's volcanic soil makes it phenomenally fertile, drawing botanists and gardeners from around the world to see its unique flora. You don't come to Nisyros for its beaches (which aren't great). You come to stand in the centre of its hissing volcano, to explore its less touristy villages, to hike along its lush slopes and to dine on amazing local produce.

GETTING THERE & AWAY

Nisyros is linked by regular ferries to Rhodes, Kos and Piraeus. Two small local ferries link Mandraki with Kardamena on Kos, and Kos Town.

GETTING AROUND
BOAT

In July and August there are excursion boats (return €10) to the pumice-stone islet of Giali, where there's a relaxing, sandy beach.

BUS

In summer, bus companies run up to 10 excursion buses daily between 9.30am and 3pm (€7.50 return) that give you about 40 minutes at the volcano. In addition, three daily buses travel to Nikea (€2) via Pali. The bus stop is located at Mandraki's port.

TAXI

For a cab call ☎ 6989969810, 22420 31460 or 22420 22420. A taxi from Mandraki to the volcano costs €20 return, to Nikea €11 and to Pali €5.

MANDRAKI ΜΑΝΔΡΑΚΙ

pop 660

Mandraki is the port and main village of Nisyros – it is a wonderful place to explore. Wander through the maze of residential alleyways, passing houses with brightly painted balconies, drying laundry and children playing outside.

ORIENTATION

The port is 500m northeast of the centre of Mandraki. Take the road right from the port and you will hit the town centre. A couple of blocks up, you'll come to a Y-junction. Head left to reach the tree-shaded Plateia Ilikiomenis, Mandraki's focal point. Head right along the main drag for signs for the monastery and castle.

INFORMATION

The Co-operative Bank of the Dodecanese has an ATM at the harbour and a branch in Mandraki.

Diakomihalis (☎ 22420 31015; diakomiha lis@kos.forthnet.gr; Mandraki) Sells ferry tickets and hires cars.

Enetikon Travel (☎ 22420 31180; agiosnis@ otenet.gr) Provides tourist information; 100m from the quay towards Mandraki.

Police (☎ 22420 31201) Opposite the quay.

Port police (☎ 22420 31222) Opposite the quay.

Post office (☎ 22420 31249) Opposite the quay.

www.nisyros.gr Info on sights, history and the environment.

GEORGE TSAFOS

Hohlakia (pebble mosaic flooring), Mandraki, Nisyros

SIGHTS

Towering over Mandraki is the 14th-century cliff-top **Moni Panagias Spilianis** (Virgin of the Cave; ☎ 22420 31125; admission by donation; ☺ 10.30am-3pm). There's not a huge amount to see, other than a few exhibits on the way up and a room lined with impressive icons, but the views from the top are spectacular.

In town, the brand new **Archaeological Museum** was due to open at the time of research. If a sneak peek was anything to go by, it's definitely worth a visit.

Above Mandraki, the impressive Mycenaean-era acropolis, **Paleokastro** (Old Kastro) has restored 4th-century Cyclopean walls built from massive blocks of volcanic rock that you can perch atop for breathtaking views. There are good explanatory notes in English throughout the site. Follow the route signposted '*kastro*', heading southwest from the monastery steps. You can drive here too.

SLEEPING

Three Brothers Hotel (☎ 22420 31344; iiibrothers@kos.forthnet.gr; s/d/studio €30/40/60; ☒) This welcoming, family-run hotel has smallish but well-maintained rooms with balconies and a few spacious, high-ceilinged studios with kitchenettes and verandas. All rooms have a small fridge and most have sea views. Next to the port, the hotel is very handy for ferries.

Ta Liotridia (☎ 22420 31580; www.nisyros -taliotridia.gr; apt €100; ☒) Along the waterfront, this stone building used to house oil presses. They're now luxurious rooms decorated in traditional style with raised beds, stone archways and classic furnishings. Expect fantastic sea views from the balcony. Apartments sleep four and have full kitchens.

EATING

Ask for the island speciality, *pitties* (chickpea and onion patties) and wash them down with a refreshing *soumada*, a nonalcoholic local beverage made from almond extract.

Restaurant Irini (☎ 22420 31365; Plateia Ilikiomenis; mains €3-6) Ignore the big tourist boards outside; dining here may make you wonder if you've entered Irini's own dining room. You'll be treated like family with big dishes of great home cooking. Try the excellent dolmadhes, aubergine salad, grilled meat and fish dishes and leave room for the amazing puddings.

Kleanthes Taverna (☎ 22420 31484; mains €6-12) On the seafront with views of the monastery and Kos, this restaurant is popular with locals for its fresh fish soup, mussels with rice, grilled beef burgers and baked feta.

AROUND NISYROS
EMBORIOS & NIKEA
ΕΜΠΟΡΕΙΟΣ & ΝΙΚΑΙΑ

Emborios and Nikea perch on the volcano's rim. From each, there are stunning views down into the caldera. Only a handful of inhabitants linger on in Emborios. You may encounter a few elderly women sitting on their doorsteps crocheting, their husbands at the *kafeneio* (coffee house).

ourpick Ainria Taverna (☎ 22420 31377; Embrosios; mains €3-12), located behind the church, is the big drawcard in Emborios. It's impossible to go wrong with this menu: the country salad, meatballs, stuffed peppers, baked cheese, tomato and aubergine, and the seafood are all truly gourmet. The bright decor of the traditional wooden building makes it a comfortable place to linger over a scrumptious meal.

In contrast to Emborios, picturesque Nikea, with 35 inhabitants, buzzes with

Lakki (crater depression), Nisyros volcano

↘ THE VOLCANO ΤΟ ΗΦΑΙΣΤΕΙΟ

Nisyros is on a volcanic line that passes through the islands of Aegina, Paros, Milos, Santorini, Nisyros, Giali and Kos. The island originally culminated in a mountain of 850m, but the centre collapsed 30,000 to 40,000 years ago after three violent eruptions. Another violent eruption occurred in 1422 on the western side of the caldera depression (called Lakki); this, like all other eruptions since, emitted steam, gases and mud, but no lava. The islanders call the volcano Polyvotis because, during the Great War between the gods and the Titans, the Titan Polyvotis annoyed Poseidon so much that the god tore off a chunk of Kos and threw it at him. This rock pinned Polyvotis under it and became the island of Nisyros. The hapless Polyvotis has been groaning and sighing while trying to escape from that day forth.

Descending into the volcano's **caldera** is other-worldly. Cows graze near the crater's edge, amidst red, green and orange rocks. A not-so-obvious and unsignposted path descends into the largest of the five craters, **Stefanos**, where you can examine the multicoloured fumaroles, listen to their hissing and smell their sulphurous vapours. The surface is soft and hot, making sturdy footwear essential. Don't stray too far out as the ground is unstable and can collapse. Also be careful not to step into a fumarole as the gases are 100°C and corrosive. Another unsignposted but more obvious track leads to **Polyvotis**, which is smaller and wilder looking, but it doesn't allow access to the caldera itself. The fumaroles are around the edge here so be very careful.

You can reach the volcano by bus, car or along a 3km-long trail from Nikia. If you get there before 11am you may just have the whole place entirely to yourself.

Things you should know: Caldera (admission €2.50; ⊙ 9am-8pm)

DODECANESE

NISYROS

JAN WLODARCZYK

Kitesurfing, Cape Prasonisi, Rhodes

↘ IF YOU LIKE...

If you like hiking through the lush terrain of **Nisyros** (p290) or renting a bike on **Kos** (p295), we think you'd like these other Dodecanese activities:

- **Cape Prasonisi** At the southern end of Rhodes, a 10km road snakes across windswept terrain to this remote and gorgeous sandy point. If you're into windsurfing, this is the place to come. The resort caters entirely to surfers and outside of the summer season it's totally shut.
- **Tilos** Basking in relative obscurity, tiny Tilos island is popular with migratory birds and avid birdwatchers. Rare species such as the Eleonora's falcon, the Mediterranean shag and the Bonelli's eagle nest here and the island is home to countless rare orchids and mammals such as sea turtles and the Mediterranean monk seal. Watch for them as you strike out on the island's countless walking trails.
- **Kalymnos** This island's spectacular limestone walls attract legions of climbers looking for seriously challenging extreme sport. There are over 20 documented climbs awaiting the adventurous, pulling in visitors from March onwards.
- **Karpathos** With some of the clearest water for snorkelling in the whole of the Aegean, consider Ammoöpi on Karpathos. Just up the road, wind- and kitesurfers head for the broad **Afiartis Bay** in droves to enjoy world-class conditions. It's also home to the annual international kitesurfing competition (www.speedworldcup.com).
- **Petaloudes** (adult €3; ☼ 8.30am-4.30pm) Better known as the Valley of the Butterflies, this is a popular sight on Rhodes. Visit in June, July or August when these colourful creatures mature, and you'll quickly see why. Come out of season and you'll miss the winged critters but you'll have the gorgeous forest path, rustic footbridges, streams and pools to yourself.

life. It has dazzling white houses with vibrant gardens and a lovely mosaic-tiled central square. At the edge of town is the **Volcanological Museum** (☎ 22420 31400; ⊙ 11am-3pm May-Sep) detailing the history of the volcano and its effects on the island. In the village's main square, **Cafe Porta Pangiotis** (☎ 22420 31285) is a cheerful, homey place to get coffee or a cool drink.

The steep path down to the volcano begins from Plateia Nikolaou Hartofyli. It takes about 40 minutes to walk it one way.

KOS ΚΩΣ

pop 17,890

With some of the Dodecanese' very best beaches, impressive archaeological sites and a lush interior, it's hardly surprising that Kos (*koss*) is such a popular destination. Kos Town has a wonderful vibe and is an excellent base, catering to everyone from upmarket tourists to backpackers after a party. When you tire of the crowds, there are plenty of places to spread out – long, sandy beaches, hilltop villages and remote coves. You won't have the island to yourself, but some things are worth sharing.

GETTING THERE & AWAY

There are regular flights to Athens, Rhodes, Leros and Astypalea with **Olympic Air** (Map p297; ☎ 22420 28330; Vasileos Pavlou 22).

BOAT

Kos is well connected to Piraeus and all the islands in the Dodecanese, as well as to the Cyclades, Samos and Thessaloniki. Services are offered by three ferry companies: **Blue Star Ferries** (Map p297; ☎ 22420 28914), **G&A Ferries** (☎ 22420 28545) and the **ANE Kalymnou** (☎ 22420 29900). Catamarans are run by Dodekanisos

Seaways at the interisland ferry quay. Local passenger and car ferries run to Pothia on Kalymnos from Mastihari. For tickets, visit the very helpful **Fanos Travel & Shipping** (☎ 22420 20035; www. kostravel.gr; 11 Akti Kountourioti, Kos Town) on the harbour.

GETTING AROUND
TO/FROM THE AIRPORT

The **airport** (☎ 22420 51229) is 24km southwest of Kos Town. An Aegean Airlines bus (€4) ferries passengers from Kos Town, leaving the airline's office two hours before the Athens flights depart. Kefalos-bound buses also stop at the big roundabout near the airport entrance. A taxi from the airport to Kos Town costs around €22.

BOAT

From Kos Town there are many boat excursions around the island and to other islands. Examples of return fares: Kalymnos €10; Pserimos, Kalymnos and Platy €20; Nisyros €20. In Kos Town these boats line the southern arm of Akti Koundourioti.

BICYCLE

Cycling is very popular in Kos and you'll be tripping over bicycles for hire; prices range from €5 per day for a boneshaker to €10 for a half-decent mountain bike. In Kos Town try **George's Bikes** (Map p297; ☎ 22420 24157; Spetson 48; per day €3) for decent bikes at reasonable prices.

BUS

The **bus station** (Map p297; ☎ 22420 22292; Kleopatras 7, Kos Town) is just west of the Olympic Air office. Buses regularly serve all parts of the island, as well as the all-important beaches on the south side of Kos. A bus to the beaches will cost around €3.60.

KOS TOWN
pop 14,750

Palm-fringed and colourful, with the Castle of the Knights picturesquely perched at its centre, Kos Town's harbour hints at the lush, vibrant town that spreads beyond it. Located on the northeast coast, Kos Town is the island's capital and main port. With an abundance of palms, pines, oleander and hibiscus, its lively squares and shopping streets are balanced with impressive Hellenistic and Roman ruins seemingly strewn everywhere.

ORIENTATION

The ferry quay is north of the castle and Akti Koundourioti is the street edging the harbour. The central square of Plateia Eleftherias is south of here along Vasileos Pavlou. What's left of Kos' Old Town is centred around the pedestrianised Apellou Ifestou.

Southeast of the castle, the waterfront is called Akti Miaouli. It continues as Vasileos Georgiou and then Georgiou Papandreou, which leads to the beaches of Psalidi, Agios Fokas and Therma Loutra.

INFORMATION

Alpha Bank (El Venizelou) Has a 24-hour ATM.

Hospital (☎ 22420 22300; Ippokratous 32) In the centre of town.

Municipal Tourist Office (☎ 22420 24460; www.kosinfo.gr; Akti Kountouriotou; ☼ 8am-2.30pm & 3-10pm Mon-Fri, 9am-2pm Sat May-Oct) General information on Kos in the office and online.

National Bank of Greece (Riga Fereou) With ATM.

Police (☎ 22420 22222) Shares the Municipality Building with the tourist police.

Port police (cnr Akti Koundourioti & Megalou Alexandrou)

Post office (Vasileos Pavlou)

Tourist police (☎ 22420 22444)

www.travel-to-kos.com Comprehensive guide to most of Kos' attractions.

SIGHTS & ACTIVITIES
ARCHAEOLOGICAL MUSEUM

Cool and calm, the **archaeological museum** (☎ 22420 28326; Plateia Eleftherias; admission €3; ☼ 8am-2.30pm Tue-Sun) is a pleasant place to take in local sculptures from the Hellenistic to the Late Roman era. The most renowned statue is that of Hippocrates; there's a 3rd-century-AD mosaic in the vestibule that's worth seeing.

CASTLE OF THE KNIGHTS

You can now reach the once impregnable **Castle of the Knights** (☎ 22420 27927; Leoforos Finikon; admission €4; ☼ 8am-2.30pm Tue-Sun) by crossing a bridge over Finikon from Plateia Platanou. The castle, which had massive outer walls and an inner keep, was built in the 14th century and separated from the town by a moat (now Finikon). These days you'll find six resident tortoises as well as performances of Hippocrates' works in the summer.

ARCHAEOLOGICAL SITES

The **ancient agora** (admission free; ☼ 8am-2pm) is an open site south of the castle. A massive 3rd-century-BC stoa, with some reconstructed columns, stands on its western side. North of the agora is the lovely cobblestone Plateia Platanou, where you can sit in a cafe while paying respects to the once magnificent **Hippocrates Plane Tree**, under which Hippocrates is said to have taught his pupils.

On the other side of town is the **western excavation site**. Two wooden shelters at the back of the site protect the 3rd-century **mosaics of the House of Europa**. On the opposite side of Grigoriou

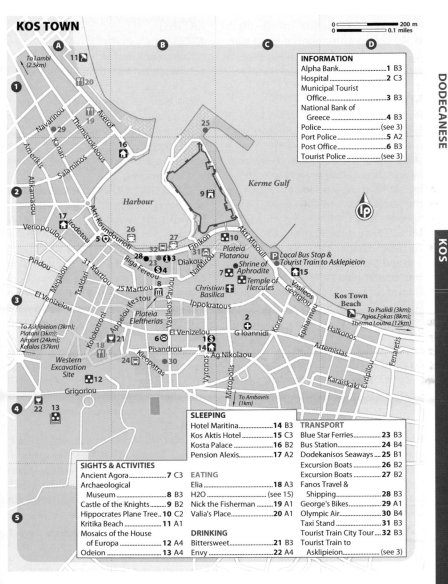

KOS TOWN

INFORMATION
Alpha Bank	**1** B3
Hospital	**2** C3
Municipal Tourist Office	**3** B3
National Bank of Greece	**4** B3
Police	(see 3)
Port Police	**5** A2
Post Office	**6** B3
Tourist Police	(see 3)

SIGHTS & ACTIVITIES
Ancient Agora	**7** C3
Archaeological Museum	**8** B3
Castle of the Knights	**9** B2
Hippocrates Plane Tree	**10** C2
Kritika Beach	**11** A1
Mosaics of the House of Europa	**12** A4
Odeion	**13** A4

SLEEPING
Hotel Maritina	**14** B3
Kos Aktis Hotel	**15** C3
Kosta Palace	**16** B2
Pension Alexis	**17** A2

EATING
Elia	**18** A3
H2O	(see 15)
Nick the Fisherman	**19** A1
Valia's Place	**20** A1

DRINKING
Bittersweet	**21** B3
Envy	**22** A4

TRANSPORT
Blue Star Ferries	**23** B3
Bus Station	**24** B4
Dodekanisos Seaways	**25** B1
Excursion Boats	**26** B2
Excursion Boats	**27** B2
Fanos Travel & Shipping	**28** B3
George's Bikes	**29** A1
Olympic Air	**30** B4
Taxi Stand	**31** B3
Tourist Train City Tour	**32** B3
Tourist Train to Asklipieion	(see 3)

is the impressive 2nd-century **odeion**. It was initially a venue for the senate and musical competitions and was restored during the Italian occupation when it was discovered, filled with sculptures (many are now in the archaeological museum).

BEACHES

On the east side of town, **Kos Town Beach** has a thin strip of sand and deep water for swimming. It tends to be dominated by the restaurants and hotels along this stretch. West of town, **Kritika**

Beach is a long sandy stretch that's polka-dotted with umbrellas in the summer. It gets crowded but is within easy walking distance of the town centre.

SLEEPING

Pension Alexis (☎ 22420 28798; fax 22420 25797; Irodotou 9; d €40-50; ✂) Going since the 1970s and with little redecoration since, these big, airy rooms have bold, mismatched wallpaper and a very homey feel. All have lovely balconies; room 4 has the best harbour view. The owner is keen to dole out local info and lets you use her kitchen. The only drawbacks are thin walls and shared bathrooms.

Hotel Maritina (☎ 22420 23511-3; www .maritina.gr; Vyronos 19; ☙ year-round; s/d incl breakfast €50/75; ✂ 🖳) The halls may feel a little down-at-heel but the rooms are very comfortable – stylish if anonymous – with lots of amenities and a small balcony. There's a huge breakfast and very friendly service.

Kosta Palace (☎ 22420 22855; www .kosta-palace.com; cnr Akti Kountourioti & Averof; d €70; ☙ year-round; ✂ 🖳 🖳) Easily spotted on the harbour's northern side, these rooms don't have a lot of character but they are spacious and impeccably clean. Some have spectacular harbour views and there's a cafe and rooftop pool. Very friendly staff; the beach is just a short walk away.

Kos Aktis Hotel (☎ 22420 47200; www.kosaktis.gr; Vasileos Georgiou 7; s/d from €140/178; ✂ 🖳 🛜) You'll fall asleep to the sound of lapping waves at this boutique hotel, set on a small beach yet close to the town centre. Very plush and very stylish, with flat-screen TVs, amazing tubs with sea views and glass balconies; you'll be well pampered.

EATING

our pick **Valia's Place** (☎ 22420 27877; www .valiasplace.gr; Averof 38; mains €3-6) Hidden behind a giant tree, this place has an old jazz club feel to it, complete with lots of wood, worn leather and old photographs. With a patio on the beach, it's a popular haunt with locals and often hosts live local folkstyle music. Fill up on drunk chicken, aubergine *boureki* (pies), salads and sandwiches.

our pick **Elia** (☎ 22420 22133; Appelou Ifestou 27; mains €4-8) With their images painted beneath the wooden rafters, you will certainly feel like you're dining with the gods here. Start with chunky bread and olive pâté and then try the pumpkin balls, grilled vegies with haloumi, pork with mustard and capers or the Byzantine chicken with leek and spices.

Nick the Fisherman (☎ 22420 23098; Averof 21; mains €5-12) This lively open-air restaurant is frequented by locals and is a relaxed place to try fresh seafood with a gourmet twist. Dishes like squid stuffed with cheese, seafood spaghetti and mussels with red sauce keep customers coming back.

H2O (☎ 22420 47200; Vasileos Georgiou 7; snacks €5-10, mains €15-20) Exceptionally stylish and ultracool, the food here lives up to the decor. Try the linguine with shrimp, peppers and ouzo, or garlic lamb with rosemary and local cheese. Or just opt for an aperitif and classy snacks on the patio.

DRINKING & ENTERTAINMENT

Kos' nightlife, geared for partying tourists, is centred a block south of the harbour, along Diakou. There's also a plethora of similar bars along the waterfront on Kritika Beach. If you're looking for clubs, they pass in and out of favour so just follow the crowds.

Waterfront views over Kos Town (p296)

ROBERT MORRIS/ALAMY

Envy (☎ 22420 00827; Grigoriou) Denlike, with cool blue cube lighting, red chandeliers and velvet sofas, local DJs pump Greek and English music out of this traditional stone building until the wee hours.

Bittersweet (☎ 22420 26003; Apellou Ifestou) Disguised as a simple crêperie from the outside, inside you'll find a lounge-like affair with moody lighting, sofas, a fantastic garden and almost anything you can dream of drinking. Not surprisingly, the music is lounge.

GETTING AROUND
BUS
Urban buses depart from Akti Miaouli and have two ticket prices: Zone A (€0.80) and Zone B (€1). For schedules, check the Local Bus Office.

TAXI
Taxis congregate at a stand on the south side of the port.

TOURIST TRAIN
In summer, a good way to get your bearings is to hop on the city's vehicular Tourist Train's city tour (€4, 20 minutes), which runs from 10am to 2pm and 6pm to 10pm, starting from the bus station on Akti Kountouriotou. You can also take a train to the Asklipieion and back (€3.50), departing on the hour from 10am to 5pm Tuesday to Sunday, from the bus stop on Akti Miaouli.

AROUND KOS TOWN
The nearest decent beach to Kos Town is the crowded **Lambi Beach**, 4km to the northwest and an extension of Kritika Beach. Further round the coast is a long, pale-sand stretch of beach, divided into **Tingaki**, 10km from Kos Town, and **Marmari Beach**, 14km west and slightly less crowded. Windsurfing is popular at all three beaches.

Vasileos Georgiou in Kos Town leads to the three busy beaches of **Psalidi**, 3km from Kos Town, **Agios Fokas** (8km) and

Therma Loutra (12km). The latter has hot mineral springs that warm the sea.

ASKLIPIEION ΑΣΚΛΗΠΙΕΙΟΝ

The island's most important ancient site is the **Asklipieion** (☎ 22420 28763; Platani; adult/student €4/3; ◷ 8am-7.30pm Tue-Sun), built on a pine-covered hill 3km southwest of Kos Town, with lovely views of the town and Turkey. The Asklipieion consisted of a religious sanctuary devoted to Asclepius (the god of healing), a healing centre and a school of medicine, where training followed the teachings of Hippocrates. Until AD 554, when an earthquake destroyed the Asklipieion, people came from far and wide for treatment.

The hourly bus 3 and the Tourist Train (p299) go to the site. It's also a pleasant cycle or walk.

MOUNTAIN VILLAGES

The villages scattered on the northern green slopes of the Dikeos mountain range are a great place for exploring. From Zia, take a left and follow signs for **Pyli**. Just before the village, a left turn leads to the extensive ruins of the medieval village of **Old Pyli** where a well-marked trail leads past the remains of houses and up to the castle. A number of the chapels on the site are currently being restored and many of the Byzantine gates and archways are still largely intact. Watch out for tortoises, too! Good footwear and a little stamina are a must. It's a great place to picnic; stock up in the grocery stores and bakeries of Pyli.

KAMARI & KEFALOS BAY ΚΑΜΑΡΙ & ΚΕΦΑΛΟΣ

Continue southwest to the huge Kefalos Bay, fringed by a 12km stretch of incredible sand. Don't be put off by the tacky strip of tourist shops, restaurants and hotels behind on the main road. These divine beaches are idyllic, backed by green hills and lapped by warm water. The stretch is roughly divided into seven, each signposted from the main road. The most popular is **Paradise Beach**, while the most undeveloped is **Exotic Beach**; **Banana Beach** (also known as Langada Beach) is a good compromise.

Agios Stefanos Beach, at the far western end, is reached along a short turn-off from the main road and worth a visit to see the island of **Agios Stefanos**. Within swimming distance, this tiny island is home to the ruins of two 5th-century basilicas and to another lovely, sandy beach.

Further down the road, you'll reach **Kamari Beach**, an elongated holiday resort strip.

PATMOS ΠΑΤΜΟΣ

pop 3040

Shrouded in spiritual mystery, Patmos has an atmosphere unlike any of the other Dodecanese. It's as if the island itself knows it's special. Even the light here is unusual, bathing the landscape in warm hues; the islanders are a mix of proud locals and long-term expats drawn by the lure of harmony. It was here that St John the Divine ensconced himself in a cave and wrote the Apocalypse (see the boxed text, p303). Since then, it has become a place of pilgrimage for both Orthodox and Western Christians and is, without doubt, the best place to experience Orthodox Easter. Beyond the tolling bells of the chapels, it's easy to locate dazzling beaches, great nosh and relaxing places to lay your head. The hard part is leaving.

GETTING THERE & AWAY

Patmos is connected with Piraeus, Rhodes and a number of islands in between through mainline services with Blue Star Ferries and G&A Ferries. Hydrofoils and catamarans also link Patmos with Samos and the rest of the Dodecanese. Boat tickets are sold by Apollon Travel (p301) in Skala.

GETTING AROUND

Excursion boats go to Psili Ammos Beach from Skala, departing around 10am and returning about 4pm.

From Skala, there are six return buses daily to Hora and four to Grikos and Kambos. Fares are a standard €1.

You can catch a **taxi** (☎ 22470 31225) from Skala's taxi rank opposite the police station.

SKALA ΣΚΑΛΑ

You may find Patmos' port town of Skala (*ska*-la), draped around a curving bay, slightly more glitzy than expected. Skala certainly sees its fair share of tourists, resulting in lots of excellent accommodation and restaurants. Despite its bustle, the people here seem to be in perpetual holiday mode and relaxing is easy.

ORIENTATION

All transport arrives at the centre of the long quay, smack bang in the middle of Skala. To the right the road leads to a narrow, sandy beach, the yacht port and on to the north of the island. To the left, the road leads to the south side of the island. From a roundabout near the ferry terminal, a road heads inland and up to Hora. The bus terminal and taxi rank are at the quay and all main services are within 100m.

INFORMATION

There are three ATM-equipped banks in Skala: the National Bank of Greece, the Emporiki Bank and the Commercial Bank.

AB Food Market (☎ 22470 34023) A well-stocked grocery store 100m along the Hora road in Skala.

Apollon Travel (☎ 22470 31324; apollon travel@stratas.gr) Ticketing for flights and ferries.

Hospital (☎ 22470 31211) Two kilometres along the road to Hora.

ZACH HOLMES/ALAMY

Road leading from Hora towards Skala, Patmos

Municipal Tourist Office (☎ 22470 31666; ☺ summer) Shares the same building as the post office and police station.

Police (☎ 22470 31303) On the main waterfront.

Port police (☎ 22470 31231) Behind the quay's passenger-transit building.

www.patmos-island.com Lots of local listings and info.

www.patmosweb.gr A slightly flashier site with history, listings and photos.

SLEEPING

At the port you'll find a small **info bureau** (☎ 22470 32899) with details on private rooms, studios and apartments for rent.

Casteli Hotel (☎ 22470 31361; fax 22470 51656; s/d incl breakfast €50/70; P ☒ ☒) With '70s retro telephones and funky tiles in the bathroom, this place is dated but well loved. Rooms aren't huge but have great views of the harbour and Hora and there's a rooftop pool.

Hotel Chris (☎ 22470 31001; www.patmos chrishotel.gr; d back/sea view €50/80; ☒) This hotel's age shows in the slightly down-at-heel lobby and halls but the renovated rooms have tiled floors and lovely wooden furniture. Some have four-poster double beds and sea-view rooms have balconies. A little pricey but well situated next to the beach with a popular cafe out front.

Kalderimi Apartments (☎ 22470 33008; www.kalderimi.com; apt incl breakfast from €110; ☒) At the foot of the path up to the monastery and secluded by trees, these gorgeous apartments have a traditional design with wooden beams and stone walls, along with lots of swish extras. A full kitchen, shaded balcony and lots of privacy make them a perfect retreat for longer-term stays.

EATING

Tzivaeri (☎ 22470 31170; mains €4-7; ☺ dinner) All old-fashioned elegance with china, a record player and black-and-white photos, this beachside restaurant serves traditional dishes. The service is fast and courteous and the upstairs looks out over the harbour.

Meltemi (☎ 22470 31839; full breakfast €5; ☺ 9am-late; ☐) Start your morning off right, filling up on home-cooked breakfasts at tables on the sand. Later in the day, come here for milkshakes, quiche and coffee while the waves lap at your toes.

Ostria (☎ 22470 30501; mains €7-12) Easily recognisable by the boat on its roof, this place doesn't look that special but packs in seafood connoisseurs all day long. Stuffed *kalamari*, shrimp with tomato and feta, and swordfish souvlaki are just a few of the tempting dishes.

Vegghera (☎ 22470 32988; mains €17-28) High-society diners head for this swish restaurant opposite the yacht marina. The cuisine is a melange of French and Greek with dishes like mushroom risotto, spaghetti with smoked turkey or shrimp on halva. Don't miss the chocolate soufflé.

DRINKING

Koukoumavia (☎ 22470 32325) Sip your cocktail at the mosaic bar of this very funky drinking hole. A great selection of music, friendly staff and unique artistic creations will keep you lingering. You'll find it a block north of the turn-off for Hora.

Arion (☎ 22470 31595) Right on the harbour, this popular spot has high-beamed ceilings, polished wood tables and looks more Cuban than Greek. Join a good mix of locals and tourists at any time of day, swaying your cocktail, beer or coffee to an eclectic mix of music.

SHOPPING

There's a creative streak running through Patmos, which leads to some interesting shopping. **Koukoumavla** (☎ 22470 32325; www.patmos-island.com/koukoumavla) has funky handmade clothing and accessories; on the harbour, **Selene** (☎ 22470 31742) has works by 40 artists from around Greece. Browse through Byzantine effigies, wooden carvings, games, pottery and jewellery. Behind the main square, **Jewel Kalogero** (☎ 22470 32453) sells locally made silver jewellery with unique designs.

HORA ΧΩΡΑ

High on the hill, huddled around the Monastery of St John, are the immaculate whitewashed houses of Hora, a legacy of the island's great wealth in the 17th and 18th centuries. A stroll through the mazelike streets evokes a timeless atmosphere.

The immense **Monastery of St John the Theologian** (☎ 22470 31398; admission free; ☽ 8am-1.30pm daily, plus 4-6pm Tue, Thu & Sun) crowns the island of Patmos. Attending a service here, with plumes of incense, religious chants and devoted worshippers, is like no other experience you'll have in Greece. Outside of services, you'll get a chance to see the intricate decor. To reach it, many people walk up the Byzantine path which starts from a signposted spot along the Skala-Hora road.

Some 200m along this path, a dirt trail to the left leads through pine trees to the **Monastery of the Apocalypse** (☎ 22470 31234; admission free, treasury €6; ☽ 8am-1.30pm daily, plus 4-6pm Tue, Thu & Sun), built around the cave where St John received his divine revelation. Inside you can see the rock that the saint used as a pillow, and the triple fissure in the roof from where the voice of God issued. The finest frescoes of this monastery are those in the outer narthex. It's also worth taking a peak at the icons and ecclesiastical ornaments found in the treasury.

A five-minute walk west of St John's Monastery, the **Holy Monastery of**

ST JOHN THE DIVINE & THE APOCALYPSE

The island of Patmos is home to the Cave of the Apocalypse where St John the Divine was allegedly visited by God and instructed to write the tell-all Book of Revelations, also known as the Book of the Apocalypse. He is often believed to be John the Apostle of Jesus or John the Evangelist, though many would dispute this due to his exile in AD 95 to Patmos by the pagan Roman Emperor Domitian. (John the Apostle would have been very, very old by then.) In the Book of Revelations, John wrote about two apocalyptic visions he had received.

'Revelation' is considered to be open to interpretation at best and is not afforded the serious scholarly study that it would seem to merit – perhaps because of the obscure and essentially hard-to-interpret symbolism of the work. Some critics have even suggested that it was the work of a deranged man. Whatever you choose to believe, it's worth visiting the cave where it all supposedly took place. Who knows – you may even have a bit of a revelation yourself.

DODECANESE

PATMOS

Vagia Beach, Patmos

IML IMAGE GROUP LTD/ALAMY

⬲ IF YOU LIKE...

If you like lazing on **Kambos Beach** (p305) and digging into excellent nosh at George's Place (p305), we think you'd like to dig your toes into the sand and your fork into the meals at these other Patmos beaches:

- **Vagia Beach** This quiet beach lies under the protected lee of the north arm of the island. Overlooking the beach is **Cafe Vagia** (☎ 22470 31658; mains €3-5; ☺ 9am-7pm) with its amazing vegie pies, hearty omelettes and local desserts, all served in a lush garden. It's especially popular with families.

- **Livadi tou Geranou Beach** Also in the north is this picturesque, shaded beach, with a small church-crowned island opposite. The road here is narrow and slightly treacherous but stunning. For lunch, stop at the cute **Livadi Geranou Taverna** (☎ 22470 32046; mains €3-5) overlooking the sea from a shaded garden.

- **Sapsila** This tiny settlement just south of Skala has a small beach offering peace and quiet. Dine at **Benetos** (☎ 22470 33089; Sapsila; mains €7-14; ☺ dinner Tue-Sun), just up the road. It's a working boutique farmhouse specialising in Mediterranean fusion dishes with an occasional Japanese kick.

- **Grikos** Also in the south, this relaxed, low-key resort has a long, sandy beach and warm shallow water. The bay is lined with tavernas and popular with yachties. At the southern end of the bay is **Ktima Petra** (☎ 22470 33207; mains €4-7), with organic, homegrown produce. The stuffed and wood-oven-baked goat melts in your mouth and the organic cheese and vegetables are scrumptious.

Zoodohos Pigi (admission free; ⊙ 8am-noon & 5-7pm Sun-Fri) is a women's convent with incredibly impressive frescoes. On Good Friday, a beautiful candle-lit ceremony takes place here.

Just east of St John's Monastery, **Andreas Kalatzis** (☎ 22470 31129) is a Byzantine icon artist who lives and works in a 1740s traditional home. Inside, you'll find an interesting mix of pottery, jewellery and paintings by local artists.

SLEEPING & EATING

ourpick **Archontariki** (☎ 22470 29368; www .arch ontariki-patmos.gr; ste €200-400) will do the trick if you're in need of a little luxury. Inside a 400-year-old building, four gorgeous suites are equipped with every convenience, traditional furnishings and plush touches.

Loza (☎ 22470 32405; starters €3-8, mains €10-19) is hard to miss as you enter Hora. With stunning views over Skala, it serves up reasonably priced salads and starters, along with some interesting mains like sweet and sour feta in filo and ouzo prawns with basmati rice. Up the stairs and left from here is the tiny **Pantheon** (☎ 22470 31226; mains €5-12) with views of the harbour. Dolmadhes, aubergine with garlic and fish are all well prepared and great value.

NORTH OF SKALA

North of Skala is the inland village of Kambos, from where the road descends to the relatively wide and sandy **Kambos Beach**, perhaps the most popular and easily accessible beach on the island. Situated on a fairly enclosed bay, it's great for swimming and you can hire kayaks and sun beds.

ourpick **George's Place** (☎ 22470 31881; snacks €3-7) is a fantastic beachside spot for lunch with a big selection of gourmet salads and snacks. The mint iced tea is very satisfying. Kick back and play backgammon, listen to the tunes and watch the waves roll in.

SOUTH OF SKALA

Petra Beach is very peaceful with sand, pebbles and lots of shade. A spit leads out to the startling **Kalikatsos Rock**. A rough coastal track leads from here to **Diakofti**, the last settlement in the south. From here you can follow a half-hour walking track to the long, sandy, tree-shaded **Psili Ammos Beach** where there's a seasonal taverna. You can also get here by excursion boat (p301).

GREECE IN FOCUS

ARCHITECTURE

ARCHITECTURE

GEORGE TSAFOS

Neoclassical architecture, Athens Academy (p310)

Get lost in Ancient Delphi or gaze up at the Parthenon and you'll quickly understand how Greece's architecture has inspired entire civilisations and spawned major architectural movements such as the Italian Renaissance. With four millenniums' worth of ruins, covering everything from Minoan palaces to Frankish keeps, exploring Greece is like delving into a natural library of architectural reference.

MINOAN MAGNIFICENCE

Our earliest glimpse of Greek architecture begins from around 2000 BC with the Minoans, who were based on Crete but whose influence spread throughout the Aegean. Minoan architects constructed technologically advanced, labyrinthine palace complexes such as Knossos (p248; see also p250).

Several gigantic volcanic eruptions rocked the region in the mid-15th century BC, causing big chunks of palaces to fall to the ground. The Minoans resolutely rebuilt these crumbling palaces on an even grander scale, only to have more natural disasters wipe them out again.

MYCENAEAN ENGINEERING

The Mycenaeans had a fierce reputation as spectacular structural engineers and expert builders of massive masonry. These rich war-mongering people picked choice vantage points for their large and austere palaces. At their zenith, the Mycenaeans had constructed over 300 supersized citadels throughout mainland Greece and the

Aegean. Usually built to a compact and orderly plan, the citadels' enclosing fortified Cyclopean-stone walls were on average an unbreachable 3m (10ft) to 7m (25ft) thick – it was believed for a time that only the legendary race of giants could have lifted such monumental blocks of stone. The famous Lion Gate at the citadel of Ancient Mycenae (p111) is the oldest monumental gate in Europe.

CLASSIC COMPOSITIONS

The classical age (5th to 4th centuries BC) is when most Greek architectural clichés converge, with the classical temple style underpinned by a refined knack for mathematics and aesthetics. Temples became characterised by the famous orders of columns, particularly the Doric, Ionic and Corinthian.

Doric columns feature austere cushion capitals, fluted shafts and no bases. The mother of all Doric structures is the 5th-century-BC Parthenon (p71), which emerged as the ultimate in architectural bling: a gleaming, solid marble crown.

The Ionic order originates from Asia Minor and features a column base with several tiers, more flutes and ornamented necking. You'll find this on the Acropolis' Temple of Athena Nike (p71) and the Erechtheion (p71).

Towards the tail end of the classical period, the Corinthian column was in limited vogue. Featuring a single or double row of ornate leafy scrolls, the order was adopted by the Romans and used only on Corinthian temples in Athens, such as the Temple of Olympian Zeus (p74).

The Greek theatre design is also a hallmark of the classical period. The original classical theatre design had a round stage to accommodate the traditional circular dance. The semicircle of steeply banked stone benches seated many thousands, but the perfect acoustics meant every spectator could hear every syllable uttered on the stage below. Visit Epidavros (p110) to test it out.

HELLENISTIC CITIZENS

In the twilight years of the classical age (from about the late 4th century BC), cosmopolitan folks started to take a very individualistic approach to life, casting their gaze towards a more decadent urban style. Wealthy citizens lavishly remodelled their homes with painted stonework, columns, marble courtyards and striking mosaics. The best Hellenistic ancient home displays are the grand houses at Ancient Delos (p212).

BYZANTINE ZEAL

Church-building was particularly expressive during Byzantium (from around AD 700). The Byzantine church design has the perfect symbiotic relationship between

◥THE BEST

DIANA MAYFIELD

Stone seating, Theatre of Dionysos (p73)

ANCIENT THEATRES

- **Epidavros** (p110)
- **Ancient Delphi** (138)
- **Odeon of Herodes Atticus** (p73; p80)
- **Theatre of Dionysos** (p73)
- **Theatre of Dodoni** (p190)

THE BEST

IML IMAGE GROUP LTD/ALAMY

Stone houses of Zagorohoria (p190)

REGIONAL ORIGINALS

- **Zagorohoria's slate mansions (p190)**
- **Hamlet of Vathia (p118)**
- **Volcanic-rock hewn village of Oia (p222)**
- **Lindos' captains' houses (p288)**

structural form and function. The original Greek Byzantine model features a distinctive cross shape and spectacular devotional mosaics and frescoes. Symbolically, working down from the dome (which is always representative of Christ in heaven), images of the Virgin are shown in the apse, with the walls decorated with images of saints or apostles, representing the descent to earth (the nave). Visit Athens' Church of Agii Theodori (p77).

FRANKISH KEEPS & VENETIAN STRONGHOLDS

After the sack of Constantinople by the Crusaders in 1204, much of Greece became the fiefdoms of Western aristocrats. The Villehardouin family punctuated the Peloponnesian landscape with Frankish castles, such as Mystras (p110). When the Venetians dropped by to seize a few coastal enclaves, they built the imposing 18th-century Palamidi fortress (p107) at Nafplio and the rock-nest protecting the enchanting Byzantine village at Monemvasia (p112).

OTTOMAN OFFERINGS

Interestingly, remarkably few monuments are left after the four centuries of Ottoman Turkish rule (16th to 19th centuries) in Greece. Those that survive include the prominent pink-domed Mosque of Süleyman (p284) in Rhodes' Old Town; the walled quarter of Ioannina with its restored Fetiye Cami (Victory Mosque; p187); and Athens' Turkish Baths (p76). The streets of Thessaloniki (p174) showcase superb Turkish-designed homes with stained-glass windows, wooden overhangs on buttresses, decorated plasterwork and painted woodwork.

NEOCLASSICAL SPLENDOUR

Regarded by experts as the most beautiful neoclassical building worldwide, the 1885 Athens Academy (Map 66–7) reflects Greece's post-Independence yearnings for grand and geometric forms, and Hellenistic detail. Other neoclassical examples include the solid marble National Library (Map 52–3), the more sedate Athens University (Map 66–7) and the meticulously restored neoclassical mansion housing the Benaki Museum (p75).

CUISINE

ALAN BENSON

Morning catch of fish, Paros, Cyclades

Steeped in ritual, Greece's culinary tradition incorporates mountain village food, island cuisine and influences from various invaders and historical trading partners. Rustic Greek cooking reflects the bounty of the land and its diverse topography. Whether it's dining alfresco at a rickety table by the sea, enjoying modern Greek cuisine in stylish Athens or eating boiled goat in a mountain village, dining out in Greece is never just about what you eat, but the whole sensory experience.

The essence of traditional Greek cuisine lies in its fresh, seasonal produce and generally simple, unfussy cooking that brings out the rich flavours of the Mediterranean. Olive oil is indeed the elixir of Greece, with extra-virgin oil produced in groves all over the country.

Vegetables, pulses and legumes – key elements of the healthy Mediterranean diet – feature prominently in Greek cooking, made tastier with plentiful use of olive oil and herbs. Meat was once reserved for special occasions but has become more prominent in the modern diet; lamb and pork dominate, though kid goat is also common. Fish has long been an essential ingredient, and is cooked with minimum fuss. The ubiquitous Greek salad (*horiatiki,* translated as 'village salad') is *the* summer salad, made of fresh tomatoes, cucumber, onions, feta and olives.

Greece's exceptional tangy, thick-strained yoghurt, usually made from sheep's milk, is rich and flavourful and ideal for breakfast with thick honey. A Greek staple is the

pita (pie), the most common being *tyropita* (cheese pie) and *spanakopita* (spinach pie).
Typical Greek pasta dishes include *pastitsio* (a thick spaghetti and meat bake) and the
hearty *youvetsi,* slow-cooked lamb or beef in a tomato sauce with *kritharaki* (orzo or
rice-shaped pasta).

Bread is a mandatory feature of every meal and is traditionally used to scoop up food
in lieu of a knife. The most common is the white crusty *horiatiko* (village) loaf.

MEZEDHES

Greeks love to share a range of mezedhes (appetisers), often making a full meal of them.
Do the same to try a whole gamut of Greek cuisine.

Common mezedhes include *keftedhes* (meatballs), *loukaniko* (sausage), *saganaki* (skillet-fried cheese) and dips, such as *taramasalata* (fish roe), tzatziki (yoghurt, cucumber
and garlic) and *melitzanosalata* (aubergine). Vegetarian mezedhes include rice-filled
dolmadhes, deep-fried zucchini or aubergine slices and *yigantes* (lima beans in tomato
and herb sauce).

Typical seafood mezedhes are pickled or grilled *ohtapodi* (octopus), marinated *gavros*
(anchovies), *lakerda* (cured fish), mussel or prawn *saganaki* (usually fried with tomato
sauce and cheese), crispy fried calamari and fried *maridha* (whitebait).

ALAN BENSON

The ubiquitous Greek salad

GREEK COFFEE

A legacy of Ottoman rule, Greek coffee
has a rich aroma and distinctive taste. It
is brewed in a *briki* (narrow-top copper
pot) and served in a small cup. It should
be sipped slowly until you reach the mud-
like grounds at the bottom (don't drink
them) and is best drunk *metrios* (medium,
with one sugar).

SWEET TREATS

Greeks traditionally serve fruit rather than
sweets after a meal but there's no shortage
of delectable Greek sweets and cakes, as the
proliferation of *zaharoplasteia* (patisseries)
will attest. Traditional syrupy fruit preserves,
ghlika kutalyu (spoon sweets), are served on
tiny plates as a welcome offering.

Other traditional sweets include baklava,
loukoumadhes (ball-shaped doughnuts
served with honey and cinnamon), *kataïfi*
(chopped nuts inside shredded angel-hair
pastry), *rizogalo* (rice pudding) and *galak-
toboureko* (custard-filled pastry). It's also
worth looking out for places selling *politiko
pagoto* (Constantinople-style ice cream).

REGIONAL COOKING

The cuisine of northern Greece is influenced by the eastern flavours introduced by Asia Minor refugees, and uses less olive oil and more peppers and spices than the rest of the country. The Peloponnese is known for simpler herb-rich one-pot dishes. As the biggest producers of olive oil, it is not surprising that the Peloponnese and Crete have the biggest variety of *ladhera* (vegetable dishes baked or stewed with plenty of olive oil).

The cuisine of the Ionian and Dodecanese islands have an Italian influence, while Cretan specialities include spiky wild artichokes, *hohlii* (snails) and *dakos* (rusks moistened and topped with tomato, olive oil and cheese). The Cyclades are renowned for their *fava* (split pea purée served with lemon juice and red onions), sun-dried tomato fritters and wild capers.

You'll find excellent cured meats across Greece, from the vinegar-cured *apaki* (Crete) to olive-oil stored *pasto* (the Mani).

> ## SAY CHEESE
>
> Greeks are the world's biggest per capita consumers of cheese, eating around 25kg per capita annually – more than the French and Italians. Widely used in cooking in both savoury and sweet dishes, cheese is also an accompaniment to most meals. Greece produces many different types of cheeses. Most are made from the milk of the nation's 16 million goats and sheep. Feta, the national cheese, has been produced for about 6000 years.

EATING GREEK-STYLE

Meals are commonly laid out in the middle of the table and shared, making it a more social dining experience. Lunch is usually the big meal of the day and does not start until after 2pm. Most Greeks wouldn't think of eating dinner before sunset, so restaurants often don't fill up until after 10pm.

While it's okay to look in the pots in the kitchen to choose your meal, and to choose your fish and get it weighed, it's impolite to start drinking before everyone's glass is full and they've done the customary toast, *'Ya mas'*. Don't insist on paying if you've been invited out – it insults your host. And drink up if offered a coffee or drinks – it's a gesture of hospitality.

FAMILY TRAVEL

KATJA KREDER/IMAGEBROKER

Water playground, Rhodes

Thinking of packing the family along? Greece is a safe and easy place to travel with children. Greek society welcomes children with open arms; the cities are often geared for families with child-friendly sights and parks, though you won't necessarily find these in smaller destinations,. Greeks will generally make a fuss over your children, who will find themselves on the receiving end of many small gifts and treats. Teaching your children a few words in Greek will ingratiate them further.

Travelling is especially easy if you're staying at a resort hotel by the beach, where everything is set up for families with children. Elsewhere, it's rare to find cots and high-chairs, although most hotels and restaurants will do their best to help. The fast service in most restaurants is good news when it comes to feeding hungry kids. Ordering lots of small dishes to share gives kids the chance to try local cuisine, and omelettes, chips and spaghetti are omnipresent. Many hotels let small children stay for free and will squeeze an extra bed into the room.

Unless you head straight for the beach, a holiday in Greece can mean a lot of walking. If your kids aren't old enough to walk on their own for long, consider a sturdy carrying backpack; unless they're of the sturdy, off-road variety, pushchairs are a struggle in towns and villages with slippery cobbles and high pavements.

Fresh milk is available in large towns and tourist areas, but harder to find on smaller islands. Supermarkets are the best place to look. Formula is available almost everywhere, as is condensed and heat-treated milk. Disposable nappies are also available everywhere.

Travel on ferries, buses and trains is free for children under four. They pay half-fare up to the age of 10 (ferries) or 12 (buses and trains). Full fares apply otherwise. On domestic flights, you'll pay 10% of the adult fare to have a child under two sitting on your knee. Kids aged two to 12 pay half-fare. If you plan to rent a car, it's wise to bring your own car or booster seat as many of the smaller local agencies won't have these.

Matt Barrett's website (www.greek-travel.com) has lots of useful tips for parents, while his daughter Amarandi has put together some tips for kids (www.greece4kids.com).

> ↘ **THE NITTY GRITTY**

- **Change facilities** Rare
- **Cots** Only available in top-end hotels
- **Health** Carry a first-aid kit and rehydration supplies
- **Highchairs** Nearly unheard of
- **Milk & Formula** Fresh milk is available in large towns and tourist areas; formula available almost everywhere
- **Nappies (diapers)** Everywhere
- **Transport** Lots of discounts; bring your own car seat for car rentals

GREECE IN FOCUS

FAMILY TRAVEL

FAMILY FUN

Most towns will have at least a small playground, while larger cities often have fantastic, modern play parks. You'll also find aquariums in many of the cities, along with play-centred children's museums. Check out the Hellenic Children's Museum (p79) in Athens, where your kids can join Greek cooking and craft classes.

Most kids enjoy climbing and exploring at ancient sights; young imaginations go into overdrive when let loose somewhere like the 'labyrinth' at Knossos (p248). Exploring Asklipieion (p300) on Kos, Ancient Olympia (p120) in the Peloponnese or climbing to the top of the rock pinnacles of Meteora (p145) will thrill parents and kids alike.

Many of Greece's beaches are ideal for families, with warm, shallow water. Others have activities popular with older children and teenagers, such as snorkelling and kayaking. And then there's the endless stretches of sand for castle building, digging and beachcombing.

FESTIVALS

Easter church ceremony held in Kalambaka (p149), Meteora

HEMIS/ALAMY

Attending an atmospheric and jubilant Greek festival or event can easily be a highlight of your trip. The Orthodox faith is the official religion of Greece, with a membership of around 95% of the population. Consequently, religious festivals flood the Greek calendar.

NAME DAYS

Christian Greeks are more likely to celebrate the day for the saint they are named after than their birthday. On a person's name day, greet them with *hronia polla* (good wishes and prosperity) and, if you go to visit or meet them out, take them a small gift. Islands and towns also celebrate the day of their patron saint with church services in historic chapels, feasting and dancing.

EASTER

In Greece, the biggest festival of the year is Easter. The festival begins on the evening of Good Friday when a shrouded bier (representing Christ's funeral bier) is carried through the streets in a candle-lit procession. Resurrection Mass starts at 11pm on Saturday night. At midnight, packed churches are plunged into darkness to symbolise Christ's passing through the underworld. The ceremony of the lighting of candles that follows is the most significant moment in the Orthodox year, symbolising the Resurrection. The ceremony ends with fireworks representing the sound of the boulder rolling away from in front of Jesus' tomb. The Lenten fast ends on Easter Sunday with the cracking of red-dyed Easter eggs, symbolising the blood of Christ and new life. The day's greeting is '*Hristos anesti*' (Christ is risen), to which the reply is '*Alithos anesti*' (truly He is risen).

GODS & GODDESSES

CHRISTINA DAMEYER

Representation of the battle between Athena and Poseidon for the honour of Guardian of Athens

Ancient Greece revolved around a careful worship of gods and goddesses. You'll find temples dedicated to them throughout the country and images of them on everything from ancient artefacts to restaurant walls. A little background knowledge can help you make heads and tails of them.

WHO'S WHO

Zeus was the heavyweight champ of Mt Olympus, lord of the skies and master of disguise in pursuit of mortal maidens. His younger brother, Poseidon, was god of the seas and master of the mists, living in a glittering underwater palace. Hera was protector of women and family; the queen of heaven is also the embattled wife of Zeus.

Goddess of love and beauty, Aphrodite was the curvy lady of the shell. When she wasn't cuckolding her unfortunate husband, Hephaestus, she and her cherubic son Eros were enflaming hearts and causing trouble.

Apollo was the god of music, the arts and fortune-telling. He was also the god of light and an expert shot with a bow and arrow. The goddess of the hunt and twin sister of Apollo, Artemis was, ironically, patron saint of wild animals.

Athena was goddess of wisdom, war, science and Guardian of Athens. Where possible, she was diplomatic in the art of war. Ares, on the other hand, was god of war, a bit of a hooligan and Zeus' least favourite offspring.

God of death, Hades ruled the underworld, bringing in newly dead with the help of his skeletal ferryman, Charon. God of craftsmanship, metallurgy and fire, Hephaestus was the deformed and oft-derided son of Zeus who made the world's first woman of clay, Pandora, as a punishment for man. Inside that box of hers were the evils of mankind.

And while you're touring Greece, don't neglect a nod to Hermes, messenger of the gods and patron saint of travellers. He's the handsome one with a winged hat and sandals.

MARVELLOUS MYTHS

The Greek religious pantheon was personified through Greek mythology. Filled with monsters, centaurs, nymphs, heroes and baddies, Greek myths make for an exciting read. Here's a taste.

THESEUS

This Athenian hero volunteered himself as one of seven men and maidens in the annual sacrifice to the Minotaur, the crazed half-bull-half-man offspring of King Minos of Crete. Once inside its forbidding labyrinth (Knossos; p248), Theseus loosened a spool of thread to find his way out once he'd killed the monster.

ICARUS

Pursued by King Minos and his troops, Icarus flew off the cliffs of Crete using wings made of feathers and wax. His father instructed him to fly away from the midday sun, but boys will be boys…glue melts, feathers separate, bird-boy drowns. And the moral is: listen to your father.

PERSEUS

Perseus' impossible task was to kill the gorgon, Medusa, whose head of snakes could turn a man to stone with a single glance. Armed with an invisibility cap and a pair of flying sandals from Hermes, Perseus used his reflective shield to avoid Medusa's stare. Having cut off her head and secreted it in a bag, it was shortly unsheathed to save Andromeda, a princess about to be sacrificed to a sea monster. Medusa's head turns it to stone, Perseus gets the girl.

OEDIPUS

Abandoned at birth, Oedipus learned from the Delphic oracle that he would one day slay his father and marry his mother. On a journey to Thiva (Thebes), Oedipus killed a rude stranger and then felled a murderous Sphinx that plagued the city, thereby gaining the queen of Thiva's hand in marriage. On discovering the stranger he'd killed was his father and that his new wife was his mother, Oedipus ripped out his eyes and exiled himself.

HISTORY

GEORGE TSAFOS

Caryatids of the Erechtheion (p71), Acropolis, Athens

Since its earliest days, the Greek landscape has been trudged across by countless invaders, occupiers and settlers. Each group has left its footprints, resulting in a culture and society that is as varied as the Greek landscape – experience the influence of the Ottomans in the north, the Italians in the Dodecanese and the Venetians in the Ionian Islands. Greece's past is very much a part of its current terrain, from ancient ruins scattered throughout the land to the origins of democracy which continue to be struggled for today.

EARLIEST DAYS

A Neanderthal skull found in a cave on the Halkidiki peninsula of Macedonia in northern Greece shows that humans have been hanging out in Greece for at least 700,000 years. Around 6500 BC, folks from the Palaeolithic times left bones and tools scattered in the Pindos Mountains, while pastoral communities emerged during Neolithic times (7000–3000 BC), mainly in the fertile region that is now Thessaly. Around

7000-3000 BC	3000-1100 BC	1700-1550 BC
Early inhabitants live a simple agrarian life, growing crops and herding animals.	Increased prosperity sees the birth of the Cycladic and Minoan – and later, the Mycenaean – civilisations.	Santorini erupts with a cataclysmic explosion, one of the largest volcanic events in recorded history.

JOHN ELK II

Setting of the Sanctuary of Apollo (p139), Ancient Delphi

3000 BC, Indo-European migrants arrived with the know-how to process bronze, sparking the beginning of three remarkable civilisations: Cycladic, Minoan and Mycenaean.

ARTISTIC & CULTURAL LEGACIES
ANCIENT CIVILISATIONS
CYCLADIC CIVILISATION
The Cycladic civilisation was a cluster of fishing and farming island communities with a sophisticated artistic temperament. The most striking legacy of this civilisation is the carving of statuettes from Parian marble – the famous Cycladic figurines. Cycladic sculptors are also renowned for their impressive, life-sized *kouroi* (marble statues), carved during the Archaic period.

MINOAN CIVILISATION
Named after King Minos, the mythical ruler of Crete, the Minoans were Europe's first advanced civilisation. Around 2000 BC, splendidly decorated palace complexes like Knossos (p248) were built, marking a sharp break from village life. The Minoans were also great seafarers, exporting goods to Asia Minor (the west of present-day Turkey), Europe and North Africa, as well as to continental Greece.

1200-800 BC	800-700 BC	800-650 BC
The Dorian tribes herald a 400-year 'dark age' in terms of international trade.	Homer composes the *Iliad* and the *Odyssey* around this time, Greece's earliest pieces of literary art.	Independent city-states begin to appear and the Greek alphabet emerges from Phoenician script.

GREECE IN FOCUS

Nobody really knows what happened to the Minoans. They may have succumbed to a massive tsunami and ash fallout from the volcanic eruption on Thira (Santorini; p219) around 1500 BC. Or perhaps a second, powerful quake a century later decimated the society. Others blame their demise on invading Mycenaeans.

MYCENAEAN CIVILISATION
The Mycenaean civilisation reached its crescendo between 1500 and 1200 BC with mainland city-states like Corinth and Mycenae. The Mycenaeans created impressive palace frescoes and documented commerce in Linear B (a form of Greek language 500 years older than the Ionic Greek used by Homer). Their most

➤ **THE BEST**

GEORGE TSAFOS

Palaestra (wrestling school), Ancient Olympia (p120)

ANCIENT RUINS
- **Acropolis** (p70)
- **Ancient Delphi** (p138)
- **Knossos** (p248)
- **Delos** (p212)
- **Ancient Olympia** (p120)

HISTORY

extraordinary legacies are magnificent gold masks, refined jewellery and ornaments; check them out in the National Archaeological Museum (p74) in Athens.

GEOMETRIC & ARCHAIC AGES
The Dorians were an ancient Hellenic people who were settled in the Peloponnese by the 8th century BC. In the 11th or 12th century BC these warrior-like people fanned out to occupy much of the mainland, seizing control of the Mycenaean kingdoms and enslaving the inhabitants. The following 400-year period is often referred to as Greece's 'dark age', however they can be credited with bringing iron with them and developing a new style of pottery, decorated with striking geometric designs.

The Dorians were followed by the Archaic period (1000–800 BC) when Greek culture developed rapidly. Many of the advancements in literature, sculpture, theatre, architecture and intellectual endeavour began; this revival overlapped with the Classical age (the two eras are often classified as the Hellenic period). Advances included the Greek alphabetic script; the verses of Homer; the founding of the Olympic Games and central sanctuaries such as Delphi (p138). These common bonds gave Greeks a sense of national identity.

By about 800 BC Greece had begun to settle into a new social and political structure. Monarchic rule was abolished in favour of an aristocratic form of government,

700-500 BC	594 BC	479 BC
■	■	■
Having originated around 1000 BC in the Peloponnese, the Spartans dominate for around 200 years.	Solon, a ruling aristocrat in Athens, is credited as being the first to initiate democracy.	The Greeks smash the Persian army under Spartan leadership. The Persian Wars are finally over.

THE SPARTANS

A dominant military power from 650-363 BC, the Peloponnese-based Spartans were held in mythic awe by their fellow Greeks for their ferocious and self-sacrificing martial supremacy, living (and very often dying) by the motto 'return with your shield or on it'.

Every male Spartiate began his military training almost from birth and was bound to military service until the age of 60. Poor recruits were weeded out early, with newborn babies who didn't pass muster being left on a mountaintop to die. The surviving children endured 13 years of training to foster supreme physical fitness and suffered institutionalised beating 'competitions' to toughen them up.

which was later replaced by a set of laws that redistributed wealth and allowed the city's citizens to regain control over their lands.

DEMOCRACY

During the Archaic Age, Athens was firmly in the hands of aristocrats when Solon was appointed *arhon* (chief magistrate) in 594 BC to soothe tensions between the haves and have-nots. He cancelled all debts and freed those who had become enslaved because of them. Solon went on to abolish inherited privileges and restructured political power, establishing four classes based on wealth. Although only the first two classes were eligible for office, all four could elect magistrates and vote on legislation. Solon's reforms have become regarded as a harbinger of the ideological democratic system found in most current Western legal traditions.

CLASSICAL AGE

Greece's golden age (6th to 4th centuries BC) brought a boom in economic and political prosperity and cultural creativity. Literature and drama blossomed with innovations like dramatic tragedies and political satire. Athens reached its zenith and founded the Delian League in 477 BC, a naval alliance based on Delos to liberate the city-states still occupied by Persia. Many of the Aegean islands and Ionian city-states swore allegiance to Athens and made a mandatory annual contribution to the treasury of ships.

When Pericles became leader of Athens in 461 BC, he moved the treasury from Delos to the Acropolis and used the treasury's funds to construct new and grander temples on the Acropolis, such as the Parthenon (p71) and the Temple of Zeus at Ancient Olympia (p120).

With the Aegean Sea safely under its wing, Athens began to look westwards, bringing it into conflict with the Sparta-dominated Peloponnesian League. A series of skirmishes subsequently led to the Peloponnesian Wars.

431-404 BC	334-323 BC	86 BC-AD 224
Sparta becomes the main enemy of Athens, sparking the two Peloponnesian Wars.	Alexander the Great sets out to conquer the known world.	Roman expansion inevitably includes Greek territory and ultimately overtakes the mainland.

HELLENISTIC AGE

In the century following the Peloponnesian Wars, the battle-weary city-states came under the rule of the Macedonian king Philip II. It was his young son though, Alexander the Great, who was determined to unite the Greeks and spread Greek language and culture throughout the wider empire. The Greeks now perceived themselves as part of a larger empire and contemporary arts, drama, sculpture and philosophy reflected this growing awareness of a Greek identity.

Hellenism continued to prosper even under Roman rule (p323) and experienced an unprecedented period of peace for almost 300 years, known as the Pax Romana. The Romans had always venerated Greek art, literature and philosophy, and spread its unifying traditions throughout their empire.

⤷ THE BEST

JOHN ELK III

Minoan frescoes, National Archaeological Museum (p75)

ANCIENT TREASURE TROVES

- **National Archaeological Museum, Athens** (p74)
- **Acropolis Museum** (p72)
- **Archaeological Museum of Iraklio** (p245)
- **Delphi Museum** (p140)

The Romans were also the first to refer to the Hellenes as Greeks, derived from the word *graikos* – the name of a prehistoric tribe.

FOREIGN RULE

ROMAN ERA

While Alexander the Great was forging his vast empire in the east, the Romans had been expanding theirs to the west and were keen to make inroads into Greece. They defeated Macedon in 168 BC at the Battle of Pydna and the Achaean League in 146 BC. In 86 BC Athens joined an ill-fated rebellion against the Romans and in retribution, the Romans invaded Athens, took off with its most valuable sculptures and claimed Greece as the Graeco-Roman province of Achaea.

THE BYZANTINE EMPIRE & THE CRUSADES

Roman rule began to crumble in AD 250 when the Goths invaded Greece, the first of a succession of invaders. In an attempt to save his empire, Roman Emperor Constantine I transferred the capital from Rome to Byzantium (present-day İstanbul) in AD 324. While Rome went into terminal decline, the eastern capital began to grow

394	1453	1460
Christianity is declared the official religion. All pagan worship of Greek and Roman gods is outlawed.	Greece becomes a dominion of the Ottoman Turks.	Medieval Peloponnese falls to the Turks, leading to centuries of power struggles between the Turks and Venetians.

GLENN BEANLAND

Byzantine fortress ruins, Mystras (p110), Peloponnese

in wealth and strength and Byzantine Greece managed to retain its stronghold over the region.

The Frankish Crusaders brought the demise of the Byzantine Empire in their mission to liberate the Holy Land from the Muslims. Driven as much by greed as by religious zeal they decided that Byzantium (renamed Constantinople) presented richer pickings than Jerusalem. Constantinople was sacked in 1204 and much of the Byzantine Empire was partitioned into fiefdoms. The Venetians, meanwhile, had also secured a foothold in Greece. Over the next few centuries they acquired all the key Greek ports and Crete, becoming the wealthiest traders in the Mediterranean.

Despite this sorry state of affairs, Byzantium was not yet dead. In 1259 the Byzantine emperor Michael VIII Palaeologos recaptured the Peloponnese and made the city of Mystras (p110) his headquarters. Many eminent Byzantine artists, architects, intellectuals and philosophers converged on the city for a final burst of Byzantine creativity.

OTTOMAN RULE

Constantinople was soon facing a much greater threat from the Muslim Ottomans in the east. When Constantinople fell under Turkish Ottoman rule in 1453, Greece became a battleground between the Turks and Venetians. Eventually, with the exception of

1684-87	1822-29	1833
The Venetians expel the Turks from the Peloponnese.	Greek Independence is declared in 1822, but the fight against the Turks continues for seven years.	Britain, France and Russia dispatch Prince Otto of Bavaria to be the Greek monarch.

the Ionian Islands (where the Venetians retained control), Greece became part of the Ottoman Empire.

Ottoman power reached its zenith under Sultan Süleyman the Magnificent, who ruled between 1520 and 1566. Although they captured Crete in 1669 after a 25-year campaign, the ineffectual sultans that followed in the late 16th and 17th centuries saw the empire go into steady decline.

INDEPENDENCE

The first Greek independence party, the underground Filiki Eteria (Friendly Society), was founded in 1814. On 25 March 1821, the Greeks launched the War of Independence. Uprisings broke out almost simultaneously across most of Greece and the occupied islands. Within a year the Greeks had captured the fortresses of Monemvasia, Navarino (modern Pylos) and Nafplio in the Peloponnese, and Messolongi, Athens and Thebes. The Greeks proclaimed independence on 13 January 1822 at Epidavros.

Regional differences over national governance escalated into civil war in 1824 and 1825, which the Ottomans took advantage of by recapturing most of the Peloponnese, as well as Messolongi and Athens by 1827. The Western powers intervened and a combined Russian, French and British naval fleet sunk the Turkish-Egyptian fleet in the Battle of Navarino in October 1827. Fighting continued until 1829 when, with Russian troops at the gates of Constantinople, the sultan accepted Greek independence with the Treaty of Adrianople. Independence was formally recognised in 1830.

THE MODERN GREEK NATION

The Greeks, meanwhile, had been busy organising the independent state they had proclaimed several years earlier. In April 1827 they elected Ioannis Kapodistrias, a Corfiot and former diplomat of Russian Tsar Alexander I, as the first president of the republic; and chose Nafplio, in the Peloponnese, as the capital.

> ### A FEMALE FORCE
>
> Laskarina Bouboulina (1771–1825) was a member of Filiki Eteria (Friendly Society). Originally from Hydra, she settled in Spetses from where she commissioned and commanded several warships used in significant naval blockades. She helped maintain the crews of her ships and a small army of soldiers, and supplied the revolutionaries with food, weapons and ammunition. While her role in maritime operations significantly helped the independence movement, political factionism within the government led to her postwar arrest and subsequent exile to Spetses, where she died. Distinguished now as a national heroine, streets across Greece bear her name.

1862-63	1863-64	1896
King Otto is deposed in a bloodless coup and the British return the Ionian Islands to Greece.	The British engineer the ascension to the Greek throne of Danish Prince William.	The staging of the first modern Olympic Games in Athens marks Greece's coming of age.

However, there was much dissension within Greek ranks. Kapodistrias was assassinated in 1831 after he had ordered the imprisonment of a Maniot chieftain. Amid the ensuing anarchy, Britain, France and Russia declared Greece a monarchy, placing a non-Greek, 17-year-old Bavarian Prince Otto on the throne in 1833. The new kingdom consisted of the Peloponnese, Sterea Ellada, the Cyclades and the Sporades.

After moving the capital to Athens in 1834, King Otto managed to alienate the independence veterans by giving the most prestigious official posts to his Bavarian court. In 1862, Otto was ousted in a bloodless coup and Britain eased a young Danish Prince William onto the throne, crowned King George I in 1863. His 50-year reign brought some stability to the country, beginning with a new constitution in 1864 that established the power of democratically elected representatives.

WWI & SMYRNA

After an initial stance of neutrality, Greece was pressured into joining the Allies in WWI, with land in Asia Minor promised in return. Despite Greek troops serving with distinction, when the war ended in 1918, the promised land was not forthcoming.

In an attempt to get what he felt was rightfully Greece's, Prime Minister Eleftherios Venizelos led a diplomatic campaign into Smyrna (present-day İzmir in Turkey) in May 1919, under the guise of protecting the half a million Greeks living in the city. Believing he had a hold in Asia Minor, Venizelos ordered his troops to march ahead, and by September 1921 they'd advanced as far as Ankara. Turkish forces, commanded by Mustafa Kemal (later to become Atatürk), halted the offensive and recaptured Smyrna in 1922, when tens of thousands of its Greek inhabitants were killed.

The outcome of these hostilities was not at all what Venizelos had in mind. The Treaty of Lausanne in July 1923 gave Turkey eastern Thrace and the islands of Imvros and Tenedos, while Italy kept the Dodecanese (which it had temporarily acquired in 1912 and would hold until 1947). The treaty also called for a population exchange between Greece and Turkey to prevent future disputes. Almost 1.5 million Greeks left Turkey and almost 400,000 Turks left Greece. The exchange put a tremendous strain on the Greek economy and caused great bitterness and hardship for the individuals involved. Many Greeks abandoned a privileged life in Asia Minor for one of extreme poverty in emerging urban shanty towns in Athens and Thessaloniki.

THE REPUBLIC OF 1924-35

The arrival of the Greek refugees from Turkey coincided with, and compounded, a period of political instability unprecedented even by Greek standards. After to-ing and fro-ing of the throne between various Danish descendents, George II found himself on the throne in 1920 but was no match for the group of army officers who

1912-13	1914	1919-23
■	■	■
The Balkan Wars erupt when Greece, Serbia, Bulgaria and Turkey wrestle each other over the territory of Macedonia.	The outbreak of WWI sees Greece eventually siding with the Western Allies against Germany and Turkey on the promise of land in Asia Minor.	Greece unsuccessfully attempts to unite the former Hellenic regions, leading to a population exchange between Greece and Turkey.

seized power. A republic was proclaimed in March 1924 amid a series of coups and counter-coups.

A measure of stability was attained with Prime Minister Venizelos' return to power in 1928, although progress was inhibited by the Great Depression and he was defeated at the polls in March 1933. The new government was preparing for the restoration of the monarchy when Venizelos and his supporters staged an unsuccessful coup in March 1935. Venizelos was exiled to Paris and in November 1935, King George II reassumed the throne and installed the right-wing General Ioannis Metaxas as prime minister. Nine months later, Metaxas assumed dictatorial powers with the king's consent.

WWII

Metaxas' grandiose vision was to create a utopian Third Greek Civilisation, based on its glorious ancient and Byzantine past, but what he actually created was more like a Greek version of the Third Reich. He exiled or imprisoned opponents, banned trade unions and the recently established

NEIL SETCHFIELD

Helmeted warrior, National Archaeological Museum (p74)

Kommounistiko Komma Elladas (KKE, the Greek Communist Party), imposed press censorship, and created a secret police force and fascist-style youth movement. But Metaxas is best known for his reply of *ohi* (no) to Mussolini's ultimatum to allow Italians passage through Greece at the beginning of WWII. When the British asked Metaxas if they could land troops in Greece, he gave the same reply, but then died suddenly in January 1941. The king replaced him with the more timid Alexandros Koryzis, who agreed to British forces landing in Greece. German troops invaded Greece on 6 April 1941 and vastly outnumbered the defending Allied troops, and the whole country was under Nazi occupation within a few weeks. The civilian population suffered appallingly during the occupation, many dying of starvation. The Nazis rounded up more than half the Jewish population and transported them to death camps.

1924-34	1935	1940
Greece is proclaimed a republic but the Great Depression counters the nation's return to stability.	The monarchy is restored and General Ioannis Metaxas adopts the role of prime minister, introducing dictatorial measures of governance.	Metaxas famously rebuffs the Italian request to traverse Greece at the beginning of WWII.

DMITRI KESSEL/GETTY IMAGES

Anti-goverment street protest in 1944

CIVIL WAR

By late 1944 the royalists, republicans and communists were locked in a serious battle for control. The British-backed provisional government was in an untenable position: the left was threatening revolt, and the British were pushing to prevent the communists from further legitimising their hold over the administration. On 3 December 1944 the police fired on a communist demonstration in Plateia Syntagmatos (Syntagma Sq) in Athens, killing several people. The ensuing six weeks of fighting between the left and the right, known as the Dekemvriana (events of December), marked the first round of the Greek Civil War. Negotiations for reconciliation between the government and the communists failed and the friction continued as civilians on all political sides were subjected to bitter reprisals and widespread intimidation and violence. The royalists won the March 1946 election and George II landed back on the throne.

In October the left-wing Democratic Army of Greece (DSE) was formed to resume the fight against the monarchy and its British supporters – they swiftly occupied a large swath of land along Greece's northern border. In 1947 the USA intervened and the civil war developed into a setting for the new Cold War theatre. Communism was declared illegal and the government introduced its notorious Certificate of Political Reliability (which remained valid until 1962), which declared that the document bearer was not a left-wing sympathiser; without this certificate Greeks could not vote and found it

1941-44	1944-49	1967-74
Germany invades and occupies Greece.	The end of WWII sees Greece descend into civil war, pitching monarchists against communists.	A right-wing military coup d'état establishes a junta, imposing martial law and abolishing many civil rights.

almost impossible to get work. The DSE continued to be a strong opponent until 1949 when the tide began to turn. The central government drove the DSE out of the Peloponnese and Yugoslavia cut the DSE's supply lines.

The civil war left Greece politically frayed and economically shattered. More Greeks had been killed in three years of bitter civil war than in WWII, and a quarter of a million people were homeless. The sense of despair became the trigger for a mass exodus. Almost a million Greeks headed off in search of a better life elsewhere, primarily to countries such as Australia, Canada and the USA.

COLONELS, MONARCHS & DEMOCRACY

Greece's political right staged a coup on 21 April 1967, establishing a military junta. The colonels declared martial law, banned political parties and trade unions, imposed censorship and imprisoned, tortured and exiled thousands of dissidents.

> ## THE GREEK ROYALS
>
> Danish by descent and English by residence, the Greek royal family fled Greece following a military coup in 1967 and the monarch was officially disposed of in 1974. While they no longer represent Greece, the family remains part of the extended Danish royal family and continue to use their titles.
>
> After leaving Greece, the family requested compensation for assets seized by the Greek Government – namely three properties, including a palace on Corfu where Britain's Prince Phillip was born. Former King Constantine II took his case to the European Court of Human Rights and was awarded €12 million in 2002.

On 17 November 1973 tanks stormed a building at the Athens Polytechnio (Technical University) to quell a student occupation calling for an uprising against the US-backed junta. While the number of casualties is still in dispute (more than 20 students were reportedly killed and hundreds injured), the act meant the death knell for the junta.

Shortly after, the junta dictatorship collapsed. Former Prime Minister Konstandinos Karamanlis was summoned from his exile in Paris to take office and his New Democracy (ND) party won a large majority at the November elections in 1974.

THE 1980S &1990S

When Greece became the 10th member of the EU in 1981, it was the smallest and poorest member. In October 1981, Andreas Papandreou's PASOK party was elected as Greece's first socialist government. PASOK ruled for almost two decades (except for 1990-93). PASOK promised ambitious social reform, and that they would close the US

1974	1981	1999
A botched plan to unite Cyprus with Greece prompts the fall of the military junta and the restoration of Greece's parliamentary democracy.	Greece joins the EU and the economy grows smartly.	Turkey and Greece experience powerful earthquakes within weeks of each other that result in hundreds of deaths.

Georgios Papandreou being sworn in as prime minister (2009)

PASOK.GR/WIKIPEDIA

air bases and withdraw from NATO. US military presence was reduced, but unemployment was high and reforms in education and welfare were limited. Women's issues fared better: the dowry system was abolished, abortion legalised, and civil marriage and divorce were implemented.

Papandreou stepped down in 1996 and his departure produced a dramatic change of direction for PASOK, with the party abandoning Papandreou's left-leaning politics and electing experienced economist and lawyer Costas Simitis as the new prime minister (who won a comfortable majority at the October 1996 polls).

THE 21ST CENTURY

The new millenium has seen living standards increase and billions of euros poured into large-scale infrastructure projects across Greece, including the redevelopment of Athens – spurred on largely by its hosting of the 2004 Olympic Games.

In 2004, the ND party won the general election, with Karamanlis (nephew of the former prime minister) as prime minister. However, rising unemployment, ballooning public debt, slowing inflation and the squeezing of consumer credit have taken their toll. Public opinion soured further in 2007 when Karamanlis' government was widely criticised for its handling of severe summer fires, which were responsible for widespread

2004	2007	2008
Greece successfully hosts the 28th Summer Olympic Games and wins the European football championship.	Vast forest fires devastate much of the western Peloponnese as well as parts of Evia and Epiros.	Police shoot and kill a 15-year-old boy in Athens, sparking a series of urban riots nationwide.

destruction throughout Greece. Nevertheless, snap elections held in September 2007 returned the conservatives, albeit with a diminished majority.

Over recent years, a series of massive general strikes and blockades have highlighted mounting electoral discontent. Hundreds of thousands of people have protested against proposed radical labour and pension reforms and privatisation plans that analysts claim will help curb public debt. The backlash against the government reached boiling point in December 2008, when urban rioting broke out across the country, led by youths outraged by the police shooting of a 15-year-old boy in Athens following an alleged exchange between police and a group of teenagers. Alleged corruption among state executives and controversy that involved land-swap deals at the expense of taxpayers have done little to increase support for ND and a general election held in October 2009 (midway through Karamanlis' term) saw PASOK take back the reins in a landslide win against the conservatives.

2009	2009	2010
Greece questions Turkey's intention to explore for oil off the coasts of Kastellorizo and Cyprus.	Conservatives call for an early general election and lose by a landslide to Socialist PASOK, under Georgios Papandreou.	Experiencing debt crisis and deep-seated recession, Greece is the subject of an EU bail-out.

NATIONAL CHARACTER

Villagers meeting over an afternoon coffee, Peloponnese

ANTHONY PIDGEON

Greece is both Mediterranean and Balkan and has long straddled East and West, so it's not surprising that Greeks have a very different character to the rest of Europe. The Greeks are undeniably passionate, fiercely independent and proud of their heritage.

Greeks have an undeniable zest for life, but aren't into making plans, with spontaneity a refreshing aspect of social life. Greeks are notoriously late; turning up to an appointment on time is often referred to as 'being English'.

Most Greeks are forthright and argumentative. They thrive on news, gossip and political debate and, while they will mercilessly malign their governments and society, they are defensive about external criticism and can be fervently nationalistic. Greeks have a work-to-live attitude and pride themselves on their capacity to enjoy life. They are social animals and enjoy a rich communal life. Greeks are unashamed about staring at strangers and blatantly discussing people around them. Few subjects are off limits, from your private life to how much money you earn.

In the major shift from a largely poor, agrarian existence to increasingly sophisticated urban dwellers, the current generation of Greeks is dealing with a massive generational and technological divide; multilingual children play games on their mobile phones while their illiterate grandfathers still get around on a mule.

Greeks have long enjoyed a reputation as loyal friends and generous hosts. They pride themselves on their *filotimo* (dignity and sense of honour), and their *filoxenia* (hospitality, welcome, shelter), which you will find in even the poorest household.

SUSTAINABLE TRAVEL

NORBERT EISELE-HEIN/IMAGEBROKER

Mountain biking through the Lasithi Plateau, Crete

Greece is dropping its devil-may-care attitude of yesteryear and belatedly becoming environmentally conscious. While the bigger picture of soil erosion, annual forest fires, illegal development and overfishing can seem overwhelming to an individual tourist, there are a number of things you can do that can help lessen your impact without compromising your holiday. Follow in locals' footsteps as they hop on buses, munch on local produce and do their bit for the gorgeous Greek environment.

As with many popular European destinations, Greece's environment is pushed to the limit each year by the massive influx of tourists. Consider when you're going to travel. Visiting Greece on the shoulder seasons – early spring or autumn – means the weather is more bearable and puts less pressure on precious resources such as food and water. This is particularly true on the islands.

Once you're there, how you get around can make a difference to the environment. Not everyone (in fact, very few of us!) have the gumption and stamina to tackle the hilly, hot terrain on a bicycle, but you can opt for local buses and trains rather than planes or rented cars, or for fast, fuel-economic ferries rather than slow gas-guzzlers.

Water scarcity is a serious problem throughout much of Greece. It's impractical to avoid buying bottled water entirely. On some of the remote and smaller islands, tap water is not safe to drink; always ask locally. When buying bottled water, choose Greek brands (which are everywhere) rather than European brands that have travelled further and therefore come with a larger carbon footprint. You can also cut down on water use by

DIVING INTO CULTURAL SUSTAINABILITY

Greece's ocean bed is a graveyard to countless shipwrecks dating back to classical times. Approximately one hundred known underwater sites are protected, however historians claim there are likely thousands more yet to be discovered.

Despite a law dating back to 1932 which asserts that all found artefacts belong to the state, divers are said to be surfacing with sculptures, jewellery, warrior helmets and more. Meanwhile, archaeologists claim that the removal of even the most seemingly mundane objects can affect and eventually destroy sites.

The moral for divers? Don't become another finned pirate. Look but don't touch.

not requesting hotels to wash your towels daily and by taking quick showers.

'Organic' and 'green' are increasingly popular buzzwords in Greece. The rise in agrotourism means more options for staying in environmentally friendly places. You'll also find increasing options for recycling and for guided activities such as hiking and cycling. As much of Greek cuisine is based on local produce, restaurant proprietors are advertising their dishes as locally sourced and organically grown. Shops also sell local, organic herbs, honey, soap and other wares as souvenirs, making it possible to support the local economy and the environment in one go.

And finally – do your bit by going to the beach! While tourism has historically caused pollution of the Greek seas, more recently it's been the motivation for cleaning them up. Greece's bathing water quality has climbed to number two in Europe by the European Commission.

TRADITIONAL MUSIC

KEVIN GALVIN/IMAGEBROKER

Fiddle-playing folk musician, Santorini (Thira)

Whether you buy tickets to a concert in an ancient theatre or your dinner in a family taverna is accompanied by the owner playing the blues, taking in some live music is an essential Greek experience. Greeks are passionate about music, with a whole gamut of styles and traditions and countless opportunities to lend them an ear.

Greece's strong and enduring musical tradition dates back to at least 2000 BC. Regional folk music is divided into *nisiotika* (the lighter, more upbeat music of the islands), and the more grounded *dimotika* of the mainland. The music of Crete, represented in the world-music scene as a genre in its own right, remains the most dynamic traditional form. Folk music can be heard in *panigyria* (open-air festivals) around Greece during summer.

REMBETIKA

Rembetika is often referred to as the Greek 'blues', because of its urban folk-music roots and themes of heartache, hardship, drugs, crime, and the grittier elements of urban life. The rhythms and melodies are a hybrid of influences, with Byzantine and Ancient Greek roots.

Two styles make up what is broadly known as *rembetika*. The first emerged in the mid- to late-19th century and is known as Smyrneika or Cafe Aman music, with haunting *amanedes* (vocal improvisations), occasional Turkish lyrics and a more oriental sound. In Piraeus, *rembetika* was the music of the underclass, when the bulk of refugees from Asia Minor ended up in Piraeus in 1922. Markos Vamvakaris, acknowledged as the

MEET THE ORCHESTRA

Ancient Greek instruments included the lyre, lute, *piktis* (pipes), *kroupeza* (a percussion instrument), *kithara* (a stringed guitarlike instrument), *avlos* (a wind instrument), *barbitos* (similar to a cello) and the *magadio* (similar to a harp).

The plucked strings of the bulbous *outi* (oud), the strident sound of the Cretan *lyra* (lyre), the staccato rap of the *toumberleki* (lap drum), the *mandolino* (mandolin) and the *gaïda* (bagpipe) bear witness to a rich range of musical instruments that share many characteristics with instruments all over the Middle East.

The ubiquitous six- or eight-stringed bouzouki, the long-necked lute-like instrument, is a relative newcomer to the scene. Its baby version is the *baglamas*, used in *rembetika*.

greatest *rembetika* musician, revolutionised the sound of popular Greek music.

The protagonists of *rembetika* songs were often the smartly dressed, hashish-smoking, street-wise outcasts who spent their evenings singing and dancing in hash dens. Although hashish was illegal, the law was rarely enforced until 1936, with the Government's attempt to wipe out the subculture through censorship, raids and arresting people carrying a bouzouki (and apparently cutting off half their slick moustaches and lopping their pointy shoes). Many artists soon stopped performing and recording, though the music continued clandestinely.

After WWII a new wave of *rembetika* performers and composers emerged, including Vasilis Tsitsanis, Apostolos Kaldaras, Yiannis Papaioannou, Georgos Mitsakis and Apostolos Hatzihristou; one of the greatest female *rembetika* singers, Sotiria Bellou, also appeared at this time. Their music later morphed into lighter *laïka* (urban folk music), with the lyrics reflecting more social and sentimental themes. It was played in bigger clubs with electrified orchestras, losing much of the essence of the original music. Interest in genuine *rembetika* was revived in the late 1970s to early '80s – particularly among students and intellectuals, and it continues to be popular today.

⤵ DIRECTORY, TRANSPORT & ISLAND HOPPING

DIRECTORY

ACCOMMODATION

There is a range of accommodation available in Greece to suit every taste and pocket. All places to stay are subject to strict price controls set by the tourist police. By law, a notice must be displayed in every room, stating the category of the room and the price charged in each season. The price includes a 4.5% community tax and 8% VAT.

Accommodation owners may add a 10% surcharge for a stay of less than three nights, but this is not mandatory. A mandatory charge of 20% is levied if an extra bed is put into a room (although this often doesn't happen if the extra bed is for a child). During July and August accommodation owners will charge the maximum price, but in spring and autumn prices can drop by 20%, and then drop even further in winter.

Rip-offs rarely occur, but if you do suspect that you have been exploited by an accommodation owner, make sure you report it to either the tourist police or the regular police, and they will act swiftly.

Throughout this book we have divided accommodation into budget (up to €80 in Athens; up to €60 elsewhere), midrange (€80 to €150 in Athens; €60 to €150 elsewhere) and top end (€150+) categories. This is based on the rate for a double room in high season (July and August). Unless otherwise stated, all rooms have private bathroom facilities. It's difficult to generalise accommodation prices in Greece as rates depend entirely on the season and location. Don't expect to pay the same price for a double on one of the islands as you would in central Greece or Athens.

DOMATIA

Domatia (literally 'rooms') are the Greek equivalent of the British bed and breakfast, minus the breakfast. Once upon a time, domatia comprised little more than spare rooms in the family home that could be rented out to travellers in summer; nowadays, many are purpose-built appendages to the family house. Some come complete with fully equipped kitchens. Standards of cleanliness are generally high. Domatia are found throughout the mainland (except in large cities) and on almost every island that has a permanent population. Many are open only between April and October.

From June to September domatia owners are out in force, touting for customers. They meet buses and boats, shouting 'Room, room!' and often carrying photographs of their rooms. In peak season it can prove a mistake not to take up an offer – but be wary of owners who are vague about the location of their accommodation.

HOTELS

Hotels in Greece are divided into six categories: deluxe, A, B, C, D and E. Hotels are categorised according to the size of

---

> ↘ **BOOK YOUR STAY ONLINE**
>
> For more accommodation reviews and recommendations by Lonely Planet authors, check out the online booking service at www.lonelyplanet.com. You'll find the true, insider lowdown on the best places to stay. Reviews are thorough and independent. Best of all, you can book online.

the rooms, whether or not they have a bar, and the ratio of bathrooms to beds, rather than standards of cleanliness, comfort of beds and friendliness of staff – all elements that may be of greater relevance to guests.

As one would expect, deluxe, A- and B-class hotels have many of the usual amenities, private bathrooms and constant hot water. C-class hotels have a snack bar and rooms with private bathrooms, but hot water may only be available at certain times of the day. D-class hotels may or may not have snack bars; most rooms will share bathrooms, but there may be some with private bathrooms; and they may have solar-heated water, which means hot water is not guaranteed. E-class hotels do not have a snack bar; bathrooms are shared and you may have to pay extra for hot water.

PENSIONS

Pensions are indistinguishable from hotels. They are categorised as A, B or C class. An A-class pension is equivalent in amenities and price to a B-class hotel, a B-class pension is equivalent to a C-class hotel, and a C-class pension is equivalent to a D- or E-class hotel.

RENTAL ACCOMMODATION

A really practical way to save on money and maximise comfort is to rent a furnished apartment or villa. The main advantage is that you can accommodate a larger number of people under one roof, and you can also save money by self-catering. This option is best for a stay of more than three days. Be prepared – some owners may insist on a minimum week's stay. A good site to spot prospective villas is www.greekislands.com.

ACTIVITIES
CYCLING

With over 4000km of coastal road on the mainland alone and 80% mountainous terrain, Greece is gaining popularity as a cycling destination. Bicycles can be taken on trains and ferries for free and there are an increasing number of tour companies specialising in cycling holidays.

Cycle Greece (www.cyclegreece.gr) runs road- and mountain-bike tours across most of Greece for various skill levels. **Hooked on Cycling** (www.hookedoncycling .co.uk/Greece/greece.html) offers boat and bike trips through the islands and tours of the mainland. **Bike Greece** (www.bikegreece .com) specialises in mountain biking, with various week-long tours for beginners and the experienced.

For lots of information and routes, check out Anthony Campbell's website at www.acampbell.ukfsn.org/cycling/greece.index.html.

DIVING & SNORKELLING

Snorkelling can be enjoyed just about anywhere along the coast of Greece. Greek law insists that diving be done under the supervision of a diving school in order to protect the many antiquities in the depths of the Aegean. Until recently dive sites were severely restricted, but many more have been opened up and diving schools have flourished. You'll find diving schools on the islands of Corfu, Evia, Hydra, Leros, Milos, Mykonos, Paros, Rhodes, Santorini and Skiathos; in Agios Nikolaos and Rethymno on Crete; in Glyfada near Athens; and in Parga on the mainland.

HIKING

The majority of Greece is mountainous and, in many ways, is a hikers' paradise. The most popular routes are well walked and maintained; however, the **EOS** (Greek

DIRECTORY

ACTIVITIES

Alpine Club; ☎ 210 321 2429; Plateia Kapnikareas 2, Athens) is grossly underfunded and consequently many of the lesser-known paths are overgrown and inadequately marked.

On small islands you will encounter a variety of paths, including *kalderimia,* which are cobbled or flagstone paths that have linked settlements since Byzantine times. Other paths include shepherds' trails *(monopatia)* that link settlements with sheepfolds or link remote settlements via rough unmarked trails. Be aware that shepherd or animal trails can be very steep and difficult to navigate.

A number of companies run organised hikes. The biggest is Trekking Hellas (www.trekking.gr), which offers a variety of hikes ranging from a four-hour stroll through the Lousios Valley to a week-long hike around Mt Olympus and Meteora. The company also runs hikes on Crete and in the Cyclades.

KITESURFING

Also known as kiteboarding, this action sport has taken off in a big way in Greece and you'll find beaches festooned with athletic surfers. The Greek Wakeboard and Kite Surf Association (☎ 69445 17963; www.gwa.gr) has details of popular kitesurfing locales. Each summer, Ammoöpi (Afiartis Bay; p294) on Karpathos hosts an international kitesurfing competition.

SKIING

Greece provides some of the cheapest skiing in Europe. There are 16 resorts dotted around the mountains of mainland Greece, mainly in the north. The main skiing areas are Mt Parnassos (p142), 195km northwest of Athens, and Mt Vermio, 110km west of Thessaloniki. There are no foreign package holidays to these resorts; they are used mainly by Greeks.

They have all the basic facilities and can be a pleasant alternative to the glitzy resorts of northern Europe.

The season depends on snow conditions but runs approximately from January to the end of April. For further information pick up a copy of *Greece: Mountain Refuges & Ski Centres* from an EOT office (p350). Information may also be obtained from the Hellenic Skiing Federation (Map pp66-7; ☎ 210 323 0182; press@ski.org.gr; Karageorgi Servias 7, Syntagma, Athens). You'll find information about the latest snow conditions online at www.snowreport.gr.

WHITEWATER RAFTING

The popularity of whitewater rafting and other river adventure sports has grown rapidly in recent years as more and more urban Greeks, particularly Athenians, head off in search of a wilderness experience.

Trekking Hellas (www.trekking.gr) offers half a dozen possibilities, including the Ladonas and Alfios Rivers in the Peloponnese, the Arahthos River in Epiros and the Aheloös River in Thessaly. Alpin Club (☎ 210 675 3514/5; www.alpinclub .gr) specialises in the Alfios River and the Evinos River, near Nafpaktos in Sterea Ellada. Eco Action (☎ 210 331 7866; www .ecoaction.gr; Agion Anargyron, Psyrri) offers rafting and kayaking on the Ladonas River, which hosted the kayaking at the 2004 Olympics, as well as on another three rivers throughout Greece.

WINDSURFING

Windsurfing is a very popular water sport in Greece. You'll find sailboards for hire almost everywhere. Hire charges range from €10 to €15 an hour, depending on the gear. If you are a novice, most places that rent equipment also give lessons.

Sailboards can be imported freely from other EU countries, but the import of boards from other destinations, such as Australia and the USA, is subject to regulations. Theoretically, importers need a Greek national residing in Greece to guarantee that the board will be taken out of the country again. Contact the **Hellenic Windsurfing Association** (Map pp66-7; ☎ 210 323 3696; Filellinon 4, Syntagma, Athens) for more information.

BUSINESS HOURS

Banks are open from 8am to 2.30pm Monday to Thursday, and from 8am to 2pm Friday. Some banks in large towns and cities also open from 3.30pm to 6.30pm on weekdays and from 8am to 1.30pm on Saturday.

Post offices are open from 7.30am to 2pm Monday to Friday. In the major cities they stay open until 8pm, and open from 7.30am to 2pm on Saturday.

In summer the usual opening hours for shops are from 8am to 3pm on Monday, Wednesday and Saturday, and from 8am to 2.30pm and then from 5pm to 8.30pm on Tuesday, Thursday and Friday. Shops open 30 minutes later during winter. These times are not always strictly adhered to. Many shops in tourist resorts are open seven days a week and keep later hours.

Department stores and supermarkets are open from 8am to 8pm Monday to Friday, and from 8am to at least 3pm on Saturday. They are closed on Sunday.

Periptera (street kiosks) are open from early morning until late at night. They sell everything from bus tickets and cigarettes to razor blades and shaving cream.

Restaurant hours vary enormously. Most places are normally open for lunch from 11am to 3pm and for dinner from 7pm to 1am, while restaurants in tourist areas remain open all day. Cafes normally open at about 10am and stay open until midnight.

Bars open from about 8pm until late. Discos and nightclubs don't usually open until at least 10pm; it's rare to find much of a crowd before midnight. They close at about 4am, later on Friday and Saturday.

CLIMATE

Greece can be divided into a number of main climatic regions.

Northern Macedonia and northern Epiros have a climate similar to the Balkans, with freezing winters and very hot, humid summers. The Attica Peninsula, the Cyclades, the Dodecanese, Crete, and the central and eastern Peloponnese have a more typically Mediterranean climate, with hot, dry summers and milder winters.

Snow is rare in the Cyclades, but the high mountains of the Peloponnese and Crete are covered in snow during the winter and it occasionally snows in Athens. In July and August the mercury can soar to 40°C (over 100°F) in the shade just about anywhere in the country. July and August are also the months of the *meltemi*, a strong northerly wind that sweeps the eastern coast of mainland Greece (including Athens) and the Aegean islands, especially the Cyclades. The *meltemi* is a mixed blessing: it reduces humidity, but plays havoc with ferry schedules and sends everything flying – from beach umbrellas to washing hanging out to dry.

Mid-October is when the rains start in most areas, and the weather stays cold and wet until February – although there are also occasional winter days with clear blue skies and sunshine.

For tips on the best times to visit Greece, see p44.

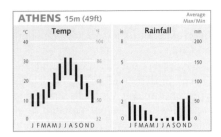

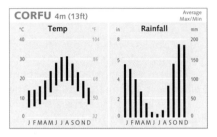

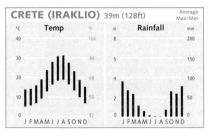

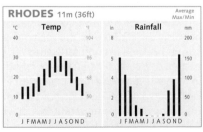

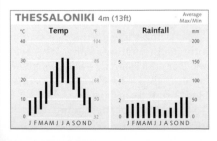

CUSTOMS

There are no longer duty-free restrictions within the EU. Upon entering the country from outside the EU, customs inspection is usually cursory for foreign tourists and a verbal declaration is usually all that is required. Random searches are still occasionally made for drugs.

You may bring the following into Greece duty-free: 200 cigarettes or 50 cigars; 1L of spirits or 2L of wine; 50mL of perfume; 250mL of eau de cologne; one camera (still or video) and film; a pair of binoculars; a portable musical instrument; a portable radio or tape recorder; a laptop computer; sports equipment; and dogs and cats (with a veterinary certificate). Restrictions apply to the importation of sailboards into Greece (see p341).

Import regulations for medicines are strict in Greece; if you are taking medication, make sure you get a statement from your doctor before you leave home. It is illegal, for instance, to take codeine into Greece without an accompanying doctor's certificate.

An unlimited amount of foreign currency and travellers cheques may be brought into Greece. If you intend to leave the country with foreign banknotes in excess of US$1000, you must declare the sum upon entry.

It is strictly forbidden to export antiquities (anything over 100 years old) without an export permit. This crime is second only to drug smuggling in the penalties imposed. It is an offence to remove even the smallest article from an archaeological site. The place to apply for an export permit is the Antique Dealers and Private Collections section of the **Athens Archaeological Service** (Map pp66-7; Polygnotou 13, Plaka, Athens).

⬎ CLIMATE CHANGE & TRAVEL

Travel – especially air travel – is a significant contributor to global climate change. At Lonely Planet, we believe that all who travel have a responsibility to limit their personal impact. As a result, we have teamed with Rough Guides and other concerned industry partners to support Climate Care, which allows people to offset the greenhouse gases they are responsible for with contributions to energy-saving projects and other climate-friendly initiatives in the developing world. Lonely Planet offsets all staff and author travel.

For more information, turn to the responsible travel pages on www.lonely planet.com. For details on offsetting your carbon emissions and a carbon calculator, go to www.climatecare.org.

DANGERS & ANNOYANCES

ADULTERATED & SPIKED DRINKS

Adulterated drinks (known as *bombes*) are served in some bars and clubs in Athens and resorts known for partying. These drinks are diluted with cheap illegal imports that leave you feeling worse for wear the next day.

Many of the party resorts catering to large budget-tour groups are also unfortunately the scene of drunk and disorderly behaviour – some of it just purely annoying and some of it frighteningly violent. Spiked drinks are not uncommon; keep your hand over the top of your glass. More often than not, the perpetrators are foreign tourists rather than locals.

THEFT

Crime, especially theft, is traditionally low in Greece, but unfortunately it is on the rise. If you are staying in a hotel room, and the windows and door do not lock securely, ask for your valuables to be locked in the hotel safe – hotel proprietors are happy to do this.

DISCOUNT CARDS

SENIOR CARDS

Card-carrying EU pensioners can claim a range of benefits, such as reduced admission to ancient sites and museums, and discounts on bus and train fares.

STUDENT & YOUTH CARDS

The most widely recognised form of student ID is the International Student Identity Card (ISIC). These cards can entitle the holder to half-price admission to museums and ancient sites, and discounts at some budget hotels and hostels. In some cases only Greek student cards will be accepted but it's always worth flashing your international student card just in case. The Euro26 card is available for anyone up to the age of 30 and which can provide discounts of up to 20% at sights, shops and for some transport. Visit www.isic.org and www.euro26.org for more details.

Aegean Airlines offers student discounts on some domestic flights, but there are none to be had on buses, ferries or trains. Students can often find good deals on international airfares.

EMBASSIES & CONSULATES

All foreign embassies in Greece are in Athens and its suburbs, with a few consulates in Thessaloniki.

Australia (Map pp52-3; ☎ 210 870 4000; cnr Leoforos Alexandras & Leoforos Kifisias, Ambelokipi, Athens GR-115 23)

Canada (Map pp52-3; ☎ 210 727 3400; Genadiou 4, Athens GR-115 21)

France (Map pp52-3; ☎ 210 361 1663; Leoforos Vasilissis Sofias 7, Athens GR-106 71)

Germany (Map pp52-3; ☎ 210 728 5111; Dimitriou 3, cnr Karaoli, Kolonaki, Athens GR-106 75)

Ireland (Map pp52-3; ☎ 210 723 2771; Leoforos Vasileos Konstantinou 5-7, Athens GR-153 34)

Italy (Map pp52-3; ☎ 210 361 7260; Sekeri 2, Athens GR-106 74)

Japan (Map pp52-3; ☎ 210 775 8101; Athens Tower, Mesogion 2-4, Athens GR-115 27)

Netherlands (Map pp52-3; ☎ 210 723 9701; Leoforos Vasileos Konstantinou 5-7, Athens GR-106 74)

New Zealand (☎ 210 687 4701; Kifisias 268, Halandri, Athens 152 26)

Turkey Athens (Map pp52-3; ☎ 210 724 5915; Leoforos Vasileos Georgiou 8, Athens GR-106 74); Thessaloniki (Map pp176-7; ☎ 23102 48452; Agiou Dimitriou 151, Thessaloniki)

UK Athens (Map pp52-3; ☎ 210 723 6211; Ploutarhou 1, Athens GR-106 75); Thessaloniki (Map pp176-7; ☎ 23102 78006; Tsimiski 43, Thessaloniki)

USA Athens (Map pp52-3; ☎ 210 721 2951; Leoforos Vasilissis Sofias 91, Athens GR-115 21); Thessaloniki (Map pp176-7; ☎ 23102 42905; Tsimiski 43, Thessaloniki)

It's important to know what your embassy – the embassy of the country of which you are a citizen – can and can't do to help if you get into trouble. Generally, it won't be much help in emergencies if the trouble you're in is remotely your own fault. Remember that you are bound by the laws of the country you are in.

In genuine emergencies you might get some assistance, but only if other channels have been exhausted. If you have all your money and documents stolen, your embassy will usually assist with getting a new passport, but a loan for onward travel is very unlikely.

FOOD

For large cities and towns, restaurant listings in this book are given in the following order: budget (under €15), midrange (€15 to €40) and top end (over €40). Prices refer to a main dish for one person unless otherwise noted in the review. For information on Greek cuisine, see p311.

GAY & LESBIAN TRAVELLERS

In a country where the Church still plays a prominent role in shaping society's views on issues such as sexuality, it should come as no surprise that homosexuality is generally frowned upon by many locals – especially outside the major cities. While there is no legislation against homosexual activity, it pays to be discreet.

Some areas of Greece are, however, extremely popular destinations for gay and lesbian travellers. Athens has a busy gay scene, but most gay and lesbian travellers head for the islands. Mykonos has long been famous for its bars, beaches and general hedonism, while Skiathos also has its share of gay hang-outs. The island of Lesvos (Mytilini), birthplace of the lesbian poet Sappho, has become something of a place of pilgrimage for lesbians.

INFORMATION

The *Spartacus International Gay Guide*, published by Bruno Gmünder (Berlin), is widely regarded as the leading authority on the gay travel scene. There is also stacks of information on the internet. **Roz Mov** (www.geocities.com/WestHollywood/2225) has info on gay health, press, organisations, events and legal issues – and links to lots more sites. Also check out **Gayscape** (www .gayscape.com/gays cape/menugreece.html).

HEALTH

A signed and dated letter from your physician describing your medical conditions and medications, including generic names, is also a good idea. For example, taking codeine into Greece is strictly prohibited unless accompanied by a doctor's certificate. See also p342.

If carrying syringes or needles, be sure to have a physician's letter documenting their medical necessity. If you are embarking on a long trip, make sure your teeth are OK and take your optical prescription with you.

INSURANCE

If you're an EU citizen, a European Health Insurance Card (EHIC; formerly the E111) covers you for most medical care but not emergency repatriation home or non-emergencies. It is available from health centres, and post offices in the UK. Citizens from other countries should find out if there is a reciprocal arrangement for free medical care between their country and Greece. If you do need health insurance, make sure you get a policy that covers you for the worst possible scenario, such as an accident requiring an emergency flight home. Find out in advance if your insurance plan will make payments directly to providers or reimburse you later for overseas health expenditures.

RECOMMENDED VACCINATIONS

No jabs are required to travel to Greece, but a yellow-fever vaccination certificate is required if you are coming from an infected area.

INTERNET RESOURCES

The WHO's publication *International Travel and Health* is revised annually and is available online at www.who.int/ith. Other useful websites include www.mdtravelhealth .com (travel health recommendations for every country; updated daily), www.fitfor travel.scot.nhs.uk (general travel advice for the layperson), www.ageconcern.org .uk (advice on travel for the elderly) and www.mariestopes.org.uk (information on women's health and contraception).

AVAILABILITY & COST OF HEALTH CARE

If you need an ambulance in Greece call ☎ 166. There is at least one doctor on every island and larger islands have hospitals. Pharmacies can dispense medicines that are available only by prescription in most European countries, so you can consult a pharmacist for minor ailments.

All this sounds fine but, although medical training is of a high standard in Greece, the public health service is badly underfunded. Hospitals can be overcrowded, hygiene is not always what it should be and relatives are expected to bring in food for the patient – which could be a problem for a tourist. Conditions and treatment are much better in private hospitals, which are expensive. All this means that a good health-insurance policy is essential.

ENVIRONMENTAL HAZARDS
BITES, STINGS & INSECT-BORNE DISEASES

Keep an eye out for sea urchins lurking around rocky beaches; if you get some of their needles embedded in your skin, olive oil should help to loosen them. You should also be wary of jellyfish, particularly during the months of September and October. Dousing the affected area with vinegar will deactivate any stingers that have not 'fired'. Calamine lotion, antihistamines and analgesics may help reduce any reaction you experience and relieve the pain of any stings. Much more painful than either of these, but thankfully much rarer, is an encounter with the weever fish. Soaking your foot in very hot water (which breaks down the poison) should solve the problem but if a child is stung, medical attention should be sought.

Greece's dangerous snakes include the adder and the less common viper and coral snakes. To minimise the possibilities of being bitten, always wear boots, socks and long trousers when walking through undergrowth where snakes may be present. Snake bites do not cause instantaneous death and an antivenin is widely available. Seek medical help, if possible with the dead snake for identification.

WATER

In much of Greece, tap water is drinkable and safe. However, in small villages and on some of the islands, this is not always the case. Always ask locally if the water is safe and, if in doubt, drink boiled or bought water. Even when water is safe, the substances and microbacteria in it may be different than you are used to and can cause vomiting or diarrhoea.

HOLIDAYS

Many sites (including the ancient sites in Athens) offer free entry on the first Sunday of the month, with the exception of July and August. You may also gain free entry on other locally celebrated holidays, although this varies across the country.

PUBLIC HOLIDAYS

All banks and shops and most museums and ancient sites close on public holidays. National public holidays in Greece:

New Year's Day 1 January

Epiphany 6 January

First Sunday in Lent February

Greek Independence Day 25 March

Good Friday March/April

Orthodox Easter Sunday April/May. Orthodox Easter Sunday falls on 4 April in 2010, 24 April in 2011 and 15 April 2012.

Easter Most sights stay open

May Day (Protomagia) 1 May

Whit Monday (Agiou Pnevmatos) May/June/July; 50 days after Easter Sunday. Schools and offices close but museums, major sites and shops usually stay open.

Feast of the Assumption 15 August

Ohi Day 28 October

Christmas Day 25 December

St Stephen's Day 26 December

SCHOOL HOLIDAYS

The school year is divided into three terms. The main school holidays are in July and August.

INSURANCE

A travel insurance policy to cover theft, loss and medical problems is a good idea. Some policies specifically exclude 'dangerous activities', which can include scuba diving, motorcycling and even hiking.

You may prefer a policy that pays doctors or hospitals directly rather than requiring you to pay on the spot and claim later. If you have to claim later make sure you keep all documentation. Some policies ask you to call back (reverse charges) to a centre in your home country where an immediate assessment of your problem is made. For more information on health insurance, see p345.

Paying for your ticket with a credit card sometimes provides limited travel insurance, and you may be able to reclaim the payment if the operator doesn't deliver. In the UK, for instance, credit card providers are required by law to reimburse consumers if a company goes into liquidation and the amount in contention is more than UK£100.

Buy travel insurance as early as possible. If you buy it just before you fly, you may find you're not covered for such problems as delays caused by industrial action. Worldwide travel insurance is available at www.lonelyplanet.com/travel_serv ices. You can buy, extend and claim online anytime – even if you're already on the road.

INTERNET ACCESS

Greece has long since embraced the convenience of the internet. There has been a huge increase in the number of hotels and businesses using the internet, and where available, websites are listed throughout this book. For a selection of useful websites about Greece, see the regional Resources information under Things You Need to Know.

Internet cafes are everywhere and many hotels also offer internet and wi-fi access, though hot spots are often located in the lobby rather than in your room. You'll also find many cafes offering wi-fi.

LEGAL MATTERS
ARRESTS

It is a good idea to have your passport with you at all times in case you are stopped by the police and questioned. Greek citizens are presumed to always have identification on them; foreign visitors are similarly presumed to by the police. If you are arrested by police insist on an interpreter (*the*-lo dhi-ermi-*nea*) and/or a lawyer (*the*-lo dhi-ki-*go*-ro). Travellers should also note that they can be prosecuted under the law of their home country regarding age of consent, even when abroad.

DRUGS

Greek drug laws are the strictest in Europe. Greek courts make no distinction between possession and pushing. Possession of even a small amount of marijuana is likely to land you in jail.

MAPS

Unless you are going to hike or drive, the free maps given out by the EOT will probably suffice, although they are not 100% accurate. On islands where there is no EOT office, there are usually tourist maps for sale for around €1.50 but, again, these are not very accurate, particularly maps of towns and villages.

The best overall maps for coverage are published by the Greek company **Road Editions** (☎ 210 345 5575; www.road.gr; Kozanis 21, cnr Amfipoleos, Votanikos, Athens), whose maps are produced with the assistance of the Hellenic Army Geographical Service. There is a wide range of maps to suit various needs, starting with a 1:500,000 map of Greece.

Hikers should also consider the *Topo* series published by **Anavasi** (☎ 210 321 8104; www.mountains.gr; Stoa Arsakiou 6a, Athens), with durable plasticised paper and detailed walking trails for many of the Aegean islands. **Emvelia** (☎ 210 771 7616; www.emvelia .gr; Navarinou 12, Athens) publishes detailed maps, including some excellent plans of the region's main towns, each with a handy index booklet. All maps can be bought online or at major bookstores in Greece.

MONEY

Greece has been using the euro currency since the beginning of 2002. There are eight euro coins, in denominations of two and one euros, then 50, 20, 10, five, two and one cents, and six notes: €5, €10, €20, €50, €100 and €200.

See inside the front cover for currency exchange rates and p43 for information on costs in Greece.

ATMS

ATMs are found in every town large enough to support a bank and in almost all the tourist areas. If you've got MasterCard or Visa, there are plenty of places to withdraw money. Cirrus and Maestro users can make withdrawals in all major towns and tourist areas. Be warned that many card companies can put an automatic block on your card after your first withdrawal abroad as an antifraud mechanism. To avoid this happening, inform your bank of your travel plans. Also be aware that many ATMs on the islands can lose their connection for a day or two at a time, making it impossible for anyone (locals included) to withdraw money. It's useful to have a backup source of money.

Automated foreign-exchange machines are common in major tourist areas. They take all the major European currencies, Australian and US dollars and Japanese yen, and are useful in an emergency, although they charge a hefty commission.

CASH

Nothing beats cash for convenience – or for risk. If you lose cash, it's gone for good and very few travel insurers will come to your rescue. Those that will, normally limit the amount to approximately US$300. It's best to carry no more cash than you need for the next few days. It's also a good idea to set aside a small amount of cash, say US$100, as an emergency stash.

CREDIT CARDS

The great advantage of credit cards is that they allow you to pay for major items without carrying around great wads of cash. Credit cards are now an accepted part of the commercial scene in Greece, although they're often not accepted on many of the smaller islands or in small villages. In larger places, credit cards can be used at top-end hotels, restaurants and shops. Some C-class hotels will accept credit cards, but D- and E-class hotels rarely do.

The main credit cards are MasterCard and Visa, both of which are widely accepted in Greece. They can also be used as cash cards to draw cash from the ATMs of affiliated Greek banks in the same way as at home. Daily withdrawal limits are set by the issuing bank and are given in local currency only. American Express and Diners Club are widely accepted in tourist areas but unheard of elsewhere.

TIPPING

In restaurants a service charge is normally included in the bill, and while a tip is not expected (as it is in North America), it is always appreciated and should be left if the service has been good. Taxi drivers normally expect you to round up the fare, while porters who help you with your luggage to your hotel room or stewards on ferries who take you to your cabin normally expect a small gratuity of between €1 and €3.

TRAVELLERS CHEQUES

The main reason to carry travellers cheques rather than cash is the protection they offer against theft. They are, however, losing popularity as more and more travellers opt to put their money in a bank at home and withdraw it at ATMs as they go. American Express, Visa and Thomas Cook cheques are available in euros and are all widely accepted and have efficient replacement policies.

PHOTOGRAPHY & VIDEO

Digital photography has taken over in a big way in Greece and a range of memory cards can now be bought from camera stores. It is possible to obtain video cassettes in larger towns and cities, but be sure to buy the correct format. It is usually worth buying at least a few cassettes duty-free to start off your trip.

RESTRICTIONS & ETIQUETTE

Never photograph a military installation or anything else that has a sign forbidding photography. Flash photography is not allowed inside churches, and it's considered taboo to photograph the main altar.

Greeks usually love having their photos taken but always ask permission first. The same goes for video cameras, probably even more annoying and offensive for locals than a still camera. At archaeological sites you will be stopped from using a tripod as it marks you as a 'professional'.

SHOPPING

Shopping is big business in Greece. At times a tourist town can look like one big shop with all kinds of goods and trinkets on display. Shops and kiosks in major tourist centres are often overpriced and it's often better to find out where the locals shop. If you have room in your suitcase or backpack there are some really excellent quality artisanal works to be picked up from small boutiques and galleries, including pottery, jewellery and metalworked *objets*.

SMOKING

In July 2009 Greece brought in antismoking laws similar to those found throughout most of Europe. Smoking is now banned inside public places, with the penalty being fines placed on the business owners.

TELEPHONE

The Greek telephone service is maintained by the public corporation known as OTE (pronounced o-*teh;* Organismos Tilepikoinonion Ellados).

The system is modern and reasonably well maintained. There are public telephones just about everywhere, including in some unbelievably isolated spots. The phones are easy to operate and can be used for local, long-distance and international calls. The 'i' at the top left of the push-button dialling panel brings up the operating instructions in English.

Note that in Greece the area code must always be dialled when making a call (ie all Greek phone numbers are 10-digit).

MOBILE PHONES

The number of mobile phones in Greece now exceeds the number of landline phones. If you have a compatible GSM mobile phone from a country with an overseas global roaming arrangement with Greece, you will be able to use your phone in Greece. You may need to inform your mobile phone service provider before you depart in order to have global roaming activated. US and Canadian mobile phone users won't be able to use their mobile phones, unless their handset is equipped with a dual- or tri-band system.

There are several mobile service providers in Greece, among which Panafon, CosmOTE and Wind are the best known. All offer 2G connectivity. Of these three,

CosmOTE tends to have the best coverage in remote areas, so try retuning your phone to CosmOTE if you find mobile coverage is patchy. All three companies offer pay-as-you-talk services by which you can buy a rechargeable SIM card and have your own Greek mobile number. The Panafon system is called 'à la Carte', the Wind system 'F2G' and the CosmOTE system 'Cosmokarta'.

Note: the use of a mobile phone while driving in Greece is prohibited, but the use of a Bluetooth headset is allowed.

PHONECARDS

All public phones use OTE phonecards, known as *telekarta,* not coins. These cards are widely available at *periptera,* corner shops and tourist shops. A local call costs around €0.30 for three minutes.

It's also possible to use payphones with the growing range of discount-card schemes. This involves dialling an access code and then punching in your card number. The OTE version of this card is known as 'Hronokarta'. The cards come with instructions in Greek and English and the talk time is enormous compared to the standard phonecard rates.

TIME

Greece maintains one time zone throughout the country. It is two hours ahead of GMT/UTC and three hours ahead on daylight-saving time – which begins on the last Sunday in March, when clocks are put forward one hour. Daylight saving ends on the last Sunday in October.

TOILETS

Public toilets are a rarity, except at airports and bus and train stations. Cafes are the best option if you get caught short, but you'll be expected to buy something for the privilege.

One peculiarity of the Greek plumbing system is that it can't handle toilet paper; apparently the pipes are too narrow. Whatever the reason, anything larger than a postage stamp seems to cause a problem; flushing away tampons and sanitary napkins is guaranteed to block the system. Toilet paper etc should be placed in the small bin provided next to every toilet.

TOURIST INFORMATION

Tourist information is handled by the Greek National Tourist Organisation, known by the initials GNTO abroad and EOT within Greece. The quality of service from office to office varies dramatically.

LOCAL TOURIST OFFICES

The EOT in Athens dispenses information, including a very useful timetable of the week's ferry departures from Piraeus, and details about public transport prices and schedules from Athens.

EOT offices can be found in major tourist locations, though they are increasingly being supplemented or even replaced by local municipality tourist offices (such as in the Peloponnese):

Athens (Map pp66-7; ☎ 210 331 0392; www .gnto.gr; Leoforos Vasilissis Amalias 26a, Syntagma; ⏱ 9am-7pm Mon-Fri, 10am-4pm Sat & Sun) See also p69.

Crete (☎ 2810 246 299; Xanthoudidou, Iraklio; ⏱ 8.30am-8.30pm Apr-Oct, 8.30am-3pm Nov-Mar) See also p244.

Dodecanese (Map p282; ☎ 22410 35226; www.ando.gr; cnr Makariou & Papagou, Rhodes Town, Rhodes; ⏱ 8am-2.45pm Mon-Fri) See also p283.

Ionian Islands (☎ 26710 22248; Argostoli, Kefallonia; ⏱ 8am-8pm Mon-Fri & 9am-3pm Sat Jul-Aug, 8am-2.30pm Mon-Fri) See also p160.

Macedonia (Office of Tourism Directorate; Map pp176-7; ☎ 2310 221 100; tour-the@otenet .gr; Tsimiski 136, Thessaloniki; ◷ 8am-8pm Mon-Fri, 8am-2pm Sat) See also p175.

Peloponnese (Info Center; ☎ 2610 461 740/1; www.infocenterpatras.gr; Othonos Amalias 6, Patra; ◷ 8am-10pm)

TOURIST POLICE

The tourist police work in cooperation with the regular Greek police and the EOT. Each tourist police office has at least one member of staff who speaks English. Hotels, restaurants, travel agencies, tourist shops, tourist guides, waiters, taxi drivers and bus drivers all come under the jurisdiction of the tourist police. If you think that you have been ripped off by any of these, report it to the tourist police and they will investigate. If you need to report a theft or loss of passport, then go to the tourist police first, and they will act as interpreters between you and the regular police. The tourist police also fulfil the same functions as the EOT and municipal tourist offices, dispensing maps and brochures, and giving information on transport. They can often help to find accommodation.

TRAVELLERS WITH DISABILITIES

Access for travellers with disabilities has improved somewhat in recent years, largely thanks to the Olympics. Improvements are mostly restricted to Athens, where there are more accessible sights, hotels and restaurants. Much of the rest of Greece remains inaccessible to wheelchairs, and the abundance of stones, marble, slippery cobbles and stepped alleys creates a further challenge. Visually or hearing impaired people are also rarely catered to.

Careful planning before you go can make a world of difference. The British-based **Royal Association for Disability & Rehabilitation** (Radar; ☎ 020 7250 3222; www.radar.org.uk; 12 City Forum, 250 City Rd, London EC1V 8AF) publishes a useful guide called *Holidays & Travel Abroad: A Guide for Disabled People,* which gives a good overview of facilities available to travellers with disabilities in Europe. Also check out www.greecetravel.com/handicapped for links to local articles, resorts and tour groups catering to physically disabled tourists. Some options:

Christianakis Travel (www.greecetravel .com/handi capped/christianakis/index.htm) Creates tailor-made itineraries and can organise transportation, hotels and guides.

Sailing Holidays (www.charterayacht ingreece.com/DRYachting/index.html) Two-day to two-week sailing trips around the Greek islands in fully accessible yachts.

Sirens Resort (www.hotelsofgreece.com/ central/loutraki/sirens-wheelchair-accessible-resort/index.html; Loutraki, Skaloma, Central Greece) Family-friendly resort with accessible apartments, tours and ramps into the sea.

VISAS

The list of countries whose nationals can stay in Greece for up to three months without a visa includes Australia, Canada, all EU countries, Iceland, Israel, Japan, New Zealand, Norway, Switzerland and the USA. Other countries included are the European principalities of Monaco and San Marino and most South American countries. The list changes – contact Greek embassies for the full list. Those not included can expect to pay about US$20 for a three-month visa.

WOMEN TRAVELLERS

Many women travel alone in Greece. The crime rate remains relatively low and solo travel is probably safer than in most European countries. This does not mean that you should be lulled into complacency; bag snatching and rapes do occur, particularly at party resorts on the islands.

The biggest nuisance to foreign women travelling alone is the guys the Greeks have nicknamed *kamaki*. The word means 'fishing trident' and refers to the *kamaki's* favourite pastime: 'fishing' for foreign women. You'll find them everywhere there are lots of tourists: young (for the most part), smooth-talking guys who aren't in the least bit bashful about sidling up to women in the street. They can be very persistent, but they are usually a hassle rather than a threat. The majority of Greek men treat foreign women with respect, and are genuinely helpful.

TRANSPORT

GETTING THERE & AWAY

Flights, tours and rail tickets can be booked online at www.lonelyplanet.com/travel_services.

ENTERING THE COUNTRY

If entering from another EU nation passports are not checked, but customs and police may be interested in what you are carrying. EU citizens may also enter Greece on a national identity card. Visitors from outside the EU usually require a visa. This must be checked with consular authorities before you arrive. For visa requirements, see p351.

AIR

Olympic Air (OA; ☎ 801 114 4444; www.olympicairlines.com) is the country's national airline with the majority of flights to and from Athens. Olympic flies direct between Athens and destinations throughout Europe, as well as to Cairo, İstanbul, Tel Aviv, New York and Toronto. **Aegean Airlines** (A3; ☎ 801 112 0000; www.aegeanair.com) has flights to and from destinations in Spain, Germany and Italy as well as to Paris, London, Cairo and İstanbul. The safety record of both airlines is exemplary. The contact details for local Olympic and Aegean offices are listed throughout the book.

EasyJet offers some of the cheapest tickets between Greece and the rest of Europe and covers a huge range of destinations. If you're coming from outside Europe, consider a cheap flight to a European hub like London and then an onward ticket with easyJet. If travelling between June and September, it's wise to book ahead.

ASIA

Most Asian countries offer fairly competitive deals, with Bangkok, Singapore and Hong Kong the best places to shop around for discount tickets.

Bangkok has a number of excellent travel agencies, but there are also some suspect ones; ask the advice of other travellers. **STA Travel** (☎ 02-236 0262; www.statravel.co.th) is a good place to start. In Singapore, **STA Travel** (☎ 6737 7188; www.statravel.com.sg) offers competitive discount fares for most destinations. In Hong Kong, **Four Seas Tours** (☎ 2200 7760; www.fourseastravel.com) is recommended, as is **Shoestring Travel** (☎ 2723 2306; www.shoestringtravel.com.hk).

AUSTRALIA

STA Travel (☎ 1300 733 035; www.statravel.com.au) has its main office in Melbourne but also has offices in all major cities and on many university campuses. **Flight Centre** (☎ 13 16 00; www.flightcentre.com.au) has its central office in Sydney and dozens of offices throughout Australia.

Thai Airways and Singapore Airlines both have convenient connections to Athens as do three of the Persian Gulf airlines – Emirates, Gulf and Qatar Airways.

CANADA

Canada's national student travel agency is **Travel CUTS** (☎ 800 667 2887; www.travelcuts.com), which has offices in all major cities. **Flight Centre** (☎ 1 877 967 5302; www.flightcentre.ca) has offices in most major cities and offers discounted tickets. For online bookings go to www.expedia.ca or www.travelocity.ca.

Olympic Air has flights from Toronto to Athens via Montreal. There are no direct flights from Vancouver, but there are connecting flights via Toronto, Amsterdam, Frankfurt and London on Air Canada, KLM, Lufthansa and British Airways.

CONTINENTAL EUROPE

Athens is linked to every major city in Europe by either Olympic Air or the flag carrier of each country. Amsterdam, Frankfurt, Berlin and Paris are all major centres for cheap airfares.

France has a network of travel agencies that can supply discount tickets to travellers of all ages. They include **OTU Voyages** (☎ 01 40 29 12 22), which has branches across the country. Other recommendations include **Voyageurs du Monde** (☎ 01 40 15 11 15; www.vdm.com) and **Nouvelles Frontières** (☎ 0825 000 747; www.nouvelles-frontieres.fr).

In Germany, **STA Travel** (☎ 01805 456 422; www.statravel.de) has several offices around the country. For online fares, try **Expedia** (☎ 0180 500 6025; www.expedia.de).

In Denmark, **My Travel** (☎ 7010 2111; www.mytravel.dk) and in the Netherlands, **Airfair** (☎ 020-620 5121; www.airfair.nl) are recommended.

UK

STA Travel (☎ 0871 230 0040; www.statravel.co.uk) has discounted tickets for students and travellers under 26, while **Flight Centre** (☎ 0870 499 0040; www.flightcentre.co.uk) offers competitive rates and also has deals for students. Both agencies have offices in most cities. Other recommended travel agencies in London include **Trailfinders** (☎ 020 7938 3939; www.trailfinders.co.uk), **Travel Bag** (☎ 0870 814 6614; www.travelbag.co.uk) and **ebookers** (☎ 0800 082 3000; www.ebookers.com). Online, check out www.charterflights.co.uk and www.cheapflights.co.uk.

The cheapest scheduled flights are with **easyJet** (☎ 0871 750 0100; www.easyjet.com), the no-frills specialist, which has flights from Luton and Gatwick to Athens. Greece's two main airlines have regular flights between the UK and Athens and offer good deals for online booking.

USA

STA Travel (☎ 800 781 4040; www.statravel.com) has offices in most major cities that have a university. For online bookings try www.cheaptickets.com, www.expedia.com and www.orbitz.com.

New York has the widest range of options to Athens. Olympic Air and Delta Airlines both have direct flights but there are numerous other connecting flights.

While there are no direct flights to Athens from the west coast, there are connecting flights to Athens from many US cities, either linking with Olympic Air in New York or flying with one of the European national airlines to their home country, and then on to Athens.

SEA

ITALY

There are ferries to Greece from the Italian ports of Ancona, Bari, Brindisi and Venice.

The ferries can get very crowded in summer. If you want to take a vehicle across it's wise to make a reservation beforehand. You'll find all the latest information about ferry routes, schedules and services online at www.greekferries.gr.

GETTING AROUND
AIR
See Island Hopping (p357) for details on flights between the mainland and the islands and between the islands themselves.

The prices listed in this book are for full-fare economy, and include domestic taxes and charges. There are discounts for return tickets for travel between Monday and Thursday, and bigger discounts for trips that include a Saturday night away. You'll find full details on the airline's website, as well as information on timetables.

The baggage allowance on domestic flights is 15kg, or 20kg if the domestic flight is part of an international journey.

BICYCLE
Cycling is not popular among Greeks; however, it's gaining kudos with tourists. You'll need strong leg muscles to tackle the mountains or you can stick to some of the flatter coastal routes. Bike lanes are rare to nonexistent and helmets are not compulsory. See p339 for more details on cycling in Greece.

BOAT
See Island Hopping (p357) for details on getting around by boat.

BUS
All long-distance buses, on the mainland and the islands, are operated by regional collectives known as **KTEL** (Koino Tamio Eispraxeon Leoforion; www.ktel.org). The bus network is comprehensive. All the major towns on the mainland have frequent connections to Athens. The islands of Corfu, Kefallonia and Zakynthos can also be reached directly from Athens by bus – the fares include the price of the ferry ticket.

The KTEL buses are safe and modern, and these days most are air conditioned – at least on the major routes. In more-remote rural areas they tend to be older and less comfortable.

Most villages have a daily bus service of some sort, although remote areas may have only one or two buses a week. They operate for the benefit of people going to town to shop, rather than for tourists, and consequently leave the villages very early in the morning and return early in the afternoon.

On islands where the capital is inland rather than a port, buses normally meet boats. Some of the more remote islands have not yet acquired a bus, but most have some sort of motorised transport – even if it is only a bone-shaking, three-wheeled truck.

It is important to note that big cities like Athens, Iraklio, Patra and Thessaloniki may have more than one bus station, each serving different regions. Make sure you find the correct station for your destination.

Fares are fixed by the government and bus travel is very reasonably priced. A journey costs approximately €5 per 100km.

CAR
No one who has travelled on Greece's roads will be surprised to hear that the country's road fatality rate is the highest in Europe. Ever-stricter traffic laws have had little impact on the toll; Greek roads remain a good place to practise your defensive-driving techniques.

Heart-stopping moments aside, your own car is a great way to explore off the beaten track. It's important to get a good road map (for more information, see p347).

DRIVING LICENCE

Drivers with an EU driving licence can drive with it in Greece. If your driving licence comes from outside the EU, Greece requires that you possess an International Driving Permit, which should be obtained before you leave home.

FUEL

Fuel is available widely throughout the country, though service stations may be closed on weekends and public holidays. On the islands, there may be only one petrol station; check where it is before you head out. Self-service pumps are not the norm in Greece, nor are credit-card pumps, so it is always advisable to keep the reservoir level up just in case. Petrol in Greece is cheaper than in most other European countries, but by American or Australian standards it is expensive.

HIRE

Hire cars are available just about everywhere, but it's best to hire from major cities where competition offers better opportunities to bargain. All the big multinational companies are represented in Athens, and most have branches in major towns and popular tourist destinations. The majority of islands have at least one outlet. By Greek law, rental cars have to be replaced every six years so most vehicles you rent will be relatively new.

High-season weekly rates with unlimited mileage start at about €280 for the smallest models, such as a Fiat Seicento, dropping to about €200 per week in winter. These prices don't include local tax (known as VAT). The major companies offer much cheaper prebooked and prepaid rates. You can also find better deals at local companies. Their advertised rates can be up to 50% cheaper, and they are normally open to negotiation, especially if business is slow. On the islands, you can rent a car for the day for around €30 to €50, including all insurance and taxes.

Always check what the insurance includes; there are often rough roads or dangerous routes that you can only tackle by renting a 4WD. If you want to take a hire car to another country or onto a ferry, you will need advance written authorisation from the hire company, as the insurance may not cover you.

The minimum driving age in Greece is 18 years, but most car-hire firms require you to be at least 21, or 23 for larger vehicles.

INSURANCE

Insurance is always included in any vehicle hire agreements, but you are advised to check whether it is fully comprehensive or third party only.

ROAD RULES

In Greece, as throughout Continental Europe, you drive on the right and overtake on the left. Outside built-up areas, traffic on a main road has right of way at intersections. In towns, vehicles coming from the right have right of way. This includes roundabouts – even if you're in the roundabout, you must give way to drivers coming onto the roundabout to your right.

Seat belts must be worn in front seats, and in back seats if the car is fitted with them. Children under 12 years of age are not allowed in the front seat. It is compulsory to carry a first-aid kit, fire extinguisher and warning triangle, and it is forbidden to carry cans of petrol.

Outside residential areas the speed limit is 120km/h on highways, 90km/h on other roads and 50km/h in built-up areas. The police have also cracked down on drink-driving – at last. A blood-alcohol content of 0.05% can incur a fine of €150, and over 0.08% is a criminal offence.

TOURS

Tours are worth considering if your time is very limited or if you fancy somebody else doing all of the organising. In Athens, you'll find countless day tours (p79), with some agencies offering two- or three-day trips to nearby sights. For something on a larger scale, try **Intrepid Travel** (www.intrepidtravel.com). With offices in Australia, the UK and the USA, Intrepid offers a 15-day tour of the Greek Islands (£1105/US$2120 plus €200) and an eight-day tour from Athens to Santorini (£645/US$1230 plus €200), including everything except meals and flights. **Encounter Greece** (www.encountergreece.com) offers a plethora of tours; a 10-day tour across the country costs €1595 while three days on the mainland is €375. Flights to Greece are not included.

More adventurous tours include guided activities involving hiking, climbing, whitewater rafting, kayaking, canoeing or canyoning. **Alpin Club** (www.alpinclub.gr) in Athens operates out of Karitena in the Peloponnese, while outfits like **Trekking Hellas** (www.trekking.gr) or **Robinson Expeditions** (www.robinson.gr) run tours from the centre and north of Greece. For more information on activity-based tours, see p339.

TRAIN

Trains are operated by **Greek Railways Organisation** (Organismos Sidirodromon Ellados; www.ose.gr), always referred to as the OSE. You'll find information on fares and schedules on the website. Information on domestic departures from Athens or Thessaloniki can be sought by calling ☎ 1440.

The biggest problem with the Greek railway network is that it is so limited. There are essentially only two main lines: the standard-gauge service from Athens to Alexandroupoli via Thessaloniki (p88), and the Peloponnese network. The services that do exist are of a good standard, and are improving all the time.

CLASSES

There are two types of service: regular (slow) trains that stop at all stations and faster, modern intercity (IC) trains that link most major cities.

The slow trains represent the country's cheapest form of public transport: 2nd-class fares are absurdly cheap, and even 1st class is cheaper than bus travel.

The IC trains that link the major Greek cities are an excellent way to travel. The services are not necessarily express – the Greek terrain is far too mountainous for that – but the trains are modern and comfortable. There are 1st- and 2nd-class tickets and a cafe-bar on board. On some services, meals can be ordered and delivered to your seat.

COSTS

For a 2nd-class slow-train trip from Athens to Thessaloniki expect to pay €28 (six hours). Ticket prices for IC services are subject to a distance loading charged on top of the normal fares. Seat reservations should be made as far in advance as possible, especially during summer. A sample 2nd-class fare for Athens to Thessaloniki is €36 (five hours). There is an additional nonstop

Athens-Thessaloniki express service for €48 (four hours).

A comfortable night service runs between Athens and Thessaloniki, with a choice of couchettes (from €20), two-bed compartments (€31) and single compartments (€54).

ISLAND HOPPING

In Greece, getting there really is half the adventure and island hopping remains an essential part of the Greek experience. Whether you're sailing into a colourful harbour, sitting on a sun-drenched deck with the surf pounding below, or flying low over the azure waters in a propeller-driven twin-engine plane, you will undoubtedly be filled with a sense of adventure and see the islands at their most tantalising.

The trade-off is, of course, that sea travel can be quite expensive these days. A bed for the night in a cabin from Piraeus to Rhodes can be more expensive than a discounted airline ticket. Nevertheless, deck class is still very reasonable, cabins are like hotel rooms and the experience of staying overnight on a boat is one you shouldn't pass up too quickly.

In the summer, lots of boats and planes connect the islands to one another and to the mainland. However, travelling at peak times and between smaller islands and island groups can take some careful planning. Many local travel agents have a good handle on the transport available and can help you build an itinerary and book all necessary tickets. Out of season, planning ahead is even more essential as the number of boats and planes diminishes considerably.

Ferry and airline timetables change from year to year and season to season, and planes and boats can be subject to delays and cancellations at short notice due to bad weather and strikes. No timetable is infallible, but the comprehensive weekly list of departures from Piraeus put out by the EOT (known abroad as the GNTO, the Greek National Tourist Organisation) in Athens is as accurate as possible. The people to go to for the most up-to-date ferry information are the local *limenarhio* (port police), whose offices are usually on or near the quayside.

A couple of very useful websites:

Danae Travel (www.danae.gr) This is a good site for booking boat tickets.
Greek Travel Pages (www.gtp.gr) Has a useful search program and links for flights and ferries.

This section deals with domestic flight and boat connections.

PRACTICALITIES
THE GREEK FLEETS

With a network covering every inhabited island, the Greek ferry network is vast and varied. The slow rust-buckets that used to ply the seas are nearly a thing of the past. Local ferries, excursion boats and tiny, private fishing boats called caïques often connect neighbouring islands and islets. You'll also find water taxis that will take you to isolated beaches and coves. At the other end of the spectrum, hydrofoils and catamarans can cut travel time drastically. Catamarans have taken to the sea in a big way; they offer more comfort and cope better with poor weather conditions.

While the largest and most popular islands tend to have airports, many of the smaller ones don't. Flights tend to be short and aeroplanes are small, often making for a bumpy ride.

ISLAND HOPPING

PRACTICALITIES

OPERATORS

WHO'S WHO IN THE AIR?

The biggest player in the sky is Olympic Air, followed closely by Aegean Airlines which often offers great discounts. Airlines often have local offices on the islands (see the relevant destination chapter for details).

Aegean Airlines (☎ 801 112 0000, 210 626 1000; www.aegeanair.com)

Athens Airways (☎ 210 669 6600; www.athensairways.com)

Olympic Air (☎ 801 114 4444; www.olympicairlines.com)

Sky Express (☎ 28102 23500; www.skyexpress.gr)

WHO'S WHO IN THE WATER?

Ferry companies often have local offices on many of the islands; see the relevant destination chapter for details of these as well as small, local ferries and caïques.

Aegean Speed Lines (☎ 210 969 0950; www.aegean speedlines.gr) Superspeedy boats between Athens and the Cyclades.

Agoudimos Lines (☎ 210 414 1300; www.agoudimos-lines.com) Ferries connecting the Cyclades and the mainland. Also travels to Italy via Corfu.

Blue Star Ferries (☎ 210 891 9800; www.bluestarferries.com) Long-haul high-speed ferries and Seajet catamarans between the mainland and the Cyclades.

Cyclades Fast Ferries (☎ 210 418 2005; www.fastferries.com.gr) Comfortable ferries to the most popular Cyclades.

Dodekanisos Seaways (☎ 22410 70590; www.12ne.gr) Runs luxurious catamarans in the Dodecanese.

Euroseas (☎ 210 413 2188; www.ferries.gr/euroseas) Linking the Saronics with services to the mainland.

Evoikos Lines (☎ 210 413 4483; www.glyfa ferries.gr, in Greek) Comfortable short-haul ferry services between Glyfa on the mainland and Agiokambos in northern Evia.

GA Ferries (☎ 210 419 9100; www.gaferries.gr) Old-style, long-haul ferries serving a huge number of islands.

Hellenic Seaways (☎ 210 419 9000; www.hellenicseaways.gr) Conventional long-haul ferries and catamarans from the mainland to Cyclades and between the Sporades and Saronic islands.

Ionian Ferries (☎ 210 324 9997; www.ionianferries.gr) Large ferries serving the Ionian Islands.

LANE Lines (☎ 210 427 4011; www.ferries.gr/lane) Long-haul ferries.

Minoan Lines (☎ 210 414 5700; www.minoan.gr) High-speed luxury ferries between Piraeus and Iraklio, and Patra, Igoumenitsa and Corfu.

NEL Lines (☎ 22510 26299; www.nel.gr) High-speed, long-haul ferries.

Sea Jets (☎ 210 412 1001) Catamarans calling at Athens, Crete, Santorini (Thira), Paros and many islands in between.

Superfast Ferries (www.superfast.com) As the name implies, speedy ferries from the mainland to Crete, Corfu and Patra.

TICKETS

TICKET PURCHASE

As ferries are prone to delays and cancellations, it's often best not to purchase a ticket for short trips until it has been confirmed that the ferry is leaving. During high season, or if you need to reserve a car space, you will need to book in advance. High-speed boats like catamarans tend to sell out long before the slow chuggers. For overnight ferries it's always best to book in advance, particularly if you want a cabin or a particular type of accommodation. If a service is cancelled you can usually transfer your ticket to the next available service with that company.

Many ferry companies have online booking services, or you can purchase tickets from their local offices or most travel agents across the country. Agencies selling tickets line the waterfront of most ports, but rarely is there one that sells tickets for every boat, and often an agency is reluctant to give you information about a boat they do not sell tickets for. Most have time-tables displayed outside; check these for the next departing boat or ask the *limenarhio*.

To find specific details on where to buy tickets and other important local information for the islands, see the specific island's Getting There & Away section in the destination chapters throughout this book.

COSTS

Ferry prices are fixed by the government and are determined by the distance of the destination from the port of origin. High-speed ferries and hydrofoils cost about 20% more than the traditional ferries, while catamarans are often a third to double the price of their slower counterparts. Caïques and water taxis are usually very reasonable while excursion boats can be pricey but very useful to reach out-of-the-way islands. Children under five travel for free while those between five and 10 are usually given half-price tickets.

Almost all islands are served by car ferries but they are expensive. If you're planning to island hop, you're better off renting a vehicle at each destination.

CLASSES

On smaller boats, hydrofoils and catamarans, there is only one type of ticket available and these days, even on larger vessels, classes are largely a thing of the

> ### FEELING WOOZY?
>
> Even those with the sturdiest stomachs can feel seasick when a boat hits rough weather. Here are a few tips to calm your tummy:
>
> - Gaze at the horizon, not the sea. Don't read or stare at objects that your mind will assume are stable.
> - Drink plenty and eat lightly. Many people claim ginger biscuits and ginger tea help settle the stomach.
> - Don't use binoculars.
> - If possible stay in the fresh air – don't go below deck and avoid hydrofoils where you are trapped indoors.
> - Try to keep your mind occupied.
> - If you know you're prone to seasickness, consider investing in acupressure wristbands before you leave.

past. The public spaces on the more modern ferries are generally open to all. What does differ is the level of accommodation that you can purchase for overnight boats.

Your 'deck class' ticket typically gives you access to the deck and interior with no accommodation option. Next up, aeroplane-type seats give you a reserved, reclining seat in which to sleep (you hope). Then come various shades of cabin accommodation: a four-berth, three-berth or two-berth interior cabin is cheaper than an equivalent outside cabin with a porthole. On most boats, cabins are very comfortable, resembling a small hotel room with a private bathroom. At the other end of the spectrum are luxury cabins with a view to the

FERRY ROUTES

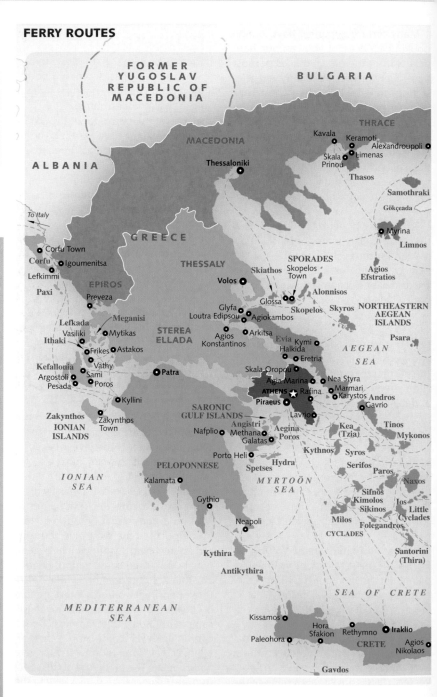

front of the ship. These resemble standard cruise-ship cabins and are generally very pricey.

Unless you state otherwise, you will automatically be given deck class when purchasing a ticket. Unless otherwise indicated, prices quoted in this book are for deck-class tickets and economy flight tickets.

CONNECTIONS

Transport information is always vulnerable to change – nowhere is this truer than in Greece. It's important to remember that ferry companies and airlines can change routes and timetables faster than a catamaran can zip between the islands. Outside of the summer season, most services are less frequent. Always check online schedules, operators or travel agencies for up-to-the-minute info.

References to 'port' in the table headings throughout this chapter refer to the port of departure, not the destination port.

INDIVIDUAL ISLANDS & MAINLAND PORTS

AGIOS KONSTANTINOS

Central Greece (mainland port)

BOAT SERVICES FROM AGIOS KONSTANTINOS

Destination	Port	Duration	Fare	Frequency
Skiathos*	Agios Konstantinos	2hr	€33	1 daily
Skiathos**	Agios Konstantinos	2hr	€33	2-3 daily
Skopelos*	Agios Konstantinos	3hr	€44	1 daily
Skopelos**	Agios Konstantinos	2½hr	€44	1-2 Mon-Fri, 2-3 Sat & Sun

*fast-ferry services
**hydrofoil services

AMORGOS

Cyclades; see also p217

BOAT SERVICES FROM AMORGOS

Destination	Port	Duration	Fare	Frequency
Aegiali	Katapola	50min	€4.50	1-2 daily
Kos	Katapola	5hr	€22.50	2 weekly
Leros	Katapola	3hr 10min	€18	2 weekly
Naxos	Katapola	1-4hr	€7.50	1-3 daily
Patmos	Katapola	2hr	€18	2 weekly
Piraeus	Katapola	9hr	€30	4 weekly
Piraeus*	Katapola	7hr 25min	€58	1 daily
Rhodes	Katapola	10hr	€25.50	2 weekly
Santorini (Thira)*	Katapola	1½hr	€32	1 daily

*high-speed services

ANDROS

Cyclades; see also p217

BOAT SERVICES FROM ANDROS

Destination	Port	Duration	Fare	Frequency
Mykonos	Gavrio	1¼hr	€10-13	4 daily
Naxos	Gavrio	4hr 10min	€15.70	2 weekly
Rafina	Gavrio	2½hr	€12-14	4-8 daily

ASTAKOS

Central Greece (mainland port)

BOAT SERVICES FROM ASTAKOS

Destination	Port	Duration	Fare	Frequency
Kefallonia	Astakos	3hr	€8	1 daily (Sami)

ATHENS

Mainland port; see also p88

AIR

Olympic Air has flights to all islands with airports, and the more popular islands are also serviced by Aegean Airlines and Athens Airways.

Aegean Airlines has eight flights daily to Rhodes, seven flights daily to Iraklio, six to Santorini (Thira), five daily to Hania, three to Lesvos (Mytilini) and Mykonos, at least two daily to Corfu and Kos and at least one daily to Chios, Kefallonia, Samos and Limnos.

Athens Airways has flights to Hania, Chios, Iraklio, Kefallonia, Lesvos, Mykonos, Rhodes and Santorini.

The following table indicates starting prices (including tax).

DOMESTIC FLIGHTS FROM ATHENS

Destination	Duration	Fare	Frequency
Corfu	1hr	€77	14 weekly
Crete (Hania)	50min	€77	30 weekly
Crete (Iraklio)	50min	€77	40 weekly
Crete (Sitia)	1hr 10min	€89	4 weekly
Kefallonia	65min	€111	13 weekly
Kos	55min	€89	14 weekly
Mykonos	40min	€77	27 weekly
Naxos	45min	€80	8 weekly
Rhodes	1hr	€77	35 weekly
Santorini (Thira)	50min	€77	35 weekly
Skiathos	50min	€71	7 weekly
Thessaloniki	55min	€77	58 weekly

BOAT

Athens' main port, Piraeus, is the departure point for an overwhelming number of island destinations. The smaller east coast ports of Rafina and Lavrio service the Cyclades and Evia. See also p88.

BOAT SERVICES FROM ATHENS to Crete

Destination	Port	Duration	Fare	Frequency
Agios Nikolaos	Piraeus	12hr	€30	2 weekly
Iraklio	Piraeus	6½hr	€33.50	3 weekly
Iraklio	Piraeus	8hr	€36-37	2 daily
Rethymno	Piraeus	10hr	€30	2 daily
Rethymno*	Piraeus	6hr	€57	1 daily
Sitia	Piraeus	14½hr	€32.10	2 weekly
Souda (Hania)	Piraeus	8½hr	€30	2 daily
Souda (Hania)*	Piraeus	4½hr	€55	1 daily

*high-speed services

to the Cyclades

Destination	Port	Duration	Fare	Frequency
Andros	Rafina	2hr	€12-14	4 daily
Amorgos	Piraeus	9hr	€30	4 weekly
Amorgos*	Piraeus	7hr 25min	€58	1 daily
Mykonos	Piraeus	4¾hr	€30.50-39.50	2 daily
Mykonos*	Piraeus	3hr	€43	3 daily
Mykonos	Rafina	4½hr	€23	2-3 daily
Mykonos*	Rafina	2hr 10min	€41	4-5 daily
Naxos	Piraeus	4¾hr	€30	4-5 daily
Naxos*	Piraeus	3½hr	€45	3 daily
Naxos*	Rafina	3hr	€43	1 daily
Santorini (Thira)	Piraeus	9hr	€33.50	4-5 daily
Santorini (Thira)*	Piraeus	5¼hr	€47-65	3 daily
Santorini (Thira)*	Rafina	4¾hr	€49	1 daily
Sifnos	Piraeus	5¼hr	€28	5 daily
Sifnos*	Piraeus	2hr 25min	€44	3 daily

*high-speed services

to the Dodecanese

Destination	Port	Duration	Fare	Frequency
Kalymnos	Piraeus	13hr	€44	3 weekly
Karpathos	Piraeus	17hr	€58	2 weekly
Kos	Piraeus	10hr	€46	4 weekly
Nisyros	Piraeus	18hr	€46	3 weekly
Patmos	Piraeus	7hr	€34	4 weekly
Rhodes	Piraeus	13hr	€53	1 daily
Tilos	Piraeus	19hr	€46	2 weekly

to Evia

Destination	Port	Duration	Fare	Frequency
Evia (Marmari)	Rafina	1hr	€7	4-6 daily

to the Saronic Gulf Islands

Destination	Port	Duration	Fare	Frequency
Hydra*	Piraeus	50min-1½hr	€28.40	10 daily
Poros	Piraeus	2¼hr	€13.30	4 daily
Poros*	Piraeus	1hr	€25.20	4-6 daily

*high-speed services

to the Peloponnese

Destination	Port	Duration	Fare	Frequency
Ermioni*	Piraeus	2hr	€30	4 daily
Methana	Piraeus	2hr	€12	1-3 daily
Porto Heli*	Piraeus	2hr	€29.50	4 daily

*high-speed services

CORFU

Ionian Islands; see also p151

DOMESTIC FLIGHTS FROM CORFU

Destination	Airport	Duration	Fare	Frequency
Athens	Corfu	1hr	€60	2 daily
Kefallonia	Corfu	1hr 20min	€39	3 weekly
Thessaloniki	Corfu	55min	€69	3 weekly

BOAT SERVICES FROM CORFU

Destination	Port	Duration	Fare	Frequency
Igoumenitsa	Corfu	1¼hr	€7	hourly
Igoumenitsa	Lefkimmi	1hr 10min	€5.60	6 daily
Patra	Corfu	6½hr	€30	2 weekly
Paxi	Corfu	3½hr	from €8.50	3 weekly
Paxi*	Corfu	40min	€16.40	1-3 daily

*high-speed services

CRETE

See also p233

AIR

Nikos Kazantzakis Airport in Iraklio receives the bulk of Crete's national and international flights, though Hania is also busy. Sitia has been pegged for expansion, but remains much less used.

To reach Crete by air from other Greek islands usually requires changing in Athens, except for some flights operated by newcomer Sky Express; the direct flight offers between Crete and other islands in the tables here are all offered by Sky Express. Note, cheaper Sky Express flights restrict baggage to 12.5kg. In the high season, it's best to book somewhat in advance, as Crete is a very popular destination and tickets may sell out quickly for the dates you wish to travel.

Remarkably, international direct flights to Crete are sometimes cheaper than flying to the island from elsewhere in Greece, even from Greek carriers.

European budget airlines are also starting to serve Crete in summer months.

DOMESTIC FLIGHTS FROM CRETE

Destination	Port	Duration	Fare	Frequency
Athens	Hania	1hr	€100	1 daily
Athens	Iraklio	1hr	€110	2 daily
Kos	Iraklio	35min	€110	4 weekly
Mykonos	Iraklio	30min	€80	12 weekly
Rhodes	Iraklio	45min	€110	11 weekly
Thessaloniki	Hania	1½hr	€120	1 daily
Thessaloniki	Iraklio	1½hr	€130	2 daily

BOAT

Crete's major ferry ports are on the north coast. Iraklio is the major one, followed by Souda (for Hania), Rethymno and Sitia in the east. The small western port of Kissamos (Kastelli) exists exclusively to service Gythio in the Peloponnese and the nearby island of Kythira.

Information given here pertains only to north-coast ports. For schedules, prices and other information involving the south-coast ports and local excursion boats, see the relevant sections of the Crete chapter (see p233).

BOAT SERVICES FROM CRETE

Destination	Port	Duration	Fare	Frequency
Gythio	Kissamos	7hr	€23	5 weekly
Karpathos	Iraklio	7½hr	€19.60	2 weekly
Mykonos	Iraklio	6¾hr	€66.50	2 weekly
Piraeus	Agios Nikolaos	12hr	€30	2 weekly
Piraeus	Iraklio	6½hr	€33.50	3 weekly
Piraeus	Iraklio	8hr	€36-37	2 daily
Piraeus	Rethymno	10hr	€30	2 daily
Piraeus*	Rethymno	6hr	€57	1 daily
Piraeus	Sitia	14½hr	€32.10	2 weekly
Piraeus	Souda (Hania)	8½hr	€30	2 daily
Piraeus*	Souda (Hania)	4½hr	€55	1 daily
Rhodes	Agios Nikolaos	12hr	€26.40	2 weekly
Rhodes	Iraklio	12hr	€27.50	2 weekly
Rhodes	Sitia	10hr	€26.40	2 weekly
Santorini (Thira)	Iraklio	4½hr	€16.30	4 weekly
Santorini (Thira)*	Iraklio	1¾hr	€41	1 daily
Santorini (Thira)	Rethymno	2hr 20min	€46	3 weekly

*high-speed services

EVIA

Evia & the Sporades; see also p225

BOAT SERVICES FROM EVIA

Destination	Port	Duration	Fare	Frequency
Agia Marina	Evia (Nea Styra)	45min	€3.50	6-8 daily
Arkitsa	Evia (Loutra Edipsou)	40min	€3.30	10-12 daily
Glyfa	Evia (Agiokambos)	20min	€2	8-12 daily
Rafina	Evia (Marmari)	1hr	€7	4-6 daily
Skala Oropou	Evia (Eretria)	25min	€1.40	hourly

HYDRA

Saronic Gulf Islands; see also p123

BOAT SERVICES FROM HYDRA

Destination	Port	Duration	Fare	Frequency
Ermioni*	Hydra	50min	€9.50	7 daily
Piraeus*	Hydra	1½hr	€28.40	7 daily
Poros*	Hydra	1hr 50min	€12.50	7 daily
Porto Heli*	Hydra	50min	€11.50	7 daily

*high-speed services

KALYMNOS

Dodecanese; see also p294

AIR

Olympic Air has daily flights to Athens from Kalymnos (€65, 20 minutes).

BOAT

Small, local car and passenger ferries leave three times daily from Pothia to Mastihari on Kos. The fast Lipsi-based *Anna Express* links Pothia with Leros and Lipsi three times weekly. There's also a daily caïque from Myrties to Xirokambos (€8) on Leros and Emborios (€8) in the north of Kalymnos. A caïque runs between Myrties and Telendos Islet (€2) throughout the day.

BOAT SERVICES FROM KALYMNOS

Destination	Port	Duration	Fare	Frequency
Astypalea	Pothia	3½hr	€11	3 weekly
Kos	Pothia	50min	€4	3 daily
Kos*	Pothia	35min	€15	1 daily
Leros	Pothia	1½hr	€7	1 daily
Leros*	Pothia	50min	€20	1 daily
Lipsi*	Pothia	1hr 20min	€20	6 weekly
Patmos*	Pothia	1hr 40min	€26	6 weekly
Piraeus	Pothia	13hr	€44	3 weekly
Rhodes	Pothia	4½hr	€20	3 weekly

*high-speed services

KARPATHOS

Dodecanese; see also p294

AIR

From Karpathos, flights with Olympic Air head daily to Kasos (€21) and Sitia (€43), twice daily to Rhodes (€28) and three times per week to Athens (€69).

BOAT SERVICES FROM KARPATHOS

Destination	Port	Duration	Fare	Frequency
Halki	Diafani	2hr	€17	4 weekly
Kasos	Pigadia	1½hr	€15	2 weekly
Milos	Pigadia	16hr	€36	2 weekly
Piraeus	Pigadia	17hr	€58	2 weekly
Rhodes	Pigadia	5hr	€22	3 weekly
Santorini (Thira)	Pigadia	11hr	€25	2 weekly
Sitia	Pigadia	4hr	€18	2 weekly

KEFALLONIA

Ionian Islands; see also p159

DOMESTIC FLIGHTS FROM KEFALLONIA

Destination	Airport	Duration	Fare	Frequency
Athens	Kefallonia	55min	€71	2 daily

BOAT SERVICES FROM KEFALLONIA

Destination	Port	Duration	Fare	Frequency
Astakos	Sami	3hr	€10	1 daily
Igoumenitsa	Sami	4¼hr	€13	1 weekly
Kyllini	Argostoli	3hr	€14	1 daily
Patra	Sami	2¾hr	€16.90	2 daily
Poros	Kyllini	1½hr	€9.90	3-5 daily

KOS

Dodecanese; see also p295

AIR

Olympic Air has two daily flights to Athens (€44, 55 minutes) and three weekly to Rhodes (€41, 20 minutes), Leros (€41, 15 minutes) and Astypalea (€47, one hour).

BOAT SERVICES FROM KOS

Destination	Port	Duration	Fare	Frequency
Kalymnos	Mastihari	1hr	€4	3 daily
Kalymnos*	Kos Town	30min	€15	1 daily
Nisyros	Kos Town	1hr 20min	€8	4 weekly
Nisyros*	Kos Town	45min	€16	2 weekly
Patmos	Kos Town	4hr	€13	2 weekly
Patmos*	Kos Town	2½hr	€29	6 weekly
Piraeus	Kos Town	10hr	€46	4 weekly
Rhodes	Kos Town	3hr	€26	1 daily
Rhodes*	Kos Town	2½hr	€30	1 daily
Thessaloniki	Kos Town	21hr	€47	1 weekly

*high-speed services

MYKONOS

Cyclades; see also p206

DOMESTIC FLIGHTS FROM MYKONOS

Destination	Airport	Duration	Fare	Frequency
Athens	Mykonos	50min	€52-103	3-5 daily
Santorini (Thira)	Mykonos	30min	€85	1-2 daily
Thessaloniki	Mykonos	1hr	€100	3 weekly

BOAT SERVICES FROM MYKONOS

Destination	Port	Duration	Fare	Frequency
Andros	Mykonos	2¾hr	€13	3-4 daily
Iraklio*	Mykonos	1½hr	€66.50	1-2 daily
Naxos	Mykonos	1¾hr	€12	1 weekly
Naxos*	Mykonos	40min	€18.50	2 daily
Piraeus	Mykonos	4¾hr	€30.50-39.50	2 daily
Piraeus*	Mykonos	3hr	€43	3 daily
Rafina	Mykonos	4½hr	€23	2-3 daily
Rafina*	Mykonos	2hr 10min	€41	4-5 daily
Santorini (Thira)*	Mykonos	2hr 10min	€38	2-3 daily

*high-speed services

ISLAND HOPPING

INDIVIDUAL ISLANDS & MAINLAND PORTS

NAXOS
Cyclades; see also p215

DOMESTIC FLIGHTS FROM NAXOS

Destination	Airport	Duration	Fare	Frequency
Athens	Naxos	45min	€62	1 daily

BOAT SERVICES FROM NAXOS

Destination	Port	Duration	Fare	Frequency
Amorgos	Naxos	3hr-3hr 50min	€11.50-14	2-3 daily
Kalymnos	Naxos	4¾hr	€19.50	2 weekly
Kos	Naxos	8¼hr	€23	2 weekly
Mykonos	Naxos	1¾hr	€12	1 weekly
Mykonos*	Naxos	40min	€18.50	2 daily
Piraeus	Naxos	4¾hr	€30	4-5 daily
Piraeus*	Naxos	3½hr	€45	4 daily
Rafina*	Naxos	3hr	€43	1 daily
Rhodes	Naxos	14hr	€32	2 weekly
Santorini (Thira)	Naxos	3hr	€15.50	5 daily
Santorini (Thira)*	Naxos	1½hr	€27.50	2-3 daily
Tilos	Naxos	9hr 35min	€23	2 weekly

*high-speed services

NISYROS
Dodecanese; see also p290

BOAT
The small local ferry *Agios Konstantinos* links Mandraki with Kardamena on Kos (€8, two hours, daily), while the larger *Panagia Spyliani* links Nisyros with Kos Town (€10, daily).

BOAT SERVICES FROM NISYROS

Destination	Port	Duration	Fare	Frequency
Kalymnos	Mandraki	2½hr	€7	4 weekly
Kos	Mandraki	1¼hr	€8	1 weekly
Kos*	Mandraki	45min	€16	1 weekly
Piraeus	Mandraki	18hr	€46	3 weekly
Rhodes	Mandraki	4½hr	€15	3 weekly
Rhodes*	Mandraki	2¾hr	€28	2 weekly

*high-speed services

PATMOS
Dodecanese; see also p300

BOAT SERVICES FROM PATMOS

Destination	Port	Duration	Fare	Frequency
Kalymnos*	Skala	1hr 40min	€26	6 weekly
Kos*	Skala	3hr	€29	6 weekly
Piraeus	Skala	7hr	€34	4 weekly
Rhodes	Skala	6hr	€40	3 weekly
Rhodes*	Skala	5hr	€46	6 weekly

*high-speed services

PAXI
Ionian Islands; see also p157

BOAT SERVICES FROM PAXI

Destination	Port	Duration	Fare	Frequency
Corfu*	Paxi	40min	€16.40	1-3 daily
Corfu	Paxi	3½hr	€8.50	3 weekly
Igoumenitsa	Paxi	2hr	€7.50	2 daily

*high-speed services

PELOPONNESE
See also the Getting There & Around section for Gythio, p115

BOAT
Boats between Galatas (Peloponnese) and the island of Poros run approximately every 15 minutes to 30 minutes.

BOAT SERVICES FROM THE PELOPONNESE

Destination	Port	Duration	Fare	Frequency
Corfu	Patra	6-7½hr	€30	4 weekly
Corfu	Patra	6-7½hr	€33	1 daily
Crete (Kissamos)	Gythio	7hr	€24	1 weekly (via Kythira & Antikythira)
Crete	Kalamata	7hr	€40	1 weekly (via Kythira)
Gythio	Kythira	2½hr	€11	2 weekly
Hydra	Ermioni	1hr	€9.50	4 daily
Hydra*	Ermioni	25min	€15	4 daily
Hydra*	Porto Heli	25min	€15	4 daily
Kefallonia (Argostoli)	Kyllini	2hr	€13	1 daily
Kefallonia (Lixouri)	Kyllini	2¼hr	€141	daily
Kefallonia (Poros)	Kyllini	1½hr	€8	5 daily
Kefallonia (Poros)	Kyllini	1hr	€10	1 daily
Kefallonia (Poros; by bus)	Patra	3hr	€18	
Kefallonia (Sami)	Patra	2¾hr	€17	3 weekly
Kefallonia (Sami)	Patra	2¾hr	€18	2 daily
Piraeus*	Ermioni	2hr	€29.50	4 daily
Piraeus*	Porto Heli	3hr 20min	€35.50	4 daily
Poros*	Ermioni	1hr	€15	3 daily
Poros	Methana	30min	€4.20	2-3 daily
Poros*	Porto Heli	1hr 40min	€19	2 daily

*high-speed services

POROS

Saronic Gulf Islands; see also p121

BOAT SERVICES FROM POROS

Destination	Port	Duration	Fare	Frequency
Hydra*	Poros	30min	€12.50	6 daily
Methana	Poros	30min	€4.20	
Piraeus	Poros	2½hr	€13.30	8-10 daily
Piraeus*	Poros	1hr	€25.20	4 daily

*high-speed services

RHODES

Dodecanese; see also p280

AIR

Olympic Air has at least five flights daily to Athens (€58), around six per week to Karpathos (€28), three weekly to Thessaloniki (€110) and two weekly to Samos (€37). Aegean Airlines also offers daily flights to Athens (€64) and Thessaloniki (€90).

BOAT SERVICES FROM RHODES

Destination	Port	Duration	Fare	Frequency
Kalymnos	Commercial Harbour (Rhodes Town)	4½hr	€20	3 weekly
Kalymnos*	Commercial Harbour (Rhodes Town)	3hr	€38	1 daily
Karpathos	Commercial Harbour (Rhodes Town)	5hr	€22	3 weekly
Kos	Commercial Harbour (Rhodes Town)	3hr	€26	1 daily
Kos*	Commercial Harbour (Rhodes Town)	2½hr	€30	1 daily
Nisyros	Commercial Harbour (Rhodes Town)	4½hr	€15	3 weekly
Nisyros*	Commercial Harbour (Rhodes Town)	2¾hr	€28	2 weekly
Patmos	Commercial Harbour (Rhodes Town)	6hr	€40	3 weekly
Patmos*	Commercial Harbour (Rhodes Town)	5hr	€46	6 weekly
Piraeus	Commercial Harbour (Rhodes Town)	13hr	€53	1 daily
Sitia	Commercial Harbour (Rhodes Town)	10hr	€28	3 weekly
Thessaloniki	Commercial Harbour (Rhodes Town)	21hr	€55	1 weekly
Tilos	Commercial Harbour (Rhodes Town)	2½hr	€15	4 weekly
Tilos*	Commercial Harbour (Rhodes Town)	2hr	€25	2 weekly
Tilos*	Mandraki Harbour (Rhodes Town)	1½hr	€24	6 weekly

*high-speed services

ISLAND HOPPING

INDIVIDUAL ISLANDS & MAINLAND PORTS

SANTORINI (THIRA)

Cyclades; see also p219

DOMESTIC FLIGHTS FROM SANTORINI (THIRA)

Destination	Port	Duration	Fare	Frequency
Athens	Santorini (Thira)	45min	€68	10 daily
Iraklio	Santorini (Thira)	30min	€85	5 weekly
Rhodes	Santorini (Thira)	1hr	€112	2 daily

BOAT SERVICES FROM SANTORINI (THIRA)

Destination	Port	Duration	Fare	Frequency
Amorgos*	Santorini (Thira)	1hr	€32	1 daily
Iraklio	Santorini (Thira)	4½hr	€24	1 daily
Iraklio*	Santorini (Thira)	1¾hr	€42	1 daily
Karpathos	Santorini (Thira)	8hr	€25	5 weekly
Kos	Santorini (Thira)	4¼hr	€28.50	2 weekly
Mykonos*	Santorini (Thira)	2hr 10min	€38	2-3 daily
Naxos	Santorini (Thira)	3hr	€15.50	5 daily
Naxos*	Santorini (Thira)	1½hr	€30	2-3 daily
Piraeus	Santorini (Thira)	9hr	€33.50	4-5 daily
Piraeus*	Santorini (Thira)	5¼hr	€47-65	3 daily
Rafina*	Santorini (Thira)	4¾hr	€49	1 daily
Rethymno	Santorini (Thira)	2hr 20min	€46	3 weekly
Rhodes	Santorini (Thira)	13hr 10min	€27	1-2 daily
Sifnos	Santorini (Thira)	7hr 20min	€13.50	2 weekly

*high-speed services

SKIATHOS

Evia & the Sporades; see also p228

AIR

During summer there's one flight daily to/from Athens (€49).

BOAT SERVICES FROM SKIATHOS

Destination	Port	Duration	Fare	Frequency
Agios Konstantinos	Skiathos	2hr	€32	1 daily
Agios Konstantinos	Skiathos	2hr	€33	2 daily *
Skopelos	Skiathos	1¼hr	€9	1 daily
Skopelos (Glossa)	Skiathos	40min	€5.50	1 daily
Skopelos (Glossa)*	Skiathos	20min	€9.50	3-4 daily
Skopelos (Skopelos Town)*	Skiathos	45min	€16	4-5 daily
Thessaloniki*	Skiathos	4¼hr	€55	1 daily
Volos	Skiathos	2½hr	€18	2 daily
Volos*	Skiathos	1½hr	€30	3 daily

*hydrofoil services

SKOPELOS

Evia & the Sporades; see also p230

BOAT SERVICES FROM SKOPELOS

Destination	Port	Duration	Fare	Frequency
Agios Konstantinos	Skopelos*	3½hr	€44	1 daily *
Agios Konstantinos	Skopelos**	2½hr	€44	1-3 daily **
Skiathos	Skopelos (Skopelos Town)	1hr	€9	1 daily
Skiathos**	Skopelos (Glossa)	20min	€9.50	4-5 daily
Skiathos*	Skopelos (Skopelos Town)	50min	€15.50	4-5 daily
Volos	Skopelos (Glossa)	3½hr	€19.50	1 daily
Volos	Skopelos (Skopelos Town)	4hr	€23	1-2 daily

*fast-ferry services
**hydrofoil services

SIFNOS

Cyclades; see also p217

BOAT SERVICES FROM SIFNOS

Destination	Port	Duration	Fare	Frequency
Folegandros	Sifnos	4½hr	€13.50	1-3 daily
Folegandros*	Sifnos	1hr	€18	4 weekly
Piraeus	Sifnos	5¼hr	€28	2 daily
Piraeus*	Sifnos	2hr 40min	€44	3 daily
Santorini (Thira)	Sifnos	7hr 20min	€13.50	2 weekly

*high-speed services

THESSALONIKI

As Greece's second city, mainland Thessaloniki has plenty of air and boat connections. It usually has hydrofoils to the Sporades as well, but these are unpredictable, so check locally. See also p183.

AIR

Some of Thessaloniki's island flights go via Athens; the following table lists direct island flights. Note that a few island flights are multistop, but don't involve change of aircraft.

DOMESTIC FLIGHTS FROM THESSALONIKI

Destination	Airport	Duration	Fare	Frequency
Corfu	Thessaloniki	50min	€75	4 weekly
Crete (Hania)	Thessaloniki	1¼hr	€100	7 weekly
Crete (Iraklio)	Thessaloniki	1¼hr	€100	2 daily
Kefallonia	Thessaloniki	1¾hr	€100	3 weekly
Kos	Thessaloniki	1¼hr	€135	2 weekly
Mykonos	Thessaloniki	1hr	€100	3 weekly
Rhodes	Thessaloniki	1¼hr	€100	2 daily
Santorini (Thira)	Thessaloniki	1¼hr	€100	3 weekly

BOAT SERVICES FROM THESSALONIKI

Destination	Port	Duration	Fare	Frequency
Kalymnos	Thessaloniki	20hr	€46	1 weekly
Kos	Thessaloniki	19¼hr	€47	1 weekly
Rhodes	Thessaloniki	25hr	€57	1 weekly

TILOS

Dodecanese; see also p294

BOAT SERVICES FROM TILOS

Destination	Port	Duration	Fare	Frequency
Kos	Livadia	3hr	€9	2 weekly
Kos*	Livadia	1½hr	€22	2 weekly
Nisyros	Livadia	1hr	€7	6 weekly
Nisyros*	Livadia	40min	€13	2 weekly
Piraeus	Livadia	19½hr	€46	2 weekly
Rhodes	Livadia	2½hr	€15	4 weekly
Rhodes*	Livadia	1½hr	€24	6 weekly
Symi	Livadia	2hr	€8	2 weekly

*high-speed services

VOLOS

Central Greece (mainland port)

BOAT SERVICES FROM VOLOS

Destination	Port	Duration	Fare	Frequency
Skiathos	Volos	2½hr	€18.50	1-2 daily
Skiathos*	Volos	1½hr	€31	2 daily
Skopelos (Glossa)	Volos	3hr	€20.50	3 weekly
Skopelos (Glossa)*	Volos	2hr	€34	2 daily
Skopelos (Skopelos Town)	Volos	4hr	€24	1 daily
Skopelos (Skopelos Town)*	Volos	2½hr	€40	2 daily

*hydrofoil services

ISLAND HOPPING

INDIVIDUAL ISLANDS & MAINLAND PORTS

↘GLOSSARY

For culinary terms, see p311.

Achaean civilisation – see *Mycenaean civilisation*
acropolis – citadel; highest point of an ancient city
agia (f), agios (m) – saint
agora – commercial area of an ancient city; shopping precinct in modern Greece
Archaic period – also known as the *Middle Age* (800-480 BC); period in which the city-states emerged from the *'dark age'* and traded their way to wealth and power; the city-states were unified by a Greek alphabet and common cultural pursuits, engendering a sense of national identity

basilica – early Christian church
bouzouki – long-necked, stringed lutelike instrument associated with *rembetika* music
Byzantine Empire – characterised by the merging of Hellenistic culture and Christianity and named after Byzantium, the city on the Bosphorus that became the capital of the Roman Empire; when the Roman Empire was formally divided in AD 395, Rome went into decline and the eastern capital, renamed Constantinople, flourished; the Byzantine Empire (324 BC-AD 1453) dissolved after the fall of Constantinople to the Turks in 1453

caïque – small, sturdy fishing boat often used to carry passengers
Classical period – era in which the city-states reached the height of their wealth and power after the defeat of the Persians in the 5th century BC; the Classical period (480-323 BC) ended with the decline of the city-states as a result of the Peloponnesian Wars, and the expansionist aspirations of Philip II, King of Macedon (r 359-336 BC), and his son, Alexander the Great (r 336-323 BC)
Corinthian – order of Greek architecture recognisable by columns with bell-shaped capitals that have sculpted, elaborate ornaments based on acanthus leaves; see also *Doric* and *Ionic*
Cycladic civilisation – the civilisation (3000-1100 BC) that emerged following the settlement of Phoenician colonists on the Cycladic islands

dark age – period (1200-800 BC) in which Greece was under *Dorian* rule
domatio (s), domatia (pl) – room, usually in a private home; cheap accommodation option
Dorians – Hellenic warriors who invaded Greece around 1200 BC, demolishing the city-states and destroying the *Mycenaean civilisation*; heralded Greece's *'dark age'*, when the artistic and cultural advancements of the *Mycenaean* and the *Minoan civilisations* were abandoned; the Dorians later developed into land-holding aristocrats which encouraged the resurgence of independent city-states led by wealthy aristocrats
Doric – order of Greek architecture characterised by a column that has no base, a fluted shaft and a relatively plain capital, when compared with the flourishes evident on *Ionic* and *Corinthian* capitals

ELPA – Elliniki Leschi Aftokinitou kai Periigiseon; Greek automobile club

ELTA – Ellinika Tahydromia; the Greek post office organisation

EOT – Ellinikos Organismos Tourismou; main tourist office (has offices in most major towns), known abroad as *GNTO*

Geometric period – period (1200-800 BC) characterised by pottery decorated with geometric designs; sometimes referred to as Greece's '*dark age*'

GNTO – Greek National Tourist Organisation; see also *EOT*

Hellenistic period – prosperous, influential period (323-146 BC) of Greek civilisation ushered in by Alexander the Great's empire building and lasting until the Roman sacking of Corinth in 146 BC

hora – main town (usually on an island)

horio – village

IC – intercity (sometimes express) train service

Ionic – order of Greek architecture characterised by a column with truncated flutes and capitals with ornaments resembling scrolls; see also *Doric* and *Corinthian*

kastro – walled-in town; also describes a fort or castle

KTEL – Koino Tamio Eispraxeon Leoforion; national bus cooperative; runs all long-distance bus services

leoforos – avenue; commonly shortened to 'leof'

Middle Age – see *Archaic period*

Minoan civilisation – Bronze Age (3000-1100 BC) culture of Crete named after the mythical King Minos, and characterised by pottery and metalwork of great beauty and artisanship

moni – monastery or convent

Mycenaean civilisation – the first great civilisation (1600-1100 BC) of the Greek mainland, characterised by powerful independent city-states ruled by kings; also known as the *Achaean civilisation*

odos – street

OSE – Organismos Sidirodromon Ellados; Greek railways organisation

OTE – Organismos Tilepikoinonion Ellados; Greece's major telecommunications carrier

Panagia – Mother of God or Virgin Mary; name frequently used for churches

plateia – square

rembetika – blues songs commonly associated with the underworld of the 1920s

stele (s), stelae (pl) – upright stone (or pillar) decorated with inscriptions or figures

stoa – long colonnaded building, usually in an *agora*; used as a meeting place and shelter in ancient Greece

⬎ BEHIND THE SCENES

THE AUTHORS
KORINA MILLER

Coordinating author; This is Greece; Greece's Top Itineraries; Planning Your Trip; Dodecanese; Greece in Focus; Directory, Transport & Island Hopping; Glossary

Korina first ventured to Greece as a backpacking teenager, sleeping on ferry decks and hiking in the mountains. She has since found herself drawn back to soak up the dazzling Greek sunshine, lounge on the beaches and consume vast quantities of Greek salad and strong coffee. Korina grew up on Vancouver Island and has been exploring the globe since she was 16, working, studying and travelling in 36 countries en route. She now resides in England's Sussex countryside while she plots her next adventure. She has been writing travel guides for Lonely Planet for the past 12 years with 18 titles under her belt.

Author thanks Thank you to the following people for their generosity of time and knowledge: Pavlos Georgilas and Y'vonne Walser of Kefallonia; Voula Karatziou-Anastasopoulou of Evia; Anna Butcher of Areopoli; Maria Ioanna Koutsoudaki and Catherine Triantis of Athens; Evelynne Bakinta of Crete; Eva Veneka and Yorgos Loukos of Athens; Vasileios Per. Sirimis of Rhodes; Petros Krountselis and Alexis Valogiorgos of Thessaloniki; Billy and Talitha Castillo of Vancouver Island; and Krista Davis of New Jersey. At Lonely Planet, a big thanks to Jo Potts, Sally Schafer, Cliff Wilkinson, Eoin Dunlevy and Herman So. And, finally, love and appreciation to my husband Paul and daughters Simone and Monique.

KATE ARMSTRONG
Peloponnese

Having studied history and fine arts, Kate headed to Greece aeons ago to view her first (noncelluloid) *kouros* (male statue of the Archaic period), and fell in love with the country. On several subsequent visits she's rubbed shoulders with many ghosts of mythical beings in the Peloponnese, her all-time favourite region. She devoured kilos of feta and olives (to the delight of locals), several pigs (to the dismay of her vegetarian partner)

LONELY PLANET AUTHORS

Why is our travel information the best in the world? It's simple: our authors are passionate, dedicated travellers. They don't take freebies in exchange for positive coverage so you can be sure the advice you're given is impartial. They travel widely to all the popular spots, and off the beaten track. They don't research using just the internet or phone. They discover new places not included in any other guidebook. They personally visit thousands of hotels, restaurants, palaces, trails, galleries, temples and more. They speak with dozens of locals every day to make sure you get the kind of insider knowledge only a local could tell you. They take pride in getting all the details right, and in telling it how it is. Think you can do it? Find out how at **lonelyplanet.com**.

and was treated to more hospitality than Aphrodite herself. When not wandering in mountainous terrains, Kate sets her itchy feet in Australia. A freelance travel writer, she contributes to Lonely Planet's African, South American and Portuguese titles as well as Australian newspapers, and is the author of educational children's books.

MICHAEL STAMATIOS CLARK   Central Greece, Evia & the Sporades
Michael's Greek roots go back to the village of Karavostamo on the Aegean island of Ikaria, home of his maternal grandparents. He was born into a Greek-American community in Cambridge, Ohio, and recently became a Greek citizen. His first trip to Greece was as a deckhand aboard a Greek freighter, trading English lessons for Greek over wine and backgammon. When not travelling to Greece, Michael teaches English to international students in Berkeley, California, listens to Greek *rembetika* (blues) after midnight and searches for new ways to convert friends to the subtle pleasures of retsina.

CHRIS DELISO   Northern Greece, Crete
Chris Deliso was drawing maps of the Aegean by the age of five, and 20 years later he ended up in Greece while labouring away on an MPhil in Byzantine Studies at Oxford. Ever since studying Modern Greek in Thessaloniki in 1998, he has travelled frequently in Greece, including a year in Crete and a long sojourn on Mt Athos. Chris especially enjoyed stumbling upon the unexpected on remote isles like Psara, imbibing heartily in the wineries of Macedonia, gawking at the vultures ripping apart carrion in Thrace, and feasting himself on those incomparable Cretan sweet cheese pies – the *myzithropitakia*.

DES HANNIGAN   Saronic Gulf Islands, Cyclades, Ionian Islands
Des first surfaced (literally) in Greece many years ago in an Aegina harbour, having jumped off a boat into several feet of unexpected water. Ever since, he's been drifting around the country whenever he can, though home is on the edge of the cold Atlantic in beautiful Cornwall, England. In a previous life Des worked at sea, valuable experience for coping with the Greek ferry system. One day he'd really like to hop round the islands in a very fast yacht with all sails set, though he would happily settle for an old caïque with just one sail. Des worked on the latest editions of Lonely Planet's *Greece* and *Greek Islands* and has written guidebooks to Corfu and Rhodes for other publishers.

VICTORIA KYRIAKOPOULOS   Athens & Attica
Victoria Kyriakopoulos is a Melbourne-based journalist who morphs effortlessly into an Athenian whenever she hits the motherland. She just clocked up her 269,010th kilometre getting to Greece, has travelled widely around the country and moved there for a while (2000–04), hoping to get it out of her system. Victoria wrote Lonely Planet's first pocket *Athens* guide in 2001, did a stint as editor of *Odyssey* magazine, covered the 2004 Olympics for international media and worked on several television shows about Greece. She returns regularly for research (and pleasure), including for Lonely Planet's latest *Athens Encounter* and *Crete*. An occasional food critic back home, when not writing or making documentaries, she is working through her extensive Greek cookbook collection. The Cuisine section of Greece in Focus was originally written by Victoria.

CONTRIBUTING AUTHORS

Gina Tsarouhas Born in Melbourne with Greek blood flowing through her veins, Gina packed her little suitcase at the tender age of four and took off for Greece. Gina flitted across various continents over the years until she discovered she could travel vicariously as an editor of travel guides, as well. When not editing she's co-authoring and contributing to all things Greek at Lonely Planet, including *Greece* and *Greek Islands*; or tending to her beloved fig and olive trees in the backyard. The Architecture and History sections of Greece in Focus were originally written by Gina.

Richard Waters Richard's first of taste of travel was as a 21-year-old driving around Central America in an old jalopy; it took him through Guatemala's civil war and gave him his first taste of wanderlust. He's been travelling ever since: across Southeast Asia, Europe, the US and Africa. His first visit to Laos in '99 brought the Hmong guerrillas to his attention and in 2002 he was among the first to creep into the Special Zone in search of their story. He's since contributed to three books on Laos for Lonely Planet. He lives with his partner, son and daughter in Brighton and works as a freelance writer and photographer for British newspapers and magazines. You can see his work at: www.richardwaters.co.uk. The Gods & Goddesses section of Greece in Focus was originally written by Richard.

THIS BOOK

This 1st edition of *Discover Greece* was coordinated by Korina Miller, and researched and written by Kate Armstrong, Michael Stamatios Clark, Chris Deliso, Des Hannigan and Victoria Kyriakopoulos, with contributions from Gina Tsarouhas and Richard Waters. This guidebook was commissioned in Lonely Planet's London office, and produced by the following:

Commissioning Editor Jo Potts
Coordinating Editor Gina Tsarouhas
Coordinating Cartographer Alex Leung
Coordinating Layout Designer Paul Iacono
Managing Editor Annelies Mertens
Managing Cartographers Shahara Ahmed, Herman So

SEND US YOUR FEEDBACK

We love to hear from travellers – your comments keep us on our toes and help make our books better. Our well-travelled team reads every word on what you loved or loathed about this book. Although we cannot reply individually to postal submissions, we always guarantee that your feedback goes straight to the appropriate authors, in time for the next edition. Each person who sends us information is thanked in the next edition and the most useful submissions are rewarded with a free book.

To send us your updates – and find out about Lonely Planet events, newsletters and travel news – visit our award-winning website: lonelyplanet.com/contact.

Note: we may edit, reproduce and incorporate your comments in Lonely Planet products such as guidebooks, websites and digital products, so let us know if you don't want your comments reproduced or your name acknowledged. For a copy of our privacy policy visit lonelyplanet.com/privacy.

Managing Layout Designer Sally Darmody
Assisting Editor Elizabeth Harvey
Assisting Cartographers Hunor Csutoros, Xavier di Toro, Joelene Kowalski
Cover Nic Lehman, lonelyplanetimages.com
Internal Image Research Sabrina Dalbesio, lonelyplanetimages.com
Project Manager Eoin Dunlevy
Language Content Branislava Vladisavljevic

Thanks to Lauren Hunt, John Mazzocchi, Daniel Moore, Laura Stansfeld, John Taufa, Juan Winata, Celia Wood

BEHIND THE SCENES

THIS BOOK

Internal photographs
p4 Cafe on Ancient Promenade with views of the Acropolis, George Tsafos; p10 View of the Parthenon at the Acropolis, Athens, Rick Gerharter; pp12–13 Streetside cafes, Plaka, Athens, Diana Mayfield; p31 Views overlooking a church and belltower, Santorini (Thira), Cyclades, Diana Mayfield; p39 Moni Agias Varvaras Rousanou, Meteora, Thessaly, Paolo Cordelli; p3, pp50–1 Outdoor cafes along Adrianou, Monastiraki, Athens, George Tsafos; p3, p93 Ruins of tower houses, Lakonian Mani, Peloponnese, George Tsafos; p3, p127 Corfu Town, Corfu, Ionian Islands, Jon Arnold Images Ltd/Alamy; p3, p163 Vikos Gorge, Zagorohoria, northern Greece, Ann Rayworth/Alamy; p3, p195 Clifftop village of Oia, Santorini (Thira), Cyclades, Shania Shegedyn; p3, p233 Old Town, Hania, Crete, Jon Arnold Images Ltd/Alamy; p3, p267 Avenue of the Knights, Rhodes Town, Rhodes, Dodecanese, Nicholas Pitt/Alamy; pp306–7 Views from Areopagus Hill of the Stoa of Attalos and Church of the Holy Apostles, Ancient Agora, Athens, George Tsafos; p337 Ferry approaching the harbour, Santorini (Thira), Cyclades, Greg Gawlowski.

All images are copyright of the photographer unless otherwise indicated. Many of the images in this guide are available for licensing from Lonely Planet Images: www.lonelyplanetimages.com.

↘INDEX

000 Map pages
000 Photograph pages

INDEX

P-T